The Experimental, Expe
Science of Self

The personal alchemy system presented here includes the foundation elements from many traditional systems of wisdom as they specifically relate to the correlating alchemies of color Rays and Lights, and the active use of imagery. This system of healing magick builds on the foundations of traditions, but is not bound by the limitations of set rules, forms, or dogmas. In *Personal Alchemy*, "rules" from the past provide correlations from the present, and experimental catalysts and materials for the future. The experiential examples of active imagery found in this book reflect several approaches to wisdom:

- Western, direct, active forms such as goal-oriented, creative visualization
- Eastern, indirect, receptive forms such as deep relaxation, no-boundary meditations
- Oriental, indirect, reflective forms such as clear-minded awareness meditations
- Natural, direct, experiential forms such as shamanic journey and vision quest
- Tibetan, holistic, synthesis forms such as harmonic attunements for Body, Mind and Spirit unity.

How you use *Personal Alchemy* depends entirely on your personal style and experience. You are free to adapt this system as you choose for the creation of your own alchemy, self-transformation, and personal empowerment. *Personal Alchemy* provides you with the foundation from which you may develop the most simple and basic or elaborate and complex system of healing magick. It is your choice.

Personal Alchemy was designed to be flexible and self-expanding. And so, indeed were you. That is the truly definitive power of personal alchemy.

About the Author

Amber Wolfe is a psychotherapist in private practice. She combines her twenty-five years of training in psychology, anthropology, and sociology with a lifetime of attunement to, and study of, the ways of Nature and earth wisdom.

Having lived in the Far East and Polynesia, and having traveled to many other areas of the world, Amber has had the opportunity to learn from many different cultures. Like the shamans of old, she strives to "make her own medicine" by blending the wealth of wisdoms and experiences encountered on her life journey into a workable potion for psychological growth and spiritual development. In her work with clients and workshop participants, she encourages others to find and follow their own paths to wisdom.

Amber is a solitary practitioner of the Celtic traditions of the Craft of the Wise, and she has created guided imagery tapes designed to evoke and support the quest for spirituality and Nature awareness. She is currently working on several projects exploring the ancient ways of earth wisdom and the psychological benefits of myth.

To Write to the Author

If you wish to contact the author or would like more information about this book, please write to the author in care of Llewellyn Worldwide, and we will forward you request. Both the author and publisher appreciate hearing from you and learning of your enjoyment of this book and how it has helped you. Llewellyn Worldwide cannot guarantee that every letter written to the author can be answered, but all will be forwarded. Please write to:

Amber Wolfe
c/o Llewellyn Worldwide
P.O. Box 64383-890, St. Paul, MN 55164-0383, U.S.A.

Please enclose a self-addressed, stamped envelope for reply, or $1.00 to cover costs.
If outside the U.S.A., enclose international postal reply coupon.

Free Catalog from Llewellyn

For more than 90 years Llewellyn has brought its readers knowledge in the fields of metaphysics and human potential. Learn about the newest books in spiritual guidance, natural healing, astrology, occult philosophy and more. Enjoy book reviews, new age articles, a calendar of events, plus current advertised products and services. To get your free copy of *Llewellyn's New Worlds of Mind and Spirit*, send your name and address to:

Llewellyn's New Worlds of Mind and Spirit
P.O. Box 64383-890, St. Paul, MN 55164-0383, U.S.A.

Personal Alchemy

A Handbook of Healing and Self-Transformation

Amber Wolfe

1993
Llewellyn Publications
St. Paul, Minnesota, 55164-0383, U.S.A.

FIRST EDITION
First Printing

Cover: Victoria Lisi
Illustrations: Merle S. Insinga, Christopher Wells
Book design and layout: Jessica Thoreson

Tarot illustrations from *The Robin Wood Tarot* © 1991 by Robin Wood. Used by permission.

Library of Congress Cataloging-in-Publication Data
Wolfe, Amber, 1950-
   Personal alchemy : a handbook of healing and self-transformation /
Amber Wolfe.
        p.   cm.
   Includes bibliographical references.
   ISBN 0-87542-890-8
   1. Color—Psychic aspects. 2. Alchemy. 3. Magic. I. Title.
BF1623.C7W65   1992
133—dc20   92-31670
                                                               CIP

Llewellyn Publications
A Division of Llewellyn Worldwide, Ltd.
P.O. Box 64383, St. Paul, MN 55164-0383

Gratefully dedicated
to

Iris: Multidimensional Goddess of the Rainbow,
Messenger of the Gods,

and to

Janie Veth: Healing Catalyst of Angelic Degree,
in whose compassionate heart dwells:

The Courage of the Lion
The Beauty of the Rose
The Honor of the Eagle
And the Wisdom of Universal Love.

Acknowledgements

I am grateful to the many people who have shared the gifts of their wisdom, their experiences, their support, and their encouragement to help make *Personal Alchemy* possible.

Special thanks to:

Bruce, for his patient nurturing, and his practical wisdom;

My children, for their boundless curiosity;

Nancy Mostad, for the treasure of her Being;

Jeanne Tiedemann, for typing and for organization far beyond any of my abilities;

Samuel Weiser, now in Spirit, teacher, stone wizard, and Earth gnome—for his vast knowledge and deep love of the Mineral World which I was privileged to experience during the last of his nearly nine decades on this earth. It is my hope that this work will honor the wisdom he imparted, and will reverence his special spirit.

Thanks also to many friends and colleagues for their support during the creation of *Personal Alchemy*. Among them are Pech Rafferty, Joan Watson, Kathy Cross, Barbara Harrison, Angie Owens, Joe and Fred, Kathy Canas, Dorothy Witherspoon, Jay Veneer, Debbie Day, Jean Underwood, Michelle Singleton, Carol and Marilyn, Jan and Paul Atkinson, Jerry and Patty Smith, John and Kara and Jonathan Starr, and "Miss Jennie" Temples.

Do Not Believe . . .

Do not believe in what you have heard.

Do not believe in traditions because they have been handed down for many generations.

Do not believe anything because it is rumored and spoken of by many.

Do not believe merely because the written statement of some old sage is produced.

Do not believe in conjectures.

Do not believe merely in the authority of your teachers and elders.

After observation and analysis, when it agrees with reason and is conducive to the good and benefit of one and all . . .

Then accept it and live up to it.

—Gautama Buddha
(From the *Kalamas Sutra*)

Contents

Introduction

The Evolution of Personal Alchemy: A Definitive Overview

"Alchemy," as most define it, refers to the empirical Medieval science which dealt in particular with the search for the universal solvent, the "alkahest," which would transmute the baser metals (such as lead) into gold.

In alchemy, a mysterious substance was thought to exist, a "philosopher's stone" or elixir which would provide a universal solution for all ills, all dis-ease, of humankind. This universal solution, or cure, was called the "panacea."

Although alchemy is not considered to be a science by some, it may well have been the only true science to exist during the Dark Ages, a time of philosophical persecution and religious domination. Every aspect of life was dictated according to the dogma of the Church. The only sciences which were allowed to exist were those which proved the doctrines accepted by the Church, or produced the substances valued by the Church.

It is understandable that the ancient alchemists were actively searching for the mysterious universal solvent to create gold. For one thing, it kept the Church supportive of their science. For another, it kept science itself "alive," experiential, and experimental. Some of these alchemists lost their lives in this time of persecution, but others managed to keep themselves and their science free—at least in their own minds.

"Science" may be defined as the systematic acquisition of knowledge through observation, analysis, and experimentation. Alchemy is an empirical science, which means it relies primarily on the process of experimentation rather than on theory. In modern times, this difference is still the subject of many academic debates between "schools" of science. In Medieval times, however, an experimental, empirical scientific attitude was considered dangerous and heretical as it encouraged new questions, new thoughts, and new possibilities.

Alchemy is an experimental science which looks at things "in a new light." During the Dark Ages, alchemy was one of the few sources of illumination that kept the light of truth and learning alive. Unfortunately, as most of us recall, another sort of illumination was all too common during the Dark Ages—the light from the fires which burned millions of witches. Symbolically, the light of truth was also consumed.

Although witches are most often thought to have been burned for their religious beliefs or their lands, many witches were also burned because they were the original experimental scientists. As such, they were not willing to relinquish their right to question and learn. Witches were healers, natural scientists, and the first personal alchemists. Some of the witches died because of their magickal or alchemical powers; however, most were persecuted because of their personal power. This was the power of individuals choosing to heed the free-minded direction of their own spirit rather that the spiritual dictates of others. Witches have always understood the alchemical power of choice.

Alchemist's Note: Lest we forget, the power of choice lies in the personal exercise and application of that choice, and not in the relinquishing of choice to others. And lest we become maudlin about the burning times, let us remember that it too was an act of choice—in some dimension. We can choose to regard the persecution as a destruction or as a transformation into the Light.

I choose to believe that many, many of the true witches chose to use the time of persecution to transform through the purification of the flame. In so doing, they were forged as a blade is, in the fire, to create a force—or a "sword" of personal and collective power. This power was for use in the then future, and the now, present time. Certainly witches were burned; but, believing as they did—and do—they're back.

"Personal" means being characteristic of or relating to an individual person. "Character" reflects a certain unique quality or aspect. "Individual" means a single indivisible unit. Choice is the action or the process of becoming an individual. *Personal Alchemy is the activation of individual choice.*

Self-transformation is self-change according to self-choice. The alchemy of choice for the individual must include an aware consciousness. This is because the Self is the subject of consciousness. The Self is never subject to the consciousness of others—unless the Self chooses. It's an individual choice.

An individual activates and projects the powers of individuality. Individuality is that special, indivisible force which emerges from a person who feels, thinks, and experiences life for themselves. The personal alchemist is one who creates his or her own life in as many dimensions as possible. This is accomplished by blending the inner, intuitive Self-nature with the outer, interactive relationship with Nature. The alchemy of this blend creates individuals who reflect the special forces of healing magick.

"Magick" is the active belief that the forces of Nature can be accessed through the use of certain rites, formulas, or behaviors. Magick involves the actions of alchemy used to access preternatural and supernatural forces. Alchemical experimentation and experiential research using the known realm of physical and metaphysical forces is the foundation of natural healing magick.

A "preternatural force" exceeds or diverges from the common order observable in Nature, yet remains connected and within the known frame of natural physical laws. Preternatural is distinguished from supernatural. A "supernatural force" is neither bound nor explained by known natural laws.

That which is supernatural is usually attributed to a divine force or order. Preternatural is a superlative force, but not outside the known realms or orders. Personal alchemy as an experimental process involves the use of both preternatural and supernatural forces.

The balance of preternatural and supernatural energies the personal alchemist uses in magick depends entirely upon independent choices. Preternatural forces reflect the observable energies and sensations such as colors, sounds, scents, and the elements as they manifest in Nature. The powers of the animal, mineral, plant, and human worlds are preternatural forces.

Supernatural forces reflect the energies that transcend the physical laws of Nature. These are the metaphysical forces which pertain to the ultimate, essential reality—the dimension we call Spirit, Source, or the Divine. These dimensions are accessed in alchemy through the use of ritual and symbolic representations of the Divine.

Magick blends preternatural with supernatural by combining correlating energies. The preternatural physical energies of a crystal, for example, correlate with and can be used to access the supernatural dimensions of Spirit. This can be accomplished through the use of ritual to access ceremonial, Spiritual hierarchies such as angelic realms, or dimensions of the Spirit guides and ascended masters. These form an essentially experiential, shamanic connection between the preternatural and the supernatural. The personal alchemists, like the shamans and the witches, work between the physical and the metaphysical "worlds," or realms. The personal alchemist uses the expressive action of magick to weave these realms together in an honorable healing manner for the good of all. The power of the personal alchemist emerges from personal experience of the energies and the realms used in healing magick. The magick forces used by the personal alchemist flow through, as well as forth, from the source.

Like the shamans and the witches, the personal alchemists are never disconnected from their magick. They are the magick reflected and manifested in their individual selves. The wise personal alchemist reflects and manifests the energies in a positive healing and self-healing manner.

The personal alchemist understands the indivisible essential unity of life's energies and the interactive relationship of all the worlds and the divine dimensions we call Spirit. In knowing and accepting this unity, the personal alchemist endeavors to create healing with magick.

The word "healing" is from the old English word "Health," which means wholeness. Healing is the process of maintaining the condition of health—wholeness. Healing does not create health; healing restores, remedies and repairs health. Healing is the maintenance force, not the creation force of wholeness. Healing in magick is the alchemy of receptive nurturance, reflective natural harmony, and the active manifestation of wholeness.

Healing magick is the force for positive transformation and empowerment. Healing magick naturally reflects a blend of the physical and the metaphysical. For the personal alchemist, health is understood as a natural harmony of Body, Mind and Spirit, and a balanced relationship between the mundane and the Divine realms of energy. This is the foundational philosophy of all healing magick, and reflects the wisdom and love of Nature as it manifests in humankind. It is a philosophy which reflects a universal truth of unity of Spirit, which has survived despite attempts made to control or destroy it.

The witches were, and are, the craft healers of magick. Their powerful healing craft caused the dominating forces of the Church to envy and fear the witches' influence over the people. Indeed, the witches sought no dominating influence over the lives of the people, it was the Church who sought control of the common people. And it was the scientists controlled by the Church who, in turn, sought control of the healing arts—and the craft of magick.

Medical "science" was emerging, and its practitioners sought the power and the influence they perceived the witches to have over the people. The influence of the Church had begun to poison the attitudes of medicine with doctrines that separated humankind from Nature and Self-nature.

According to the philosophy of the witches, disorders of the body and mind were viewed as indications of disharmony. The witches used the preternatural energies of Nature and the supernatural energies of Spirit to restore health. With herbs and minerals to heal the body, and "spells" or rituals, the witches made mind and Spirit whole once more. It was an interactive process used to restore health for and with the people. Theirs was—and is—a natural philosophy of love and wisdom. The word "philosophy," which comes from the Greek "philos" (loving) and "sophy" (wise), reflects the intentions and the energies of the witches' healing magick.

The new medical "science" held no such philosophy. Instead, these new physicians reflected the separatist attitude of the Church and its controlling dogmas. Disorders of body and mind were viewed as indications of a dis-eased evil spirit. Sickness and sorrow were seen as indications of punishment by the Divine, or as possessions by some demonic evil. The only possibility for wellness lay in complete submission to the doctrines of the Church, a debasement of the physical body, and a disconnection with the old ways of Nature, even if it meant death; this was seen as martyrdom.

So greatly enforced was this fear of the physical and natural that it caused a period of disconnection of humankind from Nature. This soon resulted in the near demise of Western culture through the ravages of plague and persecution.

Bubonic plague had been an ever-present threat since the beginning of settled civilization. However, its devastating effects had been held in check due, for the most part, to the healthful philosophy and healing practices of the old ways of Nature. When the burning times began, these healthful ways of Nature either fell silent or were silenced by force.

When this "witchcraze" period of persecution reached its peak, most of the healers had been either banished or destroyed. In an unparalleled absurdity of superstitious behavior, the rulers of the Churches decreed that not only witches, but their helping "familiars," the cats, were also evil and therefore must be destroyed.

Suffice it to say that the nature of cats and witches both reflect an independent and uncontrollable Spirit. In their stupidity—and their greed—the Church destroyed the two primary protections of Western civilization against the ravages of the bubonic plague.

This plague was carried by fleas on rats. When the cats were almost annihilated, the population of rats increased beyond a measurable rate of speed. With the witches literally under fire from the Church and the ways of Nature devalued as demonic or evil, the plague swept across the then-Western World.

The plague destroyed over a third of the population of Europe, rivaling the number of witches and alchemists destroyed. For a time, destructive forces of evil intentions seemed to "possess" the Church and the scientific intelligentsia of Western civilization. For a time, the ruling powers sought to blame the evil, sinful nature of humankind itself for the devastation, and the witchcraze escalated into a frenzy of fear and superstition. Not just known witches and healers were persecuted, but all women—and men who reflected the ways considered to be natural only in women—were persecuted.

The ruling powers of the Church found Biblical indications that women were the source of all sin, and therefore the cause of all weakness and disease. The goddess of Nature, so revered by the witches, was seen to be an evil force inherent—and suspected—in all women.

Eve had caused Adam to fall from grace, and had therefore expelled all humankind from the divine garden of Eden, the Church claimed. Therefore all women, seen as descended from Eve, were responsible for the wrath of God upon all humankind.

When this period of time had finally passed, an estimated nine million European women and many men had been destroyed. Entire cultures were uprooted and cast into chaos. In one valley in Switzerland, only two women were left out of three villages. It was a pattern repeated far too many times throughout Europe.

It was the darkest period of an Age of Darkness, when the very colors and energies of all life dimmed and fell into the shadows of a hell on Earth. But when this dark time had passed, the dogmatic powers of the Church cracked and began to fall in ruins. The faith people placed in the powers of the Church (albeit under duress), slowly began to be replaced by the philosophical rights of the people to live as free individuals. The rights of the individual to love, work, and live in personal connection to themselves, to others, and to Spirit began to emerge in the philosophies of the people.

In the tradition of the ancient bards, the medieval troubadours (travelling musicians) began to spin their tales of love, chivalry, and honor. The alchemy of their message created a gradual return to the honoring of all life. With this emerged a new view of the Divine as a loving, wise force. It was as if a force of light shone through the dark, controlling powers of the Church. Although those dark powers continued to influence much of Western civilization, their greatest weapon—fear—began to be replaced by the newly emerging philosophies and faiths of the people.

Out of the devastation, a new dimension evolved from within the mind of Western civilization. Like the forest which renews itself—ever greener, ever more powerful after a fire—the Mind of Western culture renewed itself. The Renaissance burst forth in a rainbow of colors, culture, and music; a rainbow of enlightenment reflecting the evolution of the Western Mind.

When the smoke from the fires of destruction had cleared, a new light of faith and reason shone through. Those of Nature understood this as the ultimate, essential restoration of the Health which Nature perpetuates despite attempts to control or destroy it. The way of the personal alchemist found its inception in the renewed acceptance of humanity's right to think and live for themselves.

Though the dogma of the Church still existed—and extended its control over much of the Western world—it no longer had the necessary power to influence the evolution of the Western Mind. Nature once again, as always, held the reins of power and directed the course of evolution. Slowly yet inexorably, the ways of Nature and the philosophies of love, health, and wisdom returned to empower humankind. Freedom of mind and Spirit were honored again, and the light of truth illuminated Western civilization once more.

The healing magick of Nature and Spirit was celebrated and honored once more, often within the framework of the same religion which had been abused for the purposes of control. The mysteriously impressive and beautiful forces of life were celebrated, first in art and music, then in the lives of the common people. Out of the shadows of superstition and fear, the light of understanding reflected in the colorful celebration of life itself and in the lives of the individual people.

The pursuit of personal truth, knowledge, and happiness began to be seen as a natural right, inherent to all humankind. Slowly but surely, the Renaissance brought a rebirth of the healing magick of choice.

The universal philosophies of unity and harmony which we now call "New Age" were reborn out of the ashes of the Dark Ages, and grew in the light of the Renaissance to create the age of Democracy and free thought still empowering the positive forces of world change today. This is the alchemical force of free choice reflecting the light of truth in a free mind. It is an ancient force, an eternal alchemy of harmony in Nature and Self-nature which can never be destroyed—only transformed into an even greater power for universal healing magick.

The power of free mind and free choice is an alchemy expressing the eternal positive evolution of intelligence and enlightenment in all Nature as it manifests in humankind.

Although Western civilization—and indeed the world as a shared civilization—has experienced periods of oppression and persecution since the Dark Ages, the alchemy of the Renaissance has remained. With the renewal of reverence for Nature and respect for human rights, the healing magick of positive evolution shall continue.

Essential health and harmony have been maintained. As all humankind evolves a universal philosophy of harmony, this essential health shall expand, fully restored and eternally renewed by the forces of light. Those forces include the alchemy of faith, free mind, and personal choice.

The positive forces of light emerge from a foundation of harmonious attunement with the energies of Nature and honor for the divine realms of Spirit. The eternally renewing force of light reflected in Nature and Spirit may well be the mysterious alkahest that transmutes all life to a higher form. The panacea of the alchemist's search may well be the essential healing renewal force of Nature and Spirit.

The systems for developing this universal alchemy, long hidden during the Dark Ages, burst forth in the light of the Renaissance. The alchemists who had weathered the times of persecution came forward in the new times of freedom to reveal ancient wisdoms and alchemical systems of knowledge and magick. Common to all was the acceptance of a universal energy force reflected in all Nature and Spirit, as varied in form as the colors of the rainbow.

When the either/or, black/white, good/evil dualities of the Dark Ages diminished, an expanded range of possibilities emerged in varied systems of wisdom, and in the rainbow hues of many philosophies coming to light.

When the alchemists of the Renaissance revealed the work they had accomplished and the wisdoms they had preserved during the times of persecution, one common form was found in most of their systems. This form was based on an understanding of and experiential attunement with the healing energies of color. "Color" was seen as the pure reflection of the natural and Divine energies associated with light.

After such a time of darkness, it is clearly understandable why the alchemy of light came to be reclaimed as a viable form of healing magick. From the alchemists of the

Renaissance came the renewal of ancient systems using the energies of color reflected in Rays and Lights. These reflected according to a natural order, and, it was surmised, a Divine force.

The ancient systems of natural magick evolved into what we now call the modern natural sciences. Underlying most, if not all, of these new natural sciences was the potent alchemy of energy and color. A renewed attitude of experimentation and expanded knowledge influenced these new forms of science. This influence, which remains in present times, perpetuates the acquisition of wisdom. We see this influence most clearly in the sciences which involve the exploration of the healing magick energies of color Rays and Lights. These observe, analyze, and determine experimentally the influence of light and color on the mind, and therefore the life forms, of humankind.

A "natural science" may be defined as one which explores the energies produced by and existing in Nature. The natural sciences investigate the essential alchemy of life in Nature by examining the essence, or character, of all animate forms. That which is animate is determined by its reception, activation, and reflection of energy. One of the primary determinants of life was the "light," or energy, inherent in each form or reflected in interaction with Nature. Thus, though a stone or crystal may have seemed inanimate to those who separated and devalued Nature, these came to be seen again as having a reflected energy or light in relationship to humankind.

While the energies of Rays and Lights had been studied since the beginning of time, their specific alchemy began to be understood more clearly in the light of scientific exploration which began with the Renaissance in Western civilization.

Rays and Lights are best understood in terms of the energy they reflect. The word "energy" comes from the Greek "en" (in) and "ergo" (work), meaning action or motion. Energy is also the intensity of an action and the expression of an inherent power or force. In alchemy and healing magick, specific energy forms are used to produce specific effects.

The alchemy of energy is determined by its capacity for doing work and overcoming the nullifying forces of entropy. Entropy is the stalemate of evolution and the polarization of the expansive cycles of growth in Nature and Self-nature. It may be said that the controlling dogmas of the Church that sought to restrict and structure natural growth were "the forces of entropy." The re-emergence of thought, philosophy, and free mind may be said to be the "forces of light and creation."

While both forces exist as polarities influencing the direction of evolution, it is only the insistence on viewing this natural polarity as a duality by much of humankind which can feed people's fears—and therefore empower these forces of entropy. That which we call the duality of light and dark is no more or less that the Shadows cast by the obstacles of fear, judgment, misunderstanding, and superstition.

In accepting the indivisible unity of all life, humankind may finally understand the ancient mystical wisdoms which demonstrated the dynamic polarities of life, and decry the artificial dualities that separate humankind from Nature and from Self. Ancient mystics, medieval alchemists, and modern metaphysicians all teach the same wisdom which the witches have understood and adhered to since the beginning of human consciousness. That wisdom teaches us of the ultimate neutrality of all energy.

Energy is neither good nor evil. Energy is a neutral force which, if left undisturbed, will evolve and transform in accordance with the growth cycles of Nature. What is seen as destructive in Nature is understood to be part of the eternally renewing cycle. Renewal is a force for transformation, not finality and death.

The alchemy of neutral energy when accessed and utilized is determined by the intentions of those who use it. Those who use energy in a positive manner are allies to the powerful creation forces of Nature. Those who use energy in a negative manner amplify the forces of entropy. Fortunately, these forces of entropy soon bind those who work with them, and the inevitable progress of Nature creates its own transformation.

The personal alchemist understands the power of intentions. The activation of positive intentions and creative healing magick is the Craft of the Wise. The activation of entropy and negative intentions is the Craft of the Stupid. The Craft of the Wise is the craft of the light. Reflection of this positive light forms the healing magick, the personal alchemy system of Rays and Lights.

According to alchemists who evolved into their role as natural scientists, we may define "light" as the form and the focus of radiant energy. Light is also classified as gleaming, glowing, or luminous energy. Light is the reflection of all forms of energy. It is a charge or a discharge of that energy we perceive as light. It is motion as light, form reflected as light, sensation stimulated by energy as light, as well as the pressure or force of energy we describe as its intensity, or its light.

Focused light is created by a convergence of light rays, waves or beams. Focused light reflects a concentration of essential energy. It is this concentration which produces a specific illumination, image, or effect. Focused light connects the point of origin of the energy and the point of image reflecting that energy. A "Ray" is a concentrated form of focused light.

Natural science describes a Ray as a narrow, focused beam of naturally reproducing transmitted light, to indicate its natural, spontaneous and continuous energy. A Ray is best understood as a spontaneous stream of energy emanating from and emitting a specific quality, property, or attribute.

These Rays of energy are reflected and received as color. The more intense the stream of energy, the stronger the Ray, the more recognizable the color, and the more specific the effects. The focus of energy as light determines its intensity as a Ray. The scattering of light beams produces a diffuse rather than direct effect.

The qualities of focused Rays are specific enough to have unique properties. The qualities of diffuse light are less specific, and are described in terms of their attributes or their ascribed, observed effects. An "attribute" describes the function of a quality. A "quality" describes the alchemy of an energy. A "property" specifies the unique form of a quality. Because of their interrelationships, property, quality, and attribute merge when we describe them in terms of their alchemy.

For example, the color Ray of Red:

Property	Short intense bursts of energy
Quality	Activation; thrust; stimulation
Attributes	Excitement; anger; lust; drives; blood; foundational, essential life forces

The metaphysical quality of alchemy transcends the known qualities of chemistry or physics. However, alchemy includes these scientific forms and functions with observation and analysis of its "structure," composition, and transformation of Rays and Lights as viable energies or substances. The personal alchemist reflects the empirical formulation of alchemy and approaches the healing magick of Rays and Lights as an experimental, experiential science. Alchemy as a science involves the study and utilization of preternatural and supernatural forces of energy, as we discussed.

The personal alchemist who reflects an emphasis on the preternatural forces uses the form of the healing magick called "Thanaturgy," and the philosophy of Natural science. The personal alchemist who emphasizes the supernatural forces reflects the philosophy of Divine intervention, the Theological Science, or the healing magick form called "Theurgy." The personal alchemist of today also recognizes that all forms reflect nothing more or less than the approach used by science to access the qualities, properties, and attributes of ultimately indivisible energy. That of Nature and of the Divine are seen to be of one alchemy by the modern personal alchemist.

This view is perhaps the most potent development in the evolution of science, physics, and human consciousness since the time of medieval alchemists. Of course the witches, who view the Divine as reflected in Nature, have always understood this alchemical truth. Most modern witches and alchemists have viewed the evolution of modern science with some amusement as it attempts to "discover" and measure that which has always been in existence, and is essentially immeasurable.

Some modern witches and alchemists still regard any "modern" form of science as counter to their craft because of its structured systems. These structures of science seem, to some, too close to the structures of religion so recently imposed upon Western civilization. However, it is wise for all modern witches and alchemists to refrain from this sort of separatist judgement, as it is similar to the dogmatic controlling alchemy of the Church imposed during the Dark Ages.

The modern witch or alchemist who is true to the Craft of Light understands the illumination and the evolution of an ecumenical blend. The old ways of Nature were once almost obliterated in the name of religion and the new sciences. The modern ways of Nature and alchemy will thrive with the understanding, acceptance, and illumination which emerges from accessing the common enlightened wisdom in all forms of science and religion.

Additionally, the power of forgiveness has a positive alchemical transformative effect on the enlightenment of human nature and the evolution of consciousness. After all, who but the forces of entropy seeks retribution through the persecution of thought, philosophy, science, and religion?

Remember that the alchemy of acceptance nullifies the effects of rejection most directly within ourselves as individuals. With time and patience, modern sciences will catch up eventually. This is particularly true if we give them some "trails" to follow, or provide a dimension in which we can have a "meeting of the minds."

From this we may create another Renaissance of light and consciousness unparalleled in the evolution of humankind. The energy is there for all to share. Let us honor the ancient alchemists and the witches by emulating their efforts to maintain health with an open mind—and an open heart. Harmony is created by blending energies and philosophies, not by separating or structuring them dogmatically.

The Renaissance brought important new and renewed interest in the Natural sciences and philosophies. Perhaps more important to the evolution of Western civilization, though, was the development of sciences involved in the exploration of human nature. The Ages of Reason and Philosophy which followed the Renaissance laid the groundwork on which our current New Age of consciousness has been built. Foremost in this have been the sciences and philosophies of the mind or psyche; that is, modern psychology or human sciences. The advent of modern psychology brought a newly evolved sense of value and compassion for the human condition. One of the key factors in the emergence of modern psychology was the alchemical explorations which showed underlying unity or commonalities in human nature. Prior to this, most efforts to understand the human psyche had stressed the "external" forces on rather that the internal processes of the mind. Disorders of the mind had been considered indications of negative possession by external "demons," or the result of a spell or "black art" rather than as an expression of natural, internal, mental processes.

For example, during the burning times a great fear of the witches resulted in many cases of supposed possessions, or "spells." These were blamed on women, and some men, who were accused of using the black arts of negative sorcery to control the souls of the people afflicted by their spells.

Witches have always been people of amplified magnetism and personal presence. When that presence and magnetism affected a person in the form of dreams, fantasies, or even Natural physical attraction, these were seen as attempts to possess or enchant.

Today, we still speak of someone who strikes our fancy and stimulates our fantasies as "enchanting." We recognize now that whatever images and sensations that enchanting person evokes from us are a natural reaction from our own mind and body. In medieval times, however, such misunderstood reactions often resulted in the persecution and death of those who were naturally enchanting. As the great "mother" of modern women's spirituality, Simone de Beavoir, has succinctly stated, "Some women were burned simply because they were beautiful." While some of these superstitious fears and reactions persist today, even within modern psychology, most have faded in the new light of understanding and exploration of the nature of the human psyche.

While certain factions of modern psychology continue to view the more esoteric contents and processes of the human psyche as "magical thinking" or para-psychological alchemy, many factions have begun to recover the natural magick of the human mind and the alchemy of its limitless dimensions. Without the "trial by fire" of the Dark Ages and the renewal catalyst of the Renaissance, the positive evolution of philosophy and psychology would not have been possible. Without the concept of individual human rights and the value of free mind and choice, modern psychology would have become simply another form of dogmatic mind control. Instead, despite some intra-philosophical differences, modern psychology has expanded to include in its exploration the ultimately uncontrolled free mind of the individual human psyche.

Most significant to the expanded progress of modern psychology has been the recovery of what Carl Jung called the "alchemystical" properties of the human mind. The work of Carl Jung regarding the internal contents and individual processes of the human mind as they express themselves in the realms of mental imagery is specific to the material presented in this system of healing magick. With the work of Carl Jung, modern psychology began to be an alchemical science of human consciousness and internal individual processes. Prior to Jung, much of modern psychology reflected an observation of the internal contents of the human mind, but not necessarily an honoring of its significance for the person.

Specifically, the work of Sigmund Freud, albeit an immeasurably valuable contribution to the evolution of psychology, regarded the contents of the human mind as emerging from a miasmic "swamp" of repressed sexualities.

The contents of mental imagery were basically seen by Freud as fantasies created primarily by unsatisfied people seeking to fulfill wishes of either an erotic or ambitious nature. Although Freud did recognize somewhat that the restrictions of the times he lived in influenced the nature, that is, the contents of what he called "fantasies," the dogmatic absolutism of his thoughts on the underlying sexual themes was all too apparent. According to Freud:

> *In young women, erotic wishes dominate the phantasies almost exclusively, for their ambition is generally comprised in their erotic longings; in young men, egoistic and ambitious wishes assert themselves plainly enough alongside their erotic desires.*

In short, Freud and the Freudian "schools" of psychology represented a somewhat negative viewpoint of the individual mind as, for the most part, controlled by the baser human drives. The contents of mental imagery were seen to be either conscious or unconscious reactions to these baser drives. Additionally, the human "psychic" reality was never credited by this "school" of psychology as having any real dimension of consciousness, awareness, or individual choice within its internal processes. Remembering the Dark Ages and the medieval viewpoints on the nature of the human mind, we can certainly see that Freudian theory represented little progress toward the true valuing of the individual human experience and the honoring of the inalienable rights of free mind and free choice. Ironically, Freud labeled Jung's "alchemystical" viewpoint as "occult."

Freud, it seems, was still bound by the duality viewpoint rather than the dynamic philosophy which views conscious/unconscious, male/female, active/receptive, and external/internal as parts of a single unified process. That which Freud described as occult included the same states of consciousness and contents of Nature and human nature that the ancient alchemists had viewed as being mystical, preternatural and supernatural. Like those same ancient alchemists who held fast to the inherent explorative, experimental nature of science, Jung strongly advocated the open and experiential nature of the new human science—psychology.

Jung's advocacy of the active use of individual internal images as a tool for healthful psychological growth stemmed, in part, from his personal work within the realms of his own imagination. Jung's openness to exploration of self through imagery and the mythic richness of human imaginative contents led him away from the teachings of his friend and psychoanalytic mentor, Sigmund Freud. The final break between Freud and Jung may be said to represent a significant break away from the last vestiges of medieval dogmatism and devaluation of the individual human psyche. That which Freud viewed as being the underlying foundation for the contents of the human psyche—sexuality—was viewed by Jung as simply an aspect of that multidimensional creature—the natural human being.

In fact, it was Freud's insistence that Jung never abandon the sexual theory but make a "dogma" of it which signalled the basic incompatibility of the two men—and ultimately of the two viewpoints forming the basis of modern psychology. The break became complete with Freud's urgent proposal to Jung to create an "unshakable bulwark" against the emergence of "occultism" in psychology. That which Freud viewed as being experimental and occult, Jung viewed as being experiential and transcendent, or alchemystical. Accordingly Jung wrote:

> First of all, it was the words (of Freud's) "bulwark" and "dogma" that alarmed me. For a dogma, that is to say, an undisputable confession of faith is set up only when the aim is to suppress doubts once and for all. But that no longer has anything to do with scientific judgement; only with a personal power drive . . . What Freud seemed to mean by "occultism" was virtually everything that philosophy and religion, including the rising contemporary science of parapsychology, had learned about the psyche. To me the sexual theory was just as occult, that is to say, just as unproven a hypothesis as many other speculative views. As I saw it, a scientific truth was a hypothesis that might be adequate for the moment but was not to be preserved as an article of faith for all time.

In this statement, we can see Jung's openness to and recognition of the process and flow of events and ideas which are the alchemical foundation of experiential human psychology. Furthermore, Jung's courage to stand by his personal convictions emerged from his own experiences. In the tradition of ancient alchemists, witches, and mystics, Jung advocated the value of the personal human experience as the formulation of all science, philosophy, and psychology.

Years before terms such as New Age, Aquarian Age, or Age of Consciousness became a part of Western vocabularies, Jung stood squarely against the arbitrary regulation and dogmatic definitions of the inherently personal contents of the human psyche. Jung viewed these contents or mental images as a natural emergence from a self-regulating human system with potential for the evolution of the person as an individual, as well as a part of the greater whole of humankind. This view naturally recalls the ancient holistic view of unified health and the synthesis of humankind attuned to Natural and self-Natural processes. In no small way, Jung served the purposes of human evolution as well as those who were persecuted long before his time. More than just a modern mystic, Jung was a modern personal alchemist, blending the ancient myths and philosophies with modern methods and psychologies to create a transpersonal, interconnected system of self-exploration and knowledge with universal, eternally present truths.

Like many of those persecuted before him, Jung had to withstand a period of isolation and ostracism when he broke with the established, professionally accepted thoughts and doctrines of psychology. However, in the true spirit of alchemy, Jung used this newfound "independence" to further his own exploration of the psyche and the esoteric, transcendental realms of myth, magick, and the mysteries of the human mind. Also in the tradition of the ancient alchemists, Jung strove to explore systems of myth, magick, and the mind from many different cultures. He did this in order to ascertain the underlying unity his faith in humankind's exalted potentials showed him. It was from Jung's personal alchemical blend of many seemingly "opposite" systems that the powerful form of active imagery emerged as a tool for self-transformation and personal empowerment. Jung was adamant in pointing out the eternal nature and the antiquity of his concepts. It is my personal opinion, however, that the enormity of Jung's work, his personal courage, and the influence of his philosophy on the development of psychology precludes his own disconnecting of himself. As Jung reflected in his final years:

> *When people say I am wise, or a sage, I cannot accept it . . . I never think that I am the one who must see to it that cherries grow on stalks. I stand, and behold admiring what nature can do.*

This recalls for me the Roman accounts of the Druids in the British Isles—as paraphrased, "And the wisest of them said, *this we know—that we know nothing.*" We may translate this to mean that knowledge is ultimately limitless—personal and transpersonal. Wisdom reflects the expansion and experience of all knowledge, ever constant in its continual processes of change. Regardless of the systems we adopt—or adapt—they are no more or less than reflections of the moment from which they emerged, and serve as a framework for systems of the future. It may well be said that our systems of wisdom are our own active images reflected within the ever-evolving mind of humanity; an alchemy of imagery emerging from the eternal blending of truth, Nature, and the experience of Self-nature.

The Personal Alchemy System

It is my hope that the system of alchemy and healing magick I present in this book will, in some small way, honor the efforts of those who have stood their ground—and, on occasion, staked their lives—for the inalienable human right to develop individual, personal wisdoms with all of the potential of a free mind and the power of free choice. It is also my hope that you, as the reader of this book, will honor this as simply another system of alchemy and healing magick from which you may glean material for the experimental, experiential development of your own. That is how this very system developed.

The personal alchemy system presented here includes foundation elements from many traditional systems of wisdom as they specifically relate to the correlating alchemies of color Rays and Lights and the active use of imagery. This system of healing magick builds on the foundation of traditions but is not bound by the limitations of set rules, forms, doctrines, or dogmas. In *Personal Alchemy*, "rules" from the past provide correlations for the present, and experimental catalysts and materials for the future. *Personal Alchemy* was designed to be flexible and self-expanding. And so indeed, were you. That is the definitive power of personal alchemy.

How you use this book depends entirely on your personal style and experience. You are free to adapt this system as you choose for the creation of your own alchemy, self-transformation, and personal empowerment. *Personal Alchemy* provides you with the foundation from which you may develop the most simple and basic or elaborate and complex system of healing magick. It is your choice.

Personal Alchemy also includes newly emerging material in the continually evolving metaphysical science using the energies of color Rays and Lights, and expanded applications of the use of active imagery for self-empowerment. Wherever possible, an alchemical blend of traditional (tried and true) elements with emerging (experimental and experiential) information has been used to form the intricate sets of correlations presented in this book. Many of the traditional color Rays and Lights have extensive correlations which match their qualities, attributes, and properties to other systems of healing magick. The newly emerging color Rays and Lights have correlations based on similar matches determined by extensive experimentation and the experiences of a wide variety of contemporary color alchemists working with the positive energies of Rays and Lights. It is my hope, as I know it to be theirs, that you will continue this alchemical tradition of an experiential, experimental science of Self. Additionally, I suggest that the information presented in this book be viewed as a springboard into further study on your part. This is particularly true of the magick systems correlated with the Rays and Lights. These systems are presented in their most efficient foundational forms in *Personal Alchemy* specifically to encourage your experience of learning and empowerment.

Each of the systems from which the correlations are drawn embodies an entire "school" of wisdom. I suggest that those specific correlating systems which are alchemically most potent for you stimulate more in-depth investigation. *Personal Alchemy* can be the catalyst which clarifies the methods of several systems of healing magick by providing an instructive, experiential format for working with these systems within the personal realms of your individual imagery. When you experience information fully, it becomes personal wisdom from the standpoint of personal wisdoms as they correlate with your individual experience. The extensive set of correlations in this book is presented generally and sequentially, layered one upon another in order to guide your experience of learning these as a system of healing magick. These correlations are then presented specifically in relation to each color Ray and Light to provide extensive information and elements from which you may evolve your own experience of this alchemy.

These correlations form the foundation of *Personal Alchemy* and provide a variety of ways in which to access and amplify the experience of active imagery using Rays and Lights for self-transformational, healing magick.

Personal Alchemy is divided into seven parts, foundational information through technical details. It finishes with a quick-reference resource section and bibliography.

The first section teaches the methods of this healing magick and explains the process of using correlations to create a personal alchemy of experiential self-transformation and empowerment. In this section, you will learn:

- *The Alchemy of Active Imagery*: How imagination activates our healing magick.
- *Attributes and Elements of Rays and Lights*: How qualities effect one's healing magick.
- *Harmonic and Sensory Correlations*: How sound and scent effect our healing magick.
- *Symbolic Keys and Personification Keys*: How we represent our healing magick.
- *Runic and Astrological Correlations*: How we amplify our traditional systems and our healing magick.
- *Tarot Arcana and Angelic Correlations*: How we expand our system to include other dimensions of healing magick.
- *Stone Alchemy, Healing Magick with Stones and Crystals*: How we can incorporate and focus with Mineral World healing magick.

The next sections provide alchemical information about the properties or energy patterns of focused color Rays which fall into the primary category of Red (Body), Yellow (Mind), and Blue (Spirit). Specific methods are provided to teach the process of using these color energies in healing magick and active imagery.

Personal Alchemy provides a system of healing magick which is easily adapted to your lifestyle. It provides methods of simple application for efficient and effective forms of alchemy, as well as techniques of intricate application for elaborate, extensive structures of alchemy. *Personal Alchemy* presents a system of self-improvement and self-development with the methods of a spiritual science and the metaphysics of magick. It is a system of healing magick which uses the energies of Nature and the imageries of Self-Nature to create an alchemy adaptable to numerous life styles.

Personal Alchemy, as a handbook, is designed to teach you a natural system of self-transformation and empowerment based on the use of active imagery to access the healing magick qualities of Rays and Lights. These qualities are explored with an extensive set of correlations provided to give you numerous ways in which to experience, and therefore learn, this system of healing magick.

Personal Alchemy is a blend of instructive information and experiential exercises. In order to fully access the alchemy of *Personal Alchemy* as a handbook, you will need to involve yourself in the material presented. The degree of your involvement will determine the depth of your experience, the dimensions of your magick, and the evolution of your personal alchemy. Evolve wisely, with the force of light supporting your Self-transformation and empowering your growth into wisdom.

Tarot: The Fool

*The Self/Personal Alchemist . . . always at the
beginning of the Journey of Self-Transformation.*

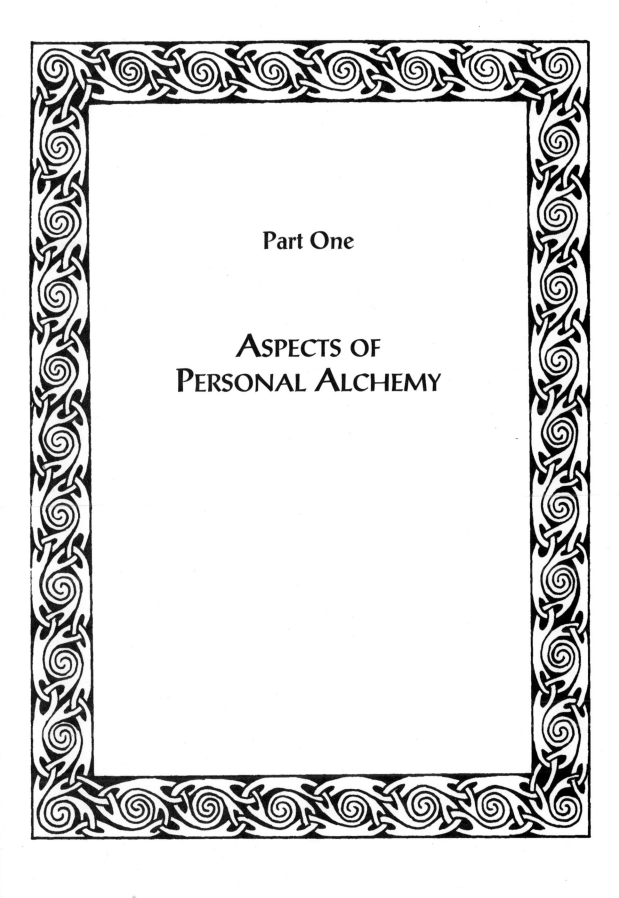

Part One

ASPECTS OF PERSONAL ALCHEMY

Chapter One

The Personal Alchemy of Imagery in Healing Magick

Arthur, for something to become tangible, for something . . . to be transported from the realm of imagination to reality and seem to fill man's physical senses, is yet an illusion.

Merlin, are you saying this realm is no more real than . . . than last night's dreams?

Yes. Yes, that is so, Arthur. The difference lies within the dimension or realm you were in when you experienced it. Many events remembered by the mind never occurred in the manner remembered. But they were experienced by the emotions, by the senses, and have thus become a part of your reality.

Arthur, remember this, for it is important. Reality is but one form of imagination. It is imagery, Arthur, imagery.

—Kara Starr
(Merlin's Journal of Time, The Camelot Adventure)

Imagery and Personal Alchemy

What does the word alchemy mean to you? What images does it bring to mind? Perhaps your imagination provides you with mental pictures.

In your mind's eye, you find yourself looking around a most unusual room. Everywhere you look are wondrous sights. Some are frightening, some are funny—all are fascinating.

The room is filled with a shimmering haze. Sunlight streams down from a high window, bringing a gentle illumination to the scene.

The walls are covered with mysterious charts, showing maps of the universe and formulas for alchemical equations. Books, both ancient and new, are stuffed into bookshelves and stacked haphazardly all around the room.

Papers and writing materials are scattered across a great oaken table as though someone had left them in a hurry.

Curious now, you move in for a closer look. You notice an ink stain beginning to form where a pen has been left, open, on one sheet of paper. You pick up the paper, feeling its coarse, thick surface. Parchment perhaps.

On the paper, someone has hastily scrawled—

Expectations !*!! * ! *
Release w/ Yellow
Realign w/ Turquoise
Balance w/ Indigo
Eureka ! X X ! !

Suddenly, you hear a slight rustling behind you, followed by the sound of sharp claws scratching, scratching, scratching.

Feeling somewhat chagrined to be snooping in this unfamiliar place, you quickly put the paper back and turn around to face the source of the noise. Across the room you see a massive mirrored wardrobe with one of its doors ajar, opening slowly—very slowly.

As the door opens slightly, you glimpse your reflection in the mirror. You realize you are holding your breath. The scratching continues in earnest now. Furious scratching noises seem to fill the room.

The last thing you notice as the mirrored door swings open further is sunlight twinkling though three glass bottles on a shelf behind you. The contents of each bottle moves and swirls visibly through the glass. You are intrigued by the colors in each bottle—yellow, turquoise, and indigo.

The scratching stops. The silence of the room is as tangible as the mists. A slight rustle is heard once more from inside the wardrobe. The mirrored door shakes, and your reflection trembles. The colors in the bottles on the shelf behind you seem to dance in the air.

A furry paw reaches around the door, claws scraping against the wood.

With a final, furious thump, the door is opened wide enough to allow the inhabitant of the cupboard to leap out and land spritely on the writing table.

A set of turquoise eyes studies you coolly, then shifts to examine the condition of its paw.

A slow rumbling sound emerges from deep inside its throat.

It appraises you once more, then speaks—**Meow!**

Well, now, what **did** you expect?

Alchemy and Expectations

Your expectation about what alchemy is will do more to influence how you use it than any other factor. It is true that alchemy is mysterious. Alchemy is an active, ever-changing process of experimentation and experience. It is an activation of the great mystery of mind and consciousness.

Alchemy is a natural science, but not an exact one. Its "potions," whether tangible or intangible, are never static. The effects of alchemical formulas are most clearly related to the unique qualities of the individual using them, as well as to the issues worked with: who you are, what you use, and how you use methods of alchemy are most important.

For example, only you can determine which of the bottles in the last image contains the potion you need to deal with your own expectations. (We all have them.) Let's clarify this a bit with some alchemical experimentation using the imagery just described. Experimenting with the content of an image to create a format for Self-transformation is an alchemical method which allows for a personal restructuring of consciousness and mindsets. Jung called this process "active imagery."

A small gray kitten leaps deftly from the table to the shelf containing the three glass bottles. The contents of each bottle moves more quickly as the kitten rubs against the glass with her soft, sleek fur. The colors in each container become brighter and brighter until their intensity threatens to burst forth from the bottles.

You feel compelled to choose one color— but which one?

At your hesitation, the kitten chooses for you. A flick of her tail sends the indigo-filled bottle plummeting toward the floor. Upon contact the bottle disappears, leaving only a cool, soothing swirl of light rising slowly from the floor.

As the indigo blue light makes its way up your body, you pick up the parchment with the magical formula for:

Expectations!!!

"Yellow for release of expectations, turquoise to amplify; indigo blue for balancing," you read aloud to the kitten. "But how is it for balance?" The kitten makes no reply, and regards you with the calm detachment of a Tibetan monk.

Indigo light swirls around your head several times, gaining in intensity. On your inhaled breath it enters your third eye area like a laser, piercing your forehead. As you exhale, indigo blue lights sparkle briefly, then vanish into the vapors of energy surrounding your body. You feel every part of your self pull together in perfect synthesis.

As the indigo fades, you find you are able to understand your feelings and your fears. You see the sum total of your experiences and expectations with greater objectivity. You confide your new-found self-consciousness in the cat until she sweeps another bottle from the shelf to catch your attention.

This time, yellow strands of light move up your body with a steady, measured pace. As these lines reach your solar plexus, they arrange themselves in a symmetrical, organized shape and begin to glow brightly. You notice the yellow pattern reflecting in the mirrored door. Though reversed, its symmetry remains the same.

You feel a quiet sense of order within. Thoughts and images of the many expectations you carry inside your mind flicker by one at a time, as though you were watching a slide show.

You find that you have the detached capacity to determine which expectations have value in your life—and which do not. Images of friends, acquaintances, colleagues, and family appear on the "screen" of your mind's eye.

With each inhalation, you focus and evaluate the expectations you place on your self and on the people in your life. With each exhalation, you release expectations which are not positive. You eliminate those expectations which show a lack of balance and perception. You have time to review these images—in order, of course—before the kitten noses the turquoise-filled bottle off the shelf.

Flashes of turquoise light sweep into your chest, sending tiny jolts throughout your entire being. For a moment you are only aware of the electric sensation this turquoise creates, then you "wake up" to a new sense of purpose. Ideas flash in turquoise lights inside your mind. A feeling of dedication and resolve brings a new sense of hope and potential for the goals you have dreamed of accomplishing and the expectations you have chosen to keep and manifest positively in your life.

As the last turquoise flashes crackle off into the mists of the room, you feel you have entered a higher, spiritual state of service. You resist the temptation to proselytize your beliefs in front of the kitten, since cats are well known for their animosity toward evangelists of any sort.

You wonder if you've "over-amplified" yourself on turquoise, and wish aloud there were some way to recreate the calming indigo lights.

The kitten rummages behind some small jars on the shelf, sniffing and discarding several before she settles on a short round container marked:

Personal! (all purpose secret ingredient for alchemy)

Curiosity being the catalyst it is, you open the bottle. A puff of smoke rises from inside and floats past your "good ear" as you lift the lid. Dismayed to find the jar empty, you look inside the lid. There you find yourself reflected in a small round mirror. The puff of smoke drifts into your ear—and a quiet little voice whispers:

Imagination!

The cat's fur stands up like velvet needles. Her eyes flash—turquoise blue—across the room. Only she knows what to expect next, if she chooses to care.

Alchemy is an experiential craft. The potency of your alchemy depends on your personal willingness to be flexible and creative with your self and with the processes of transformation in your life.

How well you change and deepen the experience of alchemy is directly related to how well you experience change, and how deeply connected you are to the center of your self. Alchemy with the active use of imagery allows you to access the dimensions of consciousness in which you can create change in your life. Active imagery is the personal use of the contents of your mind. Like the color-filled bottles, active imagery shows some of its potency before it is released, but its real alchemy is only developed through conscious use of the material which emerges.

Carl Jung called the active use of imagery a "transcendent" function, one which leads to the full realization of the self as a unique, evolved individual. An "evolved individual" is one whose processes of self-transformation have led to a harmonious, integrated state of being. Active imagery is a powerful positive method which evolves the self harmoniously with active consciousness. Personal active imagery uses the flow of emerging images, the focus of evaluating images, and formulation of manifest images. Alchemical active imagery uses the essential forces of Nature and Self-nature to establish an experimental framework within which the Self may create the foundations for experiential Self-transformation.

Alchemist's Note: Remember that which is most personal is that which is inside your own mind. Share this with your self, if with no one else. It is your right—and responsibility—to maintain a free mind. Free will may be philosophically debatable, but free mind is a given. Accept it—and make good use of it.

Imagery and Healing Magick

Active imagery reflects the alchemy of spiritual realizations, psychological rationalizations, and physical regulations. Together, these create experiential reorganization which is the alchemy of active imagery.

We might also say that healing magick emerges from your spiritual aspects—is imaged by your psychological aspects—and manifested by your physical aspects.

Healing magick uses the natural "forces" of spiritual flow, psychological focus, and physical form to create an experiential framework as the essential foundation for personal alchemy.

What images does the word "Magick" create in your mind's eye? What connection does it make with the Spiritual aspects of your self? The psychological aspects? The physical? Imagery used actively can evoke the personal synthesis of Body, Mind, and Spirit in harmonious connection, reflecting the highest aspects of Self.

Perhaps the word itself and the feel—or energy—of what magick implies has some aspects in common with these images.

Active Imagery, Spiritual Format: Empowerment Ceremony

A spiritual format in an imagery encourages us to create an image of our sacred, or magickal self. When we can image this magick Self, we can detach from it and begin to work with the energies it represents—our magick Self.

You are walking up a wide, sweeping marble stairway leading you toward a temple of magnificent beauty. Each of the many towers of this temple has a crystal spire pointing skyward to honor the presence of a higher source. The walls of this temple are mirrored with silver and trimmed with gold. An altar carved with ancient metaphysical symbols is set under a rainbow-hued skylight.

The full moon illuminates the room with a veil of white misty light. Violet and gold candles are placed on a richly embroidered cloth of emerald green silk. The misty veil of white light shimmers with a myriad of minute crystalline rainbows each time the candle flame flickers.

You approach the altar—slowly, consciously, ceremoniously. Your robes sweep across a circle painted with mysterious symbols on the cool, tiled floor. An amethyst and crystal pendant around your neck reflects the light—and the energy—of this sacred temple. Rainbows flash from the crystal, sending balanced bands of colored light around you, arcing over your head in rainbows.

Each rainbow band shoots upward, then curves down to connect with the crown of violet lights encircling your head. Your amethyst sends forth a harmonic tone which sounds like a dove crooning. Violet light shoots skyward.

You carry an incense burner; it swings rhythmically on a red velvet cord as you walk. The aroma of frankincense and myrrh creates an atmosphere of solemn purpose and a sense of anticipation in this temple of high spiritual magick. You circle the altar several times, gathering the energies of the rainbow lights into the circle of smoke you create.

You place your incense burner on the altar, and reach skyward with both hands. With each inhaled breath, you pull the crystalline lights closer to your physical body. With each exhalation, you flash rainbow lights from your fingertips. You cast these lights out into the ethers to share. Rainbows flash in the air briefly just outside your body, then flow into the realms of Spirit.

When you have absorbed the clarifying energies of the crystalline lights, you honor the experience by sending rainbows skyward in great sweeping arches. These catch in the veil of white surrounding the altar. You continue this process until the room hums with energy. As the energy builds, the hum intensifies to a tangible level.

Holding your pendant close to your heart, you speak:

> By the powers of violet rays of light which connect me to the realms of Spirit, and by the powers of green rays which open my heart to my mind and heal all disharmonies, I call forth the powers of the highest love, I call forth the nurturing abundance which is the healing Green Ray—I call forth the forces of Spirit to connect me to the highest realms of light.
>
> With these energies, I manifest a more healing distribution of love and healing throughout this world—as far as my mind's eye can travel. May I do these acts with clarity of purpose and purity of heart.
>
> I send out rainbows of light to all the world. May these be manifested by the crystal, activated by gold, borne on the veil of white. I do these acts with heartfelt intentions that abundance shall be more equitably shared by all—I call for the inspiration of spirit to connect me clearly to my purpose.
>
> May I be a channel for light and love.
>
> May my highest spiritual self reflect within my personal consciousness that I may better know my self.

Active Imagery, Psychological Format:
Release of a Binding Relationship

A psychological format in imagery encourages us to focus on the expression of our feelings. When we do so, we need to remember to listen to what we're saying. We have all the answers.

You are sitting cross-legged on the floor, facing the fireplace. Your breathing is measured and rhythmically ordered. You focus your awareness on the dancing yellow flames in front of you.

Here and there a flame leaps higher than the rest, consuming the sage brush you have scattered on the logs. As each leaf and stem blackens and turns to ash, you release your breathe slowly—purposefully—and say:

I release the relationship with _____ which has bound me for too long and impeded the cycles of my self-transformation.

I accept the responsibility for choosing this experience. I honor that all things in Nature and Self-nature have their own cycles of birth, death, and renewal. I know that these are the natural cycles of transformation as manifest in Spirit, as manifest in my Self.

My relationship with those whom I let bind me has reached the end of its cycle for me. I do not choose to renew this relationship with _____ .

I wish to release all that binds us so that we may each be free to follow our own paths in life. I can no longer walk side by side, nor can I meet at the crossroads of the inner planes of consciousness with _____ .

You sprinkle sage and cedar chips on the flames. Their scent carries you back into your memories. Each image, each emotion, each tear which emerges is a signal for you to breathe, focus and release. Feelings flow through you—unbound by each exhaled breath.

When sadness or anger seems overwhelming, you speak into the flames:

My Lady Brede, fair Briget of the sacred Orange Flame, I call upon you to give me your fires of strength and courage so I may do what I know is for the good of all.

If need be, express each feeling or thought which seems somehow "stuck" in the release process. With each expressed thought or feeling, sprinkle a few sage and cedar leaves on the fire. Focus on the flames as they consume the herbs. Watch as ashes sweep upward from the yellow flame into the smoky blackness of the chimney. Each ash represents the aspects which have bound you emotionally—and alchemically—to the relationship.

Breathe, and constantly, consciously, imagine those negative emotions shifted by your own focus and strength of intent. Release each breath with a little puff of air up the chimney to show your willingness to be an active, aware participant again in the cycles of self-trans-formation in your life. Make a personal pledge to your self to be more focused and per-ceptive. Vow to think before you act. Resolve to be more perceptive in your future relationships with others—and with your self.

You take a small black stone and hold it up to the flames until it becomes warm in your hands—and say:

With the clearing energies of Black Light, I sweep myself clean of all residues of negativity. Let this light cleanse this stone as it clears me. I charge this stone for the magical purposes of personal release.

A rush of Black Light sweeps through you, vibrating into the air around you. A glow of light spreads throughout the black stone in your hand. This dark light of release spreads its clearing energies through your body and sweeps into the black stone in your hand. The stone vibrates with a deep rhythmic pattern. You connect with this rhythm as you slowly move the dark stone downward, to touch the floor.

Your binding negativities seep into the Black Light around the stone. You close your eyes and feel these negativities drain slowly into the floor. Breathe again with focused intent. Each inhaled breath isolates a specific negativity. Each exhaled breath sends it down into the stone, through the floor and into the Earth for transmutation.

Holding the stone in your outstretched hands, you say:

> *I honor the energies of Fire and Air for the flames which have purified my personal alchemy, the process of my self-transformation, and my private healing magick.*

> *I honor the elements of Water and Earth for the clearing herbs, with which I transformed my pain and regret in personal renewed perception and resolve.*

> *I honor the energies of Spirit which bring the highest light to the cycles of my self-transformation.*

> *I honor the energies of Nature which will absorb these negativities and transmute them into nurturing energies to create new growth in my Self and others. May those I release also have new opportunities for growth and Self-nurturance.*

(If you're feeling a bit too structured with all this organized yellow, make a mental image of your negativities converted into compost. This brings the healing energies of humor.)

Focusing on the warm orange embers, you say:

> *May that which I have released be recycled in my self-transformation so that this experience will yet prove to be a cycle of positive growth.*

Reaching down again to touch the floor with your stone, you chant harmonically with the short sound of **o** as in **mom**. It is okay to laugh; it is a great form of release and rejuvenation. Simple phrases which strengthen your magick intentions are helpful, such as:

> *Gone Mom, down, gone down. No frowns Mom, gone, long gone.*

You hold the stone in your hands and take a deep breath. Blowing your released breathe across the stone, you say:

> *With this breath, I do connect with the clearing powers of Black Light energies which I see reflected in the beautiful black color of this stone and feel in its vibration. I honor the energies in this stone with which I have already released the bindings of my past relationships with _____.*

Breathe again and release without words, just the harmonic of short **o**. As you breathe and chant the harmonic for Black Light, you feel the energies of the stone begin to shift to a stronger vibration, a more intense energy pattern. You breathe softly. Feel the Black Light of release attuning the stone, and your self, to the healing magick of grounded, Earth-centered power, and say:

> *I change this stone as a symbol of my power to transform and renew myself with the forces of earth-centered release. With this stone as my talisman, I do focus my awareness closer to*

the Earth. May I ever be attuned to Her cycles of transformation and renewal. May the cycles of my own self-transformation be harmonious and flowing.

You put the stone at your feet and stand facing the fire.

You breathe deeply and whisper:

Release . . . Release . . . This is as I please.

You breathe again, and turn slowly to your right until your back is to the fireplace.

Your cycle has begun from a new position—180 degrees from where you began. You are unbound and released. You are renewed and reborn to your Self.

Holding your arms outstretched at shoulder level, you slowly give your self a hug. You reach out again and say:

I embrace the rebirth of my self at each point of transformation in my life. I call forth the Golden-Green Ray to bring its energy into the cycles of my self. I have released that which I allowed to bind me. I seek to renew my relationship with Self, Nature, and Spirit. I embrace and accept the Golden-Green of Nature's cycles.

As you speak, a pattern of energy builds in your outstretched, circled arms. You embrace the renewal energies of Nature. A Golden-Green ball of light forms, slowly building in clarity and intensity.

Breathe and make the image real. The Golden-Green energy flows into your body, cleansing you, clearing you—and preparing you for your next cycle of self-transformation. You absorb the Golden-Green energies of renewal. You honor your self and express your gratitude for the positive self-transformation you have created.

Take time now to have a quiet cup of tea. Celebrate the change you have created in your life. You have turned the wheel of Self from release to renewal. In some realm of time and space (inner-time and inner-space) you have experienced rebirth. An old way of being has just died—a new way of being has just been born.

Active Imagery, Physical Format:
Attunement for Healing Magick

A physical format is an imagery which encourages us to make friends with our body. Active imagery requires:

- Receptive consciousness
- Conscious activation
- Self-reflective conscience

Take a long, slow, soothing breath. Hold it for a moment, then release. Focus on the center of your Self. Experience that quiet inner place where you feel most grounded, balanced, and in charge of your self.

Now release your breath slowly with focused awareness, and pause for a moment before taking your next breath. During this pause, examine the sensations of your physical body. In the quiet pauses between the inhalation and exhalation of breath you can feel your physical energy patterns. Focus on the flow of essential life fluids; the electric forces of the central nervous system. Breathe again. A muscle twitches, signalling impatience or fatigue. Another muscle relaxes, signalling receptivity. You note your own sensations as you continue taking slow, deep breaths, pausing each time to examine the feel of energies moving through and around your body. You observe calmly, with detachment. Each bodily sensation is acknowledged, then released—as surely as you release your breath. Pains or discomforts are observed but not emphasized.

You continue to breathe in a calm, steady pattern until your body's energies become ordered and harmonious. You feel the strength and structure of your body—your physical vehicle—the container, for now, of your eternally recycling Spirit.

As you consider the abilities and the gifts your body brings, you feel gratitude and honor for the physical aspects of your self. You bless your connection to Spirit as it reflects in your physical body. You spend a few moments being aware of the wonders of your body. You are in gratitude for this wondrous "soft machine" which is your body. As you steady your breath, you muse on these thoughts and say them to your self either silently or aloud:

I accept my body as a gift which has wondrous abilities.

I honor my body as a physical vehicle in this life—and time.

I honor my body as a vessel of the highest light, and a channel for the forces of healing magick.

I honor my body as the reflection of my processes of self-transformation.

May my body and mind reflect a balanced relationship of unconditional positive regard.

May the balanced connection of Body and Mind bring me to a place of harmonious attunement with the realms of Spirit.

May the highest lights of Spirit, the multifaceted dimensions of Mind, and the self-healing structures of Body blend with alchemical perfection in the healing magick of my self-transformation.

May my magick bring healing energies to my self from within, and catalyst the alchemy of self-healing.

May my work with others also reflect the light of the highest good for all I encounter.

May I be a vessel of light; of truth. May I be a catalyst for the healing of my self—and for the alchemy of self-healing in others.

When you have found a deep, centered place within, you stand and stretch slowly several times. You feel the strength of your body building with each stretch. You stand relaxed and shift your awareness to the ground below you. Bending slowly toward the ground, you say:

I connect with the energies of the earth to bring support to my self-transformation. I honor the physical nature of the earth as I do the nature of my self—in the physical—on this Earth. I honor this physical form for the sensations it brings me; I honor the tangible power of the physical self.

You straighten your body gradually, taking deep, slow breaths as you go. You feel each point along your spine line up. Each vertebrae seems to stack itself upon the one before it, aligning your spine. You are creating a clearer physical pathway along which the energies of healing magick may flow. As you rise, you say:

I accept that the energies I work with must come from me—and through me—to create the alchemy of transformation in my self, and to catalyst the self-transformative healing process of others with whom I work.

You reach up as high as you can and take a deep, healing breath. Your fingertips tingle as you stretch. Your muscles feel warm, healthy, vibrant, and strong. You release your breath slowly and say:

I reach into the skies above me to gather the energies of spiritual realms for my self-transformation. I honor the infinite energies and powers of the highest Self.

I honor the great indefinable mystery of the spiritual energies. I accept what I cannot know, yet still feel manifested in me.

I honor the intangible power of the Spiritual Self.

Breathing deeply, you stretch "into spirit" once more. Releasing your breath very slowly, you bend toward the ground once more.

Breathing steadily, you straighten up, and hold your arms outstretched at heart level.

Now take one last deep, conscious breath. As you do, you tighten all the muscles of your body. You hold your breath and keep your muscles tightened (not strained), until you feel a warm, invigorating energy. You feel awake, alert, and activated.

Now release this last deep breath consciously. As you do so, relax all the muscles of your body. Pausing for a moment before you resume your regular breathing pattern, you examine the sensations of your physical body. You feel relaxed, reflective, and receptive.

You continue to stretch and bend with an alert, receptive consciousness until you feel empowered by the harmonious energies of Body, Mind and Spirit manifest in your Self.

When you have completed your experience with this attunement imagery, rest and reflect on the sensations, images, and emotions which emerged for you. To help your self-reflection, ask your self these questions. These questions help you evaluate—and therefore activate—the experience of your imagery in your life.

- Within the realm of my self—in this imagery—What did I experience of significance? Physical sensations? Emotions? Images? Colors? Thoughts?
- When those significant experiences emerged—What was I doing? How did each action make me feel? How do these correlate? How do they go together?

When you have evaluated your imagery, you can allow the images you choose to re-emerge for active restructuring. When you restructure your imagery, you activate the transformational process of Self-structure.

The Metaphysical Alchemy of Active Imagery

Imagery is active in every aspect of our self-transformation. Imagery is all that we experience in the metaphysical realms. Imagery is our way of identifying our impressions of everything we experience in the physical realms, as well.

Regardless of how tangible or intangible an energy may be, we will experience it ultimately because of our abilities to create imagery. That which we believe to be tangible may only be defined as such by our image of it. That which we believe to be intangible may only be so because of our lack of images for it.

To more fully explore and experience the alchemy of active imagery, we must be willing to distill all life to its most potent force—energy. Everything is energy—everything. Everything is energy—constantly moving, changing, transforming energy. Energy is most clearly defined by its type of movement, or vibrational rate. A specific rate of combination of different rates may be called a frequency, a sound, an energy pattern, a color, or an imagery. "Personal imagery" is the active reflection of energy patterns within the Self. We often refer to these patterns or "frequencies" quite simply as "energy." We speak of how an experience felt—but we are actually expressing the effect of the energy patterns of that experience on our own personal pattern of energy.

We say that someone or something has good or bad "vibes" because of our impressions of its energy, or frequency. We create imagery to define its effect on ourselves. Even those energy patterns which we define as ourselves and others are identified by our interaction with our self and others—and our image of that experience. The duality of "either/or" is also an image, not a manifest structure.

Metaphysically speaking (esoterically perhaps), we become what we experience. This happens when we accept that all things are no more or less than energy patterns created from our own imagery. The more we seek to make these energy patterns tangible, the more a part of us they seem. This is because all things share one potent force—energy. All things, all conscious realms, are already a part of us—ever have been—ever shall be. Life is an eternal present of energy patterns vibrating at different rates of speed. These we call past, present, future—and label with other arbitrary designations such as my self—and with other internal and external names.

When we work with imagery consciously, we are actively restructuring an energy pattern as it is defined by our image of it. When we change the image of our self, we change with that image. This is called "cognitive restructuring" in psychology. When we change our cognitions (or thoughts and images), we change ourselves. This, in turn, changes others—whether we have an understanding of that change or not. When we change our energy, it affects the energy in everything else. How could it not?

Jean Houston describes this process as such: "When someone in New York coughs—someone in New Delhi sneezes."

This may seem far-fetched to us, unless we consider how a stone thrown in a pond creates ripples all the way across. Even if we can't see the ripple, the vibration carries on.

When we connect with an energy pattern, its effects ripple through us. When we activate an imagery and bring it into focus, it becomes more tangible. The more tangible an image is, the more manifest it becomes. Our imagery becomes metaphysically real when we accept its physical reality. We do this by accepting the ultimate indivisible nature of all things. When we accept that all aspects of life are made of energy vibrating at different rates or frequencies, we begin to understand how we can use that knowledge to make conscious changes in our own energy patterns. We can "change our own vibes," so to speak. Timothy Leary tells us, "We're only as old as the last time we changed our mind."

Whether we can understand this great mystery or not, we have the ability to create imagery about it. When such imagery is personalized by many, it becomes more potently alchemical for our self-transformation. When an imagery is shared by the masses, its energies become more manifest.

For example, world peace is an imagery describing our impression of an energy pattern whose primary vibrational frequency is different from the frequency of war. However, since peace is still defined by its relationship to war, the energy pattern of war remains.

If this is not clear, try a little experiment. First of all, breathe slowly and release your breath. Focus your awareness inward to your place of inner vision. Imagine a cool Blue light in your mind's eye. Blue is cool and soothing, not like Red which is hot and stimulating. Blue is the energy pattern we need to be calm, cool, and collected. Blue can balance the activating catalyst of Red. Focus on Blue and ignore the Red when it emerges in your mind's eye. Don't let Red get your attention or it may get the energies we want to use for Blue. Remember, no Red. Focus on receiving Blue. Focus on not seeing Red.

Did you manage to not see Red? Even if you did, it required a lot of focus and energy. That fed the Red!

To metaphysically create the energy pattern of world peace, the imagery of global unity is used. Why? Because in creating the concept or energy pattern of unity, the action or rate of that energy strengthens. The action of unity is connection and communication. When we speak of global harmony we are describing the action of unity as an energy pattern—or force field.

We might say that the harmonic of peace is unity. This harmonic is created from the many personal imageries of peace as they manifest in the various vibrational rates, or energy patterns we call people. Metaphysically speaking, the lone individual who "lives a life of peace," creating, amplifying, and integrating an energy pattern of peace by the manifestation of peaceful self-transformation does more for the creation of world peace than all the groups of people who make pictures of peace, while at war within themselves.

It has been said that every act with an intent is a magickal act. Metaphysically, an action must be more than a passing ripple at the edge of a pond. To be potent, an action must be the stone thrown at the center of the pond, with clear intention to create ripples. Imagery is the alchemical expression of our intentions. It emerges from our impressions of self and evolves through our interaction with the images we created. The more we understand the many patterns within the one primary force, which is energy, the more we can define and utilize energy patterns for self-transformative healing magick. The way we learn to understand energy patterns is to define them as they relate to us in imagery.

We see energy patterns as color—we sense energy patterns by their tangibility—or by their tangible effect on us as individuals. Certain aromas give us a tangible expression of energy through our associated experiences with their scent. Symbols have long been created to express concepts or energy patterns. The energies of Nature have formed into patterns or frequencies so tangible to us that we have created deities to represent our imagery of their form. In turn, these forms become a key for connecting with the energy pattern it was defined to represent originally.

Elaborate systems of both mundane and arcane wisdom have been created to represent, through the active use of imagery, all the aspects and attributes we identify as frequencies of this primal energy force that is life.

In accepting our selves as no more or less than an active imagery of our life energy, we begin to acquire the detachment and the will to change our lives. This we can do by changing our imagery, and thus the patterns of energy which we call our Self. The imageries we create with detachment must then be experienced with a focused attachment to our personal, alchemical experience of that imagery and its energies. We deepen the experience of our imageries with multi-sensory, multi-modal processes such as ritual, ceremony, and the personal psychodrama of inner vision and active imagery. We do all this to create the alchemy of our self-transformation. Alchemy is transforming; the alchemy of active imagery reflects in our creative, self-creative experience.

Milton Erickson, the great psychiatrist and father of modern hypnotherapy, once asked a young client a question no one had thought to ask. He said, *"How will it be when you have changed?"*

In asking this, Dr. Erickson shifted the focus from the standard, "How are you going to change?" which focuses the awareness on just the responsibility for and the possibility of change, to a format which focuses on the results of change. Change becomes a given as the client creates a new image which assumes change.

If you want quality personal alchemy, you will need to make the time to develop quality personal knowledge. This will require you to have a positive experimental attitude, courage for self-transformation, willingness to learn, and the curiosity necessary to keep exploring and changing. This is necessary so your alchemy won't become stagnant.

We begin by understanding the form of alchemical blends. Some blends are simple combinations of a few elements. Others are more complex, with a multitude of alchemical elements. There are also blends which seem to reflect the energies of one specific element. In this case, the additional elements in the blend serve as a catalyst; a means of activating, developing and empowering the specific element reflected.

Just as we begin to obtain self-knowledge by discovering the strongest aspects of our Self, we begin our alchemical explorations by studying each of the strongest elemental energies we can recognize. With this system of personal alchemy, the strongest alchemical energies are those of the Rays and Lights. These are also called "color energies"— reflections of the highest Light.

We are also reflections of that Light. Our task as personal alchemists is to create the blends we need for positive self-transformation; to create the positive transformation of all the worlds.

Chapter Two

Rays and Lights: Attributes and Placements

1. Everything is alive.

2. We're all relatives.

—Vine Deloria

In the truest sense of the word—Colour—is life. The splendid symphony of colour which we see manifested on all sides of the Universe is the visible expression of Divine Mind.

—S. G. J. Ouseley

When I was learning to experience and understand the alchemical properties of Rays and Lights, I was told it might be helpful to relate them to people. A story was told to illustrate this point. I have taken this story, and with Irish poetic license, embellished it a bit.

You have three people. One of them is a Red Ray person, one is a Yellow Ray person, and the other is a Blue Ray person. You give each of them an equal amount of wood, building materials, tools, and instructions to build a bookcase.

The Red Ray person builds a bookcase immediately. It is finished. Great; it is done. It is just excellent. Well, it may lean a little bit. It rocks a bit here and there, but it is finished. It is completed. It is built. Therefore, the Red Ray person is finished with the bookcase.

The Red Ray person has a physical, creative approach. His/Her set of sensory urges keeps looking for new stimulations, new experiences, and new challenges to find and conquer. The Red Ray person may be pushy, but has to keep things changing. Red represents the energies of thrust, drive, and physical structuring.

19

Now the Yellow Ray person is still reading the instructions and is measuring and remeasuring the materials. Once in a while the Yellow Ray person will saw a little piece off a length of wood. Then the Yellow Ray person will measure again, and reread the instructions.

Eventually, the bookcase gets built. Of course it is perfect; it is SO precise. All the angles are perfect. Everything is perfect. It isn't certain whether or not the Yellow Ray person is going to let anyone put books on this bookcase. Still, it is a "perfect" bookcase. The Yellow Ray person is finished with the bookcase until it needs dusting. Daily, of course.

Yellow Ray has a mental, organized approach. This approach is a linear, divided schedule for life. The Yellow Ray person may be picky, but gives fine precision to things. Yellow represents the energies of precision, awareness, and mental structure.

Meanwhile, the Blue Ray person isn't worrying about the bookcase—or the materials—or the instructions. Why? The Blue Ray person knows a secret.

That secret is: if the bookcase is really needed, sooner or later someone will come along and build it.

If the Blue Ray person gets to keep the bookcase, that's fine. If not, that's fine, too.

Blue Ray has a spiritual, universal approach. The Blue Ray person has glimpsed the greater universal pattern, and has detachment and objectivity. The Blue Ray person may not seem to get anything done, but he or she helps teach us about the flow of energies and the universal patterns. Blue represents the energies of wisdom, cosmic flow, and spiritual patterns.

The universal pattern Blue Ray speaks of is somewhat less familiar to both Red Ray and Yellow Ray. Nevertheless, Red Ray says he created it; Yellow Ray says she gave the pattern order. What Blue Ray knows is that everyone created and ordered the greater pattern, as well as all the little patterns which make up the greater universal pattern.

When Blue Ray speaks about Self-creations, this means the universal Self—not just one's particular self. Sometimes Blue Ray is misunderstood. But when Red Ray stops being pushy and Yellow Ray quits systemizing everything, then they can see the pattern, too. This may be a quick glimpse to start, but enough to create all kinds of blends. Awareness of the greater "Universal Self" pattern increases the awareness of one's Self pattern, as well as attunement to the greater pattern of Life.

Once in a while Red Ray, Blue Ray and Yellow Ray synthesize in perfect alchemical balance. Each of their energies is equal in proportion to the rest. Then we have synthesis. (This synthesis is represented by the Indigo Ray, which we will discuss later.) Synthesis is the alchemical action which brings the energies of Body, Mind and Spirit in harmony.

Synthesis, like all alchemy, is not static. Synthesis also lasts for just a moment. Why? Because Red Ray, Yellow Ray, and, of course, Blue Ray, are needed just for who they are (if they, or we, can figure that out). Together, Red, Yellow and Blue create the harmonious synthesis of life. This process of synthesis maintains each aspect in active, reactive relationship to the others. How? Each aspect serves as a catalyst for the others.

This little story provides a good way to begin understanding how the energies of Rays and Lights work. Generally, the Yellow Ray is mental. The Red Ray is physical. The Blue Ray is spiritual. Of course, it is difficult to find somebody, or something, completely pure in its Ray. We are all combinations of energy. We are each patterns of energy, interacting together as an alchemical blend, creating a myriad of new energy patterns which form the constantly evolving pattern of the Universe.

The Alchemy of Rays and Lights

In addition to the primary rays Red, Yellow and Blue, there are the secondary rays of Green, Orange and Violet. Then there is the synthesis Ray of Indigo, which is actually a blended Ray. Indigo is made up of Red, Yellow and Blue in perfect balance—some say with Black and White, as well. (Here Black and White represent the classic duality, the dichotomy of Dark and Light.)

Primary Rays

Primary Rays may be defined for our purposes as one-part energy patterns. While we can rarely find someone or something which does not reflect a combination of energies, we can find this type of energy in the primary Rays—Red, Yellow, and Blue.

It is the primary nature of these Rays which enables us to correlate them to the energies of Body, Mind and Spirit synthesis.

Body	Red
+Mind	Yellow
+Spirit	Blue
Synthesis	Indigo

perfect balance of the three

These correlations let us know that Red Ray energy will have a primarily physical (Body) effect; Yellow Ray, a mental (mind) effect; and Blue Ray, a devotional or Spiritual effect. This also helps us set the tone for imagery and healing magick. Together, Red, Yellow and Blue can create an Indigo harmony in our work. Separately Red, Yellow and Blue can help us specify the energy to work with.

Alchemist's Note: Indigo is the synthesis Ray. The blend which creates Indigo is unique in its equal proportions. It is the action of these three—Red, Yellow, and Blue—which reflects the synthesis energy of Indigo. Indigo is the only blended Ray which can currently be identified as having this unique proportion of primary energy patterns blending together in equal combination.

Reflecting all that is Body, Mind and Spirit synthesis, Indigo Ray has an energy pattern which is as direct as any one of the three primary patterns in includes. This makes it more properly understood as a synthesis Ray with direct focused physical, mental, and spiritual effects, rather than a blended Ray which generally has a more etheric, psycho-physical (Mind/Body) effect.

As the newer blended Rays are strengthened by our alchemical awareness and experimental application, they may prove to have as direct an effect as the "original" blended Ray, Indigo. It took humankind time to activate the "third eye" energies of Indigo synthesis. Who knows what forms of evolution will occur as we actively seek etheric energies in the connection with the newer blended Rays and the diffuse energies of light?

Secondary Rays

Secondary Rays reflect the combination of two energy patterns.

> **Red + Yellow = Orange**
> **Yellow + Blue = Green**
> **Blue + Red = Violet**

However, these secondary Rays reflect more than a two-part energy pattern. The alchemy of the secondary Rays is that their particular energy pattern includes all of the energy patterns of each part—two in equal combination—as well as the energy pattern created by this combination of the two parts.

For example, the formula for Green Ray is:

> **Blue + Yellow = Green + Green**

This means that Green Ray contains all the energies of Blue, all the energies of Yellow, and all the energies created by the combination of Blue and Yellow energies.

The creation of Green amplifies the energies of Green over the energies of Blue and Yellow. We might say that Green is dominant and manifest, while both Blue and Yellow are recessive, or latent. This tells us what energies are subtle influences in the work we do with Rays and Lights. In this case, Green is direct in its effect, but both Blue and Yellow also influence the alchemy of Green with a more subtle effect.

Green Ray Alchemy

     2 parts Green
   +1 part Blue
   +1 part Yellow
     4 part energy pattern which reflects Green Ray directly as well as Blue Ray and Yellow Ray indirectly.

The more in-depth our information is about the energy patterns of the Rays and Lights with which we work, the more we can create an in-depth experience of self-transformation. We often know how energies affect us directly, but we also need to be aware of the subtle effects as well. We can weave the subtle effects into our active imagery to support or amplify the direct effects.

Suppose my intention is to work with the Green Ray energies for healing. I could simply focus on the Green Ray with an imagery.

As you stretch and bend your body, feel each muscle move in harmony with all of the others. If you feel a dis-harmonious, or "painful" muscle, take note of it. Detach and observe the reaction of your body to this sensation. Do not give energy to the pain. Give energy to the creation of Body/Mind harmony with imagery.

Breathe deeply and relax for a moment. Imagine a warm Green salve rubbed into that muscle by a friendly healing spirit. Feel the healing warmth of Green—soothing—bringing harmony to Body, Mind and Spirit/Self.

I could support the Green Ray imagery with subtle additions such as:

Focus your awareness on the center of your body as you bend. Imagine a Yellow beam of light streaming through your body, bringing awareness and mental focus to your body consciousness.

Each breath you take, each stretch, each bend, each move you make expresses your self in harmony with your body. Breathe consciously; move with expression. As you inhale and stretch, imagine a fountain of cool Blue Light bubbling up inside your throat. As you exhale, imagine the bubbly Blue Light splashing back into the fountain, keeping you cool and refreshed.

Blend subtle and direct energies to amplify your healing magick and activate your imagery. Understanding how these energy patterns work helps us know how to work with them. The more information you have about the actions and the attributes of Rays and Lights, the more able you will be to use them imaginatively.

For example, our Green Ray imagery can be a useful exercise, as we have shown in the previous example. However, with a bit of alchemy and imagination, our Green Ray imagery can become an in-depth experience.

You are walking along a perfect beach in your own island paradise. Lush tropical foliage covers the mountains. Clouds catch on the mountain peaks. The sand is warm beneath your feet. A seabird calls to you from the wide, clear sky and flies out toward the deep waters of the ocean, beyond the reef. A cool sea breeze sweeps through the palm trees towering over you, and rustles though the banana trees as you pass by. Breathe deeply, and absorb the harmony of this place in Nature. Absorb the healing beauty of Nature. Experience your own island paradise.

What colors did I mention? Careful! Trick question! The real question is what colors did I imply? Also, what energy patterns were implied but not defined? What was the direct energy being used? What did you experience?

Here is another version of the same imagery using a more overt (or direct) form. You decide how each version differs in its effect on your self.

You are walking along a perfect pale Yellow beach in your own island paradise. Lush tropical foliage covers the mountains in rich shades of emerald, lime, and kelly Green. Bright White clouds catch on the peaks, casting deep Green shadows across the mountaintops. The sand is warm and golden beneath your suntanned feet. A White-winged seabird calls to you from the wide, clear Blue sky and flies out toward the deep Blue waters of the dark ocean beyond the White caps along the reef. A cool breeze sweeps in from the azure sea. Palm trees, towering over you, dance and sway. Their deep Green fronds flash brightly against the vast Blue tropical sky. The sea breeze rustles through the gleaming, Green satin leaves of the banana trees as you pass by. Their ripe Yellow fruit can just be glimpsed, peeking out from within the cool Green folds of the banana leaves.

Breathe deeply, and absorb the healing Green harmony of this place of abundant natural beauty. Experience the soothing Blue calm of the seas, and the warmth of the tropical sun. Absorb the expansive Green beauty of your experience. Breathe, relax, and be in harmony with the beauty of your self and Nature.

For practice, try using the same alchemy of Green Ray energy pattern to create the healing magick of prosperity in your life, using Yellow or Blue as supports.

> How did the direct imagery differ from the subtle form for you?
> ↞ Hint: Yellow Ray reflects organization, focus, and mental abilities.

> How are these attributes needed to help create prosperity and receive energies?
> ↞ Hint: Blue Ray reflects expression, will, devotion, and balance.

> How can these attributes be used to develop an alchemy for prosperity and to activate energies?
> ↞ Hint: Green Ray reflects an expansive energy pattern.

> How does that energy pattern relate to prosperity?

How can the movement, or flow of an energy be used in healing magick to duplicate its effects?

↰ Hint: Dance and active celebrations create and emulate a mood, energy, or emotion. Be involved in your own magick. Make it real for your self. Green Ray is expansive and abundant. To access its energy, you must recreate it in your self. This in turn will activate its creation in your life.

Seven Chakra System

The seven chakra system is based on the use of specific energy points and patterns which correlate with the vital energies of life.

A "chakra" is a connecting channel between the physical and the etheric, or auric bodies. In the classic North Asian systems there are seven major chakras, connecting with the physical body in specific placements which correspond to the location of the seven major glands. Each of the seven major chakras correlates with one of the seven Rays. Each chakra point "matches" the color Rays in the energy it produces.

Perhaps you are already familiar with the seven chakra system. Chakras are the energy points on the body. If you already know this system, you will certainly recognize the Red, Yellow, Blue, Green, Orange, Violet and Indigo as parts of that traditional system.

Maybe you haven't thought about it in a while, or are fairly new to it. Since this is not the primary subject of this book, let's review it only briefly. There are many fine books on the chakra system available for more information. Several are listed in the Bibliography.

The chakra system has to do with energy centers on the physical body which connect to the etheric or outer bodies. These centers are connective channels for energy to move around, within, and throughout our total being. These chakras, or energy centers, have specific, strong vibrational frequencies.

The first physical energy center is the Root Chakra. This relates to Red Ray energy.

The second center is the Sacral Chakra. This relates to Orange Ray.

The third center is the Solar Plexus Chakra. This relates to Yellow Ray.

The fourth center is the Heart Chakra. This relates to Green Ray.

The fifth center is the Throat Chakra. This relates to Blue Ray.

The sixth center is the Brow Chakra. This relates to Indigo Ray.

The seventh center is the Crown Chakra. This relates to Violet Ray.

These are the traditional chakras, most likely familiar to you already. Remember that fixed traditions can give us one way to approach the energies. Traditions need not determine the outcome of your creations, but they can help provide elements which are often useful reference points for your own healing magick.

   The seven chakra system is a foundation for the alchemy of Rays and Lights in healing magick. Each chakra serves a specific energy function. The seven chakras together create and maintain a balanced flow of life's essential "current." An improperly functioning chakra affects the flow of this current, creating an imbalanced energy pattern which manifests as dis-ease of the Body/Mind connection. Knowing this, we can work with the correlating Rays to keep the energy patterns harmonically functioning and the current of life flowing clearly. This current may be actively imaged as an energy line connecting us shamanically, experientially, to the Earth and Spirit realms. This Earth and Spirit connection is maintained by the current of energy which runs through our bodies (as in the spinal cord network—central nervous system). The chakras "control" the flow of this energy.

   In order to determine the cause of chakra imbalances, the personal alchemist first becomes familiar with the feel, action, frequency and interaction of all the chakras. This requires study, experiential research, and a true willingness to develop a personal intuitive

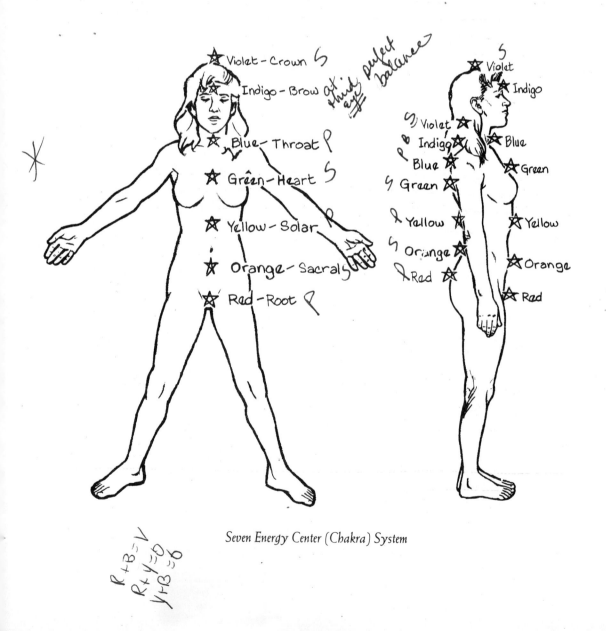

Seven Energy Center (Chakra) System

style. Remember that intuition means "inner-teacher." You are your own inner-teacher; be a good student of your self.

In this book, the seven chakras are specified according to their corresponding Rays (by color). To develop a more through understanding of the chakras, I suggest that you experiment with the information correlated with each of the seven Rays. This is located in the chapters on each color.

These seven Rays have the added benefit of an identifiable physical correlation in the body. Because of this, the seven chakras and their correlating Rays provide a framework from which to experience the less familiar blended Rays, as well as the diffuse Lights. These blended Rays and Lights affect the physical in an indirect manner, from the etheric outer bodies. The realms of imagery and healing magick allow us to connect and correlate physical points and effects for the purposes of our alchemy.

The seven Rays with their seven correlating chakras give us a more manifest physical experience of the energy patterns of Rays and Lights. From this we may explore the less tangible etheric energies of the blended Rays.

Seven Chakra Empowerment Exercise

If the seven chakras are unfamiliar, you may need your chakra placement charts.

Breathe deeply, and focus your awareness on your physical body. Stretch as you inhale. Relax as you exhale. Continue this until your body feels comfortable to you. Inhale to connect with the physical aspects of your self, and exhale to connect with the etheric aspects of your self. Breathe . . . Stretch . . . Relax.

Connect with Physical

Connect with Etheric

Connect with Physical

Breathe . . . Stretch . . . Relax

Now find a comfortable position, one in which your back is well supported.

Breathe, and imagine a ball of warm White light forming just above your head. Inside that ball of light are threads of color, sparkling brightly. You see Violet, Red and Green; Blue, Orange and Yellow. You notice the deep Blue of Indigo at the center of this ball of White light. Breathe and feel the Indigo bring your energies into synthesis. Breathe deeply, and focus on the feel of that warm light shining just above your head.

Breathe again. Feel the warm White light enter your body, just at the top of your head. As it does, a vibrant thread of Violet encircles the crown of your head, signifying your divine right to connect with Spirit consciously for self-transformation and healing magick.

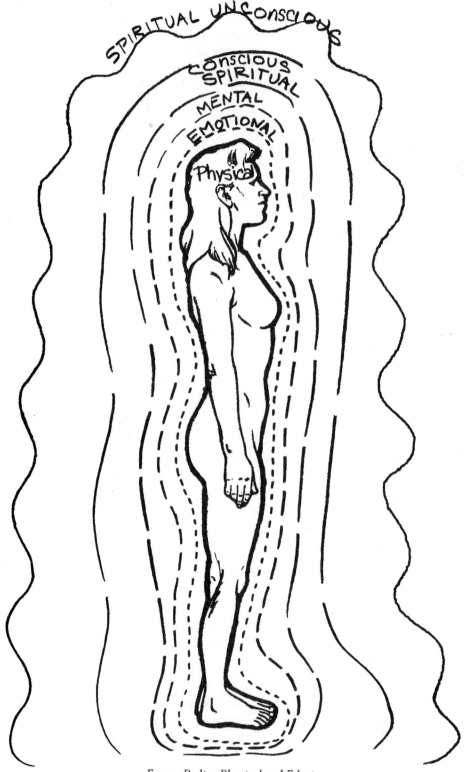

Energy Bodies, Physical and Etheric

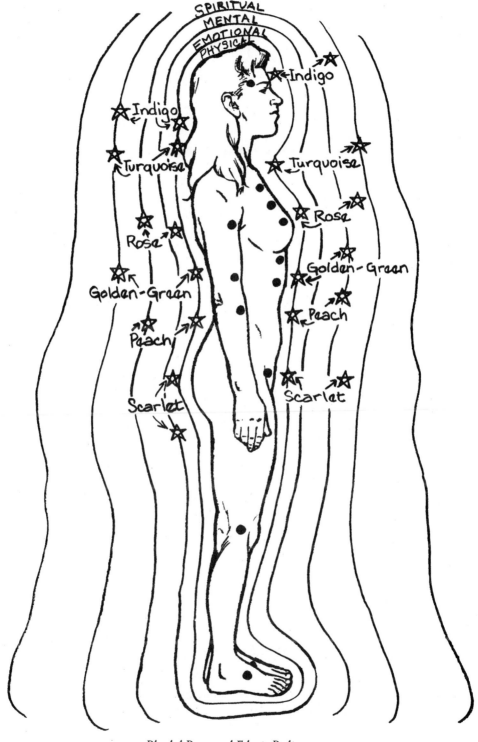

SPIRITUAL
MENTAL
EMOTIONAL
PHYSICAL

Indigo

Indigo

Turquoise

Turquoise

Rose

Rose

Golden-Green

Golden-Green

Peach

Peach

Scarlet

Scarlet

Blended Rays and Etheric Bodies

Excrcise 't
con't

The warm White light moves slowly around to gather at the center of your forehead. An intense thread of Indigo begins to form a small spiral, spinning over your third eye area.

For a moment there is only the quiet force of synthesis and your Self. The Indigo spirals into your body at the center of your forehead. As it does, all thoughts, words, deeds, dreams, sensations, and emotions spiral inward. You feel your self coming together with calm detachment. You observe the senses and images of your self-transformational process arrange themselves in a pattern which is both harmonious and chaotic, as is life. Breathe and recognize the synthesis of being centered within the deepest realms of your Self—and consciousness.

Breathe again—and slowly release. The warm White ball of light follows the Indigo spiral into your third eye area. Breathe deeply and absorb the healing alchemy of White and Indigo. Breathe again—and release your breath slowly. As you exhale, the ball of White healing light emerges from inside your throat. Along with the White ball of light are threads of Blue, flowing upward.

Breathe, swallow, and focus your awareness on your throat. Feel the cool Blues—the electric, cobalt, robin's egg, sky Blue, crayon-box blues—of your memory express themselves almost willfully. Breathe, and laugh out loud. Now again—with expression. The Blue threads intensify, then softly melt into your throat area. Breathe, swallow, relax and receive.

The White healing light drifts slowly down your chest, and stops to rest on your heart area. Emerald lights flash and swirl inside the ball of White. The warm White energies begin to trace a circle of light around your heart area. Breathe, and focus your awareness on your heart area. Breathe again. Focus on your inner vision. Create an image in your mind's eye of someone you truly love. As you bring your loved one's image into focus, you feel Green energy loosen from the ball of White, and expand in wide circles from and around your heart. Brilliant Green energy flashes from the center of your emotions. Experience the healing, nurturing love of Green.

The ball of White light expands along with the Green energies. Circles of Green and White expand from the center of your self in an ever-widening pattern. Breathe, and allow this alchemy of White and Green to expand outward. Share the healing energies of Green with the world, or with someone who simply means the world to you.

Breathe again with measured pace. Count to four as you inhale, count to four as you hold your breath, count to four as you release your breath, and count to four before you take another breath. Repeat this rhythmic pattern of breathing until you feel a quiet, centered focus within your self.

Feel the shift of energies as you move from expansive Green to the focus of Yellow. As your focus sharpens, shift your awareness to the center of your body, at waist level. Breathe deeply and consciously. Reach within the center of your self with each breath.

As you reach within, feel a warm Yellow glow begin to radiate out from the center of your body. As the glowing Yellow emerges, it is illuminated by the ball of White light gathering to form just outside the center of your body. Breathe, and focus on the feel of Yellow. As your focus increases, the intensity of Yellow becomes stronger. You feel alert, aware, and sharp. You feel perceptive and clear-minded. Focus on the experience of Yellow.

Breathe again, and slowly absorb the Yellow glow into your body. Feel it there, illuminating your thoughts, awakening your mind. As the Yellow is absorbed, the ball of White light spreads out across your tummy. The White light warms and comforts you. Breathe, and enjoy the healing comfort of this White blanket of light covering your tummy.

Breathe again, and slowly release. The White light seems more tangible to you now. You notice it is gathering its form together again. You feel its gentle gathering energies pulling upward. Breathe, and focus on this pull. As you do, you feel the warm, gentle fire inside your body, just below your belly button. This warm fire brings you feelings of inspiration and vitality.

Fiery threads of Orange begin to emerge inside the ball of White light. Breathe and focus on the clear, warm energies of Orange. Feel the Orange energies of vitality begin to spread throughout your body. Each breath you take brings more Orange into focus. Each breath causes the White ball of light to expand. Breathe and focus until your whole body is surrounded with warm White light interwoven with threads of vital, intense Orange.

Feel the vital, healthy energies of Orange spread over your body like warm honey, bringing nutrients for all the systems of your physical body.

Breathe, and focus on the Orange threads. With each inhalation the Orange intensifies like a gentle flame, empowered by your breath. With each exhalation the Orange threads weave themselves into your body.

With each new inhalation the ball of warm White light lifts gradually from your body and gathers form again just above your head. Breathe, and slowly release your breath until all the Orange threads have woven themselves into your body.

Breathe, focus, and relax. Shift your awareness to the ball of White light swirling once again just above your head. Feel yourself bathed in the healing energies of warm White light. Breathe and receive. Focus on consciously receiving healing energies and releasing any tensions. Breathe consciously until you feel clear and receptive.

Begin to shift your awareness. Begin to feel your awareness as energy moving downward slowly from the White light above your head, to the area just below your pubic bone. Feel the deeper rhythms of this part of your body. Breathe, and focus on that deep, pulsing rhythm in the lower half of your body. Each breath intensifies the pulse until you feel completely connected to the deep, personal rhythm and the deep rhythms of the Earth. Breathe again, and release your breath into the ball of White light above your head. Breathe very slowly and focus on a wide beam of pure White light reaching down through your body, connecting you to Spirit above and Earth below.

Down through the center of your crown and past your third eye, the beam of White light travels. Breathe and focus as the White light rushes downward inside your throat. Feel the beam of White expand briefly as it passes directly through your heart. Feel the healing light spiraling in tendrils all around the central core of your self. Breathe, and focus the White beam into a smooth column of light as it passes down through the center of your body. Feel the White light clearing a path through your Self. Feel its gentle vibration begin to connect with the deeper rhythms pulsing in your body.

Steady and strengthen the rhythm of your breathing until each breath is a great upward and inward sweep of energy. Breath of life—prana—moves into your Self with each breath you take. Each breath sends the White column of light vibrating down into the rhythm of your essential Self.

One more long, slow, deep breath, and the column of White Light connects with the ground beneath you. Inside your body, White Light expands until it covers your spinal cord and reaches upward into the ethers above your head. The milky White Light intensifies, then begins to clear, until the column becomes crystalline. The vibration of the crystal column of light matches its tone to the rhythms of your essential Self. You breathe and release all tensions with consciousness.

As you focus your energy, the crystal beam of light grows bright and clear. The rhythm of the Earth vibrates in the crystal confines of the magickal column of light. You feel the vibrations of the Earth moving up through the Crystal Light, charging your body with power. A flash at the base of your spine shoots upward, showering you with fiery sparks of light. A gentle warmth around your pubic bone grows hot, intense and insistent. Another flash scatters sparks into the ethers surrounding your body. With a sharp intake of your breath, you open to the pure lifeforce empowerment of Red.

Red fiery lights explode and sweep up through the crystalline beam. Each breath you take carries the Red fire higher through your self. Each point the Red energy passes through awakens to a new power; a new potential. Each vibration increases and each color intensifies as you channel the essential energies of lifeforce upward through your body— and on to Spirit realms. The crystalline column glows fiery Red with the energy it contains.

A blast of Red bursts the top of the crystalline column connected with the realms of Spirit just above your head. The Red fiery light inside the column softens quickly to Rose, then palest pink, and finally to a cool, milky White. Your body still rocks from the activation catalyst of pure Red Ray.

You breathe to steady your self. Vibrations shimmer outward into the ethers, sending waves of heat to fuel the lifeforce of all living things. The ground beneath your feet rumbles, shifts, and is silent.

Breath,e and focus your awareness on the cool White beam of light extending from just above your head to just below your feet, on the Earth. Breathe, and consciously pull the White Light down from the Violet crown of Spirit, out from the Indigo spiral of synthesis, and on, flowing down through the Blue waves of will and expression. Focus on burning the White Light through your heart area. The energy moves around and around the Green circles of healing. Breathe, and focus the flow of White as you enter the Yellow structures of perception at your heart. Breathe again, and let the cool White Light sweep through the Orange flames of health and creativity in your Self. Breathe, and slowly pace your self and your energies down through your body with the beam of White.

Breathe, and focus on the cool White Light as it detaches from your body, just below the pubic bone.

A stray ember flashes briefly as it detaches; you release the beam of White Light into the Earth beneath your feet. You tremble slightly as the cool White beam disappears into the heart of Mother Earth. A final long, slow, deep breath—and you are complete. All the energy centers of your body are activated; alert, but not anxious.

You reach down to touch the ground. With the release of your breath, you whisper your thanks for the essential current of life which connects you to Spirit and to the Earth, through the Self and the physical vehicle that is your body.

Alchemist's Note: The correct pronunciation for this word is "chakra" with a "ch" as in "channel" or "chocolate." This information came straight from the "Hindu's mouth," so to speak (several times, in fact, before I stopped softening the sound when I said it).

Consider that the soft pronunciation "shakrah" doesn't have the same mood, tone, or frequency as the more active form, "chah-krah."

Now consider the effect that a change in harmonic tone has on a pattern of energy. How we say a word can affect the meaning and the alchemy it has.

Finally, consider that unless you've never heard the word before, you already pronounce it one way or the other (probably "shakra," as most do). So why not use these different pronunciations to soften, soothe, or seal a "shakra" and to connect, catalyst, or charge a "chah-krah." "Shakra" softens, "chah-krah" activates.

To those for whom the word "chakra" is from their native language, I beg your pardon. Being "Kell-tic" and not "Sell-tic," I can sympathize. The Saxons softened the harmonic energy of the word Celtic, but not the harmonic of the breed (or of the Brede). The harmonic energies of the chakras will "speak" for themselves as we experience their energy patterns in our personal alchemy. The new harmonic energies created by the blending of Eastern and Western philosophies will also speak for themselves in our shared experiences and the shared evolution of universal alchemy.

Blended Rays

Blended Rays reflect a blend of three or more energy patterns in varied, unequal combinations. Indigo has been worked with for some time in traditional systems. While Indigo is also called a blended Ray, it is more appropriately defined as a synthesis Ray, as its action is one of bringing together, or synthesizing, Body, Mind and Spirit. Indigo is made up of equal proportions:

 Indigo: Three equal parts of Red, Yellow, Blue
(Some influence from the energy patterns of Black and White Lights)

Some newer Rays have come into focus fairly recently. These Rays, both the traditional and the newer ones, are conveniently described in terms of color, as that is with what they most clearly and consistently harmonize. Color is used as a correlating guide to approach the energy of a Ray. This is also true of any energy aspect, such as issues of over-organization (too much Yellow), aggression (too much Red), and delusional detachment (too much Blue). We will discuss these manifestations of Ray disorders as we proceed. The blended Rays (or etheric Rays) reflect the following combinations:

Scarlet: Primarily Red with Blue and some Yellow
(Suggests influence from Gold and Black Lights)

Rose: Primarily Red with Violet and some Blue
(Suggests influence from Silver, and White Lights)

Peach: Primarily Yellow with Red and some Blue
(Suggests influence from Silver and Gold Lights)

Golden-Green (or lime Green): Primarily Green with Yellow and Orange
(Suggests influence from Gold, Black, and Brown Lights)

Turquoise: Primarily Blue with Green and some Yellow
(Suggests influence of Gold and White Lights)

As with secondary and synthesis Rays, blended Rays reflect more than just the simple total of their combined energies. The blended Rays reflect an amplified emphasis on the energy pattern which is created by the alchemical gestalt, or combination, of the parts.

We can speculate that it is this which gives these blends the focused, direct energies of a Ray. The other Rays (primary, secondary, and synthesis) have specific connection points on the physical body—the seven major chakra points. These connections to the physical help to manifest the "force and the form" of the seven chakra Rays.

There are few, if any, physical points which correlate specifically to the blended Rays. However, these blended Rays may have a connection to the minor chakra points. These points occur where nerve networks cross and interweave intricately. The energies created by these networks are reflected as blended energy patterns. Thus, the blended Rays may be seen as a reflection of these "minor chakra" points just as the seven chakra Rays reflect specific energy patterns in the Body, Mind and Spirit. The blended Rays reflect their force and form in the etheric bodies, and affect the physical indirectly through the mental process of imagery.

Interestingly, the newer blended Rays seem to reflect our global blending as people, powers, and philosophies. Like us, that blend is still creating its own alchemy. We can all experiment with old or new systems in which to use these blends in order to strengthen and support the processes of creative unity.

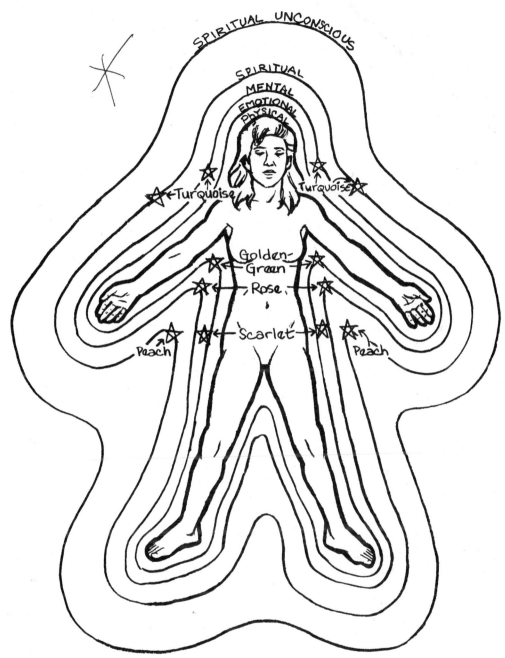

SPIRITUAL UNCONSCIOUS

SPIRITUAL

MENTAL

EMOTIONAL

PHYSICAL

Turquoise ← Turquoise

Golden-Green →

Rose

Peach ← Scarlet → Peach

Blended Rays Etheric Placement

The Lights: Sky Lights and Earth Lights

In addition to the primary, secondary, synthesis, and blended Rays which are direct focused energies, there are the diffuse, or subtle, energies. Using the analogy that focused Ray energies are the strongest, most tangible threads in the weaving of our life "fabric," then these diffuse energies are more like the finer, almost intangible threads. These diffuse energies are called Lights (or outer Rays, by some).

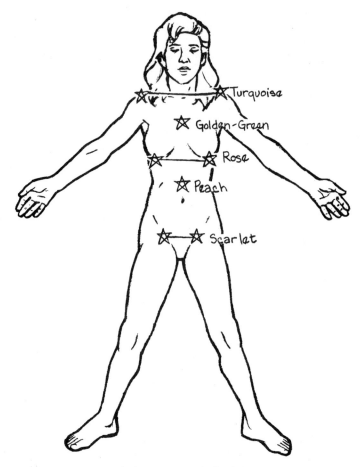

Minor Chakra Points and Blended Rays

Some of these Lights are sensed in the upper aura; that is, in the upper levels of the etheric bodies closely surrounding the physical body around the head and shoulders and the upper parts. These upper aura Lights have more to do with the realms of Spirit, and I call them Sky Lights. They are are White, Rainbow, Crystal, Spirit, Silver and Gold.

Other Lights are found in the lower aura; that is, in the lower levels of the etheric bodies, closer to the earth. These are the earth connectors. They are Brown, Black and Gray, and I call them Earth Lights.

Alchemist's Note: Focused energy patterns which are intense and direct are called Rays. Diffuse elemental energy patterns which are amorphous and free-floating are called Lights.

A Quick Review

While the energy patterns we call Rays and Lights are inherent in every aspect of life, they are most familiar to us in their form as color. We see, and image, energy as color. We even experience color's effect on our Body, Mind and Spirit system. But to understand the full alchemy of color we need to understand that color is simply one designation, one way that the energies of life and the highest Light are manifested. These energies can manifest as sound, symbol, and sensations, as we shall explore later.

The newer blended Rays have no specific energy points or set placement on the physical body, as in the traditional chakra system. However, we can correlate them etherically to certain energy centers and physical areas on the body in order to maximize their effectiveness for healing magick.

We might arbitrarily say the seven chakra Rays work more from the physical bodies outward into the etheric bodies. Remember, the etheric bodies are the subtle bodies, or the auric bodies. These include the area beyond what we consider to be the boundary of our physical bodies.

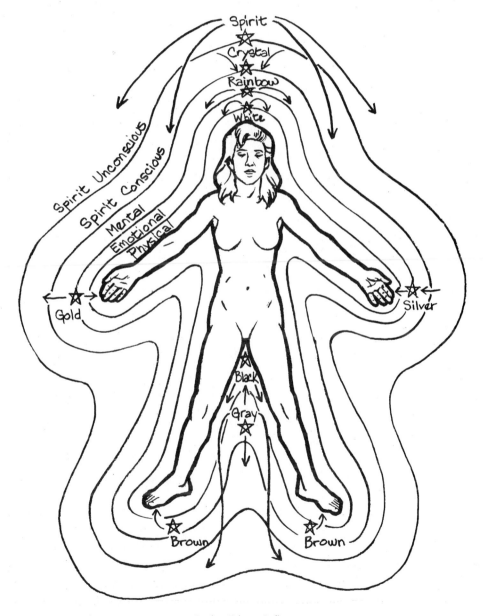

Lights Etheric Influences

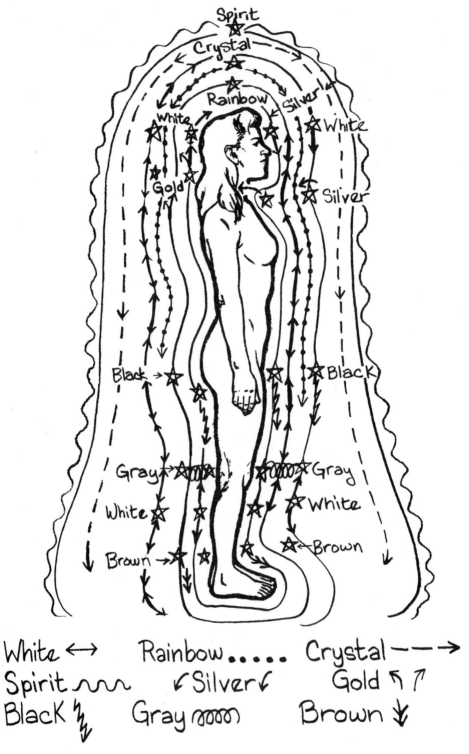

Sky and Earth Light Placement

We might also say that the blended Rays, particularly the newer ones, work from the etheric inward to the physical. However, these are arbitrary boundaries, divisions which are designated in order to work with the energies more specifically and effectively.

The elements of alchemy are not, ultimately, separate. The divisions we make are still part of the Body, Mind and Spirit connection. Remember that our divisions are arbitrary, but useful. This is especially true when we are learning. (When is that not?)

As personal alchemists, we are learning all the time. Alchemy is an active science, an art, a craft. It is wise to continue learning.

Although we may recognize that sound and light can influence us psychologically, most of us have not conceived that our psychological aspect, like our physical structure, may be nothing more or less than a configuration of energies.

—W. Brugh Joy, M. D.

Attributes of Rays and Lights

As colors and their associated qualities are perceived and experienced, one's vibrational frequency is increased, which allows more and purer color qualities to be discerned, manifested and experienced. This increases the vibrational frequency, again allowing purer color qualities to be experienced.

—William David

Each Ray or Light has specific qualities which we refer to as attributes. Metaphysically speaking, an attribute is the vibrational frequency of an energy which is most related to the specific manifestation or pattern of that energy. In other words, a similar or supportive "match" of "intangible" energies and "tangible" forms a correlation of energies. Red, for example, has fiery, activating energies. Blue has water, and soothing energies. Yellow has a mental, focusing energy. When we work with any energy pattern, we tap its frequency and manifest its effects in many ways.

For example, the color red produces a bright, intense, active etheric, emotional experience. The Ray Red produces a driving, thrusting energy in a primarily physical form.

From this, we can begin to see how the use of the color red, in combination with the Ray energies of Red, may be used to access, activate, and amplify both the emotional experience, and the physical form.

> Personal emotional experience
> + Alchemical energy patterns
> Personal alchemy experience

The auric healer of the occult school works in three ways, by thought transference, by influencing the aura of the patient, and by encouraging the right emanations. In short, he attempts to set up vibrations in the mind of his patient through concentration; his thoughts on certain hues will (so he hopes) build up his own aura and thence act directly on the aura of his patient; and this, in turn, will arouse corresponding vibrations in the mind of the patient—and thereupon effect the cure.

—Faber Birren

As you read the following list of attributes, consider first the emotional experience you have associated with the following Rays and Lights as colors. Next, consider the attributes of the Rays and Lights as they manifest in relationship to your experience.

Basic Attributes of Rays and Lights

Rays and Lights reflect and amplify specific identifiable energy patterns.

Rays	Basic Attributes of Rays	
Red Ray	Lifeforce	Thrust, drive, physical nature
Scarlet Ray	Balance	Yin/Yang, androgyny, patterning
Rose Ray	Temperance	Harmony, unity, moderation
Orange Ray	Vitality	Health, self-control, creativity
Peach Ray	Peace	Activating right action, communication
Yellow Ray	Intellect	Ordered perception, mindfulness
Golden-Green Ray	Rejuvenation	Renewal, metamorphosis
Green Ray	Expansion	Healing, growth, abundance
Turquoise Ray	Dedication	Active service, self-determination
Blue Ray	Expression	Devotion, inspiration, idealism
Indigo Ray	Synthesis	Integrating wisdom, ceremony
Violet Ray	Spirituality	Transformation, Karma, transmutation

Lights	Basic Attributes of Lights	
White Light	Healing	Transmitter, positive medium
Rainbow Light	Blending	Realignment, distribution of energies
Crystal Light	Clarity	Protection, Empowerment
Spirit Light	Source	Transcendence, purity, creator
Silver Light	Receptivity	Lunar, serenity, Yin
Gold Light	Activation	Solar, stimulation, Yang
Black Light	Release	Transmutation, shielding, filtering
Gray Light	Flexibility	Balanced, stable, friendly
Brown Light	Earth-Connected	Attuned to Nature and self-nature

Alchemy and Philosophy

Carl Jung speaks of alchemy as a process of "boundless amplification." In alchemy, it is important to accept the philosophical view that everything is created from a blend of energies and energy patterns. Some of these we call natural, or foundational elements: Air, Fire, Water, Earth and Spirit (Ether). Other energy patterns we call Rays, Lights, color, sound, vibration, mental imagery and symbolic keys. The philosophy of personal alchemy reflects the personal evolution of the alchemist.

Some blends of energy seem more philosophically and physically tangible to us, others less so. In alchemy and philosophy tangibility is not an issue in determining the properties or the value of any thought or energy used. The issue in philosophy and alchemy is the exploration of the energy patterns and processes of life itself. The purpose of alchemy is to obtain knowledge about the properties of energy, and to utilize that knowledge to effect self-transformation. The purpose of philosophy is to obtain self-knowledge for self-transformation.

To consciously and philosophically create the most positive alchemy for self-transformation requires personal knowledge of as many energy patterns and personal processes as possible. The greater the knowledge, the greater the alchemy and the philosophy. In this case, greater refers to the quality of the knowledge, the philosophy and the alchemy, not the quantity. That's positive personal alchemy.

> *Consciousness is dispersed throughout the Universe on rays of energy vibrations with each ray having its own vibrational rate and distinct set of life qualities.*
>
> —William David

The attributes of a Ray or Light reflect its specific frequency, or energy pattern, we can actively use in imagery and healing magick. Here is an example of healing magick using the attributes of Rose Ray temperance.

Breathe deeply. Hold your breath for a moment, then slowly release it. Take a dark pink or Rose colored marker and begin to draw small circles. Remember that the circle is the shape of harmony and oneness. Muse or meditate on the concept of harmony and oneness. Breathe again, and close your eyes. Continue to draw circles with your eyes closed. Focus your awareness on your inner vision. What image emerges? Put your marker down and focus inward to your "mind's eye."

Draw circles of Rose in your inner vision. Imagine all the circles forming into one large Rose-colored ball of light. Breathe deeply. Hold the image of the Rose-colored ball in your mind's eye. Know that within that ball of Rose-colored light exists all the energies you need to bring harmony into your life. Know that within your self, this quality of harmony already exists. Breathe deeply, and imagine the Rose-colored ball of light becoming brighter and clearer.

Breathe again, and shift your awareness to the area around your heart. Imagine the Rose-colored ball of light being absorbed directly into your heart with each breath you take. Feel the Rose energy as moving circles of harmony deep within your heart.

Absorb what you need from Rose Ray for harmony in your own life. If you choose, send out Rose Ray for world harmony by imagining a beautiful Rose-colored ball of light surrounding the planet. If you wish to send Rose Ray to someone else, focus on an image of them in your mind, or write their name with the Rose-colored marker. Breathe deeply, and renew Rose Ray within your heart. Hold your breath and imagine the person in your mind.

Surround the image of that person in Rose Ray. Release your breath slowly; let the image of the person and the Rose Ray fade. Imagine Rose Ray floating outward from your heart, carrying with it the energy of harmony for the good of all.

(Take time to note your reactions to Rose Ray, particularly how it made you feel. Also note what images, other than the ones suggested in the example, came into your mind. Personal images are the keys to deeper personal alchemy and to Self-understanding.)

Knowing the alchemy of a Ray or Light enables you to determine the type of imagery to create for your healing magick. The natural elements provide a foundation for the deeply experiential, active imagery we call shamanic journeys, or vision quests. Use these examples to experience the elemental energy of Blue Ray. Notice the suggestions of the elements in the imagery which reflect the energies of Water and Spirit. Design some Blue Ray healing magick using these examples for practice.

> Beautiful waves of music vibrating through crystals in a temple of healing.

> An ancient holy well sheltered in the embrace of a lone oak tree, silhouetted against the sky.

> A sacred pool of water deep within the forest on a moonlit midsummer's eve—and an ancient goddess.

> A mountain brook in winter—its waters rushing over snow covered stones—ice crystals sparkling in the midwinter sun.

> A bear wading into the shallow waters of a clear stream in search of spring salmon.

Natural Elements and Key Issues

Rays and Lights reflect alchemical blends and frequencies which can be correlated to the energy patterns of natural, foundational elements. These frequencies can be recognized and accessed. Examples for each element follow.

Spirit: Right action, oneness
The All, multidimensional unity, universal purity, Divinity, Source, transcendence, joy, highest vibrational energies of love, order, wisdom, life, Heaven, the Godhead, Supreme Being, The Force, The Light, highest vibrations and frequencies of all "matter" and energy, The Great Mystery, angelic realms, ascended masters, Spiritual teachers. In the Spirit realm or in the mundane world.

Air: Perception, communication
Intellect, self-development, awareness, mental acuity, mental stimulation, illumination, enlightenment, concentration, inspiration, expression, mindfulness, thoughts, ideas, philosophy, evolution of intelligence, expansion of mind, DNA codes, brain activity, meditation, focus, clarity, order from chaos, organization, psychology, vision, imagery, divination, the Philosopher, developmental teacher. In Spirit or mundane form.

Fire: Sensation, regeneration
Strength, protection, courage, faith, trust, self-determination, creation, activation, will, control, physical movement, exercise, dance, sensuality, physical communication, relationships, privacy, elusiveness, vulnerability, innocence, purity, beginnings, birth, growth, change, force, thrust, drive, transformation, anger, lust, pride, confidence, security, self-image, sensory awareness, lifeforce, enthusiasm, motivation, empowerment, the Guardian, activator, teacher. In Spirit or in the mundane world.

Water: Intuition, healing
Inner knowing, dreams, Shamanic journeys, spiritual quests, guides, inner teachers, internal wisdoms, introspection, deeper states of consciousness, emotions, love, feelings, personal patterns, balance of energies, female/male, receptive/active, Yin/Yang, personal androgyny, emotional love, soul connections, past lives, attunement, psychism, "sixth sense," catharsis, source of renewal, spiritual sustenance, nurturance, blessings, gifts, abilities, the Muse, nurturing teacher. Within the realms of Spirit or in mundane form.

Earth: Knowledge, moderation
Wisdom, ritual, ceremony, magick, the arcane, occult, secrets, symbols, sacred knowledge, teachings, learning theories, history, sciences, physics, metaphysics, universal awareness, religions, spirituality, the Path, asceticism, devotion to higher causes, spiritual evolution, abundance, prosperity, practicality, land, materialism, business, money, work, success, increased capacities, mundane matters, life planning, patience, temperance, schedules, curriculums, applications of knowledge, practical wisdom, stability, the Sage or civil authoritarian, teacher, guide. Spirit or mundane form.

Alchemical Exercise

Elemental Energy	Key Attributes
Blue Ray	Expression, will, healing, spiritual devotion, growth, inner guidance

(Blue Ray Reflects the alchemy of Water + Spirit)

Water	Intuition, healing, inner guidance
Spirit	Highest expression of devotion and will, spiritual growth

Alchemical Combinations of Natural Elements in Correlation with Rays and Lights

Five elements: Spirit, Air, Fire Water, Earth
Twelve Rays: Red, Scarlet, Rose, Orange, Peach, Yellow, Golden-Green,
                     Green, Turquoise, Blue, Indigo, Violet
Nine Lights: White, Rainbow, Crystal, Spirit, Silver, Gold, Black, Gray, Brown

Assume the alchemy of Spirit is Spirit and begin. Primary element first; secondary added:

Spirit	Spirit Light
Spirit and Air	White Light
Spirit and Fire	Crystal Light
Spirit and Water	Violet Ray
Spirit and Earth	Black Light
Air and Spirit	Peach Ray
Fire and Spirit	Rainbow Light
Water and Spirit	Blue Ray
Earth and Spirit	Golden-Green Ray
Air and Fire	Yellow Ray
Air and Water	Rose Ray
Air and Earth	Gray Light
Fire and Air	Orange Ray
Water and Air	Silver Light
Earth and Air	Indigo Ray
Fire and Water	Scarlet Ray
Fire and Earth	Red Ray
Water and Fire	Turquoise Ray
Earth and Fire	Gold Light
Water and Earth	Green Ray
Earth and Water	Brown Light

Healing Magick Examples

When we begin to recognize how many aspects and qualities are attributed to the various natural elements, we begin to see how many aspects of our Self-transformation we can effect as we become familiar with the energies of Rays and Lights.

Here are some healing magick examples showing how to select Rays and Lights for specific situations, according to their natural elements.

Suppose that you are feeling somewhat light-headed and floaty. In other words, very airy. Breathe deeply for a moment and really experience feeling airy, light-headed and floaty.

Imagine your Self floating freely just above the top of a large oak tree. Enjoy the experience for a moment. Imagine a color for this experience. Perhaps its a light sky Blue, or maybe a shining Silver, or a shimmering lavender.

Breathe again, and absorb all you need from the colors you see as you are free-floating above the large oak tree in your image.

Now shift your awareness to the colors of the leaves on your oak tree. Image these clearly in your inner vision. Some of the leaves are Green, some are Brown. These are natural, earthy colors, refreshing and centering. Breathe, and focus on the different shades of Green in the leaves. Begin to get a feel for the Green color of the leaves; feel the strength of that Green.

Now focus on the many shades of Brown in the leaves, as well. Notice how the browns are also present in the branches of that tree. Trace the many shades of Brown down the trunk of your oak tree. Notice how the browns become darker and deeper in tone as you image the roots of your tree in your mind's eye.

Breathe deeply, and imagine your self sitting at the base of your oak tree, absorbing the healing, centering energies of Green Ray and Brown Light. Breathe deeply, hold your breath, and focus on your image of the oak tree. Release your breath slowly and let the image fade. Feel yourself embody the central healing energies of the image. Be the grounded, rooted oak. Be centered in your own Strength.

(When you have finished, take time to note specifics about your image. Draw your oak tree with markers, and note any different reactions to the colors used. For example, Green may make you feel more expansive or active, Brown may feel more grounded and sedate.)

Now let's suppose you are working with someone who is feeling very agitated, charged up, or angry at the moment. In other words, too fiery. Even if you are hoping to work on the reasons for the overly fiery feelings, it is advisable to soothe or focus the person's feelings first so they may become centered enough to communicate.

Begin by having the person breathe very fast for a few moments, then deliberately slow the breathing down. Pace the person by breathing with them; breathe in concert with the person. Then shift the pace of breath slowly with focus.

Repeat the process of fast breathing. This time have the person focus on a image of the color Yellow. Have them calmly imagine a meadow filled with light Yellow flowers—clear, bright, and airy Yellow flowers.

Breathe deeply together. Have the person focus on the Yellow while they slow their breathing. Have them shift their center of awareness to the center of their body (up from the lower, fiery areas associated with anger).

Instruct them to breathe steadily and imagine clear, bright Yellow Ray streaming into the center of their body, bringing focus and calm.

Now breathe again together slowly, with long, deep breaths. Have the person shift their center of awareness up into the area around their throat. Have them imagine a cool Blue light streaming into their throat and flowing downward to soothe their fiery feelings.

Have them take a deep breath, and absorb the soothing Blue Ray as though they were enjoying a long, cool drink of water. Resume slow, steady breathing and encourage the person to express their feelings. First, discuss the experience of the Ray colors, noting the difference between feeling cool and focused rather than fiery and agitated. Stress the fact that the person had indeed "cooled themselves down" and has the tools to use next time—the focus of Yellow Ray and the soothing expressiveness of Blue Ray.

Now discuss the reasons for the fiery state with which they began. If the person becomes agitated, simply breathe, focus with Yellow, and soothe with Blue.

Suppose you wish to increase prosperity in your life. You see that issues of prosperity correlate with the element of Earth. In checking your natural elements of Rays and Lights, you find that Green Ray, which is also the color of money, has an element of Earth along with the element of Water.

From this you can create and image of Green Ray flowing like water all around you, empowering you with the energies of growth and prosperity. Imagine that flow of Green Ray entering into your work, your bank account, or your wallet! This helps bring prosperity into manifestation. Focus and "earth" the energies of prosperity. Feel your self to be "grounded" in success.

Perhaps you need to "fire up" that prosperity rather quickly. Add the Gold Light energy pattern of activation which has the natural elements of Earth (for prosperity, remember?) and Fire (for thrust and power).

These works of healing magick may be done through imagery or with objects of the color Rays and Lights you are using. For example, on a piece of paper write or draw your wishes for prosperity (specifically please—it is best for focus). Save these for further focusing, or burn the paper to ceremonially send out the energies of prosperity. There are countless ways to deepen your connection to and therefore your experience of the Rays and Lights by simply using your imagination.

Suppose you wish to deepen your understanding of the spiritual parts of your life. What Rays and Lights might you use?

Of course, Spirit Light is the clearest example with a natural element of Spirit, but Spirit Light is ultimately unmanifest and needs to work in relationship to other more manifest energy patterns such as Green, Blue, or Violet.

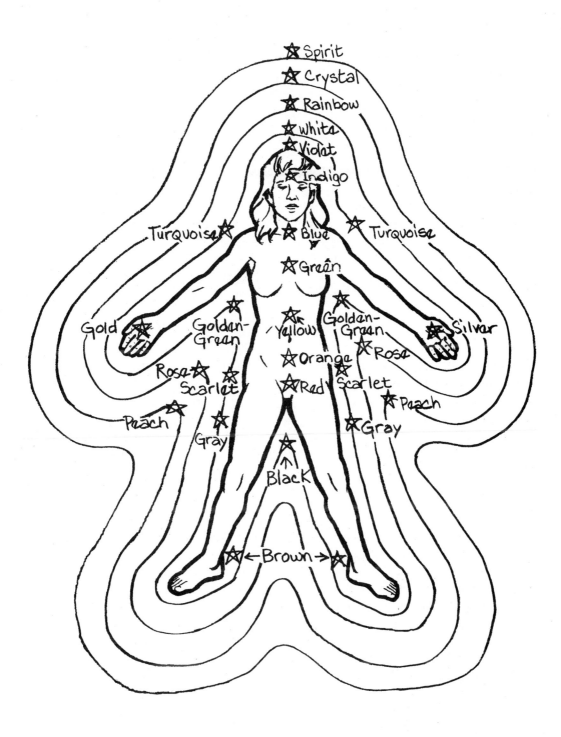

Sample of Cumulative Color Harmony

Try starting with Green Ray for a deep emotional connection to your spiritual path:

Green Ray = Earth and Water
Earth = heartfelt, Water = emotional

Next shift to Blue Ray for devoted expression of your spiritual path:

Blue Ray = Water and Spirit
Water = expression, Spirit = devoted

Next shift to Violet Ray for spiritual transformation in your life:

Violet Ray = Spirit and Water
Spirit = Spiritual, Water = transformation

Note that the natural element of Water is correlated with each of the Rays used for deepening Spiritual connection. Water has the attributes of healing, emotionality, and inner knowing, which are all qualities which deepen the personal experience of spirituality.

To work with Spirit, imagine the Rays of Green, Blue and Violet moving upward from your heart into the "heavens" above your head. Imagine these Rays lifting and transforming themselves into pure light and energy. Breathe, and absorb the energy of the highest spiritual light. Know that each time you breathe you deepen your connection to Spiritual realms. To remind your self of your connection to Spirit, simply focus your awareness on your breathing. Make each breath a ceremonial intake of Spiritual energies.

Exercises using Placements and Attributes of Rays and Lights

Suppose you wish to strengthen a romantic relationship?
↞ Hint: don't forget Green Ray to connect the hearts.

Suppose you need to study or write a project?
↞ Hint: Don't forget Blue Ray to help with expression.

Chapter Three

Harmonetrics and Aromatic Keys

Harmonetrics is the science of refining the ability to run the gamut of major and minor scales simultaneously, to explore the cacophony of existence, and pluck the appropriate sequence—to finish the score; to masterfully create new dimensions for further creation. The mundane "music of the cosmos" is the arcane expression for L-I-F-E, and the proper weaving of an endless score. You are the composer. You must perform your own composition.

—Stardragon

Harmonic Alchemy

Harmonetrics utilizes the harmonic (or the vibration) of sounds to activate energy patterns in alchemy. The vibration of a specific harmonic has a frequency, tone, or pitch all its own. These frequencies correlate with the energies of all aspects in Nature. This is particularly so with the energies of Rays and Lights.

The alchemy of harmonics is activated by attuning to the energies of Rays and Lights through the use of specific sounds. The appropriate combination of harmonics and specific Rays or Lights can create an intense, clear source of energy which deepens the power of the energies used.

A way you can quickly attune your self (as well as your stones or crystals) with harmonics is simply by going through the vowel sounds. We all know these from grammar school: **a, e, i, o, u.** When you get to **u,** stretch it into an **oo** sound for an alchemical effect.

Red Ray

The harmonic key for Red Ray is the sound of long **e** as in **she.**

Red Ray energies are very direct and physical. When using the harmonic **e** for Red Ray, focus on the physical, bodily experience of the energies.

To activate with the harmonic **e**, breathe rapidly in and out of the mouth while chanting the long **e**. This is similar to some breathing exercises used in natural childbirth. The strong physical energies of Red Ray in combination with harmonic breathing creates a natural way to transmute pain and support the body during life changes.

After you have become familiar with the bodily sensation created by harmonic breathing with Red Ray energies, you can begin to pace the flow to suit your specific needs. For example, a simple charge-up exercise can be performed by simply breathing rapidly while chanting the harmonic **e**. Any excessive energy can be dispelled by finishing the rapid breathing with a deep inhalation and exhalation which is short, strong and direct, as though you were blowing out a candle.

To amplify the harmonic breathing with Red Ray, add the use of appropriate words which match the sound of long **e**.

For example, while breathing rapidly, substitute the word "Energy" for the harmonic of long **e**. Repeat the word while "panting," being sure to draw out the last sound: **Ener geee . . . Ener geee . . . Ener geee.**

To dispel any excess energy, make deep inhalations and exhalations while chanting the word "Release." This time, draw out the sound of both long **e**'s and pace down slowly: **Reee leeese . . . Reee leeese.**

After you have activated Red Ray and released excess energies, you can resume natural breathing patterns and begin to focus on specific words for specific effects. Further examples for Red Ray harmonic energy patterns, as well as for all other Rays and Lights, are found in the individual chapters.

> *For example, when one learns to produce harmonious sound vibrations and mentally direct them inwardly toward the physical body centers, a rearrangement for balancing and centering is acquired which permits greater and more effective energy flow. Harmonious sound vibration directed with appropriate mental thought disrupts negative qualities and transmits them into positive qualities.*
>
> —William David

Harmonic Correlations

Primary Rays

Red	Harmonic **e** as in **she**
Yellow	Harmonic **ah** as in **father**
Blue	Harmonic **o** as in **boat**

Secondary Rays

Green	Harmonic **a** as in **say**
Orange	Harmonic **eh** as in **bet**
Violet	Harmonic **u** as in **sun** (This can also be lifted a bit higher and go from the short **u** in **sun** to **oo** as in **moon**)

Blended Rays

Scarlet   Harmonic **i** as in **ice**
Turquoise   Harmonic **aw** as in **draw**
Golden-Green   Harmonic **i** as in **sit**
Rose   Harmonic **y** as in **why** (It's not like **ice**, it's like **why**; a different vibration)
Peach   Harmonic **a** as in **sat**

Indigo

This synthesis Ray has the sound of **om**. **Om**, the chant of **ohm**, can be used for any stone to awaken its energy. It is an all-purpose chanting harmonic. In **om**, the **o** is physical and the **mmm** is spiritual. When you make this sound in balance, you can balance out these energies. If you need a little more physical energy, stretch out the **o**. If you need a little more soothing or spiritual energy, stretch out the **mmm**.

Sky Lights

The harmonic key for the Sky Lights is the sound of **m** as in **me**. This harmonic is higher pitched and far more variable than the deep **m** of the Indigo harmonic **om**.

Earth Lights

The harmonic key for the Earth Lights is the sound of (short) **o** as in **mom**. This harmonic **o** is moderately deep in pitch but not as much as the harmonic (long) **o** of Blue Ray, or the harmonic **om** of Indigo. Variations of this harmonic are best sung or chanted with a sedate, grounded energy.

Alchemist's Note: Alchemy is often catalyzed by the use of symbolic keys. Images and symbols such as Merlin, the tower, the dragon and the cauldron, are mythic, symbolic keys for our use. Words are also harmonically symbolic at times. Look for the alchemical message in these words: **magick, imagery, imagination, magus, magician, magi** and **mage**. The root of these words and the variations of form and meaning reflect a common energy pattern.

Here's a hint:

Imagination

I   magi   nation

Sometimes the harmonic as well as the symbolic energies of a word can provide alchemical keys. The power of a word has magick when used consciously.

The alchemy of sounds and words provides a method to create subtle, complex effects—for example, puns and double-entendres.

Here's another hint:

Druid

Drew   It

An exercise in word symbology is to read poetry, plays, or prose which are magickal for you with the intention of uncovering the subtle, as well as the direct, influences of the harmonic and symbolic alchemy in the words.

From this you can determine the magick of what you read in terms of its energy patterns. When we speak of written or spoken language as "colorful," we are referring to its effect on our personal imagery.

For an example of healing magick using word symbology and harmonics, imagine yourself to be a great magician, one whose powers are so strong that you can create whatever you need simply by using your imagination. Your imagination is magick.

As a great magician, you know that your imagination is your most powerful, potent alchemy. This is because you know that "what your mind can conceive, your will can achieve." When you distill the concepts of your mind into an expression of your will, you create the words of magick for your personal alchemy. For you, the word "imagination" becomes a symbolic focus point, or word mantra. A "mantra" is a personal, talismanic sound or symbol. Words make effective mantras.

Begin by writing and sounding out the word. Sound it out slowly, phonetically: i—maji—na—shun. In this word alchemy, we have the sounds of short i, long a, and short u.

In checking the harmonic correlations chart, you will find this gives the word the following Rays and Lights in sequence: Golden-Green, the Sky Lights, Peach, Scarlet, Green and Violet. Imagine these as colors vibrating into the ethers as you speak. In checking your lists of Ray and Light attributes, you will find this gives the word "imagination" these attributes, or magickal qualities: renewal, the Spirit qualities of the Sky Lights, peace, balance, expansion and spirituality—a magickal blend.

If you work with the word "imagination" while visualizing each Ray and Light and focusing on their qualities, you will have soon developed a connection between the colors, energy patterns and harmonic alchemy.

Experiment with other words. Consider words which are magickal for you. Check the harmonics and find out what attributes are in the harmonic energy pattern of those words. Use images of color, light, and sound to amplify the power of your words of magick.

Consider the ancient wisdom often attributed to the Druids that stresses the power of the spoken word. Remember also that the Druids gave us the phrase, "Don't put it in writing," and relied on the oral tradition to pass wisdom from generation to generation. Then as now, the power of the word had to come from more than just its defined meaning. Words can be the most powerful forces of healing magick, as words create energy.

The power of a word used with intent and focus sets up a sound wavelength, or harmonic pattern. That pattern correlates with certain physical, psychological, and spiritual qualities. These qualities also correlate with the specific energy patterns of Rays and Lights. Because of this, the intonation of a word, which is a group of sounds in sequence, or the harmonic of a single sound, can set up an energy pattern just through the harmonic which correlates with that pattern. This is the alchemy used in written and spoken imagery, ceremony, music, and poetry.

In other words, whether you have realized it or not, the sounds you make and the words you speak already have an alchemical effect. When you speak a word with focused intentions, and awareness of the qualities of that word, you have spoken a word of Magick. This effect is well-known to poets and magicians.

For example, the word "rage" has as its primary harmonic the sound of long **a**, which correlates with the Green Ray of healing. Since Green Ray energy center is the heart area on the physical body, we can begin to see some interesting tie-ins with the energy pattern of rage being heart-related. This can also give us clues as to what energy patterns to use in dealing with the issues of rage when they are presented to us.

Experiment with different words to discover their particular harmonic energy patterns. Its fun to do this with names. For example, "Betty" (Beh—tee) gives us the feeling of someone rather active, and interestingly correlates with the Rays of Orange (short **e**) and Red (long **e**). Both Orange and Red are physical and active energy patterns, representing the attributes of vitality and lifeforce. What is the harmonic of your name? How about your magickal name?

Pay attention to key words that you hear your self or someone else say often or with particularly strong emotions. Make a note of these key words. Do a bit of harmonic alchemy on them to find out what energy patterns are being created. Create new energy patterns with new words and harmonic chants designed to balance or support positive self-transformation.

Always consider other individual's concept of a word as well as your own. Personal concepts and interpretations affect the meanings of words, symbols, and colors. What something means to you may have little or no relation to what it means to someone else. Consider this when you work with the harmonic expressions of others and your self.

Give the alchemy of word symbology some thought; that's the way of the personal alchemist. Examine the harmonic poetry of lyrics in your favorite music.

Sensory Keys

To be awake is to be alive.
—Henry David Thoreau

Our senses are indeed our doors and windows on this world, in a very real sense the key to the unlocking of meaning, and the well spring of creativity.
—Jean Houston

Knowledge is obtained from the conscious synthesis of information. Wisdom is obtained from the positive use of that knowledge for the good of all. Wisdom is supported by the experience of being guided in our self-transformation by inner knowing, as well as external information.

The deeper the connection to inner knowing, the clearer the connection to the source of all knowledge and elements of universal alchemy. The clearer the connection to universal alchemy, the greater our skills of personal alchemy. The greater our skills of personal alchemy, the more frequent our opportunities for information, inner-knowing and wisdom. It's a positive cycle on the spiraling path to Source.

So long as the positive pursuit of information and experience continues, personal alchemy is the crafting of self-transformation. Information well-gained provides a strong element for your personal alchemy.

The brain is the "organ of the mind." It is our physical computer and vehicle of life experiences as well as the "soft machine" which controls all our natural functions.

Much of the information we obtain about our self and our environment is stored in the brain. This information is accessed basically through the use of sensory keys. Sensory keys include those things which stimulate the five primary senses and give us vital information with which to structure our lives, our imageries, and our realities.

The five primary senses are correlated with the first five chakra points (or energy centers) on the physical body. Interestingly, the sixth (or psychic) sense is related to the brow chakra (or energy center) of the third eye. As you remember, at this point the energies of Body, Mind, and Spirit (Red, Yellow and Blue) synthesize (Indigo).

Primary Sense	Natural Element	Energy Center
Smell	Earth	Root center
Taste	Water	Sacral center
Sight	Fire	Solar plexus center
Touch	Air	Heart center
Sound	Spirit (ether)	Throat center

Multimodal Processing of the Senses

Color associations exist by the score. Man finds in the hues of the spectrum emotional analogies with sounds, shapes and forms, odors, tastes. Color expressions work their way into language symbolism, tradition, and superstition.

—Faber Brown

In alchemy, we stimulate our primary senses through the use of sensory keys such as incenses, oils, herbs, flavors, music, candles, fabrics and color—lots of color. We call this stimulation of sensory keys "multimodal processing." That is the use of many (multi) forms (modes) to stimulate our senses and catalyst the alchemy of self-transformation. Jean Houston says, "The brain loves ritual." Ceremony and ritual use sensory input to deepen the experience. The alchemist uses ritual for this experiential quality in healing magick to deepen the effects and expand the abilities of the brain, as well. Expanded brain potential and increased abilities activate personal evolution, and in turn, the evolution of all brain and mind consciousness.

All of this sensory stimulation "wakes up the brain," allowing us to deepen our experience of the energies with which we are working. The more we focus on our personal experience, the more sensitive we become to the energies of Rays and Lights.

The primary sense which is most related to the development of physical information is the sense of smell. In my opinion, the use of sensory keys designed to catalyst information through the sense of smell is the most useful, convenient and expedient method to deepen the experience of the elemental energies. The use of specific scents creates an aromatic key to stimulate the brain and create the mood (or mindset) of healing magick and alchemy. An aromatic key, properly correlated with a "match" of energy patterns or attributes, creates a deeply experiential imagery because the scent directly stimulates the physical (brain) as well as subtly stimulating the etheric (mind).

For example:

- You enter a small thatched hut, deep in an ancient forest. From a cauldron on a hook in the fireplace comes the scent of . . . .

- You wake in a cool, dark room that you have never seen before. The heavy scent of jasmine fills the air. What do you see?

Aromatic keys are most effective when they evoke experiential images. For instance, have you ever walked through a rose garden on a warm summer day? Do you remember what it smelled like? How did it make you feel? With a little energy pattern alchemy, we can correlate the wonderful scent of roses with the Rose Ray of temperance and harmony. Didn't the rose garden make you feel in harmony with Nature, even just for a moment?

Smells have a deep physical connection for us as human beings. When we have made associations with certain smells and certain emotions or events, they stay with us longer than most other sensory associations we have made. The smell of a rose today can "transport" you back to that rose garden of yesterday. It can also evoke those same feelings of harmony, particularly when accompanied by focused imaging of the Rose Ray. You may not always have time to "stop and smell the roses," but you can evoke the healing magick of that experience with aromatic keys in your imagery.

Note that the natural element of Earth is associated with the sense of smell. This links experience to the physical body and transmits information to the brain directly and efficiently. Smell is the most primal sense.

The following list of sensory keys correlated with Rays and Lights adds another way to deepen the experience of your personal alchemy. These are a blend of traditional and personal correlations. Experiment with other ways to create alchemical sensations in your healing magick and imagery. Remember: the Rays and Lights give us color for seeing, the harmonics give us sound for hearing, the aromatics give us scents for smelling, and can provide flavors as well, for tasting.

The alchemy of color, sound and scent can create an atmosphere in your imagery which is as personally alchemical as the atmosphere created in ritual, ceremony or the magick of Nature. We can stimulate the senses in imagery that allow us to "touch" new dimensions of Self.

Just remember, any aromatic key which is personally alchemical for you will always be most effective for your work. The diffuse energies of Lights can be evoked without a specific match. In all cases, use keys which work best for your self.

Aromatic Keys

Rays	Ray Incense
Red	Cinnamon
Scarlet	Cloves
Rose	Floral
Orange	Ginger
Peach	Fruity
Yellow	Sandalwood
Golden-Green	Herbal or minty
Green	Bayberry
Turquoise	Bay laurel
Blue	Thyme (tranquility)
Indigo	Jasmine (temple incenses)
Violet	Lavender, lilac

Sky Lights	Sky Lights Incense *(Interchangeable)*
White	Frankincense
Rainbow	Myrrh
Crystal	Almond
Spirit	Vanilla
Gold	
Silver	

Earth Lights	Earth Lights Incense *(Interchangeable)*
Black	Patchouli
Gray	Sage
Brown	Woodsy

While having a variety of sensory keys (such as scents) to select from is quite useful, it is not essential. A specific aromatic key can be used to activate categories of similar energies. Experiment to determine which keys evoke similar moods or types of energies for you. Here are some healing magick examples using the aromatic keys, harmonics, and attributes of Rays and Lights.

For ceremonial synthesis (Indigo) and Spiritual Light (Sky Lights) work you can use incenses (or oils) with jasmine, and any of the Sky Lights incenses (frankincense, myrrh, almond or vanilla).

Light the jasmine incense, and breathe slowly and quietly. After your breathing has steadied, begin to chant the harmonic of Indigo, **om.** Close your eyes and focus your center of awareness on the center of your brow at the place of the third eye.

Visualize deep Indigo blue energy turning slowly in a small circle around your third eye area. Continue to chant the harmonic of Indigo, **om.** Imagine the Indigo Ray energy pattern gently pulling all your focus into the slowly spinning circle on your brow. Breathe, and center your self. Focus your awareness on the synthesis energy of Indigo. Feel your self "coming together."

Now light one of the Sky Light incenses. Breathe slowly, inhale the scent, and release your breath in an arch above your head. Fan the smoke from the Sky Lights incense upward around your head, and in an arch over your upper body.

Breathe deeply. Imagine the Indigo Ray energy pattern lifting from your brow area and spreading outward to join the smoke of the Sky Light incense. Imagine the energy pattern of Indigo connecting with the light, Spirit energies of the Sky Lights as they arc over your physical body and into the ethers, or the aura surrounding your body.

Breathe again and focus on the Indigo Ray coming back into the center of your brow. As the Indigo Ray slowly spirals back in, imagine it bringing all the Sky Lights energy: White, Rainbow, Crystal, Spirit, Gold and Silver.

Slowly spiral the Sky Lights into your third eye area as though you were casting liquid lights into the waters of a deep magickal well.

Finish by chanting the Indigo Ray harmonic **om,** or by chanting (in whisper) the word "synthesis." Feel your thoughts, personal emotions and physical energies come together in harmonious synthesis with spiritual flow.

Meditate on Indigo, and note other images which may arise for you.

For Shamanic clearing and Earth connection (Earth Lights), burn a woodsy incense or anoint a candle with patchouli oil.

Breathe deeply and focus your center of awareness close to the Earth (at your feet if you are standing, or your tail bone if you are sitting). Breathe, center, and focus on the scent you have chosen.

Shift your awareness to your inner vision. Imagine a veil of Black Light sweeping away all your negativities such as little pains, irritations, and distracting thoughts. Let these negativities seep into the ground with the veil of Black Light. Focus your concentration on the inhalation of your breath. Feel the deep earth energy of the woodsy scent. With each exhalation, more negativities are released to seep into the ground with the veil of Black Light.

After you have "swept" your self clear with the Black Light veil, concentrate on inhalation. With each inhalation of breath, imagine warm Brown Light emerging from the earth, bringing stabilizing, empowering energy patterns which connect you to the Shamanic powers of the planet Earth. Let the scent carry you into the energies of the Earth.

Continue breathing in warm, supportive Brown Light energy until you feel centered, empowered and connected to the planet Earth.

Finish by imagining threads of Brown Light, like roots, connecting you to the supportive powers of the Earth.

To remind yourself of your rooted connection, simply chant the harmonic of Brown Light, short o as in **Brown**. Whenever you need the energies of a shamanic, Earth-centered experience, let the scent you used here provide you with a "quick trip."

Since a variety of aromatic scents can be complicated to collect, fewer scents can be used to evoke similar energy patterns. You can use the word alchemy of imagery to specify which particular energy is being used. Experiment for your own alchemy.

Five Selected Incenses Systems

> **Red**—Spicy (blends of cinnamon, cloves, etc.)
> > Red
> > Rose
> > Scarlet
> > Orange

> **Yellow**—Sandalwood (single note)
> > Peach
> > Yellow
> > Golden-Green
> > Green

> **Blue**—Jasmine (single note)
> > Blue
> > Turquoise
> > Indigo
> > Violet

Sky Lights—Frankincense/Myrrh (single or blend)
>White
>Rainbow
>Crystal
>Spirit
>Gold
>Silver

Earth Lights—Woodsy (blend of cedar, evergreen, etc.)
>Black
>Gray
>Brown

Another convenient system for aromatic keys is to divide them into three primary categories of Body, Mind and Spirit. This can provide an alchemy for the transformational synthesis of Self. Here is a healing magick example for Body, Mind and Spirit with keys. You will need three varieties of fragrant oils (spicy, woodsy, and floral) and one White votive candle.

Breathe deeply. Find a quiet place within your self. Focus your center of awareness on the steady rhythm of your breath. Light the candle. Focus on the flame and the sound of your breath for a few moments until you feel centered and calm.

Imagine three concentric rings of White and colored light surrounding your self. The ring closest to your self represents the physical body, and has a few threads of Red mixed in the White. The middle ring represents mind, and has Yellow. The outer ring of White Light represents Spirit, and has Blue.

Take the spicy oil and put a few drops on the candle, near the wick. Inhale the spicy scent, and focus on the inner ring of White Light you have imagined around your body. Imagine that ring of White healing light merging into your physical body, bringing you strength and health. Focus on the feeling of a strong healthy body. Breathe, and exhale slowly.

Breathe again, and take the woodsy oil and place a few drops near the candle wick. As you breathe in the woodsy scent focus on the middle ring, now just outside your physical body. Imagine that ring of White Light merging slowly into your physical body, bringing the focused, calm energies of a quiet mind. Breathe, and experience.

Finally, take the floral oil and repeat the procedure. This time, let the last ring of White Light merge into your body, bringing the power and the protection of Spirit into your self. Contemplate, and note your reactions.

In the example just given, the various scents stimulated large groups of Rays and Lights by subtle sensory activation. Yet this required only the specific rings imagery of White Light as a transmittal medium for the qualities needed for Body, Mind and Spirit healing magick.

Three Selected Aromatic Keys Systems for Approaching Mind/Body/Spirit Work

These divisions are arbitrary, useful to focus, but not fixed in effect. Experiment.

Mind	Woodsy blends
Body	Spicy blends
Spirit	Floral blends

Mind   Woodsy blends (most specifically compatible Ray is Yellow)

Scarlet	Rainbow
Peach	Brown
Yellow	Turquoise
Indigo	

Body   Spicy blends (most specifically compatible Ray is Red)

Orange	Gold
Golden-Green	Silver
Green	Gray
Red	

Spirit   Floral blends (most specifically compatible Ray is Blue)

Violet	White
Blue	Spirit
White	Black
Crystal	

Exercises

1. Decide which incenses (or blends) would work well to encourage communication in a group or with another individual.

   ← Hint: Larger groups may need calming aromatic keys first. Debating groups may need more than usual!

2. Decide how you would strengthen someone's vitality level using aromatic keys, specific Rays and/or Lights and harmonics.

   ← Hint: Sometimes vitality needs an activating energy pattern, sometimes a balancing or ordering energy pattern for better distribution.

3. Decide which natural element would correlate most strongly with the development of focus and concentration. Choose Rays and Lights which are appropriate for focus and concentration and contain the natural element you started with. Add harmonics and aromatic keys.

4. Decide on a harmonic tone (or word) for inner knowing and psychic receptivity. Design a short healing magick example which deepens the experience.

Answers: Of course there are a number of ways each of these questions could be answered. Check yours against mine to see where we are in agreement. Where we were not, check your information. If you still agree with your answer, then you're right. If something works for you, use it. If it doesn't, change it. Experiment.

1. Thyme, fruity blends, floral blends; also sandalwood, sage, and vanilla. (To figure out exactly why, work backwards from the aromatic key charts.)

2. Orange Ray, with Gold, possibly Red, to activate; and Scarlet, Yellow or Rainbow to reorganize the flow of vitality. A spicy blend would provide an activating aromatic key to accompany the Rays and Lights. A single note incense such as sandalwood or clove would provide for a more structured energy pattern. Use words such as "strength" and "health" for general Orange Ray harmonics. Add words such as "activate" or "accelerate" to fire up vitality, and words such as "order" and "balance" to regulate the energy patterns of vitality.

3. Use Air for mental aspects such as focus and concentration, with the element of Earth for a supportive, centering energy pattern. To develop focus and concentration, use Yellow Ray, Indigo Ray, and Gray Light; possibly Brown Light as well, for grounding. Figure out why I chose these, if you haven't already, and correlate with harmonics and aromatic keys.

4. Harmonic word symbol such as "summer" (short **u** for spirituality); with Violet Ray. Add Earth Lights (short **o**) for centering (with Brown) and releasing distractions (with Black), as well as for being flexible enough to listen (with Gray). Focus on the meaning of the word as well as harmonics. Add Indigo, **om**, and say "Summer Home," etc.

Chapter Four

Symbolic Keys and Personification Images

All Things have the nature of Mind.
—Gautama Buddha

The symbol is not a sign that veils something everybody knows. Such is not its significance; on the contrary, it represents an attempt to elucidate, by means of analog, something that still belongs entirely to the domain of the unknown, or something that is yet to be.

—Carl Jung

Symbolic keys and personification images rise from our personal mindset, or have already risen out of the Mind of Humankind. Fundamentally, personal symbols are representations of the self-psyche; the mindset of the individual. Social symbols represent the cultural psyche, and Spiritual symbols represent the Mind of the Universe according to personal, social and cultural interpretations of Spirit realms.

Ancient alchemical symbols and personifications (or deities) are focused frequencies of energy (or thought forms) with great potency for connecting us to the dimensions of Universal Mind and the deepest human wisdoms. Personal personifications represent our individual images, as well as the deification we bring to our experience of life's energies.

The energy pattern of a symbol is always greater in intensity than the catalyst (or the cause) that produced the symbol in the first place. The creation of a symbol "imprints" its energy pattern etherically, and encodes an energy pattern into the personal group or Universal Mind. Each time the symbol is used, its energy pattern becomes less etheric and more manifest in Nature. As we know, that which we energize with intent grows stronger and more effective. Symbols are both keys to energy patterns and manifestations of that energy. When symbols are misused or misunderstood for long or intense periods of time, the energy field around that symbol changes; sometimes the basic energy pattern is affected. This makes alchemical use of that symbol very tricky.

Other times, symbols are able to "shift" with the flow of the times. With some alchemical research, you can find that most symbols which have done a bit of "shape-shifting" of their meanings according to cultural philosophies and interpretations still retain the energy patterns they were originally created to represent.

Symbolic keys and personification images include those manifestations of elemental energies which connect us to our "sixth sense." In turn, that psychic, intangible level of awareness leads us toward a greater connection to our etheric bodies. Our etheric bodies are also called our "auric bodies," or "aura."

As we connect more clearly to our etheric bodies, we expand our connection to and awareness of the highest dimensions of Universal Alchemy. From these dimensions, we can access the highest qualities of elemental energies—and wisdom for the alchemy of self-transformation.

The symbol of a Sun—often correlated with Red, Orange, Yellow or Gold—has several meanings. It represents active force, overt personality, "male" energy, and the generative energy patterns of life. It can also represent anything from a social, "sunny" welcome to one of the ancient solar gods such as Lugh, Mithras or Apollo. The Sun can also represent the more devic or natural element energy patterns found in the growth patterns of Nature. One of the ancient solar harvest gods is still referred to today as "John Barleycorn" to signify the life-giving effect of the Sun's energy on the crops. Thus, the Sun still is the symbol for the "life of the fields."

The symbol of the Moon—correlated with White, Blue, Violet or Silver—also has several meanings. It represents the cycles of life; the emotional, mystic, inner qualities of personal energy patterns. It can also represent anything from a social, arcane, or mystical sign, to one of the ancient Lunar goddesses such as Diana, Selene or Hecate. The Moon can also represent the devic energy patterns of nature, such as the ebb and flow of tides. These in turn can be correlated with the emotional patterns in people. It is interesting that someone infatuated is still called "Moonstruck" or in the act of "Mooning."

Note how long symbols, their names, and their meanings retain their alchemical attributes within our consciousness and our language. Even when the form of a symbol changes to reflect social changes, it can actually increase alchemically as it relates to the "current" of the present.

Symbolic Keys

Classic symbols and keys come with an established alchemy that is sort of an instant blend of energies—simply add your Self. Classic symbols are the circle, the cross, the star, and other established social and religious symbols which represent shared beliefs.

Similar causes (other things being equal) have similar effects, and similar psychological situations make use of the same symbols, which on their side rest on archetypal foundations, as I have been shown in the case of alchemy.

—Carl Jung

Sometimes established symbols carry confused interpretations. In other words, the misuse of symbols can create an unpleasant etheric energy field which can mask the true alchemy of the symbol. Fortunately, many of these energy masks are simply that—masks to be removed, revealing the true nature of the energy in the symbol. Your personal clarity of intention and purpose is the best tool to access the true energy of any symbol or personification image.

Solar Wheel of Life

The Swastika evolved from a solar wheel symbol for life. When the Nazi Party came into power in Germany, they chose to use the same solar wheel, but reversed it to form the infamous Swastika. Reversing an established symbol alchemically causes a reversal of that symbol's associated energy pattern.

Swastika

In essence, the Swastika reversed the ancient Wheel of the Sun which represented life. When reversed, the symbol came to represent death. This reversal and its associations are so strong that even now the ancient solar wheel is immediately mistaken for the Swastika by most people. Because of this, the symbol of the ancient solar wheel can no longer clearly be used to represent the energy patterns of life and personal empowerment.

Sigel

Another example of symbols made infamous by the Nazis is the insignia of the dreaded SS troops. The Sigel, which represents pure force, power, and thrust, was doubled and placed side by side. This, in effect, metaphysically amplified the power of the rune Sigel into a force not controllable even by its creators. When combined with the already reversed energy pattern of the Nazi party as represented by the Swastika, the SS insignia became a force for death.

Doubled Sigel

It is interesting to speculate that if the ancient Wheel of the Sun with its original positive energy patterns had been the symbol of a political party—and if some members of that political party also used a pair of Sigel runes to represent the power—would that force have brought mass healing?

Unfortunately, like other symbols whose physical as well as representative qualities have been actively misused or even consciously debased, the potential use of those symbols has been severely limited, and using them can be risky.

It is always a good idea to research the origin of symbols to let you know what is present on the positive side. It will also let you know what to avoid, release, or work out, if there is a negative side to or association with that symbol.

An established symbol with strong energy patterns can be reversed for healing magick. So long as the purpose is pure and the intentions are positive, this will establish a new form without taking away from the original alchemy of the symbol. In fact, the original form may benefit from the additional dimensions of energy associated with it in reversed form. This makes a symbol's alchemy more like a wheel or sphere than a flat, fixed pattern.

Rune of Protection

An excellent example of this is the development of the peace symbol by the philosopher (and modern Druid) Bertrand Russell during the 1950's. Russell took the ancient rune of protection and reversed it to represent peace. Then he enclosed the reversed rune in a circle to represent unity, harmony, and the focused power of the magick circle.

Peace Symbol

Bertrand Russell's rationale for this act of modern alchemy was that our pre-occupation with protection was leading us to emphasize militaristic power. This in turn often led to the use of force as an automatic response.

Since this symbol was developed just after World War II and the Korean War, it is understandable how the times were right to shift the energies toward peace. War had just devastated a great part of the world's lands and cultures; the atomic bomb had been used as well, bringing the world to a new recognition of the need for an active force for peace.

It is also interesting to note that Bertrand Russell used the Germanic rune to activate this force for peace. Germany, as you know, had been both devastated and divided as a result of World War II. Much of the responsibility for World War II can be attributed to the rise of the Nazi party in Germany. They, too, used a reversed symbol.

Consider how these two acts of modern alchemy with symbols have changed the world. The peace symbol has gained in strength since its creation, despite attempts to malign it with absurd interpretations such as those who say it represents a "broken" Christian cross. No doubt this absurd interpretation is fully accepted by those who still serve, and are therefore bound by, the energies of the Swastika. Seems to me they have "broken" that cross within themselves—if it was ever there.

Imagery with Symbols

The following set of symbols provides a guide for developing your own. These symbols or symbolic images classically represent energies that correlate with the energy patterns of Rays and Lights. As always, let personal symbols emerge in your own imagery work; be sure to consider the shape, mood, and implied action of any symbol you use. A symbol which evokes the energy of a Ray or Light will be most effective alchemically.

Symbolic Keys

Red	Feathered arrow, drum, drop of blood
Scarlet	Double-edged sword, justice scales, Yin/Yang symbol
Rose	Wreath, links in a chain, full-blown rose
Orange	Flame, control panel, cauldron
Peach	Peace symbol, handprint, keystone arch
Yellow	Obelisk, pagoda, maze
Golden-Green	Flower bud, spoked wheel, tiny sprout
Green	Heart, evergreen tree, money sign
Turquoise	Shield (badge), staff, sword
Blue	Music note, grail, wave
Indigo	Equilateral cross, sailor's knot, Egyptian eye
Violet	Lotus blossom, temple, star (five- or six-point)
White	Pyramid, clouds, feather
Rainbow	Rainbow, solar system (galaxy), beribboned maypole
Crystal	Quartz crystal point, crystal ball, wand
Spirit	Eight-point star (or other religious symbol), wings, crown
Gold	Sun, male symbol, rocket (fireworks)
Silver	Moon, female symbol, basket
Black	Theta symbol, footprint, candle
Grey	Spiral, road sign or X, river
Brown	Tree with roots, shell, seed pod

For Spirit Light, I suggest the use of several symbols: an eight-point star, wings, and a crown, plus a personal Spiritual or religious symbol. I often choose one of three traditional crosses associated with the Christian religious philosophy.

The Celtic Cross (or World Cross) emphasizes the circle of harmony and wheels of life which continue to turn and flow while connected to Earth.

The Maltese Cross emphasizes the action of energy flowing out from the center in a direct, balanced manner. This cross can stand or turn in every direction and remain the same. It cannot be reversed, and thus contains no inherent duality.

The Crusader's Cross emphasizes the eternal motion of life, with the equilateral crosses each representing wheels of life within the greater wheel of the Universe. This cross cannot be reversed, but does represent separate action within one Universal force.

If I am doing Spirit Light work with the intention of bringing harmony and healing into manifestation, I choose the Celtic Cross as the focus while receiving from the realms of Spirit. This is because the Celtic Cross has one line or axis which is longer, reaching down to connect with the Earth from within the circle of Universal Harmony. For me, this is a very shamanic version of the Cross.

For Spirit Light work with the intention of generating energy patterns or power from Source, I choose the Maltese Cross to focus on and bring forth the Spirit from within the center of my Self. It is also symbolic for me in that the Maltese Cross has eight points, like the Druidic eight-point star. These points represent the Wheel of the Year and the eight sacred festivals of Nature celebrated by the Craft of the Wise. These are Samhain, Yule, Candlemas, Spring Equinox, Beltane, Summer Solstice, Lammas, and Autumn Equinox.

If I am doing Spirit Light work with the intention of activating a part of my life, a project, or a process of Self-transformation, I choose the Crusader's Cross to get all the "wheels" turning. A new project or process in my life is invariably approached with the attitude of being a new crusade; an honorable, Spiritual venture—and sometimes, quest. The more specific you are with a particular symbol, the more accurate and effective you can become in your healing magick. This is why you must work with symbols personally to determine your individual reaction to them. Regardless of what they may mean to anyone else, symbols which personally and potentially reflect an energy pattern, a certain feeling, or an association for you will always be effective.

Alchemist's Note: It is interesting to me how often I have been chided for using the Christian crosses for symbols of the Spirit. "A Christian Witch?" I am asked. To which I am wont to reply, "Why the Hell not?" Christian Witch or Druidic Christian—both contain the energies of Light (Christ) and Wisdom (Witch and Druid).

To me, the symbolic use of crosses has far more ancient meanings than those which have emerged fairly recently (historically speaking) in traditional Christian philosophy. Crosses are symbols of energy patterns, nothing more or less. The word "Christ" means "light," or in some interpretations, "The Light."

Indeed, it is often easier to access the energy patterns of a symbol than it is to wade through the doctrines of a religious philosophy. For me the Calvary Cross, which is like a "+," and the Catholic Crucifix do not work at all, possibly because they do not have the centrifugal, circulating pattern I find in the other crosses. Since I am far more Druidic-

Christian than Judeo-Christian, I'm bound to be more attuned to any symbols which have the energy pattern of the wheel, reflecting the cycles of Nature.

One shape I find changing in alchemical symbolism is the circle surrounding the pagan woven star, or the neo-pagan version of the pentagram. The circle around the woven star represents the unity of the neo-pagan movement. It is valuable as a symbol for networking and solidarity, but it sometimes makes me feel as if I should hold hands with someone as I work healing magick.

I find I work more effectively with the older pentagram, the five-point woven star called the "Witches Foot." It has no circle, yet it has the magical implications of both the wheel and the woven star. The choice is simply a matter of personal alchemical preference.

I have noticed a newer version of the neo-pagan pentagram emerging which reflects yet another nuance on the emerging pattern of that symbol. The points extend beyond the confines of the circle, and the woven star superimposed on the foundation of the circle seems to reflect a more independent energy pattern. This emerging pentagram could well be used to represent those in what has been called the Solitary Alliances.

A "Solitary Alliance" is a loose network of those who practice healing magick with the common goal of bringing global unity and harmony, as symbolized by the circle. They are free to weave healing magick on their own as symbolized by the star extending above and beyond the circle, yet springing from a higher unity of purpose—the universal circle.

We have delved into these symbolic examples to give you a feel for the energy patterns reflected in symbolic representation. When your familiarity with a symbol's energy is strong enough, you can choose it as a focus for a wider variety of Rays and Lights than with which it was originally correlated. Be experimental (with positive intent, of course).

The action, movement or prevalent energy pattern of a symbol can be used to direct the flow of energies in healing magick. This can be done in a variety of ways: focusing on the symbol, drawing it, making its motions in the air, moving energies in a pattern like the symbol, or laying out stones or candles in its pattern. You will want to be experimentally creative with whatever you use to deepen the experience of your work.

Symbolic Key Exercise

Select a symbol from the list. Try them out one at a time to start:

> Cauldron
> Egyptian eye
> Yin/Yang
> Rainbow
> Equilateral cross

Draw the symbol you have selected, or image it in your mind.

Focus meditatively on the symbol you have selected.

Observe the sensations, images, energies, emotions, thoughts and wisdoms the symbol evokes for you. Make notes before proceeding.

Amplify the experience of the symbol by combining it with its correlated Ray or Light. Observe any changes in your experience of the elemental energy.

Deepen the experience and bring it into the physical by adding the sensory key correlated with the Ray or Light that, in turn, correlates with the symbol. Observe your personal reactions to the alchemical blend of Rays or Lights, sensory keys, and symbolic keys.

Personification Images

In Light I Work.
In Truth I know Reality.
In Vision I have Sight.
In Knowing I am Wise.
In Deities I am Personified.
In Self I am Source.

—Lyn Waters

However we may picture the relationship between God and Soul, one thing is certain: that the Soul cannot be "nothing but." On the contrary, it has the dignity endowed with consciousness of a relationship to Deity. Even if it were only the relationship of a drop of water to the sea, that sea would not exist but for the multitude of drops.

—Carl Jung

Some "living" symbols or "personified" images become alchemical keys because their energies reflect universally felt emotions or a universally accepted truth. In this manner, humankind deified the forces of nature and the patterns of life as gods. This is particularly true when we personify (or deify) an image, or when the primary energy patterns manifest clearly in a historical, religious, or mythic personality such as the Merlin, the Buddha, or Mother Nature.

When we personally deify an energy pattern we honor our part, however small, in the relationship to the divine. We experience that energy pattern as part of ourselves and part of the universal self, as well. The alchemy of imagery allows us to create workable images of the energies we experience. Sometimes these are shared and symbolic for others; sometimes they're purely personal. It is their effect that we consider in our alchemy.

For example: Merlin, or—more appropriately—The Merlin, represents a powerful symbolic alchemy or multidimensional frequency pattern (vibrational blend). This alchemy has long been sustained within the Mind of Western Consciousness as well as within the Universal Mind. Words like "magick," "alchemy," and "Druid" evoke the image of Merlin for many people.

Although the existence of several "Merlins" has been documented, it is the personification of the image which perpetuates the energies of magick and alchemy. Merlin, or rather The Merlin (the falcon) was an official title for the most influential Druid. Historically, The Merlin was the spiritual, philosophical, and personal advisor to the royal rulers. The power of The Merlin was second only to that of the throne.

Alchemist's Note: Sometimes we happen on a symbolic key or personification image that unlocks the flow of elemental energies quickly. I call this "reaching Merlin's tower." Merlin's tower is reached by finding, focusing on, and following the map to our own mind. The route we follow on this map takes us through the physical codes of our being—the DNA. The keys to these codes are the symbols and personification images that are most personally alchemical and transformative. Select your personal symbolic keys from "the classics" as well as from those newly-evolved and/or created by your Self.

Symbolic, personified images to the degree found in the Merlin are archetypal. An "archetype" is an original or primary pattern, as you may already know. Merlin, to the Western mind, is the Alchemist, the Sorcerer; the classic archetype of the wise old man.

Archetypes may retain their purest energies or power within what Jung called the "collective unconscious." However, these energies are far more available to our collective and personal consciousness than we may realize. With the alchemy of imagery and the evolution of our magickal consciousness, we can connect with energy patterns in many realms. Imagery is an active vehicle allowing us to link multidimensionally with sources of wisdom and information within the many dimensions of our mind, using our brain to access these sources. After all, the codes are kept in the brain as well as every cell. Explore within to find maps to collective consciousness.

Throughout history some personalities have manifested powerful archetypal energies. As is the nature of humankind, these personalities often became mythological figures, or deities. Often, the original alchemy and the original historic personality merged with others of similar archetypal energy. The historical Merlin became the Mythic Merlin. These mergings created the deified energy patterns we call the gods.

Sometimes the symbolic image of the personality is a complex alchemical blend of ancient origins, such as the Merlin. Other times, the symbolic alchemical energy patterns of the personified image seem to be emerging synchronously, such as Gandhi and the global consciousness of peace. Gandhi was "well-timed" with his appearance and work.

It is valuable to spend time reflecting on the many dimensions of mythic, symbolic, and personified images to provide a catalyst for knowledge about the workings of universal alchemy. Ask yourself how your favorite mythic personality may have emerged.

The Merlin, although commonly (and incorrectly) considered to be more fantasy than fact, symbolizes several magickal symbolic keys for much of Western consciousness. Merlin has come to represent the magick that much of the Western World was forced to reject when the Christian Church began to structure the teachings of Christ to suit their political power-seeking purposes. It may be that our mythic Merlin, who remained in the tree or the cave during persecution times, was kept safe in our minds.

Mahatma Gandhi, on the other hand, reflects a blending of East and West in philosophy and consciousness. Gandhi has a more global alchemy because of the connections of the West in the East. From the blend of universal alchemy manifested as Gandhi, emerged a personality catalyst for the greater good of all consciousness, particularly that of humankind in regard to peace. Although our Western mindset calls Gandhi's philosophy "passive resistance," it is more accurately "receptive resistance."

When I worked with the energies of Peach and Peach Ray, the images and philosophy of Gandhi emerged. I chose to correlate Peach Ray—admittedly a most complex Ray—with Gandhi—a complex being. Peach Ray has the elemental energies of active peace, while Gandhi used the elemental energies of love and peace to catalyst transformation for the good of all. The catalyst energy of Gandhi's personality and the alchemy of his actions combine to give us a universal image; a symbolic key to universal alchemy.

The activation of peace has become a part of our global consciousness. It is interesting to speculate on the alchemical relationship between the activation of global peace and the emerging archetypal energies surrounding the historic personality, Gandhi.

It is also interesting how a reflection of that same elemental Peach Ray manifested in Martin Luther King, an activator of peace and a student of Gandhi's philosophy. Noting these correlations can give clues to the alchemy of history and the evolution of humanity. A personified image can be a powerful catalyst for self-transformation. Consider that when you use such an image, you are able to "walk in the footprints of giants." When you use personification images, you can become the force and the Source of that image. Just use your imagination—potently.

These simple exercises, which you may make as elaborate as you choose, ensure that all of the natural elements are in harmonious balance as you work your healing magick. Amplify your imagery with your personal image of the Merlin.

Merlin—Correlated with Violet Ray for the spiritual powers of the Magician/Alchemist and the symbolic representation of the woven star.

Breathe deeply, and imagine yourself as the Magician/Alchemist connecting with the powers of the spiritual realm. Using a wand or your first two fingers, trace the outline of the woven star (or another personal symbol).

- Trace the symbol to the East to bring all the attributes of the Natural element, Air, into your healing magick.
- To the South, for the attribute of Fire.
- To the West, for Water.
- To the North, for Earth.

Then return to the East. Reach high above your head and trace a woven star to represent the natural element of Spirit.

Make the woven stars again, and add Rays and Lights to amplify the energy patterns of the natural elements and to deepen the experience. When you work with the personification image of Merlin, you personify the powers associated with The Merlin.

- To the East, trace the woven star and focus on Yellow Ray in a woven star pattern to amplify the mental aspects of the natural element, Air. Call forth all the powers of Air for your alchemy.
- To the South, focus on Scarlet Ray in a woven star pattern for personal balance and the proper flow of receptive and active energies. Call forth the forces of Fire for your imagery.
- To the West, focus on Silver Light in a woven star pattern to increase inner knowing and psychic receptivity. Call forth the powers of Water for your healing.
- To the North, focus on Gold Light in a woven star pattern to activate the attributes of the natural element of Earth such as practicality, success, prosperity, and wisdom. Call forth the forces of Earth for your ritual and ceremonial magick.

Return to the East, then face upward. To Spirit realms, focus on Rainbow Light in a woven star pattern to bring in a balanced distribution of energies as they are needed in your healing magick. Call forth the realms of Spirit to empower your process of self-transformation.

As always, amplify these examples with correlating harmonics, symbols and sensory keys to increase depth and effectiveness. Remember, even if you think you can't make magick, you know the Merlin can. Be the Merlin.

Gandhi—Correlated with Peach Ray and the symbolic representation of the handprint.

Light a peach-colored candle.

Breathe deeply, and imagine your self as an active communicator of peace and receptive (or passive) resistance to violence. Imagine what it felt like to be Gandhi (or to be Martin Luther King, another catalyst for peace in modern times). Feel the inner drive of Spirit in the activation of peace.

Hold up your right hand, palm flat as though you were greeting someone. Make a circle slowly to the right, extending your hand anew each time you turn.

Say to your self or out loud:

> *I extend the hand of peace to all the world around me. I send the Peach Ray of peace and active communication to all the world, that we may begin to work in unity for the common goal of world peace.*

As you turn the circle (as many times as you want), specify to which areas or persons you are sending the Peach Ray energy patterns. It is nice, but not essential, to do this geographically. Here are some suggestions:

Add Turquoise:

> *I extend a hand of peace and send out the Peach Ray to the East, for China, that they may find peace and liberty.*

Add Golden-Green:

> *I extend a hand of peace and send out the Peach ray to the South, for the Amazon peoples, that they may find peace and renewal for their natural resource, the tropical rain forests.*

> *I extend a hand of peace and send out the Peach Ray to the West, that there may be natural communication and a sharing of wisdom between the Native American tribes and the New American tribes.*

> *I extend a hand of peace and send out the Peach Ray to the North, for Grandmother Twylah, that she may have all the strength of her mission as peaceful communicator and teacher.*

Finish by blowing out the candle.

This is very effective with peace songs in the background.

The following exercise serves to put you in a psychological place where you can be comfortable expressing your self with color, by drawing or imagery.

Georgia O'Keefe—Correlated with the Rainbow Light for the Artist/Expresser and the symbolic representation of the rainbow.

Get out paper, markers or crayons in at least seven rainbow colors: Red, Orange, Yellow, Green, Blue, Indigo and Violet.

Light a White candle and focus on the flame for a few moments while you center your self and steady your breathing.

Imagine how it felt to be a unique expression of art and color like Georgia O'Keefe. Imagine having all the colors of the rainbow for your personal expression. Imagine having the power to express your self creatively.

Pick up your markers and draw a seven-banded rainbow. Carefully color in each band, paying close attention to the way each color makes you feel; focus on the Rainbow you have drawn. Allow words and feeling to emerge from your mind, such as: **promises, harmony, sunny skies after the rain, happiness after the pain. . .**

Trace each band of color in the rainbow with your finger to get a feel for the energy pattern. Then take a marker of that same color and begin to draw a landscape either under your rainbow or on another piece of paper. Yes, you can do this; you're the Artist/Expresser. For the purposes of this healing magick imagery, you are Georgia O'Keefe. Let the colors talk. Here are some suggestions on using the rainbow colors for your landscape:

> With Red, draw mountains (or hills) bursting up from the ground.
>
> With Orange, draw the ground itself spreading out beneath the mountains.
>
> With Yellow, draw a pattern of yellow flowers sprinkled carefully across the ground and up the mountain side. Yellow takes time, so focus.
>
> With Green, draw the spiralling circle shapes of bushes and plants expansively over your landscape.
>
> With Blue, draw the flowing water of a little stream running through the mountains and across the ground.
>
> With Indigo, draw the cool mountains, gathering in the shadows of evening falling over your landscape.
>
> With Violet, draw the last color of the evening sky above the mountains, and small violet flowers sprinkled in randomly with the yellow blossoms in your landscape. Also draw violet swirls in the blue water of your mountain stream.

This is a useful way to practice with the energy pattern of the Rays and Lights. You can include as many Rays and Lights as you choose. It is also helpful as you become familiar with the flow of specific Rays and Lights to spend time sketching with that movement in mind. We did this with the landscape you drew, as Artist/Expresser. Get the picture?

> **Red:** thrust up from the ground
> **Orange:** spread out across it
> **Yellow:** organized in a pattern
> **Green:** in expanding circles
> **Blue:** flowed in a stream
> **Indigo:** gathered and shadowed
> **Violet:** down from the sky and reflected in the patterns of Nature

Now try that landscape again, with feeling. If Red mountains and Orange ground seems strange to you, remember, you're Georgia O'Keefe; you're not bound by convention. Express the unique patterns of your self with art, or with living life as an art or craft.

Alchemist's Note: Some of the Lights are difficult to depict in terms of color. This is particularly true for Crystal and Spirit Light. For these I use symbolic patterns such as tiny crystal points for Crystal Light, and symbols such as eight-point stars or crosses for Spirit Light. You can also write the words "Crystal Light" in a precise, linear, crystalline fashion and the words "Spirit Light" in a flowing, random pattern. The Seneca Wolf Clan uses dotted lines to represent the magnetism of crystals as one of Nature's colors.

Representations of Crystal and Spirit Light

The following list of personification images provides a correlation with Rays and Lights. When you work with personified images, take time to focus on your reactions. If another mythic, historic or personal figure emerges as a correlate for the elemental energies, make a note of it. Experiment to develop your personal alchemy.

PERSONIFICATION IMAGES
(Mythic, Historic, Modern, Multi-dimensional)

Red	Essential Warrior	*Mars/Ares*
Scarlet	Warrior/Adventurer	*Robin Hood*
Rose	Active Healer	*Mother Theresa*
Orange	Creative Muse	*White Goddess*
Peach	Receptive Resistor	*Mahatma Gandhi*
Yellow	Teacher/Sage	*Gautama Buddha*
Golden-Green	Transcendental Naturalist	*Emerson/Thoreau*
Green	Creator/Nurturer	*Mother Nature*
Turquoise	Revolutionary Humanist	*Thomas Jefferson*
Blue	Spiritual Poet/Bard	*Krishnamurti/Talesin*
Indigo	Prophet/Oracle	*Edgar Cayce*
Violet	Magician/Alchemist	*Merlin*
White	Receptive Healer	*Mary, Mother of Gods*
Rainbow	Artist/Expresser	*Georgia O'Keefe*
Crystal	Guardian Angel	*(Individual)*
Spirit	Christ/Avatar	*Jesus/Buddha/Krishna*

(PERSONIFICATION IMAGES continued)

Gold	Provider/King	*Arthur*
Silver	Counselor	*Guinevere*
Black	Shaman/Medicine Teacher	*Hermes*
Gray	Dancer/Athlete	*Greek Olympian*
Brown	Earth Reverend	*St. Francis*

Personal images are those we personify and project in our personalities. These reflect personal alchemy in one type of dimension. Those images personified from the collective imagery, either conscious or unconscious, reflect cultural, societal, planetary, and universal dimensions of alchemy. What we personify is experienced within the framework of our self-knowledge so as to work with their elemental energies in a closer, more experiential manner. This can be a valuable tool for self-transformation.

To connect with the archetypal energies of a mythic, symbolic figure, integrate the experience into your personal imagery as alchemically as you can. Be mythic. Personify powers of Nature and Self-nature.

Imagine yourself as Ares—Lifeforce, the Mythic Warrior. You stand amidst the rubble of limitations in your life. The smoke of transformation drifts upward from the smoldering fires of personal truth. Structures of your Self rise and fall even as you breathe in the force of life—prana.

Obstacles to growth and healing blow away; ashes in the winds of change. The drive, the courage, and the will to live flow through your being. The power of lifeforce circulates, blood-red, through all aspects of your Self.

Red Ray Personification: Ares, the Mythic Warrior

Figure Activating Lifeforce using Mars (Ares) Imaging

Lifting a burning ember from the eternal flame of life, you begin to build anew the fires of self-transformation time and time again. You are the mythic warrior, the essential activator of your own creation. You receive the Red Ray energies of Lifeforce with each breath you take and each step you make in the creation of your Self.

Here is a cumulative healing magick example using each of the aspects discussed so far: Rays and Lights, attributes, natural elements, harmonics, sensory and symbolic keys and personification images. Imageries can be as structured or free-form as you choose. When they are free-floating—let them. When you can experience an imagery without structuring it, you have accessed another realm of personal power. This one is from a personal musing ceremony of mine, and is a bit more free-flowing and poetic in form. Since it is a ceremony for the Muse, the poetry is, as always, Hers.

Courting the Muse

Lady, I've felt your inspiration warming the stone-cold cauldron of my creativity with your divine fire.

Lady, my mind rejuvenates to feel you near, and my spirit soars on wings of violet trimmed in golden light.

But, Lady, my body aches for sleep, and my bones feel as though they belong to someone else.

This day, anyway.

Another day, Lady, perhaps another day.

It's not that I can't feel your sacred fires filling me with visions, and hope, lots of hope.

It's just that I feel like an old car; today, a 1953 Buick, I think.

I used to feel like a Bentley. Or a Jaguar.

But you see, Lady, I'm running on the fumes of faith, and my vitality is a cosmic quart low.

Still, I see you have begun to heat my cauldron with your humor and your grace.

I feel the fires of the forge and the lifeforce rhythm of your craft.

"The rhythm of the heat." "See me, Feel me, Touch me, Heal me." So many songs, and all to you, Lady, eventually.

Soothe me, Lady, heal me with the sweet waters of will power that I may express your poetry, your songs, your wit.

Help me to breathe in clearly and purely enough to blow away the ashes in my mind.

Lady, I know there are embers under the ash—it has ever been so—

Once you come, and I am a-mused once more.

Lady, I see the flickering flame emerge within my vision.

I feel your fires of inspiration turn my cauldron from black to glowing red.

Oh, Lady, how it tempts me to dance the night away, beating my drum and howling at the moon.

But, Lady, I have learned to bank that fire so it does not consume me.

So, Lady, shall we do just a little Irish Jig? I hear the penny-whistle and harp singing out the notes to soothe and cool my spirit.

This is a time for focus. Lady, this I know. Abide awhile.

I'll light a little candle, Lady, and watch the flame dance to the lovely lilting pipes.

For you, Lady, I reach within for the mechanism to control this vehicle, albeit classic, that I inhabit.

A switch here, a dial turned there, and the music flows into melody, the poetry into prose.

Lady, a few drops of ginger in your candle to spice the flame—a chant

> To let it be, let it flow
>
> No worry, no fret, no sweat
>
> All words, direct, inspect
>
> Inject, circumspect, elect, digest
>
> The best manifest easily
>
> Lady, White Goddess, destiny, in me
>
> Let it Be, for me, the best
>
> No jest, no test, true to me
>
> Inner fires, vitality
>
> Inner vision, creativity
>
> With Cauldron wisdom, objectivity
>
> So mote it be!

And so it is.

Let the candle burn, Lady—but please, not at both ends—while Body, Mind and Spirit blend in harmonious celebration of You.

Now let's see if you can track the alchemy I used. Here are key words to give clues and confirm what you've probably guessed.

Muse	**Creativity**
Lady (Goddess)	**Fire**
inspiration	**cauldron**

What Ray is being worked with so far? If you had already guessed Orange, you are correct. Now notice that even though the Orange Ray energy pattern is the primary focus of the ceremony (or ballad), other issues also need the attention of different Rays and Lights. Here are some more key words:

mind	**violet**
rejuvenates	**Spirit soars**
wings	**golden light**

Why? Here is a breakdown:

> **Mind**: refers to Yellow Ray focus needed to give structure to creative flow.
>
> **Rejuvenates**: refers to Golden-Green Ray renewal (and in some cases, resurrection of creative inspiration).
>
> **Spirit soars; wings**: refer to the intangible yet essential connection to the source of all energy.
>
> **Violet**: refers to Violet Ray (coming with Spirit energy to connect with Spiritual realms, yet remaining in the physical—as is the nature of Violet Ray).
>
> **Golden Light**: refers to the energies of activation which shape all works.

To summarize, at this point in the ceremony of healing magick I felt the "heat" of new inspiration. From this I focused, began turning the wheels anew in my mind, then offered up my willingness of mind and Spirit to connect with higher realms of Spirituality.

So what's next? Here are a few key words we'll do as we go:

> **Body**: refers to physical strength.
>
> **Fires, visions, hopes**: refers to depleted Red Ray.
>
> **Fires of the Forge; Life force; the rhythm of the heat**: all refer to the process of building up Red Ray.
>
> **Songs, soothe, heal, waters, will power, express**: refer to the balance of Blue Ray.
>
> **Clearly, purely**: refers to Crystal Light for clarity in the work.

At this point in the ceremony, I shift the focus back to Orange Ray to strengthen the energy pattern. Orange Ray is represented in these words (and others):

Lady	**cauldron**
embers	**a-mused**
flickering flame	**inspiration**

Next, a burst of Red Ray to get those creative energies physically moving. Note that I work with Red Ray just a little at a time because of its intensity. Red Ray is represented in these words (and others):

glowing red	**dance**
beating my drum	**howling at the Moon**

Next, a return to Blue Ray to help creativity flow in balance. Then Blue, Red, Orange and Yellow shift back and forth described in terms of music, dance, focus and the now gentle candlelight of creativity. These also refer to the activities involved in the creative process: music, dance, focus, etc.

From this point, I focus specifically on Orange Ray with a bit of Blue Ray for an approximate flow of expression. In focusing on the Orange Ray strongly, I use the correlated aspects as keys to deepen and regulate the creative process.

You will probably recognize the Orange Ray key words easily:

control	switch
dial	Lady
ginger	spice
flame	

These are followed by harmonic word symbology using the Orange Ray harmonic of short **e**. Can you also see how the words chosen directly relate to the process of creativity and inspiration?

The ceremony ends with a statement of the original intention, in particular the words "vitality" and "creativity," and a gentle reminder about keeping up physical strength and the harmony of Body, Mind and Spirit blending.

We've discussed this example in detail to give you an idea about how healing magick ceremonies can flow and still incorporate all that is needed for the attributes or situations you are working with.

Ceremonial poetry does not have to meet with the approval of your English literature or grammar teacher. (Good thing!) It only has to meet with your personal approval. How you weave together your healing magick will change according to your own transformations and the differences in situations.

Don't be afraid to be wrong; your good intentions will keep you from causing any problems. And, finally, don't be afraid to use humor. Humor is a sacred gift of Mother Wit wrapped up in a peach-colored package, and we already know how special Peach is. Be an active communicator with your personal alchemy. You'll enjoy it so much more than being too stuffy or formal. It won't work anyway, if the flow of healing magick doesn't come from within your heart.

Personification Images Exercises

Design a healing magick example for flexibility using your self as the representative symbol for Gray Light, the Dancer/Athlete.

↞ Hint: Don't forget to power up or warm up like Dancers and Athletes do (and cool down, too).

Design a ceremony for two romantic partners searching for a more heartfelt relationship.

↞ Hint: Lots of relationship problems stem from blurring of sex role boundaries. And remember, what you balance in a relationship you must also balance within each partner, and of course, within your self.

Chapter Five

Runic and Astrological Correlations

The runes and holy signs may be used as focal points for evocatory magic and meditation as well as self-transmutation and mystical communication.

—Edred Thorsson

Each rune symbolically represents a force in nature and a quality of the human soul. When used rightly, runes can affect the subjective, inner world of thoughts and feelings, and the outer, objective environment. Both are one from the magical viewpoint.

—Donald Tyson

Astrology complements everything in psychology because it examines the facts of the planetary influences on the conscious and the subconscious, providing a guideline towards harmony of mind, body and spirit.

—Sybil Leek

Astrology is a language of universal principles, a way of perceiving form and order in the life of an individual person, a way of symbolizing each individuals' oneness with universal factors.

—Stephen Arroyo

All symbols—in fact, all systems—are representations of simple or elaborate energy patterns. Traditional systems are the result of alchemical experimentation and expression from what we call "the past." It is wise to remember that traditional systems may become a foundation of present and future alchemies.

Traditional systems are used today to access specific energy patterns or frequencies (pools of energy) and to use these as elements for alchemy. The perpetuation of traditional systems has created energy patterns easily accessed by the modern personal alchemist for use in the present, rather than being bound to patterns of the past.

The traditional systems presented here are in their most basic forms. Many fine books are available on numerous traditional systems. The task of the personal alchemist is to create by actively gathering information from all available resources. Experiment with both the past and the future in order to create the present—the eternal present.

The following correlations are based on research, personal experience and experimentation with these systems. Use these as a catalyst for your own experimentation; feel free to disagree. Your personal experience and experimentation creates your personal alchemy—after all, what else truly could?

The Alchemy of Runes

Runes were never a purely utilitarian script; right from their adoption into Germanic usage they served for the casting of lots, divination, and other rites. Communication among people remained a secondary function of runic writing throughout its long history; much more common was the use of runes to invoke higher powers to affect and influence the lives and fortunes of men.

—R. W. V. Elliot

Northern Celtic runes (British, Nordic and Germanic) are "living symbols." Runic symbols are "hot," or active, in the alchemical sense. Used in healing magick, their energy pattern is encapsulated, potent, and "spring-loaded." Ancient in origin, runes retain power for modern alchemy and healing magick.

The energy pattern of runes is lean and focused. This is not to say runes are not complex alchemically; indeed, they are. Runes, like the Northern Celtic cultures from which they emerged, are direct and forceful. When paired with correlating and supporting Rays and Lights, runes can be the lasers of your healing magick.

ᚠ

Os (Ansuz)

The rune Os (Ansuz) symbolizes the highest realms of Spiritual communication and guidance from the Divine. When paired with Indigo Ray, it brings Spiritual synthesis and consolidation of wisdom. Used ceremonially with Indigo, Os (Ansuz) can be activated to open channels to wisdom from what some call helping Spirits, guides, inner teachers, or ascended Spiritual masters. With Violet Ray, a more angelic, structured order of Spiritual wisdom is accessed. Crystal light with the rune Os (Ansuz) can be used to clarify messages received, intuitions, and divinations or readings which are confusing.

A simple way to activate Os (Ansuz) is to draw it downward in the ethers with sweeping motions to symbolize its powers coming from the highest spiritual realms. Imagine the rune created in the ethers in the color of the Ray or Light. Amplify with harmonic and sensory keys for multi-modal programming, and flesh out the experience to awaken the potency using dance, music, candles, and other correlating keys.

Man (Mannaz)

The rune Man (Mannaz) has an energy pattern similar to Yellow Ray with focus, perception and organization. The rune, however, symbolizes a more active energy pattern than Yellow. Man (Mannaz) can amplify Yellow Ray order into methods for strategic planning. This rune, drawn in yellow or gold, can be used to activate personal power and control of one's life patterns. Imagine having an empirical power over the order of your life patterns. Restructure and redesign your self-transformation with this detached observation and ordered control.

Peord (Perth)

The rune Peord (Perth) represents a spiritual gateway, blessing or initiation. This rune can be combined with Rainbow Light to stimulate a fuller experience of healing transformation in Body, Mind and Spirit. The pattern of this rune can be traced in scented oil along the traditional seven energy centers at the spine. At each center, use the energy pattern of Rainbow Light to redistribute the flow of the essential seven energies as represented in the prismatic rainbow: Red, Orange, Yellow, Green, Blue, Indigo and Violet.

As each energy center and its traditional Ray correlate are focused, the energy pattern of each point is adjusted into harmonious flow so Body, Mind and Spirit may positively transform and evolve. Rainbow Light is then used to smooth each energy center and to balance the flow at each point activated by the "gateway" energy pattern of the rune Peord (Perth). To seal, a Rainbow veil of Light is cast throughout the etheric bodies and into the physical to keep the essential energy centers ordered with a balanced, flowing distribution of energy.

The rune Peord (Perth) correlated with Rainbow Light can ceremonially announce intentions toward self-healing and self-development through initiation into the Rainbow path. This means the personal alchemy involved in spiritual self-transformation is taken from all systems of wisdom reflecting the light of Universal Alchemy.

For a ceremonial rune, paint the rune Peord (Perth) as a rainbow with watercolor markers or paints. After you have placed all seven rainbow colors side by side in the shape (or energy pattern) of the rune, blend the lines with water where they touch each other. This blending represents the unified flow of Body, Mind and Spirit wholeness. The water symbolizes the personal emotions and inner wisdoms involved in the process of self-healing and self-transformation, and the Spiritual experience of Self-initiation. The Rainbow symbolizes the gateway of light leading to Source and reflected in the self.

Gyfu (Gebo)

The rune Gyfu (Gebo) represents the highest gift of Spirit realms. When correlated with Spirit Light, it can provide a connection point for the indefinable experiences of Spirit. When used with any Ray or Light, Gyfu brings forth the highest power and gifts the energy pattern contains. Shamanically, Gyfu (Gebo) can be used to attune to the manifest elements of Nature—Air, Fire, Water and Earth. The rune itself becomes the symbolic vehicle of the element of Spirit.

To attune to the shamanic powers of Nature, also called the devic energy forces, you can ceremonially embody the rune. To do this, stand in the position of this rune (the figure of an X) and call forth the energies of Nature. Your Self as Gyfu symbolizes that you honor the gifts of Nature as well as your gifts of healing magick on behalf of Nature.

You may do this generally by facing the rising sun or moon and celebrating the gifts of Nature and your sacred connection to its powers. You may also do this specifically by calling upon each element and its attributes, making the ceremony as elaborate or simple as you wish.

You need only remember that in embodying the element of Spirit you become far more powerful in your Self-transformation. Spirit transforms purely, so it is important to use the alchemy of Gyfu (Gebo) with clear intentions. You cannot block or hold the flow of Spirit, you can only accept its gifts and be transformed positively.

Experiment with music until you find some that makes you feel especially sacred, powerful and gifted from Spirit. Create a ceremonial celebration of your personal alchemical relationship with Spirit within the highest dimensions of your self. The gift you bring to your self with Gyfu and Spirit Light is the gift of self-acceptance. Stand in the posture of the rune Gyfu (Gebo) as you listen to the music you have chosen to represent your gifts of power from Spirit, made manifest through Self.

Let the music flow through you. Listen to your body, let it move as it chooses to express a more physical connection of Spirit to Self.

Runic Correlations: Germanic and Northern Celtic (British)

Only one thing is certain: beyond all the efforts of scholars to encompass them, the Runes remain elusive, for they are Odin's gift, and sacred.

—Ralph Blum

These are the runes I use most frequently in correlation with specific Rays and Lights. Experiment with these, then create your own correlations. It is helpful to draw the runes in the color of a Ray or Light whenever possible, or carve or paint runes on stones and crystals. Stones are excellent for "matching" runes with Rays and Lights. Use these as focus tools for healing magick or divination. Use watercolors for stones or crystals to amplify their alchemy with Rays and Lights. This is particularly effective with crystalline forms of any stone and with clear quartz crystals, as crystals amplify energy patterns. The energy of the specific stones adds an element of Earth to help manifest the healing magick. Or use the colors Red, Gold and Black, which have long been associated with the Celtic runes as they provide additionally sharp focus. Can you figure out why these colors are attuned to runes? (Hint: dramatic energy patterns equal dramatic symbolic representations.)

RUNIC ACTIVATORS

Ray and Attribute	Runes	Runic Attribute	Symbol
Red: Lifeforce	Sigel (Sowelu) Tyr (Ger.) Teiwaz (Brit.)	Essential power, warrior	⌁ ↑
Scarlet: Balance	Thorn (Thurisaz) Beorc (Ger.) Berkana (Brit.)	Catharsis, chaos balance	Þ ß
Rose: Temperance	Os (Ansuz)	Benevolence, communication	ᚠ
Orange: Vitality	UR (Uruz)	Potency, courage, strength	ᚢ
Peach: Peace	Ethel (Othila)	Unity, allegiance, consolidation	ᛜ
Yellow: Intellect	Daeg (Dagaz) Man (Ger.) Mannaz (Brit.)	Study, facts, self-knowledge	ᛞ ᛗ
Golden-Green: Renewal	Ger (Jera)	Harvest, cycles, transformation	ᛡ
Green: Expansion	Feoh (Fehu)	Abundance, prosperity, growth	ᚡ
Turquoise: Dedication	Eoh (Eihwaz)	Readiness, service, power	ᛇ
Blue: Expression	Wyn (Wunjo)	Spiritual gain, joy, self-achievement	ᚹ

Ray and Attribute	Runes	Runic Attribute	Symbol
Indigo: Synthesis	Lagu (Laguz)	Inner wisdom, magic, mystery	ᚱ
Violet: Spirituality	Ken (Kano)	Guidance, spiritual opportunity	ᚲ

Light and Attribute	Runes	Runic Attribute	Symbol
White: Healing	Eolh (Algiz)	Shield, assistance, protection	ᛉ
Rainbow: Blending	Peord (Perth) Daeg (Ger.) Dagaz (Brit.)	Distribution, initiation, chance	ᛈ ᛞ
Crystal: Clarity	Tyr (Teiwaz)	Truth, spiritual judgment	↑
Spirit: Source	Gyfu (Gebo)	Unity of self and Self, gifts	X
Silver: Receptivity	IS (ISA) Lagu (Ger.) Laguz (Brit.)	Inner journey, secrets, mystery	ǀ ᚱ
Gold: Activity	Man (Mannaz) Wyn (Ger.) Wunjo (Brit.)	Self-activation, achievement	ᛗ ᚹ
Black: Release	Haegl (Hagalaz)	Transmutation, change, disruption	ᚺ
Gray: Flexibility	Nyd (Nauthiz)	Endurance, persistence, resolve	ᚾ
Brown: Connection	EH (Ehwaz)	Transportation, movement, vehicle	ᛗ

I find the alchemy of runes and Rays potent in healing magick. The alchemy of runes (which are direct) and Lights (which are diffuse) requires more focus than is necessary with Rays. The focused energy of a Ray is an active "match" for the direct, dynamic energy of runes, particularly with the primary Rays of Red, Yellow and Blue. Secondary Rays Orange, Green and Violet can require a bit more focus. The blended Rays of Rose, Peach and Golden-Green require more focus than Scarlet and Turquoise, which are alchemically "hot" like the runes.

Those already working with runes may find your correlations are different from mine. The "encapsulated" energy patterns of runes makes then effective keys for many healing magick purposes. If you already work with runes, I suggest you match your image or interpretation of that rune's power with a Ray or Light that suggests a similar energy pattern or correlation.

For example, in correlating Peach Ray and the rune Ethel (Othila), I know that both Ray and rune represent fairly complex energy patterns in and of themselves. The striking commonality for me was the similar flow of reflective yet interwoven energy patterns. Both had a weaving energy pattern, like Celtic knotwork or pages from the Book of Kells. The shape of the rune itself suggests the beginning of an interwoven pattern.

Ethel (Othila)

The rune Ethel (Othila) is used to represent issues such as unity, allegiance, consolidation, familial ties, homeland, legacies and inheritances. I have correlated Ethel (Othila) with the Peach Ray whose attributes such as peace, activation of right action, and communication worked well with the use of the rune Ethel (Othila).

Knowing these aspects of Peach Ray and the rune Ethel (Othila), for which sorts of issues would you use their alchemy? (Hint: the shared "weaving" energy pattern is the most potent aspect.)

This rune and Ray combination would work well for any sort of gathering, meeting, or collective work which requires diplomacy and structured action. For me, the peaceful active communication of the Peach Ray, with the familial ties and allegiance aspects of the rune Ethel (Othila), in combination with the energy pattern of weaving creates a powerful alchemy to use for uniting families and groups. This can be for the temporary purpose of doing healing magick as a circle, or for a more permanent consolidation of families, groups, or communities.

Here's a healing magick example weaving a workable unity into healing magick groups (or families) with Peach Ray and the rune Ethel (Othila).

You will need one index card for each person in the group, and one peach-colored marker. Use light pink or light orange, if need be.

Have each person draw the rune Ethel (Othila) on one side of the card, and the peace symbol on the other. Have each person write their name inside the rune and their birthdate inside the peace symbol. This will take some time, but it is important that each person

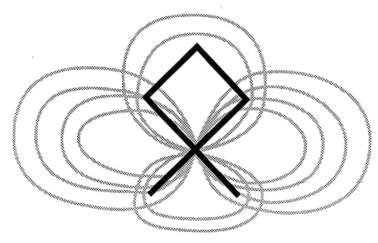

Rune Ethel (Othila) and Peach Ray

write their own. Small children can have help so long as they still get to make their own "mark" on the card. (After all, just because you can't read it doesn't mean it isn't right.)

Have the group form a circle around a small altar which you have wisely prepared ahead of time. On this altar have two White candles flanking one Peach candle (soft orange, tan or soft pink will do in a pinch). Also have a fire-proof bowl or cauldron, matches, an incense burner, and several sticks of incense. Use Peach if you can, but fruit blends or soft florals will be fine. Sandlewood is also conducive, but may be too meditative for active communication. Place all the index cards with the runes and peace symbols on the altar.

Have the group settle in a circle and begin to center their energies and steady their breathing. Have them sit or stand as you choose. If this is a large group the process will take time, so have them sit.

If you haven't already done so, light the candles and cast a circle of White Light around the room, surrounding the group. The group is now actively called the circle because the circle of light has been cast and the energy pattern of unity activated. The emphasis on the harmonic and word symbology of "circle" helps create harmony in any group work.

If you have no experience of casting a circle of White Light, here's a simple way to do it. Stand facing the candles on the altar, and hold out your right arm with the first two fingers pointing straight ahead. Imagine a beam of pure White Light emanating from your fingers. Turn clockwise slowly until you have made a full circle.

You can also imagine a gossamer veil of White Light descending from Spirit realms to protect your circle. White Light can be used to weave the circle together by connecting each person to the others. Either do this from person to person around the circle, or weave a web connecting each person to every other person in the circle. For this alchemy of Peach and Ethel (Othila), the circle is a good way to start creating unity. If you choose to create a web, make the circle of White Light first.

When you have cast your circle of White Light, go around the circle clockwise and have each person send a thread of White Light to the person across from them first, then to the people on either side of the person directly across. In other words, if Tom, Dick, and Harriet are sitting across the circle from John, John would send a thread to Dick, then to Tom, and then to Harriet. When all the threads are sent, make several circles to hold the web.

This is invariably chaotic, and can be helpful in bringing humor into this healing magick. You can create the web from the center of the circle if you or the group require a more structured approach.

After you have cast a circle of White Light or woven the web, have your group link arms and breathe quietly in unison. Ask them to imagine the pure White circle of Light entering into each of them—and into all of them as a circle. The circle becomes the Light, a pure medium for transmitting healing magick energy patterns. If you use the web, have them imagine its White connecting pattern.

Next, beginning with your self, imagine a clear, warm beam of Peach Light emanating from each individual in the circle. Each emanation of Peach streams from the etheric body just outside the physical body, from the solar plexus to heart level.

Now imagine each beam of Peach Light becoming stronger in its vibration, brighter and more intense, until its energy pattern focuses into the power of the Peach Ray. Imagine these Rays interweaving within the circle, forming new patterns and new lines for communication.

Breathe again in unison. Focus on a clear Blue Ray streaming from each person's throat area with every exhaled breath. Imagine the Blue Ray interweaving with the Peach Ray to bring the powers of expression into the circle.

Have the circle take a deep breath in unison to absorb energies of White, Peach and Blue.

As the group exhales, have them unlink arms, and be seated if they have been standing.

Stand facing the candles on the altar and declare your and the circle's intentions. It is best to use your own words, but here's a suggestion:

> I declare this circle to be cast for the purpose of creating harmony and cohesive unity among the people here. In so doing, I declare that a greater unity within this circle be for the good of all within this circle and beyond it. May our unity as a circle empower the greater, universal circle of Light workers. May our healing magick extend its positive power to those in need. We share the energies of peace and harmony so their full powers may come into manifestation.
>
> I declare myself as a vessel of this healing magick. May the powers of peace and communication flow through me for the greater good of the circle.

Have the group repeat the last two statements.

Next, take the index cards from the altar. As you read the name on each card, have that person come forward into the circle. Have him or her state their intentions for the workings of the circle. Then each person should return to their seat, cards placed in front of them, Ethel (Othila) side up and facing into the circle.

The intentions stated by the members of the group can echo the declared workings of the circle, or be more personal. After each person has returned to their place in the circle, breathe quietly together for a few minutes and honor the intentions which have been expressed.

You may honor these intentions with a harmonic tone. Have the circle breathe in unison, and on the exhalation have each person intone a personal note. As the tones blend, raise the level. Repeat a few times for harmonic unity. If this is a large group, you may need a break here. If so, set a time limit in order to keep the focus on your healing magick. Silent breaks can also be effective; tell the circle to muse on their feelings or images. When the break is over, sit in a circle again. Beginning with the first person who came into the circle and moving clockwise, let each person expand upon their intentions, or simply communicate their feelings at the moment. Let each person speak for the space of seven deep breaths (you can assign someone to pace and measure the breaths), and let no one else speak during that time. If you choose, you may pass a crystal, a wand, or a "talking stick" to symbolize that the person with it has the right to speak—and no other.

(In a healing magick ceremony for unity, there are no "facilitators" or group therapy leaders. However, this can be adapted for those types of situations. Simply include that intention at the beginning of your circle—with the agreement of the group, of course.)

For the first turn of the circle, have each person communicate personal feelings—from the heart—about their personal Self. This is not the time to talk about any other person, or make a response to any comment made by another in the circle. The idea is to encourage personal self-expression and not to "get personal" with another—yet.

Some circles require a few go-rounds with these "Self-only" conditions before the emotions are settled enough to express personal comments about others in the circle. The benefit of this is that it disperses the static of hurt feelings, anger, or pride as well as reducing the bindings of dependencies often found in groups. If these sorts of static begin to build, whether expressed verbally or experienced as tensions, take time to breathe in unison, and have each person focus on the rune Ethel (Othila) and the Peach Ray energy pattern of peace and communication entering the circle.

When communication begins to flow more peacefully, have each person state in the positive how they would like something in the group to change. For example:

> I would like to have others in the circle help me by acknowledging my suggestions and my right to make them.

Instead of:

> Nobody ever pays any attention to my ideas—especially Tom, Dick, and Harriet!

If you have a fairly cohesive group, you may find that Tom, Dick, and Harriet will reply positively on their turn when they understand the communication had been related (if not directed) to them.

They may reply:

> *I would like the circle to help me become more tolerant of other people's ideas.*

Or:

> *I would like the circle to help me learn to listen patiently and peacefully, even to things I don't agree with.*

Instead of:

> *If I have to listen to that bliss ninny's wild ideas one more time . . . !*

Continue the process of communication with a positive, patient attitude. It is amazing how much can be actively communicated in a peaceful manner—with peaceful manners!

However, should a conflict arise which seems stalemated, you may have to negotiate. In these cases it is useful to agree that differences, acknowledged but not judged, will not interfere with the healing magick of the circle. You'll need a great deal of Peach Ray energy patterns for some negotiations. Should an agreement not be reached, then the members in conflict are asked to withdraw from the circle for the moment so this does not create interference in the positive flow of energies unifying the circle. This time out of the circle can be an opportunity for those in conflict to resolve their differences.

Most people can make the peaceful compromises needed to work within a circle, especially when their opinions have been communicated and honored without judgment or ostracization. If a person chooses to sit outside the circle because of unresolved differences, it shows that he or she honors the healing magick enough to step out of the way. Those choosing to sit outside a circle can ceremonially represent the greater circle, supporting the work with light and love. Those who choose to "stand their ground" can also serve as superb "psychic guards," as they are often fiercely protective by Nature.

At best, a ceremony for unity and group cohesiveness will empower the strength of the circle and each individual involved. Sometimes this involves some emotional upheaval, which is part of active communication. Also at best, these ceremonies can lead to the dissolution of groups whose connections were based on unhealthy or unethical motives.

When you invoke the powers of peace with Peach Ray and the rune Ethel (Othila), you invoke the full force of active peace. This force can forge the positive, temper the pure, and slice away that which impedes its progress. It does this clearly, for the greater good of all. You can remind your group of that alchemy when working on the unification of a circle for healing magick.

Peace is a tremendously complex and active process, requiring constant maintenance. But it is blessed work. If your group has survived its new-found communication for an hour or so without imploding—or exploding—it is time to unify ceremonially.

Begin a final round of peaceful communication for the strength of the circle. Also acknowledge any of those outside the circle focusing with positive intentions and supporting the work. Have the circle stand, cards in hand, and take one step backward. This widens the circle and allows any who have been out to rejoin the group. This is symbolic of being part of the larger, greater, universal circle.

Beginning with your self and moving clockwise, have each person bring their card to the altar, one at a time. Have each person show the group their card, peace symbol up, with their birthdate. Encourage each person to declare their intentions to work the healing magick of peace with their unique gifts, as symbolized by the specific birth-dates. For example:

> *I, Harriet, born on the 12th of April, bring my strong Aries sense of purpose to the healing magick works of peace.*

For those unfamiliar with their specific astrological attributes, their personal strengths are expressed. For example:

> *I bring my love of animals to the healing magick works of peace.*

Or:

> *I bring my skills of organization to the pursuit of peace, through the use of networking and active communication with others involved in healing magick.*

Have each person light their card in the flame of the center (Peach) candle and place it in the fire-proof bowl as a personal pledge and shamanic gift to spirit realms.

When all the cards have been burned, have the circle hold hands while you blow out the candles. Chants or harmonic tones from the circle help activate the alchemy. Repeating the words "peace" or "unity" is fine.

Close by acknowledging the power of the healing magick and the unity of the circle. For example:

> *This is a circle of unbroken peace. We release our hands, but not our connection to the works of healing magick. We are free to be separate individuals working together, bound only by universal love and the common goal of manifesting peace for the good of all.*

Follow this with time for fun. Don't over-process or replay the experience; keep the energies light and flowing. Save and record personal reactions for your self, or for future ceremonies of peaceful, active communication.

Rune alchemy can be expanded or distilled according to your style and relationship with the runes. Runes can be swift activators for some. If your connection with the runes is "hot," you won't need elaborate ritual or ceremony to use them in your work. You may find that the runes' energies are ahead of you in focus. Catch up!

Exercises using Runic Activators with Rays and Lights

Suppose you wish to send the energy pattern of prosperity to someone in need of financial help.

↤ Hint: An activator Light and a transmittal medium energy pattern can be very supportive to this process.

Suppose you have been depleted in your vitality. In addition to a positive health plan, you wish to have a symbolic reminder to activate the energy pattern of vitality in your life.

↤ Hint: Sometimes not being receptive to an energy pattern is the cause of its depletion. Activation without receptivity produces a lot of wasted energy which never manifests because it's never effectively received.

Suppose you wish to release negative influences and prevent them from returning.

↤ Hint: Positive transmutation is eternal; banishings can lapse.

Astrological Correlations

In alchemical terms, astrology describes the natural patterns and effects of stellar, solar, and lunar cycles as they manifest on the earth and are reflected in human attributes, or patterns of living. Astrology as a "meta" science is an intricate system which provides a "map" of energy patterns as they cycle through the galaxy, and a set of correlations describing the influences of these patterns and their cycles.

The alchemical blend of astrological aspects (patterns and cycles) which is present at the specific time and place of birth reflects in the energy pattern of those born at that time. In other words, the "map" reflects within each person.

Astrology is familiar to most in its "sun sign" form. This identifies the solar cycles in relation to the zodiac, or constellation patterns. As the sun represents the dominant activating force, the emphasis on sun sign astrology is understandable. However, the true alchemy of astrology is far more complex and valuable as a system which symbolizes the intricate order of life's patterns.

For our purposes in this book, we will use the solar and the lunar aspects to correlate astrological energy patterns with Rays and Lights. Sun sign astrology provides us with information about the external and activating energy patterns of an individual. Lunar or "moon sign" correlations give information about the internal, receptive and reflective energy patterns of an individual.

Solar: An alchemical pattern based on the sun sign most often reflects the outer, "conscious" elements of a personality.

Lunar: An alchemical pattern based on the placement of the moon most often reflects the inner, "subconscious" elements of a personality.

The exception to this occurs when the sun sign (solar) is less intense in its energies than the moon sign (lunar). For example, Solar Libra with a Lunar Aries may have an overt personality more like its lunar sign (Aries).

The alchemy of astrology in combination with Rays and Lights amplifies the natural frequency of a solar, lunar, or planetary aspect. Furthermore, the natural frequencies of specific astrological patterns can be used to simulate a similar energy alchemy for use in personal transformation.

For example, an Aquarius whose natural frequencies reflect a solar Turquoise Ray and a lunar Red Ray can vibrate at an intense rate, and can benefit from accessing the natural frequencies of a Taurus. To do this, the Aquarius focuses on the solar Green Ray and lunar Rose Ray of Taurus, as well as the solar Brown Light, which correlates so well with Taurus' earth-centered alchemy.

This process can also be used in relationships to help further communication and understanding between signs. This alchemy requires the activity of the solar and receptivity of the lunar to integrate the two for balance.

Suppose a couple has requested your help in positively transforming their relationship with healing magick. In this couple, one is an Aquarius, the other a Taurus. Using just this basic astrological information, you can begin to get a feel for personal energy patterns, as well as the dynamics of their relationship. This can give you an "educated guess" from which to devise a method to help their positive transformation.

Begin by familiarizing yourself with the natural elements and their attributes in both Aquarius and Taurus. Make notes so you can have this information easily accessible, perhaps like this:

Solar Aquarius

Natural element	Air
Attributes of Air	Perception, communication, inspiration, mind, intellect, philosophy

Solar Taurus

Natural element	Earth
Attributes of Earth	Knowledge, moderation, organized wisdom, stability, practicality

From this we can begin to see that Aquarius has an energy pattern of aspects which are somewhat intangible and difficult to "pin down," or define. The Taurus also has some intangible aspects, but even these seem to reflect in a energy pattern which emphasizes a tangible form. In other words, if both were given a theory to work with, the Aquarius would be apt to create a philosophy around it; the Taurus would be apt to create a structure where by the theory would find practical application.

Alchemist's Note: One way to understand the natural elements is to humanize or personify their energy:

Air is the explorer, inventor
Earth is the builder, maneuver
Water is the healer, nurturer
Fire is the proctor, warrior

Since we are working with the solar astrological attributes, we note these are overt aspects of each person's energy pattern. The Aquarius is an active, perceptive communicator; the Taurus an active, knowledgeable moderator. Change attributes into active form to get the sense of each energy pattern's movement. The Air of Aquarius can create a pattern as quickly changeable as the wind, while the Earth of Taurus makes it as slowly changeable as the mountains.

As you "muse" on these, begin to deepen your connection to the couple and imagine how their energy patterns work together. You can experience the flow of these patterns by accessing or attuning to them through Rays and Lights correlated with each sign.

> For solar Aquarius—Turquoise Ray
> For solar Taurus—Green Ray

Since Turquoise Ray is an etheric blended Ray which contains Green, you can see a shared connection. As Green is an all purpose healing Ray, heart-centered in its energy pattern, you can assume it will be useful in your healing alchemy (If you can get your Aquarius to move from mind to heart).

Expand your alchemical information to include other solar aspects correlated with each sign, such as:

For solar Aquarius with Turquoise Ray

Shared aspects	Service
	Self-determination
	Asceticism
	Idealism
	Universal devotion
	(+ Gold Light = Dedicated Activator)

For solar Taurus with Green Ray

Shared aspects	Heart-centered
	Harmony
	Communication
	Self-healing
	Expansion
	(+ Brown Light = Grounded Healer)

Alchemist's Note: Remember that the Lights represent the less focused, diffuse energy patterns which support the Rays. The Light correlated with each astrological sign represents those supportive patterns which lend subtle, intangible form, yet are important to the alchemy of the signs themselves.

For example, the basic activating attributes of Gold Light enhances the attributes of Turquoise and support the energy pattern that is Aquarius, the Dedicated Activator. The basic connecting attributes of Brown Light support the energy pattern that is Taurus, the Grounded Healer.

Comparing the aspects of each sign, you find a common denominator of caring that points to the heart-centered energy pattern of Green Ray. In Taurus, the Green Ray is more direct and centered. In Aquarius, the Green Ray is diluted in its influences as it is only a part of the energy pattern which makes up Turquoise.

You may deduce that the Aquarius generally expresses caring in dedication to "higher" ideals and intangible, airy issues of the mind and spirit. The Taurus generally expresses caring in dedication to working closer to home; relating to the mundane, tangible objects that he or she can use. Taurus is interested in tangible, earthy methods which relate to issues of Body, Mind and Spirit.

To understand a bit more about the natural elements affecting the energy patterns of this couple we do a bit of alchemical arithmetic:

Aquarius = Air
Turquoise Ray = Water and Fire
+ Gold Light = Earth and Fire

Taurus = Earth
Green Ray = Water and Earth
+ Brown Light = Earth and Water

Because you can get some further alchemical clues to the inner self from checking the lunar correlations of each sign, you may factor these in as well.

Lunar Aquarius = Red Ray
Lunar Taurus = Rose Ray

Lunar Aquarius = Air
Red Ray = Fire and Earth
+ White Light = Spirit and Air

Lunar Taurus = Earth
Rose Ray = Air and Water
+ Gold Light = Earth and Fire

From these solar and lunar correlations with astrological attributes and natural elements, we can make educated guesses about these individuals and their relationship:

• The Aquarius has all of the natural elements, including Spirit, but is primarily a blend of Air with Fire.
• The Taurus has all as well, except the natural element of Spirit, but is primarily a blend of Earth with Water.

On the surface, this looks like a perfect arrangement for a couple. One brings Air and Fire (with some Spirit), the other brings Earth and Water (without Spirit). Natural elements for a strong relationship exist, but some healing magick can help this develop more fully by understanding the potential dynamics as well as the present ones.

For example, perhaps Aquarius will become bound into being the Air and Fire of the relationship, and Taurus the Earth and Water. This could lead to an imbalance in each of the individuals, affecting the relationship.

Each individual must not rely on the other to provide natural elements they lack, but to catalyst the development of these needed elements. In this way the relationship creates harmonious energy patterns and prevents the unbalanced stresses of mutual dependency.

Based on the information you already have about this couple—and on the alchemical analysis of the energy patterns and dynamics of the relationship—how would you use Rays and Lights to aid their positive transformation?

Here are some suggestions:

- Work with their connection to Green Ray so they can experience sharing their energies in a harmonious, heart-centered manner. Encourage loving statements and lots of hugs while using Green Ray as a starting point.

- Have Aquarius experience Green Ray in a more grounded, "earthy" fashion, as Taurus does. Add Brown Light for a devic woodland green. This will help connect Aquarius to the natural element of Earth.

- Have Taurus experience Green in a more airy, etheric manner, as Aquarius does. Have Taurus clarify Green with Crystal or White Light until it becomes more etheric and less bound to the physical. This gives Taurus the experience of working with less tangible energy patterns.

- Have Aquarius work with Turquoise Ray until it can be brought from the etheric into the physical and back easily. This gives Aquarius a tangible centering point for working with the energy pattern of Turquoise.

- Have Taurus and Aquarius sit facing one another. Taurus focuses on sending out Green Ray into the ethers between the heart centers on their physical bodies. Aquarius focuses on Turquoise Ray, also in the ethers beyond the heart center. Next, Taurus focuses on Green becoming Turquoise, and Aquarius focuses on Turquoise becoming Green. Each focuses on absorbing and exchanging the solar astrological energy patterns of the the other.

- Have Taurus focus on receiving Rose Ray into the heart center from the etheric bodies. Rose Ray will help Taurus develop the attributes of the natural element of Air, and will aid in communicating with the "airy" Aquarius.

- Have Aquarius focus on receiving Red Ray in the root center within the physical body at the base of the spine. Have Aquarius imagine Red Ray as connecting lines or roots leading from the physical body into the ground. Focus this at the feet as well as the base of the spine. This will help Aquarius develop the attributes of the natural element of Earth, and will aid in communicating with the "earthy" Taurus.

- Have Taurus focus on receiving Red Ray directly up the spine to "fire up" the earthy energy pattern. This will help Taurus attune to the higher intensity of the Aquarius energy pattern, help develop the needed element of Fire, and aid in communicating with the fiery, quick-paced aspects of Aquarius and Red Ray.

- Have Aquarius focus on Rose Ray, which has the attributes of the natural element of Water and the energy pattern of temperance. This will help Aquarius become more attuned to the patterns of moderation and heart-centered energies of Taurus.

It is advisable to share the results of your alchemical information gathering and analysis. Let the subjects be an active part of their own process. Using astrological attributes with Rays and Lights allows the couple to form a system of communication which becomes the foundation for strengthening their relationship.

Working with Rays and Lights with astrological signs can give individuals a chance for greater understanding of each other's energy patterns. Rays and Lights can be used to create an experience of "being" a different energy pattern or set of patterns than you are—astrologically.

This sharing can be an essential part of any healing magick done with someone else. Astrological information about your self and the person you're working with can give some valuable ways to connect.

Astrological Attributes

Astrology . . . it is rapidly wearing away the stigma attached to fortune-telling, and emerging in the psychology-minded twentieth century as an essential cog in the machinery of man's understanding of himself.

—Grant Lewi

Astrological Sign	Solar	Lunar
Aries	Essential Activator	Zealous Transmitter
Taurus	Grounded Healer	Harmony Activator
Gemini	Renewal Medium	Peaceful Activator
Cancer	Devoted Receptor	Healing Seeker
Leo	Creative Activator	Vitality Receptor
Virgo	Active Organizer	Grounder Spiritualist
Libra	Harmony Medium	Friendly Balancer
Scorpio	Centered Balancer	Devotion Seeker
Sagittarius	Friendly Peacemaker	Renewal Activator
Capricorn	Synthesis Seeker	Ordered Connector
Aquarius	Dedicated Activator	Essential Seeker
Pisces	Spiritual Receptor	Synthesis Medium

ASTROLOGICAL ATTRIBUTES CORRELATED WITH RAYS AND LIGHTS

Ray or Light	Solar	Lunar
Red	Aries	Aquarius
Scarlet	Scorpio	Libra
Rose	Libra	Taurus
Orange	Leo	Gemini
Peach	Sagittarius	Leo
Yellow	Virgo	Capricorn
Golden-Green	Gemini	Sagittarius
Green	Taurus	Cancer
Turquoise	Aquarius	Aries

Ray or Light	Solar	Lunar
Blue	Cancer	Scorpio
Indigo	Capricorn	Pisces
Violet	Pisces	Virgo
White	Gemini	Aries
Rainbow	All signs	
Crystal	All signs	
Spirit	All signs	
Silver	Cancer	Pisces
Gold	Aries	Leo
Black	Capricorn	Cancer
Gray	Sagittarius	Libra
Brown	Taurus	Scorpio

Solar Signs

Astrological aspects and attributes can be used quite effectively to:

Determine the external, overt energies of a personality by sun sign.
　　Examples:
　　　　　Solar sign Leo = outer personality of the creative activator, leader (Fire)
　　　　　Solar Virgo = active organizer (Earth)

Determine the dominant activating energies of a time cycle by the placement of the sun.
　　Examples:
　　　　　Sun in Leo = energies for external creative activation (amplified Fire)
　　　　　Sun in Virgo = energies for structuring, activating organization (amplified Earth)

　　Since the cycle of Leo represents the time of the Sun's greatest strength in relation to Nature's cycles of growth, you can begin to see how this manifests in Self-nature. Astrology reflects the complete cycles of Nature of which "what's in the start?" is simply one part. Solar astrology gives us clues to the primary activation pattern of an individual and a specific period of time.

Lunar Correlations

Determine the internal receptive energies of a personality by moon sign.
　　Examples:
　　　　　Lunar sign Aquarius = inner personality of the essential seeker (Air)
　　　　　Lunar Aries = zealous transmitter (Fire)

Determine the subtle, receptive and reflective energies of a time cycle based on the placement of the moon.

Examples:

Moon in Aquarius = energies for seeking essential inner-self (receptive, reflective Air)

Moon in Aries = energies for transmitting receptivity, zealous Self-reflection

We can use the primary energies of astrological aspects to find further clues in non-traditional yet alchemical ways. Try using the lunar correlation to represent the inner-self qualities of a sun sign.

Examples:

Solar Capricorn = synthesis seeker (activated Earth)

Lunar Capricorn = ordered connector (receptive, reflective Earth)

This tells you that in the Capricorn, the overt qualities of seeking to gather, integrate, and synthesize, and the subtle inner qualities of connecting, structuring, and ordering are present. The Earth element of Capricorn provides a practical, grounded approach.

This tells you that the Capricorn is gathering and synthesizing energies and experiences in life in an ordered, structured manner. The Capricorn likes to put things together in an orderly fashion—primarily to provide a sense of inner structure. Capricorn is Self-connected; Capricorn actions are ordered toward Self-integration. The Earth element of Capricorn can be balanced with Air, Fire and Water to encourage communication.

This gives you further clues to the "Nature" of the astrological signs. Information of this kind can be woven into effective healing magick with astrological correlations.

Chapter Six

Tarot Arcana and Angelic Correlations

It is important to remember that the very purpose of the Tarot is to eliminate the necessity for language or other constructs of that sort, to cut through the verbiage and get right to the heart of the matter.

—F. D. Graves

The function of ritual, as I understand it, is to give form to human life, not in the way of a mere surface arrangement, but in depth.

—Joseph Campbell

Tarot: Major Arcana Keys

The Tarot, particularly the major keys (or major arcana), was originally created as a method of symbolically representing and preserving occult wisdom; it has since developed into a system of divination. As alchemists, we can use the arcana of Tarot for both symbolic focus and divination.

For example, the selected Tarot symbol of the Empress can be used to focus the Green Ray energies of Nature with its growth and abundance.

The emergence of images of the Empress, or the appearance of the select Tarot card in a divination (or reading), can signal a shift in the energies of growth and Green Ray in the alchemy of personal transformation. This shift can be a "need" which signals receptivity, or a "deed" which signals activation.

Here is an in-depth ceremonial healing magick example using major arcana keys correlated with Rays and Lights. Those who are familiar with ceremonial work may find it more useful to skim the detailed information for new ideas. This ceremony may be seen alchemically as the detailed structuring of a magick imagery through the use of physical and external environmental actions, as well as etheric and inner-self environmental reactions and cognitive restructuring.

A Ceremony in Celebration of the Empress

Gathering Your Ceremonial Objects

Set a date on your calendar at least seven days from when you decide to do this ceremony. This ceremony is particularly effective when the Moon is waxing and energy is building; however, it may be done anytime.

During this period of time, you may make active preparations for the ceremony. This will give a sense of positive anticipation; waiting for a significant, self-transformational event. This process is your symbolic representation of the Empress in her aspect as the fertile, pregnant mother nurturing new life within her womb. It also represents the planet Earth and the growth cycles of Nature. Practice using these images in relationship to your self. This is personally empowering while you prepare for this ceremony of self-growth and self-transformation.

Approach the coming ceremony in a harmonious manner. Take time to collect what you need with consciousness rather than hastily assembling things at the last moment. You will need:

Candles
Four or five White, one Silver, one Gold, one Green, one Rose
Or four or five White, one cool color (not Green), one warm color (not Rose), one Green, one Rose
Or four or five White, one Green, one Rose
Or two White, one green, one Rose

Incenses and scented oils
For Green: bayberry or an evergreen mix
For Rose: rose or a floral mix
For White (optional): vanilla or a minty mix

A clear chalice
A crystal goblet or a simple wine glass

A tray or a shallow basket

The Empress card
From your Tarot deck

Flowers
Roses, if possible; but any soft-petal, gentle flower will be fine

A green plant
An ivy, if possible; or any strong, healthy, mature, non-deciduous plant

Salt
> Sea salt is nice but not essential

Drinking water
> Spring or mineral water is preferred

Fresh fruit
> One sweet apple, if possible; one sour lime or lemon

A light-colored feather or a fan
> White is preferable

A mirror

You will also need to have on hand
> A small knife for slicing fruit
> Matches (or a lighter) and an ashtray
> Notebook and colored markers
> Several small bowls and saucers
> A sheet, blanket, cape or large shawl
> Candle holders and incense burners

Optional extras
> Personal ceremonial objects, particularly those which correlate well with the Empress and Green Ray, such as symbolic jewelry or figurines representing the nurturing forces of Nature, the Earth-Mother Goddess
> Crystals, stones, and gemstones, particularly ones which are clear, White, Green, or Rose
> Ribbons, trimmings, scarves, bandannas
> Objects from nature such as driftwood, dried flowers, green leaves, shells or coral
> A heart shaped object or symbol
> Money, preferably a "greenback dollar" or a hundred pennies
> Picture of your self (one you like!)
> Glass marbles, clear or Green
> Glycerine and Rose water, or Rose-scented lotion
> Music or gentle environmental sounds

Alchemist's Note: By now you may be wondering how you can "afford" this ceremony either financially or in terms of time. This is a natural question for those not familiar with the use of creative "kitchen witchery." This means being abundantly clever at making do with what you have on hand, and buying what you need. For the things you do need to buy, remember that something which is expensive is not necessarily valuable.

Collecting simple, inexpensive items for your ceremonial alchemies can be an invaluable experience in harmony with the Green Ray energies of prosperity and abundance. Being in harmony here means neither exploiting nor ignoring but attuning to a healthy, balanced flow.

If you have elaborate and expensive items that you wish to use in your ceremony, then do so. It is far more in tune with the energy patterns of Green Ray and the Empress to enjoy what you have than to hoard it away.

Even if you are able to buy expensive items for your ceremonial alchemy, consider shopping for things which are simple and inexpensive. A share of what you have saved can bring its own measure of abundance to someone who really needs it. That sharing is in and of itself a ceremony of celebration for the Empress and the Green Ray energies.

If you do have to buy ceremonial items, here are a few tips on how to do it with thrifty "kitchen witchery."

Candles

The most simple White household candles can be used. You can even make Gold and Silver candles with a little school glue and dime-store glitter. Packs of larger birthday candles in pastel colors or White will do for a shorter ceremony. Votives which are not scented cost far less than those which are. Since you're going to use incense and scented oils anyway, you can use plain, unscented candles. Candles in various holiday colors (such as Red, Green and White) are invariably on sale right after holidays. Church supply stores are also a good source for inexpensive candles and other items which you can use ceremonially. Use small saucers or even baby food jars as candle holders. Drip a little wax to stick the candle to the surface, then fill with salt or sand to hold it steady.

Incenses and scented oils

Most large discount department stores now have a respectable variety of these. Take time to pick those whose scent is subtle and real, rather than overly strong and artificial. Cone incense generally lasts longer and does not require special holders. Use small saucers, ashtrays, or even shells to burn cone incense. Stick incense can be stuck in a small jar filled with salt, rocks, or marbles to hold the stick in place.

An all-purpose scented oil can be made with vanilla (or almond, etc.) extract mixed into baby oil or a light vegetable oil. A personal oil can be made with your cologne mixed with these oils, as well. Expensive scented or perfumed oils can be diluted with light vegetable oils and retain more than enough scent for your use. As scent is the key here, perfumed oils are more than adequate. These cost far less than natural essential oils. Oil of rose or mint is far more expensive than rose- or mint-scented oils. Essential oils do have an added healing quality, but you do not need them for all your healing magick. Collect a few for specific physical benefits, such as oil of jasmine for "third eye" meditations, but feel free to use your own creations as well.

Altar cloth

This can be a remnant from a fabric shop, an old sheet or pillow case, or old table liners and lace from a second-hand store. It can even be wrapping paper or art tissue with white paper doilies, if need be. See if you can find a creative way to recycle these paper products, or burn them when the ceremony is finished to release the healing magick energies symbolically into the ethers. Wrapping paper, art tissue and doilies can also be used to decorate your altar with cut-out symbols such as hearts, flowers, "angels," etc. Be creative.

Ceremonial Preparation

Use the time before the ceremony to study the aspects of Green Ray and to "muse" on their alchemical correlations to the Empress. As you collect and prepare the ceremonial objects, do so with the healing, nurturing alchemy of Green Ray and the Empress in mind. This prepares you for the healing magick to come, just as you prepare the items you plan to use. As you choose and prepare each item for this alchemy, you begin the process of dedicating or changing each thing with the energies even before the ceremony begins.

Remember, it is your action in combination with your intentions which creates healing magick. Preparation sets off a vibrational frequency which in turn creates a force field, or energy pattern, that provides a foundation for your work. The more focused your intent and ceremony, the more powerful the alchemy.

If at all possible during the week before your ceremony, try to spend as much time outside in Nature as you can. If weather prevents this, visit a plant nursery instead to start attuning to the Green Ray energies of growth and the Nature energies of the Empress.

If you are planning to buy a new plant for your ceremony, the nursery visit will give you a wider selection. Choose a plant with "spirit," one you feel attuned to strongly. A new plant really ought to have time to adjust to its new home before you do ceremony with it, so choose your plant early.

Preparation Schedule

Six or seven days before ceremony

Make a list of what you have and what you need

Get out your tray or basket to use as a collection point

Select your plant and place it in the optimal location for growth
> Since plants are living, animate objects, you shouldn't feel too strange about telling it your intentions. This creates a bond between your self and a living representation of the energies of Nature (your plant!). Spruce up your plant, if need be, and nurture it tenderly.

Study the attributes of Green Ray, Rose Ray and White Light
> Write these on index cards using colored markers, or use colored paper. These papers can also be cut in shapes that are ceremonially symbolic: hearts, evergreen trees, flowers, runes, etc. Place these in an envelope and store them on your tray.

Collect the items you have on hand
> Wash and dry each item with your consciousness focused toward the ceremony. Put these away on your tray, covered with a clean cloth (a towel is fine).

Select some music for your ceremony

It should express the attributes of Green Ray and the Empress to you. Instrumental music is generally easier to work with, but significant lyrics can add to the energy being used; for example, "The Rose" by Bette Midler. Environmental or New Age music which is especially evocative of Nature's energies is a good choice. For example, "An English Country Meadow" by Environments.

Try to listen to this music a bit each day before your ceremony, but only when you can focus on the energies you will be working with. If you are musically inclined or poetic, let these listening times encourage you to develop your own music and poetic images to evoke the Empress and Green Ray. Use the harmonics of Green Ray to develop this music or poetry. Review the attributes you have written down while you listen. Incorporate them into your poetry.

Begin a healing regime for your body

Increase the amount of water you are drinking. Clear your system with fresh fruits and vegetables. Take your vitamins. Begin to cut down on spices, heavy foods, liquors, unnecessary medications, and red meat. The healing alchemy of your ceremony will be far more effective if you help with clearing your self ahead of time. Do this with a positive attitude.

Four or five days before ceremony

Pull the Empress card from your Tarot deck and stand it up in front of your plant

If you do not have a Tarot deck, use all four queens from a regular deck of playing cards. Stack these up together with the Queen of Hearts on top to symbolize the Green Ray heart-centered energies, as well as those of Rose Ray. You may also use a picture which symbolizes the Empress for you, or draw one yourself. If you have symbolic jewelry which evokes the Empress Mother Nature, place it on or around the plant to "charge up" with Nature's Green Ray energies. Goddess figurines, crystals and stones may be placed by the plant for the same purpose. Focus on Green Ray for a moment each time you walk by the plant. Begin to acknowledge the presence of the Empress as symbolized by the Tarot card or picture you have selected.

Prepare any oil mixtures which you have decided to make

Check these once or twice a day to see if the scent needs to be more potent. If so, add more, with intent. Begin to associate the scent you have created with the ceremony to come.

Prepare your candles

You may choose to carve symbols, runes, or words in your candles which correlate with your ceremonial intentions. For example, Green candle may have dollar signs, or the words:

Growth   Healing   Luck   Abundance

or Rose candle may have a heart-shaped symbol, or words such as:

| Love | Unity | Communication |

Gold (or warm-colored) candle may have a Sun or Mars (Male symbol), or the word "Activation."

Silver (or cool-colored) candle may have a Moon or Venus (Female symbol), or the word "Receptivity."

Preparation for White candles varies according to the candle arrangement.

If you choose to use only four candles in your ceremony—two White, one Green, one Rose—then you may carve the symbols for activation and receptivity in the White candles. Burn some of the incense you will be using for ceremony. Inhale while you carve the candles.

If you are using six candles—four White, one Green, one Rose—then carve the symbols, names, or attributes of the four manifest natural elements in the White candles (Air, Fire, Water, and Earth).

If you use a fifth White candle, it will represent the natural element of Spirit. Use personal Spiritual symbols, the rune Gyfu (Gebo), or carve the word "Spirit."

If you are not using a candle to represent each attribute or natural element, it doesn't mean that you will be missing any of those energy patterns. Candles provide a focus for whatever you want in the healing magick of your ceremony. The natural elements and the attributes can be symbolized or evoked in a number of ways using their correlations.

Choose the candle arrangement which suits you best. Some people prefer a multitude of candles representing as many aspects as possible; others find this chaotic. Some prefer to focus on just one candle at a time. This is a matter of personal style and also relates to the type of ceremony.

For Green Ray with the Empress, the minimum number needs to be four candles, so there can be a four-quartered circle. Green Ray has a circular, spiralling energy pattern. Using a circle of candles helps symbolize as well as connect to the energy pattern. Consider the patterns you are creating with light and energy when you arrange and burn candles ceremonially.

Two or three days before ceremony

Select your altar table and location

Move the plant with the Empress, symbolic jewelry, figures, stones, crystals, etc. to that table—with intentions focused on the coming ceremony.

Complete the collection of all the items you will need for your ceremony

Place these together on or around your tray, and near the altar location.

Alchemist's Note: If you have the sense that you are slowly circling in toward your ceremony, moving just a bit closer with each new preparation, you are right. This slow, inward circling brings you into a centered, harmonious state of being. This is especially important in working with Green Ray, which expands outward in circles in a powerful energy pattern. It is also important for you to be centered when you work with the natural elements and the Empress representing the strong devic forces of Nature.

You may wish to oil your candles now in the preparation for the ceremony, though some prefer to do this just prior to it. Either way is equally effective. If you oil your candles a few days before ceremony, you will have to wrap them or store then in an airtight container. If you oil them just prior to ceremony, you may find your focus is distracted by the last-minute ceremonial preparations. In either case, I suggest you play the music you have selected, and spend some time focusing on the Empress card, your plant, and the symbolic items you have chosen while you oil your candles. Remember that each time you connect one attribute, activity or ceremonial item to any others, you strengthen your own connection to the energy pattern, as well as the purpose of your healing magick.

To oil your candles, begin with the White ones first. This is because White is a healing, protecting medium through which the more intense energies of Green and Rose may flow. Whether you are using one oil for all your candles or have correlated these individually, focus on the White of the candle for this most clearly represents the energy pattern of White Light. This is true even if you have carved other aspects into your candles. All these still must be transmitted through and by White Light.

Next, oil the Rose candle which is representative of the blended, etheric Rose Ray. Then oil the Green candle. This sequence represents moving inward toward the center of Self and the center of Nature. White is a diffuse Light, Rose is an etheric Ray, and Green is a heart-centered Ray with a direct physical connection to a specific energy center.

Finish oiling your candles with the Silver (or cool), then the Gold (or warm). This brings the balance of receptivity and activation into the healing magick.

If you are using two White candles to represent receptivity and activation, you may oil them twice; once for their White Light attributes, then one of them again specifically for receptivity, and the other for activation. In between these, oil the Rose and Green. This will help give you the sense of spiralling inward, even with a single circle of candles.

One way to oil a candle is to start at the middle of the candle's length and smooth oil upward towards the tip, then downward toward the base. This symbolizes the connection of Spirit (upward) to matter (downward). It also represents your intention to bring into being and manifest your intentions through your personal connection to Spirit realms.

Oil may also be spiralled from the base up for reaching into Spirit, and from the tip down for connecting with the devic energies of Earth. Be sure to balance one-directional spirals with etheric energy patterns that contain either both directions or the complement to the spiral pattern you're using in your main candles.

In this case, one-directional spirals going upward would be appropriate for Rose and for Gold (or warm); downward would be appropriate for Green and Silver (or cool). White candles contain the two directions, symbolizing White Light's receptive and active energy patterns. Rays and other Lights are both received and activated through the healing medium of White Light.

Being specific about something as intangible as energy patterns helps make them more tangible to us. This makes them easier to work with in a more focused, conscious matter. The more we experience these nuances of energy patterns, the more we learn to understand our own patterns and our relationship to the universal pattern of life.

24 to 36 hours before ceremony

Ceremonially announce that a countdown has begun

Do this simply by facing each direction (E-S-W-N) and stating your intentions
to perform a ceremony in celebration of the Empress at a specific time. Invite all
helping energies to begin gathering. Advise all blocking energies to be gone
from the sacred ceremonial space you are creating.

If you have scheduled your ceremony during a waxing moon, emphasize the
gathering of helping energies. During a waning moon cycle, emphasize the
clearing and banishing of blocking energies.

Clear your space in both a mundane and spiritual manner

Tidy up to remove distractions from your ceremonial area. Dust, sweep, or vac-
uum, at least around your altar space. Remember, you are going to ceremonially
invite the Empress into your personal space. Prepare your self and your area with
the attitude of receiving natural royalty.

For a more etheric, spiritual clearing, burn incense or herbs, such as sage or
thyme. Whatever you use, be certain to announce your intentions to clear the
area in preparation for ceremony.

Begin to shift your personal consciousness

Shift into a more ceremonial state of self-awareness. Whenever you can, focus on
breathing in to receive positive healing energy, and breathing out to release
negative blocking energy.

Limit your social contacts during this time

Even our most supportive friends and family members can be distracting to our
personal alchemical focus. Assume the attitude that you are entitled to this
sacred time. A healing magick ceremony is like a sacred, spiritual retreat into
Self. Everyone has the right to this kind of personal empowerment time. Your
personal empowerment helps empower others around you. Ceremonies such as
this one are truly for the good of all.

Eat simple, natural foods

Do so with conscious gratitude to Nature for the "fruits of the earth" which sustain you. This will help your physical body shift toward ceremonial attunement.

A few hours before ceremony

Unplug the phone if at all possible

Play music

Use that which you have selected for your ceremony, or which is conducive for
relaxation and ceremonial consciousness.

Set up your altar in a quiet, ceremonial fashion

You have all the time you need to do this with joy. For those who are unfamiliar with this process, here is a step-by-step system for setting up your altar for this ceremony.

- Collect all that you will need for your ceremony. This includes your notes and "study materials." Remember that we are all students while we are here on the planet making our "earth-walk," as the Seneca say. Clear everything off your altar table (or surface).

- Stand facing your altar table and cast a circle of White Light around your sacred area, your home, your community, etc. Focus the strength of this circle inward toward your self and your personal environment. Announce your intentions to create a private, ceremonial space.

  For issues or individuals who continue to "cross your mind" as you prepare this private space, surround them with Light. Send out beams or circles of White, Green, and Rose Lights to keep them safely and lovingly separate from your personal healing magick time.

  If something or someone is particularly resistant within your mind, surround them with a bubble of Violet Light. This transmutes the resistance to its highest spiritual good and separates you from its cause, as well as its effects, for this ceremonial period of time. Learn to take a positive power over the resistance and distractions within your own mind, and the power will manifest in the mundane as well.

- Unfold your altar cloth (and lace covering, if you have one) and drape it over your altar. This cloth now represents yet another circle or veil of White and etheric healing Lights.

- Place your plant in the center of your altar table. This represents Nature as the central source of all nurturance on the planet Earth. This is the Empress and Green Ray reflected in all of Nature. This is the Earth.

  Place the Empress card, symbolic jewelry, figures, etc., in and around the plant. This represents Nature as we express Her image with sacred spiritual symbols. These symbolize the heart center of Nature. Arrange the fruit and flowers around the center of your altar. These represent the nurturing beauty that is the Empress and Green Ray. (Sliced fruit can be kept sealed, if need be, until ceremony begins.)

  Place your mirror on the altar, close to the center, so that you may see your reflection as you face the Empress card. This represents the Empress as she is reflected in you personally.

  Embellish your altar center with crystals, stones, magical tools and decorations personally symbolic of your connection to the abundance, expansive love, and power that is Nature, reflected in the Green Ray, symbolized by the Empress.

- Place a small bowl of water and one filled with salt on your altar table. These represent the flow of Spirit (water) and the structure of matter (salt).

  Place your chalice filled within drinking water on the altar. This represents the healing purity in all Nature.

Place your incense, with lighter nearby, on the altar. This represents the divine force of Spirit and the fires of creation manifesting in the physical body.

Place your candles on the altar using a clockwise sequence or circle. This represents the gathering of energies for ceremony.

Adjust and arrange your altar until it is both aesthetically pleasing and alchemically balanced—if the arrangements I have suggested don't feel right for your altar, change it until it does feel right. That is the privilege and the power of personal alchemy. You choose what is right for your self; for your own ceremony. When the altar is arranged, cast a veil of White Light over the entire sacred space to seal and protect while you finish ceremonial preparations.

- Take a leisurely bath or shower. Make this as personally refreshing as you can. A healthy amount of personal pampering is very much a part of the Empress and Green Ray. Listen to music as you bathe and dress with a relaxed, receptive consciousness.

  Dress ceremonially; or not at all, as you prefer. Remember, it is not what you have to wear that counts, it is how you wear what you have. For this ceremony I suggest using a sheet, blanket, cape or shawl over simple clothes which will keep your body temperature comfortable.

  My basic criteria for ceremonial garb is a combination of comfort and color. Embellish your ceremonial garb as you please. Just make sure your garb reflects a harmonious, balanced abundance instead of a contrived, materialistic one. Be as simple or as elaborate as you naturally feel.

- Go into the sacred area you have created. Drape your sheet or cape around your self to represent your personal private space. Sit facing the altar; breathe and meditate quietly for a few minutes to center yourself.

  Do this without music, if you can. Focus on the "music" of your breath and the rhythm of your heart beat. This process of deep ceremonial focusing has been called "entering into the silence" by Twylah Nitsch. Spend the moments before you begin ceremony by shifting your awareness inward. Focus on the great mystery which awaits as we enter into the silence. Breathe, and receive healing energies.

The Ceremony

Alchemist's Note: A personal ceremony is the most potent, alchemically. The following ceremony is a guide line, or a catalyst, for creating your own. Please adapt alchemically. Personally, of course.

Start your ceremonial music. If possible, walk in a clockwise (deosil) circle around your sacred space three times. Let your first circle be widest, the second halfway to the altar area, and the third a close circle around the altar itself. These may be drawn in the ethers encircling the altar, if need be.

On the outer circle, say:

> *I call upon the energies of Spirit to encircle this sacred spa,e and to flow through my self and my healing magick.*

On the middle circle, say:

> *I call upon the energies of Mind to awaken consciousness and catalyst awareness in my self.*

On the inner circle, say:

> *I call upon the energies of Body to connect me physically to this healing magick and to the rhythms of Nature in my self.*

Look up and say:

> *I call for the energies of Body, Mind and Spirit within my self to join together harmoniously.*

> *I call for the personal power that this harmony of Body, Mind and Spirit brings to me.*

> *I grant permission to myself to receive this harmony, and I grant permission for all helping guides to aid me positively in this healing magick.*

Light your ceremonial incense correlated with White Light.

Fan the smoke from your incense in a clockwise circle around your self and your altar.

Stand facing the altar and say:

> *I am here in celebration of the Empress. I come to honor my own connection to this divine force of Nature, and my personal reflection of the Green, Rose and White Lights.*

> *I am _____(your name or a magickal name you have chosen).*

> *I am here to celebrate and reflect the powers of Nature. I celebrate the Empress as Nature; divine personification of the feminine principle. I celebrate the many faces of the Lady/ Goddess as they reflect in the cycles of Nature. I honor the activation of the male principle and the many faces of the Consort/Lord of Nature's powers. I ask His protection as I work my healing magick with the forces of the Lady of Nature.*

> *I honor all the energies of the stars, the sun, and the moon as they reflect in Nature, and therefore, within my self.*

> *I seek clear connection to the energies of the Earth as they reflect the feminine. I seek connection to Nature as it reflects the Goddess.*

> *I seek connection to my self as I reflect the goddess in Nature.*

> *I honor and celebrate the nurturance of Nature as it reflects in the Green Ray. (Focus on Green Ray)*

I honor this image of Nature's powers as it reflects the Empress. (Focus on the Empress card)

I honor the harmonious balance of Nature. I honor her Love. (Focus on Rose Ray)

I celebrate myself as a vessel of Light and a living channel of healing magick. (Focus on White Light)

Imagine Green, Rose, and White swirling Lights encircling your sacred space. Focus Green and Rose Ray into beams of light entering your heart center.

Imagine the Empress image entering your mind.

Light your White candles, move in a deosil circle, and say:

I call forth the healing magick powers from the natural elements, and from the guardian Spirit keepers in each direction.

Face each direction (go West—North—East—South). Say:

I call upon the powers of the West and the element of Water to flow through my self, bringing healing emotions and inner vision to my work.

I call upon the powers of the North and the element of Earth to support my self-transformation with Sacred knowledge and practical wisdom.

I call upon the powers of the East and the element of Air to awaken my creativity, illuminate my mind, and focus my intentions.

I call upon the powers of the South and the element of Fire to catalyst my growth, feed my faith, and strength my personal courage.

I call upon the powers of Spirit to guide me toward the highest good.

I call upon the powers of the planet earth to nurture and sustain me in my quest for self-transformation.

I call upon the powers within my highest self to come forth and empower my personal alchemy.

I call upon the alchemy of all aspects of Self in Mind, Body and Spirit, all aspects and elements of Nature, all aspects and elements of Nature, all aspects of life to be in harmonious attunement.

I call forth this harmonious attunement from within my self.

Light Gold (warm) and Silver (cool) candles. If you are using White for these aspects (as well as others), simply indicate Gold (warm) energies with your right hand and Silver (cool) energies with your left.

Facing the altar, reach out your right hand to the Gold (warm) candle and say:

> *I honor the powers of activation within my self and my work. May they catalyst my creativity and stimulate my self-transformation.*

Still facing the altar, reach out your left hand to the Silver (cool) candle and say:

> *I honor the powers of receptivity within my self and my work. May they open me to realms of sacred energies and reflect the source of intuition.*

Wait for the space of a few breaths, and say:

> *I honor the balance of activation and receptivity within my self, and the harmony of my being.*

Focus your awareness on the image of the Empress illuminated by the candles you have lit, and say:

> *I call forth all forces of energy to be in harmonious attunement to strengthen my connection to the heart of Nature's gifts and the source of Her powers. May this harmonious attunement reflect from within myself. May my healing magick reflect the positive intentions of a pure heart in concert with a clear mind.*

Light your ceremonial incense for Green Ray energy. If you are using only one incense, focus on that. Light the Green candle, focus on Green Ray energy, and say:

> *I call forth all qualities of the Green Ray as they are shared and reflected in the Empress, Lady of Nature.*

> *As I intone each quality, may its sound awaken these powers within this sacred space and in so doing, awaken these powers within my self.*

Abundance

Growth

Expansion

Healing

Nurturance

Love

Harmony

Alchemist's Note: Remember that sound is alchemical, and intone these qualities with focused intention. This strengthens the energy patterns of those qualities in your life. Focus on receiving and activating these qualities through your self, not as specifics, but as great surges of power. Let these words flow forth form your heart as well as your mouth.

Light your ceremonial incense for Rose, or focus on the scent of the all-purpose incense. Light the Rose candle, focus on Rose Ray, and say:

> *I call on the qualities of Rose Ray to support my heartfelt connection to the Empress as Lady of Nature. I call forth Rose Ray energies to bring temperance to the expansive energies of Green Ray.*

> *As I intone each supportive quality of Rose Ray, may its sound awaken those qualities in my work and in my self.*

Temperance

Perception

Communication

Intuition

Healing

Fan the smoke of your incense (one or all) until you feel encircled sensorially by the scents. Imagine the wisps of smoke as threads of energy weaving the qualities of White, Green, and Rose around you.

If you choose, now is the time to take a few moments to place specific intentions into the energy patterns of White, Green and Rose.

For example, you might say:

> *I call forth White Light that I may be a more receptive medium for the healing energies I need for Self-transformation and for changes in my relationship to others.*

or:

> *I call forth Green Ray that prosperity and abundance may increase in my life, as my attunement to the powers of Nature grows stronger.*

> *I ask for a specific beam of Green Ray to enlighten my career and expand my opportunities for positive financial growth.*

or:

> *I call forth Rose Ray that I may be better able to communicate my feelings to the ones I love. May I also be more intuitive about their feelings, as well as I am learning to be perceptive about my own.*

Alchemist's Note: Whether you make specific requests or state these as intentions, do this as though you were having an audience with the Empress. She "hears" you as well as you "hear" your self. Listen to what you say. You may surprise your self.

Stand facing the Empress card, and say:

> *Lady of Nature's powers, I ask your help in my healing magick. May my requests and my intentions be empowered by your abundance. May my needs be met by your nurturance, and my wants be tempered by your love and understanding.*

Look at your reflection in the mirror, and say:

> *Vessel of Nature's powers, I offer my own efforts in the crafting of my healing magick. May my strength of Spirit and my expressions of will support the Divine powers of abundance. I pledge to temper my wants and needs with conscious self-nurturance, self-love, and self-understanding.*

> *Empress, Lady of Nature's powers, I offer myself as a reflection of you as you are, in turn, a reflection of me.*

Stand facing the small containers of salt water. Take a pinch of salt, sprinkle or stir it into the water three times and say, in sequence:

> *Salt and water, in blending be for me symbolic of Spirit manifest in matter, manifest in me.*

> *Salt and water, in blending be for me the creation of magick manifest in my wishes, manifest in me.*

> *Salt and water, in blending be for me a connection to the qualities of the Empress, manifest in Nature, manifest in me.*

Breathe deeply. Focus on images of your specific intentions for a moment while you hold your breath. Surround these images of your intentions with White, Green and Rose circles of Light.

As you release your breath, let the images and colors fade into the ethers. This releases your intentions into the higher realms of consciousness and activates the alchemy of magick and manifestation.

Alchemist's Note: You may need to do this a few times if your "wishes" are a bit abundant in and of themselves. If you do, remember to acknowledge the role of the Goddess in Nature as represented by the Empress. Also, a few straight-forward requests or statements of need are far more more potent in their focused energy than are elaborate wishes or expressions of greed.

Stand facing your chalice. Squeeze the lemon (or lime) juice into the water in your chalice, and say:

> *Lady of Nature's powers, I am healed by your love, and strengthened by your spirit.*

> *I drink from your waters of life, and receive nurturance from the fruits of the earth.*

> *I do this in celebration of thee as you reflect yourself in me. This I do in gratitude for all I have received.*

Drink from your chalice and eat some of the fruit on your altar. Remember, you're ceremonially "sharing." Leave some food and drink as a symbol of your willingness to give as well as receive.

At this point, you may spend as much time as you please "visiting" with the Empress. This is the time for activities such as reading poetry, shamanic journeying, musing, dancing to the music, meditating, imaging out loud, sketching, or simply being in attunement with the Lady of Nature's power.

Here is a personal journal excerpt of ceremonial imagery which celebrates the powers of Nature in the many faces of the feminine.

Visions of the Goddess

Take a deep breath. Begin to focus your awareness on the rhythm of your breath. Imagine the gentle beating of your heart. Calm . . . peaceful . . . the rhythm of your lifeforce. Listen for the sound of your breathing. Allow it to carry you into a deeply relaxed state of awareness. Listen for the rhythm of your breath.

The time has come to meet the Goddess.

The Goddess in your self . . . time to know your self as Goddess.

Time to meet the power of woman in your self, the YIN.

Breathe deeply. Allow your mind to form images of goddesses.

Ancient and wise.

Listen for the sound of their voices.

Catch their fragrances . . . lavender . . . jasmine . . .

Ancient musk.

Imagine celestial, gossamer goddesses sweeping past you.

Breathe to energize the image. Allow your mind to form images of a myriad of goddesses.

Some quietly serene.

Some powerful and raging.

Some gentle and Nurturing.

Some goddesses like Earth mothers.

Notice the vibrations from the different images.

Ethereal goddesses float by like veils in a breeze.

Dark goddesses of power . . . deep, alchemical.

Feel the Nature goddesses of rain and thunder.

The goddess of the moon sails by in the night sky.

Breathe gently. Allow the images to swirl around you. Begin to bring your goddesses into focus.

Perhaps your goddesses are ancient.

Fertility goddesses . . . round with Earth energy. Perhaps your goddesses come to you like the gentle touch of a butterfly's wing, quietly kissing you with power as they flutter by.

Here now is a warrior goddess. Stalwart . . . brave . . . fierce in her righteousness.

Allow the goddesses to come and encircle you . . . each in her own aspect. Each quietly presenting a gift of power.

Perhaps you will receive a necklace . . . an amulet . . . a feather . . . a crystal . . . a flower . . . a storm.

Breathe deeply and focus on the goddesses in your image. Allow them to present you with gifts. Make this real for your self.

Listen as they speak to you. Take all the time you need to absorb the vibrations they send through you. Breathe, and absorb the full power of the goddesses . . . power of their aspects . . . power of your self as Goddess.

Energize your image and listen carefully as they speak. Which goddess aspect is speaking most clearly to you? Remember this, as it reflects that aspect within your self.

The goddesses encircle you. Allow them to whirl slowly around you. Perhaps they are chanting your name. Listen as they chant to the rhythm of your heartbeat. Breathe deeply. Quietly absorb this rhythm.

The goddesses slow their dance. They encircle you . . . quietly gazing into your eyes. Look around you. Breathe life into your image. Feel the energy begin to shift. The goddesses join hands and close the circle.

Feel healing energy come into your being. Breathe deeply. Notice colors in the energy swirling about.

Receive this power. This is your right . . .your honor . . . your privilege. Empower your self.

Know each of the goddesses in her aspect.

Mother Earth goddesses.

Ethereal goddesses . . . warrior queens . . . huntresses.

Dark goddesses of wisdom and power.

Know by your image all these are manifestations of your self. When you have imaged the goddesses, you have taken that which is inside of you out to look at. To know. You are the Goddess.

Go deeper into your image. Breathe and go into the All. Go as a goddess.

Go as the goddess of the New Moon. Young Artemis. Diana, the huntress . . . the warrior.

Go as Selena of the Full Moon. Mother nurturer.

Go as Hecate. Wise woman, crone of the Dark Moon.

Go together, three in one, to come face to face with the depth of your own power as Woman. Image the essential power of the female aspects. This is the power of the Earth, deep and abiding. It is the power of the ocean . . . the tides . . . the winds . . . the rains.

Know that the power of Nature is the power of Woman.

Know the power of Woman in your self.

Breathe again slowly and gently. Allow the image to lighten. Hear the sounds of birds gently singing. Know the depths of woman wisdom.

Mother Nature . . . Woman Nature . . . Woman Spirit.

Listen for the voices of Nature. Know that the power of Nature is in the sound of running water and singing birds. In all nature.

Know that to empower yourself, all you need do is listen for the sounds of Nature. Smell the fragrances of Nature. Feel the warmth of the earth. Taste the nectars of Nature. Look all around you for Nature's colors. Be at one with nature.

Mother Nature . . . Woman of Power.

Know the nature of yourself and you will know wisdom.

Breathe gently and let your image fade. Be at peace with your self. Know the nature of your being. Be awake. Be aware.

Each of the Major Arcana represents a distinct principle, law, or element in Nature. These are drawn from a repository of symbols and images common to men in all ages from what has been called the "collective unconscious."

—Eden Gray

Each must discover his own way into the non-verbal world of the Tarot . . . No precise definitions can be given to them. They are pictorial expressions which point beyond themselves to forces no human being ever completely understands.

—Sallie Nichols

MAJOR ARCANA KEYS

Rays	Arcana	Elemental Energy
Red	The Emperor	Lifeforce, Thrust
Scarlet	The Lovers	Balance, Yin/Yang
Rose	Temperance	Moderation, Self-unity
Orange	Strength	Vitality, Self-control
Peach	The Hierophant	Activating right action
Yellow	The Magician	Perceptive ordering
Golden-Green	Death	Renewal, Metamorphosis
Green	The Empress	Growth, Abundance
Turquoise	The Hanged Man	Service, Self-determination
Blue	The Chariot	Idealism expressed
Indigo	Judgment	Integrating wisdom
Violet	Justice	Spiritual choice (karma)

Lights	Arcana	Elemental Energy
White	The High Priestess	Transmitting medium
Rainbow	Wheel of Fortune	Energy distribution
Crystal	The World	Clarity, Empowerment
Spirit	The Star	Joy, Transcendence
Silver	The Moon	Receptivity, the Yin
Gold	The Sun	Activation, the Yang
Black	The Tower	Release, Transmutation
Gray	The Hermit	Centered flexibility
Brown	The Devil	Earth connecting

Self/Personal Alchemist	The Fool	Open-minded explorer

Angelic Dimensions and Ceremonial Alchemy

In reality, angelic beings are composed of pure cosmic energy, although writers and psychics picture angels in manlike forms, for that is the shape they adopt in their dealings with humanity.

—Michael Howard

As we expand our personal alchemy, we begin to unlock doors to even higher realms of Body, Mind and Spirit. In these higher realms, we connect with the guidance energies of universal alchemy. The realms of universal alchemy are most often reached through ceremony, ritual, dreams, meditation, and other spiritual endeavors. In these realms, we find the angelic dimensions.

Interacting with angelic dimensions is a fairly mysterious process. Since we don't really know how to define angels, we tend to be more definite about how we approach them. What we do know with great certainty is that what we call angels brings the protection and the power of the highest Light to all our work.

All spirituality and magick has a protocol of its own. When you are seeking for the highest guidance possible in the development of your personal alchemy, it is useful to do so with your best "metaphysical manners." I find this to be particularly true when seeking the help of the angelic realm—at least when you're new to it. Even when you're not, there are times you simply feel it is more appropriate to be formal or traditional.

I find it is easiest to think of angels as dimensional diplomats in the service of the highest Light. The personal alchemist who allies with the angels finds that allies in the Light surround us all. Remember that you, too, are a dimensional diplomat. Approach the angelic realm as an ally, and you will connect with a true source of power and guidance.

Alchemy is an active magick. Whether we think we are confining ourselves to the alchemy of our self-transformation or not, our active alchemy affects—and is affected by—universal alchemy. When we work with the energies of Rays and Lights on a personal level, we are connecting with those same energies on the universal level, as well. This is why it is advisable to have access to guidance from the angelic dimensions. Open to angelic dimensions and be open with angels to ensure communication. Let them know your true inner self. After all, isn't that where you met them, anyway?

Working with angelic guides is somewhat different than working with Spirit guides at first. To me, angelic dimensions in the spiritual realm are a bit like a giant corporation, with fixed, hierarchal positions and department "heads." Spirit guides are more personal, flexible, and independent in their positions. Angelic beings, particularly those traditionally associated with specific issues and selected rulership of times, have energy patterns which emphasize the general aspects of those issues and those times for everyone. Spirit guides, particularly those known best—if not only—by ourselves, have energy patterns which emphasize our individual processes of self-transformation.

Personal Spirit guides can be useful in connecting you with angelic dimensions. This can show personal willingness to be guided by the less understood forces of Spiritual wisdom. It also reflects your faith in accessing higher realms while still maintaining your trust in your Spiritual self. It is through the higher self that we connect with the mysterious energies and wisdoms which are called angels. Your Self is a spiritual connection.

Once you have become familiar with the angelic experience, you may find you have some "wings" of your own. Although there are a number of systems which are quite specific in their instructions for contacting angels, I feel that the heartfelt ceremonies you create are more personally effective. I do feel that the traditional times and aspects correlated with specific angels can be useful elements for your "angelic" alchemy. These times and aspects can provide the loom on which you may weave your alchemical creation, and enjoy the experience of ceremonial imagery.

If you are still hesitant about approaching the angelic realm (or even if you're not), I suggest the film *The Milagro Beanfield War*. It is a beautiful portrayal of how real angels are. Another image of angels came from a friend who explained angelic "wings" as rays of purest light and energy arising from within the heart of the angel. Wings or light beams notwithstanding, angels represent pure, clear energy patterns we may access for our work. Angels reflect our images of their energy. In turn, their image is a reflection of the angelic qualities within ourselves. Remember, like attracts like. To attract an angel, be like an angel. If you know how to be like an angel—where do you suppose you learned how?

When I learned to use angelic beings in my ceremonies of healing magick, I was told to approach these beings as "pools of focused light" with a spiritual consciousness which connects to, and through, our own spiritual consciousness. This connection serves us most clearly through our more formal works of healing magick ceremony and ritual.

Much of what I was taught seemed to present angelic beings as ultimately benevolent, but somehow remote and inaccessible except through very specific rituals, as found in high magick. While these types of ritual appeal to some, they left me feeling that there was far too much emphasis on pomp and circumstance, and far too little on the power and the glorious energy patterns angelic beings represent.

When I worked with these angelic beings in a less formal, more "friendly" manner, I found far greater results. An attitude of respect and honor, combined with an open heart, resulted in a much clearer connection for me than the intricate formality of ritual. This, again, is a personal choice.

For those who find high magick and elaborate ritual rewarding, I suggest an in-depth study of the Enochian traditions concerning angels. For those who feel comfortable with a flowing, ceremonial approach, I suggest that your personal attunement to these angelic beings of Light will serve you well. As you work with these angelic beings, feel free to create your own image of what angels are.

Whether winged beings of highest spiritual order and hierarchy, or pools of focused light and consciousness, or even metaphysical energy patterns created from the common issues and thought forms of humankind, angelic beings bring an incomparable dimension of spiritual power to healing magick.

Here are the ten angelic beings I was first "introduced to." As you read about each one, note any images, colors, or sensations you have. These can be useful in connecting to the powers and the energy patterns of the angelic realm.

SPECIFIC ANGELIC BEINGS OF LIGHT (ARCHANGELS)

Michael (Me-ki-el): Archangel of Mercury
Activation, strength, power, career, finances, personal achievement

Raphael (Ra-fi-el): Archangel of Mercury
Communication, writing, expression, intellect, creativity, healing

Anael (A-na-eel): Archangel of Venus
Relationships, love, marriage, friendship, music, art, beauty

Gabriel (Ga-bre-el): Archangel of the Moon
Psychism, intuition, clairvoyance, women's cycles, birth, conception

Samael (Sam a el): Archangel of Mars
Protection, courage, strength, metal workings, physical activation

Sachiel (Sah-shee-el): Archangel of Jupiter
Money, success, wealth, prestige, luck, love, health

Cassiel (Cah-see-el): Archangel of Saturn
Karmic patterns, properties such as land and houses, aspects of old age

Auriel (Aw-ree-el): Archangel of Uranus
Cosmic forces, magick, the arcane, sacred wisdom, inspiration

Asariel (A-saw-ree-el): Archangel of Neptune
Maritime matters, the sea, tidal patterns of the inner self, clairvoyance, the occult

Azrael (As-ray-el): Archangel of Pluto
Transformation, death, the afterlife, hidden or missing "treasures"

These ten angelic beings are further correlated with specific colors, alchemies and energy patterns. From these traditional correlations and alchemical experimentation, a useful system can be established to access angelic realms through the use of Rays and Lights.

Some of the following correlations are still somewhat arbitrary and experimental. Yet each has been carefully "matched" in order to amplify the energy patterns of both. Let your own experience of these angelic beings help you create correlations for your own personal alchemy. Remember, even the most revered traditions began as educated, yet still arbitrary, descriptions based on physical and metaphysical experience and experimentation.

ARCHANGELS CORRELATED WITH RAY AND LIGHT ENERGY PATTERNS
(Archangel indicates a ceremonial formality here rather than a hierarchal position)

Rays	Archangel	Shared Alchemy
Red	Samael (Mars)	Protection, Courage
Scarlet	Gabriel (Moon)	Balancing cycles
Rose	Anael (Venus)	Harmony, Love
Orange	Michael (Sun)	Motivation, Achievement
Peach	Anael (Venus)	Relationships, Harmony
Yellow	Raphael (Mercury)	Intellect, Communication
Golden-Green	Azrael (Pluto)	Transformation
Green	Sachiel (Jupiter)	Success, Prosperity
Turquoise	Sachiel (Jupiter)	Success
	Asariel (Neptune)	Vision
Blue	Asariel (Neptune)	Consciousness, Vision
Indigo	Cassiel (Saturn)	Karmic patterns
Violet	Auriel (Uranus)	Universal alchemy

Lights	Archangel	Shared Alchemy
White	All Angelic Dimensions	Healing
Rainbow	Cassiel (Saturn)	Order
	Auriel (Uranus)	Alchemy
Crystal	All Angelic Dimensions	Clarity
Spirit	All Angelic Dimensions	Source
Silver	Gabriel (Moon)	Intuition, Receptivity
Gold	Michael (Sun)	Achievement, Activation
Black	Azrael (Pluto)	Transformation
Gray	Raphael (Mercury)	Communication, Healing
Brown	Cassiel (Saturn)	Karmic Earth patterns

Angelic beings have long been correlated with specific days and times. These correlations, having been used metaphysically for such a length of time and with such intensity of purpose, have created specific energy patterns which we can utilize for our ceremonial work.

Alchemist's Note: The "rulership" of certain days was originally correlated to the seven "heavenly bodies" which were the known planets at that time. These were the Sun, Moon, Mars, Mercury, Jupiter, Venus and Saturn. These were correlated to the days of the week— Sunday, Monday, Tuesday, Wednesday, Thursday, Friday and Saturday.

We can hear this correlation better in the romance language of French:

Dimanche	Dios, Sun
Lundi	Luna, Moon
Mardi	Mars
Mecredi	Mercury
Jeudi	Jupiter
Vendredi	Venus
Samedi	Saturn

In English—a language which evolved from the combination of Greco-Roman, Gaelic Celt, and Brythonic Celt—the days of the week reflect not angelic beings, but Nature gods and goddesses in the Northern European pantheon:

Sunday	The Sol's day
Monday	The Mani's day
Tuesday	Tiw or Try's day
Wednesday	Woden's day
Thursday	Thor's day
Friday	Freya's day
Saturday	Seaters's day

It is also interesting that the later discovery of the planets Uranus, Neptune and Pluto led to a sharing of the rulership of certain days rather than a restructuring of the seven-day week. If these planets had been discovered much sooner, we may have had to contend with a ten-day week.

When the seven-day week evolved as a set system, it reflected a known structure of nature; i.e., the seven "heavenly bodies." This system of seven was, and still is, reflected in many arcane or metaphysical systems. The most obvious examples of this are the seven chakras, the mystical seven veils of consciousness, and the seven colors of the rainbow.

As our knowledge of Nature, our Self, and our Universe expanded, the systems of seven became flexible enough to incorporate our evolved awareness. Ancient systems such as the sacred sevens serve as foundations for our alchemy. We can learn from these systems, but we cannot be bound by them. We have expanded our abilities of perception. Our systems must evolve with our own expanded abilities. Any good system allows for growth and change—as does Nature itself.

TIMES AND ASPECTS

Gabriel	Archangel of the Moon
Day	Monday
Times	5-6 AM
	1-2 PM
	9-10 PM
Aspects	Psychic gifts, intuition, the cycles of women (and the female aspects of men, as well)
Color energies	Silver, White, Rose, Blue, Crystal, Spirit and sometimes Scarlet for Yin/Yang balance
Candle colors	White, silver, blue
Samael	Archangel of Mars
Day	Tuesday
Times	6-7 AM
	2-3 PM
	10-11 PM
Aspects	Courage, protection (particularly from violence), organization, mechanical affairs
Color energies	Red, White, Orange, Black, Gold, Crystal, Spirit and sometimes Yellow for order
Candle colors	Red, orange, white
Raphael	Archangel of Mercury
Days	Wednesday, Saturday
Times	7-8 AM
	3-5 PM
	11-12 PM
Aspects	Communication, writing, mental abilities, intellect and some healing
Color energies	Yellow, White, Gray, Black, Crystal, Spirit and sometimes Indigo for synthesis
Candle colors	Yellow, white, gray
Sachiel	Archangel of Jupiter
Days	Thursday, Sunday
Times	12-1 AM
	8-9 AM
	4-5 PM
Aspects	Money, business, social position, luck, opportunities for financial success
Color energies	Green, White, Violet, Gold, Crystal, Silver, Spirit and sometimes Turquoise for service and zeal
Candle colors	Green, white, violet

(TIMES AND ASPECTS continued)

Anael	Archangel of Venus
Days	Friday, Monday
Time	1-2 AM
	9-10 AM
	5-6 PM
Aspects	Love, relationships, art, beauty, poetry, music, harmony
Color energies	Rose, White, Peach, Blue, Silver, Crystal, Spirit and sometimes Orange for creativity
Candle colors	Rose, white, peach
Cassiel	Archangel of Saturn
Days	Saturday, Monday
Times	3-4 AM
	11-12 AM
	7-8 PM
Aspects	Real estate, homes, land, karmic patterns (personal and universal)
Color energies	Indigo, White, Brown, Green, Black, Crystal, Spirit and sometimes Rainbow for sorting energy patterns
Candle colors	Indigo, white, brown
Michael	Archangel of the Sun
Days	Sunday, Thursday
Times	4-5 AM
	12-1 PM
	8-9 PM
Aspects	Careers, achievements, ambitions, motivation and life tasks
Color energies	Orange, White, Gold, Violet, Crystal, Spirit and sometimes Brown to ground Sun energies
Candle colors	Orange, white, gold
Auriel (Uriel)	Archangel of Uranus
Days:	Monday, Wednesday
Times:	2-3 AM
	10-11 AM
	6-7 PM
Aspects	Magick, devotion, alchemy, sudden changes, astrology, universal cosmic consciousness
Color energies	Violet, White, Indigo, Blue, Spirit, Crystal, Silver and sometimes Rainbow for sudden changes
Candle colors	Violet, white, indigo

(TIMES AND ASPECTS continued)

Asariel	Archangel of Neptune
Days	Monday, Saturday
Times	(none traditional)
	I use times ruled by Auriel or by Gabriel, whose energies are compatible with the aspects of Asariel
Aspects	Vision, inner journeys, personal cosmic consciousness, water, oceans, secrets
Color energies	Silver, White, Blue, Black, Indigo, Violet, Crystal, Spirit and sometimes Turquoise for clarity and energy
Candle colors	Silver, white, blue
Azrael	Archangel of Pluto
Days	Thursday, Saturday
Times	(None traditional)
	I use times ruled by Cassiel, whose energies are compatible
Aspects	Transformation, death, spirit worlds, earth journeys, stones, crystals, minerals
Color energies	Black, White, Brown, Silver, Red, Gray, Spirit, Crystal and sometimes Violet for healing with minerals, stones and crystals
Candle colors	Black, white, brown

Ancient keys to the realms of universal alchemy were formed by combining an alchemical blend of sensory, environmental and symbolic elements. Ancient systems have also unlocked the doors to universal alchemy with combinations of elements that have become traditional forms of alchemy. These provide a foundation for our own alchemy, and a set of keys with which we may unlock our own doors to universal alchemy. Often, these traditional systems provide times, days, colors, aspects, issues, and intricate patterns of correlations. Some of these are useful, some are outdated and binding. It takes personal experience and alchemical experimentation to decide what works for you.

Personal alchemists make their own magick and ceremonies. When you start combining traditional keys with your own alchemy, you enable your self to catalyst powerful new blends. It is always advisable to seek guidance from the highest energies when you are doing any works of magickal or healing alchemy. With faith in our own inner-knowing, we can use both ancient and new symbols and systems of alchemy.

Exercises Using Tarot Arcana and Angelic Correlations

1. Design a brief ceremony for the empowerment and protection of the oceans.
   ⤙ Hint: Angels can work together to provide support to each other and to your magick.

2. Design a brief ceremony to bring fertility to a marriage. (With the couple's permission, please!)
   ⤙ Hint: An activating force can catalyst specific issues.

3. Design a ceremony to help settle a will in dispute.
   ⤙ Hint: Communication will surely be another source of dispute in this matter.

4. Design a ceremony to empower military forces and bring swift victory.
   ⤙ Hint: Wars invariably cause death somewhere.

There are no set ways to design the ceremonies I have suggested. However, the energy patterns correlated with specific angelic beings can be activated best when most clearly "matched" to the issues at hand. Here are my suggestions for designing the preceding ceremonies.

1. Asariel for matters involving the sea, with Samael for protection, and possibly Raphael for healing.

2. Gabriel for women's cycles, conception and birth; with Anael for relationships, marriage, and ether. Michael for activation or Sachiel for luck.

3. Cassiel for property matters with Azrael for uncovering the "hidden" inheritance; and Raphael for communication or Anael for relationships.

4. Samael for courage, protection and the military hardware, with Sachiel for those whose time of transformation (death) comes with the activation of military force. Also Cassiel for karmic patterns and destiny.

Here's another exercise which will require a bit more effort.

Angelic Novena

> Design a novena—an honoring ceremony for each of the sacred seven days of the week and their angelic "rulers." Choose specific candle colors, correlating Rays or Lights, stones, crystals, magical tools, and issues which correspond to these seven.
>
> ← Hint: Each Ray or Light chapter has specific angelic correlations, and the resource section has a consolidated list.

Start with Monday to open your self to receptivity, inner wisdom, etc. Finish with Sunday to activate your connection to these angelic beings and their powerful alchemy. Be creative and spontaneous. Angels have more connection to your heart-felt expressions than prepared prayers. Remember, angels are prepared for you.

Whenever rulership of a day is shared by two (or more) angelic beings, emphasize the original or primary "ruler" of the day, but acknowledge the others who also correlate with that day. The purpose of this novena is to connect to and not to petition heaven. You need not supply specific prayers or invocations unless you choose.

If you wish to create a "just slightly spontaneous" ceremony, you can use notes. These will give you the information you need without rigidity. For example, use a format like this. (Expand and embellish as you choose)

> **Wednesday: Raphael, to honor communication, intellect, creativity and healing.**
>
> **Burn a yellow candle to focus.**
>
> **Acknowledge the shared influence of Auriel to bring magick forces supporting the powers correlated with Raphael.**

This novena format may be used for any of the "sacred seven" energies such as the Rays or planetary correlations. It may also serve as a self-dedication ceremony, or for a specific, timed build-up of energies. Some issues require an extended period of focus, and for these the novena format is helpful.

Chapter Seven

Stone Alchemy

A human being is a star's way of looking at stars.
—Peter Russell

Stones are manifestations of light and life, colors, textures, vibrancy, transparency, clarity. For me their beauty is magical, mystical, mysterious. They are the stars in the earth in which the qualities of clarity and light have been bestowed.

—Daya Sarai Chocron

The process of using stones for attunement is based on the philosophy of Nature which holds that all of life is energy. This energy is interwoven into a fabric we call the Universe, of which we are all an integral and important part. Each aspect of our Selves is like a thread of energy in this great weaving of life. When we attune to or harmonize with these threads of energy, we are strengthening the threads of our own lives. That's the metaphysics of Self-transformation.

Each thread of energy has an individual vibration which we can use for holistic wellness—the harmony of Body, Mind and Spirit. Each stone is a finite piece of energy we can use for its own special vibration. When we attune to the energies of a stone and make use of its qualities and vibrations, we are attuning to a personal energy—an aspect reflected in our Self. The metaphysics of minerals is a form of trans-personal alchemy using natural elements.

When we combine a stone and its strongest correlating Ray and/or Light, the effect can be as intense as a laser beam or as gentle as moonlight. This depends on four primary factors:

- The quality of the Ray or Light itself
- The degree of our intent and our concentration
- The potential vibrational intensity of the energies in the stone itself
- The specific use and placement of the stone—on the body, around the body, or in our environment

We can learn to recognize the potential energies in a stone by its basic color. Then we can narrow the focus of this energy to attune to the more intense vibrations of the Ray or the more diffuse Light energies which the stone best reflects. In this way, we can use stones to direct specific energies in healing processes and the personal enhancement of the Self.

Each of these factors is also a thread in the weaving of our lives. Each strengthens the processes of self-healing and self-transformation. How we weave these together expresses our personal alchemy—the magickal blend that is our Self.

Alchemist's Note: This process works through the stone's energy in its relationship to the energies in and around the Self. It is purely an interactive process. A stone can support and facilitate our attunement to the energies it contains—and to the energies we are working with in our Self—but only if we accept responsibility in the process of Self-healing and Self-empowerment. It is not the energy patterns in each stone which create healing magick, it is us using the stones to reflect ourselves.

Creating a Working Collection of Stones

> *You may be drawn to a particular stone—attracted to it, desire to have it or wear it. You probably need what the stone has to offer, and the information it has to give you. Listen to what your body is telling you. You are intuitively sensing the vibration of the particular stone, and its effect on your personal energy pattern or being.*
>
> —Phyllis Galde

It is not necessary to buy expensive stone samples. Most come in a variety of forms, from rough or natural, to tumbled, cut or faceted. I suggest starting with the least expensive forms. You can add others later, if you choose. Additionally beneficial is that smaller stone or mineral samples which fit in the center of your cupped palm are of a useful size.

To begin, if you want to work with the basic seven Rays or energy centers (chakras) system we discussed, you could use these stones:

Ray	Primary attribute	Stones
Red Ray (First energy center)	Lifeforce	snowflake obsidian red jasper red coral
Orange Ray (Second energy center)	Vitality	carnelian amber fire agate
Yellow Ray (Third energy center)	Intellect	citrine topaz tigereye

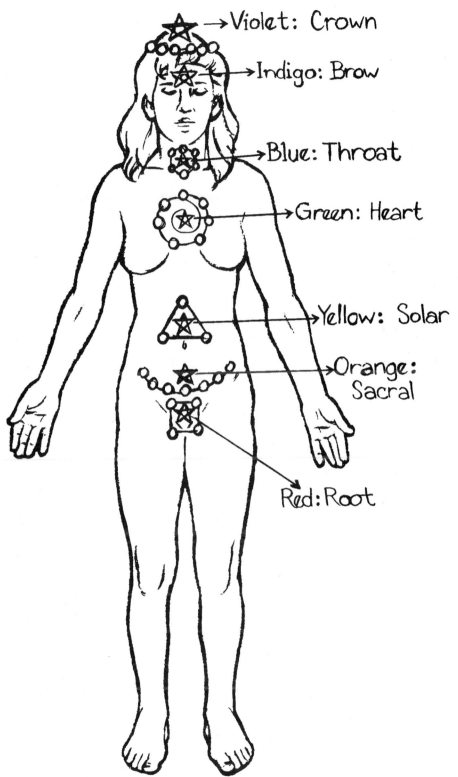

→Violet: Crown

→Indigo: Brow

→Blue: Throat

→Green: Heart

Yellow: Solar

Orange:
Sacral

Red: Root

Seven Energy Center (Chakras) Stone Placements

Ray	Primary attribute	Stones
Green Ray (Fourth energy center)	Expansion	emerald malachite aventurine
Blue Ray (Fifth energy center)	Expression	blue lace agate sodalite celestite
Indigo Ray (Sixth energy center)	Synthesis	sapphire azurite lapis
Violet Ray (Seventh energy center)	Spirituality	fluorite amethyst sugilite (royal azule)

If you also want to work with the newer blended Rays, you can use these stones:

Ray	Primary attribute	Stones
Scarlet Ray	Balance	watermelon tourmaline garnet
Rose Ray	Temperance	rhodonite rose quartz
Peach Ray	Peace	rhodochrosite unikite
Golden-Green Ray	Rejuvenation	peridot jade
Turquoise Ray	Dedication	turquoise chrysocolla

The stones used with the Sky Lights primarily affect the higher-level etheric bodies and upper chakra/power centers, but can be used for all Body, Mind and Spirit work:

Light	Primary attribute	Stones
White Light	Healing	milky quartz white agate
Rainbow Light	Blending	crystals with rainbows abalone

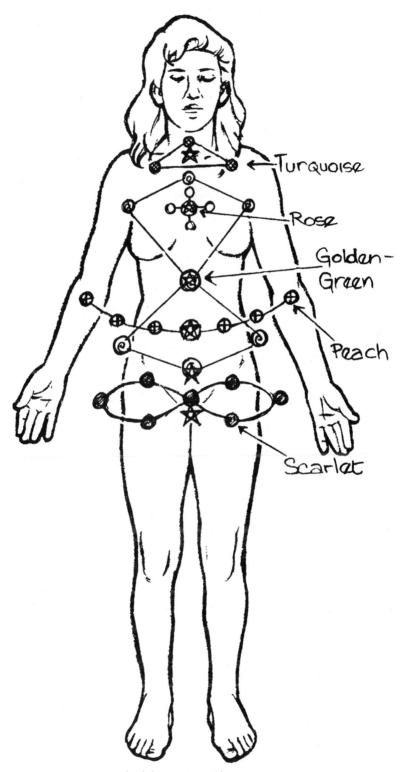

Blended Ray Stone Placement

Light	Primary attribute	Stones
Crystal Light	Clarity	clear crystal point double-terminated crystal
Spirit Light	Source	quartz cluster twin crystals
Gold Light	Activation	rutilated quartz gold
Silver Light	Receptivity	moonstone silver

The stones used with the Earth Lights primarily affect the lower-level etheric bodies and base chakra/power centers, but can be used for all Body, Mind and Spirit work. These stones include:

Light	Primary attribute	Stones
Black Light	Release	Apache tear snowflake obsidian
Gray Light	Flexibility	hematite granite
Brown Light	Earth Connections	smoky quartz petrified wood

If you are just beginning to collect and work with stones, here is a selection you can experiment with using the Rays and Lights we've discussed. Many of these can be used for other Rays and Lights. This is a basic experimental kit, for now.

BASIC TEST KIT

Stones	Correlating Rays and Lights
Snowflake obsidian	Red Ray, Black Light
Carnelian	Red, Orange and Peach Rays
Rose quartz	Scarlet, Rose and Green Rays
Tigereye	Yellow Ray, Gold and Brown Lights
Jade	Golden-Green and Green Rays
Sodalite	Blue and Indigo Rays
Blue lace agate	Rose and Blue Rays, Gray Light
Unikite	Peach and Green Rays
Amethyst	Indigo and Violet Rays
Moonstone	Silver and Gray Lights
Apache tear	All Earth Lights
Clear quartz crystal	All Sky Lights

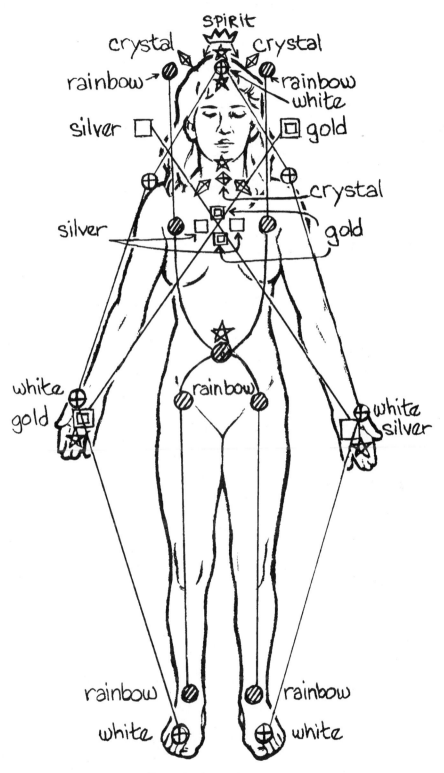

Sky Lights Stone Placement

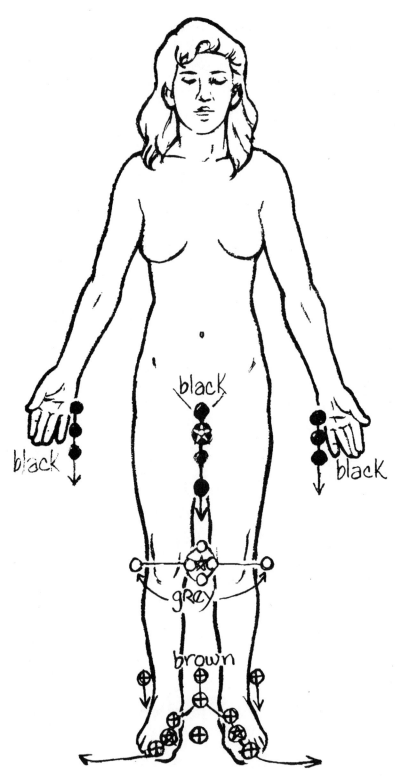

Earth Lights Stone Placement

Each stone selected for this system has a variety of energies, or properties, which combine to create an alchemical blend. This blend is the key quality of the stone.

For example, the properties of a garnet create a primal vibration which affects transformation by connecting with the physical drives as well as the emotional, mental and spiritual aspects of transformation.

A watermelon tourmaline has similar properties, but affects the transformation process more clearly through its inherent, balancing energies. Cinnabar provides stabilizing energy in a more mental, meditative fashion.

Together or individually, the garnet, watermelon tourmaline and cinnabar create an alchemy which correlates to the Scarlet Ray vibration of balance.

KEY STONE QUALITIES

Red	ruby	Divine Fire Stone
Lifeforce	red coral	Shamanic Stone
	jasper	Protective Stone
Scarlet	garnet	Primal Stone
Balance	watermelon tourmaline	Balance Stone
	cinnabar	Meditative Stone
Rose	alexandrite	Transformative Stone
Temperance	rose quartz	Harmony Stone
	rhodonite	Physical Stone
Orange	amber	Magnetic Stone
Vitality	carnelian	Action Stone
	fire agate	Courage Stone
Peach	rhodochrosite	Peacemaker Stone
Peace	unikite	Healthful Peace Stone
Yellow	citrine	Organization Stone
Intellect	tigereye	Practical Stone
	topaz	Brain Stone
Golden-Green	peridot	Antibiotic Stone
Renewal	jade	Contemplative Stone
	serpentine	Centering Stone
Green	malachite	Strength Stone
Expansion	aventurine	Good Luck Stone
	emerald	Healer Stone

(KEY STONE QUALITIES continued)

Blue Expansion	sodalite blue lace agate celestite	Supportive Stone Sensory Stone Intellectual Stone
Turquoise Dedication	aquamarine turquoise chrysocolla	Purity Stone Sacred Earth Stone Resolution Stone
Indigo Synthesis	azurite lapis sapphire	Truth Stone Penetration Stone Laser Stone
Violet Spirituality	fluorite royal azule (sugilite) amethyst	Catalyst Stone Mastery Stone Source Stone
Sky Lights **White** Healing	milky quartz white agate	Transmitter Stone Receptive Stone
Rainbow Blending	rainbow crystals abalone	Order Stone Filter Stone
Crystal Clarity	clear quartz double-terminated crystals (clear)	Clarity Stone Direction Stone
Spirit Source	clear quartz clusters	Four Council Stones
Silver Receptivity	silver moonstone	Lunar Stone Absorbent Stone
Gold Activation	gold rutile quartz	Solar Stone Activator Stone
Earth Lights **Black** Release	Apache tear snowflake obsidian	Mystery Stone Grounding Stone
Gray Flexibility	granite hematite	Foundation Stone Guidance Stone
Brown Connection	smoky quartz petrified wood	Transmuter Stone Bridging Stone

Stone Care

Any time you identify with a stone or color, and what it can do for you, that in itself is a building process and what you're building is a more balanced, happier you. The cells of your body will attune and respond to it.

—Marie Cornelio

Caring for stones also reflects your style of caring for your self. It varies accordingly to the newness of the relationship between you and the stones in general, or a specific stone. It takes a little time to get a feel for it. Use your natural style as a guideline. If you have an ordered style, set up a schedule for stone care; not a rigid structure, but a flowing pattern—like the fabric of the universe. That way, you are open to change.

If your style is free-flowing, go ahead and be a little structured with the care of your stones at the start. Once you have the feel of the stone's special energy, you will be able to determine its needs by working with it for a while.

Interestingly, some stones seem to work best with more structured care, and others with less; you will have to experiment with this your self. Trust that you are sensitive enough to know how to structure this relationship.

Moon Cycle Care Schedule

If you want a simple, effective system to get started with stone care, use the cycles of the moon. Bear in mind that you are clearly caring for your Self; your stones represent you.

Waning moon

When the moon is waning—getting smaller—it is a time for cleansing. This does not mean you cannot cleanse the stones any other time, but the waning moon is a good time for general cleansing.

Dark of the moon

No moon—it is the time for deepest release and cleansings.

New moon

A crescent—it is time to begin charging the stones; activating and working to awaken the energies.

Waxing moon

As the moon grows fuller in the sky, focus on the energies in your stones becoming stronger.

Full moon

It is time to celebrate and bring the energies fully into their power. This time is especially effective for crystals and highvibration gemstones.

I prefer stone care to be a fairly casual process. For one thing, stones do not necessarily need to be cleaned as much as some people say they should or must be. As I see it, we are often too caught up with the idea of stones needing constant cleaning. When you think about it, that's a rather negative viewpoint. It is a bit like the disease model philosophies of medicine and psychology; it assumes negativity. Be positive.

It is quite satisfactory to cleanse when you have used a stone for something intense, severe, or just plain hard work. To cleanse a stone, simply run it under a little water. A word of caution: chalky stones can disintegrate with too much water. Just sprinkle them lightly with a few drops, or mist them gently. Dry these immediately.

A very absorbent or receptive stone such as moonstone may need some additional cleansing. This is particularly true if the stone has absorbed a great deal of negativity. In this case, cleanse with salt water. A tiny bit of salt in a few cups of water can go a long way. Many stone "handlers" say that too much salt can be damaging to the stone. Don't drown it—dip it. You can repeat the process until the stone "feels right" to you again.

Solar Cycle Care

The cycles of the sun are expressed in the schedules of religious festivals. For instance:

Yule (Winter Solstice)	Return of the Light
Easter (Spring Equinox)	Resurrection of the Light
June (Summer Solstice)	Empowerment of the Light
Lammas (August 1st)	Gift of the Light

Natural Elements in Stones

Another approach to take to stone care is to consider the natural element of the stone. Each stone has an element assigned to it, either traditionally or through alchemical experimentation, or often by both. These elements are Earth, Air, Fire, Water and Spirit.

ELEMENTS AND ATTRIBUTES

Ray or Light Energy Point 1	Stone	Element	Attribute
Red	ruby	Fire	Divine Fire Stone
	red coral	Water with Fire	Shamanic Stone
	jasper	Earth with Fire	Protective Stone
Scarlet	garnet	Air and Earth	Primal Stone
	watermelon tourmaline	Air	Balance Stone
	cinnabar	Earth with Water	Meditative Stone
Rose	alexandrite	Air with Spirit	Transformative Stone
	rose quartz	Air and Earth	Harmony Stone
	rhodonite	Earth	Physical Stone
Energy Point 2			
Orange	amber	Earth with Fire	Magnetic Stone
	carnelian	Earth and Fire	Action Stone
	fire agate	Fire and Earth	Courage Stone

(ELEMENTS AND ATTRIBUTES continued)

Ray or Light	Stone	Element	Attribute
Peach	rhodochrosite	Earth with Spirit and Fire	Peacemaker Stone
	unikite	Earth with Fire	Healthful Peace Stone
Energy Point 3			
Yellow	topaz	Air	Brain Stone
	citrine	Air with Spirit	Organization Stone
	tigereye	Earth	Practical Stone
Golden-Green	peridot	Air	Antibiotic Stone
	jade	Earth with Spirit and Air	Contemplative Stone
	serpentine	Earth	Centering Stone
Energy Point 4			
Green	emerald	Air and Earth (Some with Spirit)	Healer Stone
	malachite	Earth	Strength Stone
	aventurine	Earth	Good Luck Stone
Energy Point 5			
Turquoise	aquamarine	Air with Spirit	Purity Stone
	turquoise	Earth	Sacred Earth Stone
	chrysocolla	Earth with Air	Resolution Stone
Blue	celestite	Air and Spirit	Intellectual Stone
	sodalite	Earth	Supportive Stone
	blue lace agate	Earth with Air and Spirit	Sensory Stone
Energy Point 6			
Indigo	sapphire	Air	Laser Stone
	azurite	Air and Earth with Spirit	Truth Stone
	lapis	Earth with Spirit	Penetration Stone
Energy Point 7			
Violet	amethyst	Air (Some with Air) (Some with Spirit)	Source Stone
	fluorite	Air and Spirit	Catalyst Stone
	royal azule (sugilite)	Earth and Spirit	Mastery Stone

(ELEMENTS AND ATTRIBUTES continued)

Ray or Light	Stone	Element	Attribute
White	milky quartz	Earth and Spirit	Transmitter Stone
	white agate	Earth with Spirit	Receptive Stone
Rainbow	rainbow crystals	Spirit and Air	Order Stone
	abalone	Water and Earth	Filter Stone
Crystal	clear quartz	Spirit	Clarity Stone
	double-terminated crystals (clear)	Spirit with Air	Direction Stone
Spirit	clear quartz clusters	Spirit	Sacred Four Council Stones
Silver	silver	Earth with Water	Lunar Stone
	moonstone	Water	Absorbent Stone
Gold	gold	Earth and Fire	Solar Stone
	rutile quartz	Air and Earth	Activator Stone
Black	Apache tear	Earth with Spirit	Mystery Stone
	snowflake obsidian	Earth	Grounding Stone
Gray	granite	Earth	Foundation Stone
	hematite	Earth with Fire	Guidance Stone
Brown	smoky quartz	Earth and Air	Transmuter Stone
	petrified wood	Earth	Bridging Stone

For example, if you have an earthy, dense vibration stone—such as most jaspers—you can run it under water, but it may not be all that Earth element stone needs. Put it in a potted plant or outside in the ground for a while. Earth element energies move slowly, so leave it a day or more. You can leave it there until you need it again without hurting it. Actually, you will be helping the stone, because it is in its element.

Beginning to clear up a bit? Good. The personal alchemist may not have absolute clarity, but it is there for the asking and for the experimentation.

It may certainly be argued that all stones have the element of Earth, since that's where they came from (for the greater part, anyway). When in doubt as to the elements of any stone, place it in the Earth.

Here is a guideline for stone care based on the natural elements.

Natural Element Stone Care

Fire Stones

Run through water, then place in the sun to dry and recharge. Also, you can pass these quickly through a candle flame to activate.

Water Stones

Place in soil briefly. Rinse, then place in the moonlight to recharge. Also, you can place in rainwater or dip in natural bodies of water.

Earth Stones

Rinse, dry, then place in soil or salt to recharge. Try burying these at the base of a tree for additional energies.

Air Stones

Dust lightly with salt or soil. Wipe clean, then place in an open window or on a porch. Try putting these outside on a windy or stormy day. ZAP!

Spirit Stones

Rinse, or use the salt and soil method, if you want. I prefer to smudge these stones in the smoke of burning herbs, such as sage or thyme. Recharge with ceremony. Also, place these stones in full moonlight whenever possible.

When in doubt, use the ceremonial approach. All aspects and elements benefit from ceremony. The primary element to use in ceremony is Spirit. Spirit always empowers appropriately.

For an alchemical effect you will need to consider that you are working with pure energies of colors, Rays, Lights, people and stones. Alchemy requires precision whenever possible. Alchemical precision arises from awareness and perception. Be sensitive to the energies.

Attuning with the Natural Element of Stones

It is a great help in strengthening the energy of your stone if you try to match the vibration (or energy) of its natural element. The following is a basic guideline for doing this. If you don't know the natural element of a stone, try to determine how you feel about it, or how it feels to you.

- A Fire stone may make you feel charged up
- A Water stone may make you feel soothed
- An Earth stone may make you feel grounded or centered
- An Air stone may make you feel alert or clear
- A Spirit stone may make you feel uplifted or empowered

These are ideas to catalyst your own experimentation; I do not use a fixed system as there are too many factors to take into account. I feel a fixed system does not allow these factors the freedom to emerge.

When deciding on natural elements, let your sensitivity sharpen your focus and assure your aim. It is useful to place all stones in soil for cleansing and recharging their energies. It is effective—but is it precise?

For example, if you have a crystal or a high vibration gemstone whose elements may be more precisely Air or Spirit, then putting it in soil isn't quite enough. For a stone to be an alchemical catalyst, its energy patterns and natural elements need enhancement. That crystal or gemstone may actually need ceremonial care. If ceremony is not immediately convenient, go ahead and put the stone in soil; it can wait until you have time for ceremony. You can also empower it simply (though temporarily) by chanting the harmonic scales such as the vowel sounds, or the all-purpose **om** and inner focusing with Indigo Ray.

When you wish to ceremonially attune to any stone, it is best to concentrate on strengthening your connection to the energies in the stone. Pull Ray or Light energies through the stone and through the Self from the Universal Self. This catalysts the connectors and strengthens the energies. The empowering process takes over naturally. (This is also the basis for a lot of alchemical healing.)

The only fixed requirement I would support is the need to be sensitive. If any method, including your own, says you should do one thing but your senses tell you another, I suggest following your senses. Your sensitivities reflect your inner-knowing most clearly. In general:

- Emotional issues have a Water element
- Business issues have an Earth element
- Mental issues have an Air element
- Protection issues have a Fire element
- Ceremonial issues have a Spirit element

Balanced Methods of Stone Care and Attunement

The element of a stone need not bind you to a certain way of caring for it and working with its energies. It is good to match the stone's vibration to understand its element, but be sensitive to other energies and needs; the stone may need balancing with another approach.

Here are some balanced methods examples:

- A Water stone which has been used for a lot of emotional work can be very "soggy." Put it out in the sun or on the hearth of the fireplace. Sit there your self for a while to warm up.
- An Earth stone which has been used for a lot of business work can be very "weighted" down. Take it outside for a walk on the beach, in a meadow, or any wide-open space in Nature. You have to go with it, of course!

- An Air stone which has been used for a lot of mental work can be very "rigid." Take it to the zoo or for a walk in the woods. Observe wildlife. Connect with the healing magick energies of earth together.
- A Fire stone which has been used for a lot of protective work can be very "fierce" and intense. Put it in a natural body of water or on the porch during a gentle rainfall. Cool your self down, a bit, too.
- A Spirit stone which has been used for a lot of ceremony work can be very "blissy" and erratic. Put it outside on the ground or at the base of a tree. Stay outside until you have grounded your Self.

Whenever possible, stay with the stone until you both feel better. By now, I am sure you know how that relationship works as an interactive, self-reflective process.

> *Why are all people instinctively attracted to stones?*
> *We, as human beings, are perceptive to our role in Nature, but need to be awakened to the*
> *depth of the universal system and cannot totally escape from it.*
> *Our lessons in Life are to awaken our intuitive powers to verify this Truth.*
> *Therefore, we collect stones, not really knowing the power behind this attraction.*
>
> —Twylah Nitsch
> (Seneca Wolf Clan Mother)

Here are some healing magick examples designed to increase your attunement to stones and crystals, and your experience working with correlating Rays and Lights.

The Alchemist's Tower

Imagine that you are standing at the base of a rocky hill. At the top of the hill is a round tower—tall, reaching into the sky. It is made from the same stone as the hill and seems to rise straight from it. In front of you is an old oaken door, which opens directly into the hillside. You open this door and step into a dark hallway, lit only by the light of a few candles.

As you walk down the hallway, you see great chests filled with stones. The stones are black and gray and brown.

You recognize the glisten of hematite; the sparkle of smoky quartz; deep-black obsidian—some opaque and some translucent. You see many other stones. Some of them you know, some you have yet to meet.

You make your way into another hallway. In the center is a spiral staircase reaching all the way to the top of the tower. As you look up, you see small rooms off to the sides all the way up. Go up the stairs, into the first room. Again you find chests filled with stones; red and scarlet and rose. You recognize rubies and the deep fire of garnets. You see jaspers with their rich red; and bright, sparkling corals. You see rose quartz, gentle and pink. You see many other stones which are pink and scarlet and rose and rich red. Again, some of these you know, and some you have yet to know.

Go up the staircase again to the second room. There you find stones of orange and peach. You see amber with its gentle fire, and the richer fires of carnelians and fire agates. Rhodochrosites sparkle with their own peachy-pink kind of crystal. You see unikite with its green and peach together, and many other stones in these warm, loving tones you have yet to explore.

You go up the stairs and into the third room. There you find stones of yellow and golden-green. Topaz greets you, and citrine glows golden. You see peridot, with its own golden-green fire. Jade and serpentine both are serene. You see the richness of golden tigereye.

You go further up the stairs to a fourth room. Here you find green and turquoise stones. You see the emerald with its majesty; rich malachite and aquamarine with their cool serenity. Turquoise greets you—and chrysocolla, with it's hot/cool colors. There is aventurine with its deep, rich green; and many others you have yet to meet.

You move on to the fifth room. Here you are greeted by blue stones—cool blue stones. There is celestite with blue crystals glistening. You see the gentle lavender blue of blue lace agate and the deeper, rich blue of sodalite. These you know—and others, too. Some you have yet to meet.

You continue up the stairs to the sixth room. There you find indigo stones, dark and rich. Sapphires sparkle. Azurite calls you with its deep vibration. Lapis shines with royal blue. There are a few others—some you still need to acquaint your self with.

On you go, up to the seventh room. There you find stones in violet and purple. There are amethysts in many different shades, from lavender to deep violet. Fluorites speak with their own special colors—lavenders, cool deep purples, and blues. You see the royal azule with its own red-purple, and a few others.

Go up to the top of the staircase. There is one more room; you open the door at the very top. You can see that the roof is made of a large crystal glass.

You take time to look around. You are in a round room encircled with windows and filled with crystals of all sizes and shapes. Some of these crystals have rainbows sparkling in them, some are clear. Some crystals are milky and translucent, some have golden fibers. All of these are placed in bowls of gold and silver.

You feel their crystal energy around the room. The crystals sparkle in the light from the windows, and from the window at the top of the tower, which lets in Light from the Universe.

On one windowsill is a small white dish carved from white agate. In the dish are beautiful moonstones. As you pick it up, you notice a stone is carved with a symbol most sacred to you; you realize this moonstone is for you.

Across the room is a chair by another window, and on that chair is a magic cloak in your most favorite, special color. This cloak is decorated with symbols—the moon, the sun, the stars, and symbols of the zodiac. You know this is the cloak of an alchemist. This is your cloak. It is up to you now to make magick, to use the energies of the stones. All of these—and many more—are waiting for you.

Use your own energies . . .

> And the energies of the Lights . . .

> And the Rays around you . . .

To create magickal Self-healing and magickal Self-enhancement.

You are the weaver. You create the fabric of energy that is Life . . . that is Creation.

Now it is time for you to make your Magick . . .

> And to grow in Power.

You are the magickal alchemist.

> You are the creator of your own Life.

> So mote it be . . .

> And

> So it is.

Healing Alchemy

Root Chakra—Red Ray (Includes Scarlet Ray and Rose Ray)

Red Ray energy disorders manifest around the root chakra or the first energy point. If Red Ray energy is pooling or constricting, disorders such as anger, rage, impatience, frustration and agitated insecurity emerge. With this sort of situation redirect the flow of Red, but balance and soothe it at the same time with Rose Ray. Put your rose quartz or rhodonite on the heart. Next, balance the energies by putting some green stones around to soothe the heart. Take some blue stones to put on the throat and on the brow. Focus on Blue Rayon the brow center. (Moving into Indigo might be a little intense.)

Shift the focus to the area around the root center and begin to pull the Red Ray energies upward gently. Bring in Red stones to activate. To absorb some negativity, use Black stones to help release negativities into the earth energies.

Suppose your Red Ray problem is one of depletion. In other words, not enough Red Ray is getting in, the person is not connected with it, or it is not cycling correctly. Red Ray is a thrusting, flowing process, like a car engine. If there is a depletion of Red Ray, then the sort of disorders you are going to see are general depression and debilitation, anemia, ongoing fatigue, nerve and skin disorders—a lack of essential vitality.

What you want to do in this case is energize and bring in the Red Ray. The Red Ray is not connecting, so you are going to have to attune to it, bring it into focus, and get that chakra point channeling that energy.

If you have this kind of depleted blood disorder or all-over etheric depression, go ahead and use your more intense Red Ray stones right away. Just pulse them a little at a

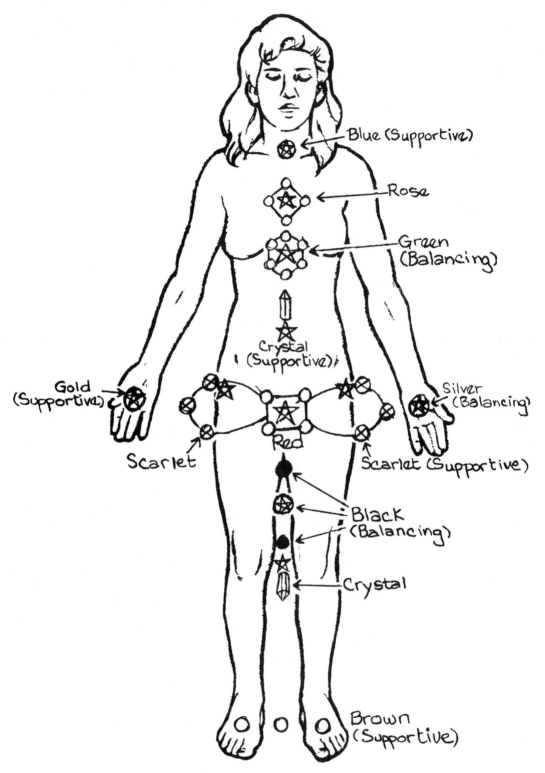

Root Center: Red Ray Layout

time. This is a good time to use Scarlet Ray with a garnet, Red Ray with a ruby, or either with high vibration crystals. However, it is still a good practice to balance these with gentle heart chakra green stones, such as malachite or emerald.

With Red Ray depletion, it is quite effective to use rutilated quartz. Start at the root center and move all the way up the spine several times, concentrating on the energy flowing into the body through the etheric; through the energy center activated by the rutile quartz.

Exercises

- Which one sensory key would you choose to correlate for this example?
- What three images or symbols would you choose?
- How would you finish this example so that focus and mental abilities benefitted from this as well?

Sacral Center—Orange Ray

For the sacral energy point correlated to Orange Ray, pooled or constricted energy creates disorders such as repression, inhibitions and fear. Release these inhibitions with Gray or Silver, and open your repressive channels to expression with Peach and Orange. Peach is a very peaceful, friendly energy in combination with Gray Light. You could also use rhodochrosite and unikite because they have Green Ray. Peach, Gray and Green in combination emit healing energy.

If you feel the problems of inhibition stem from family issues (which many inhibition problems do), try using carnelian. That will help clear out "bad scripts." These things can be traumatic at times, so protect the heart from the emotion by putting your green stones or rose quartz on the heart. Bloodstone would also be an excellent choice for this. The red in bloodstone is courageous and the green is healing.

You can also use citrine when activating Orange energy. Citrine is very good for personal courage and for good fortune; it is the "golden touch." A person who is repressed and inhibited probably needs a little good luck.

If there is too little Orange Ray energy, you get digestive depletion disorders like vitality drains, colitis, kidney and splenic problems; things of that nature. This means the body etherically and physically is not processing the toxins correctly; not enough Orange is present to vitalize and move this energy through properly.

Redirect this energy flow and revitalize by attuning purely at first to the Orange Ray. Try fire agates for pulling Orange energy straight up from the root chakra, steering through the Orange. Carnelians are also excellent for this.

Too much Orange Ray can also manifest as a digestive disorder. When you know you are working with digestive situations, make sure there isn't a burning or abrasion. If you have that burning, start by soothing first with blues and greens. Put turquoise on the area affected. Chrysocolla is also quite good for this. Bring in sodalite as a good balancing, stabilizing stone. Later, try using azurite or royal azule to balance and complement the Orange energy. Azurite and royal azule can help with the "why" of disorders and provide clarity for healing.

Exercises

- How would you adapt this for an agitated person whose depletion of vitality stems from a constant state of being off-center and not grounded?
- How would you adapt this to bring vitality to a loving relationship?
- If you had only clear crystals to use, how would you "charge" them with the Orange Ray?
    - ↞ Hint: What is the harmonic for Orange?

Solar Point—Yellow Ray (Includes Peach Ray and Golden-Green Ray)

Disorders of this point from overuse or constriction sometimes manifest as mental overload, mania, fear, and nervous strain disorders. Sometimes this may appear to be brain drain, but it is actually brain overload. (Like "Tilt" on a pinball machine.)

Recharge the mental capacities, but make sure you are soothing the over-stimulation and the overload at the same time. Try Yellow Ray and Golden Light with amber, particularly if it is a very yellow amber, purifying in its energy. This is also a good place to use tigereye, because it grounds while it energizes. Tigereye is not too intense. After all, an over-stimulated mind does not need any more intensity. While you are recharging the mental capacities with amber and/or tigereye, soothe over-stimulation with something like blue lace agate or sodalite. These are both solid, hard-working stones.

If you are going to use something as intense as topaz to recharge your Yellow Ray, put on the sodalite or blue lace agate before you start working with the more intense stone. Then pulse the topaz while the denser vibration stones give balance and support.

You can use amethyst, as well, to counteract brain drain. Violet Ray can be effective in healing inefficient use of Yellow Ray energy. Sometimes Violet Ray and amethyst can be too cosmic or heavy. If so, go back to blue lace agate or sodalite. Remember that amber is a good bridge; it is a great healing clarifier for all aspects of Mind, Body and Spirit. This is quite useful in this particular case with Yellow Ray.

In the solar plexus, there are sometimes disorders such as intestinal viruses and colds. That is the physical body manifesting the strain, saying, "Pay attention to me." Activate healing and energize the whole body by surrounding it with a sunny golden yellow. Citrine is perfect for this. While you are doing this, you can also concentrate on pale yellow. Bathe all the tissues with pale yellow and a light golden color. Use amber for this, or citrine or rutile quartz.

Exercises

- How would you ensure that a person not become too mentally fixed, but rather have an active blend of heart and spirit energies?
- What sensory key would you choose to increase receptivity for focus? Which one would activate this focus?
- How would you use Lights to bring flexibility and balanced distribution to the process of mind and intellect?

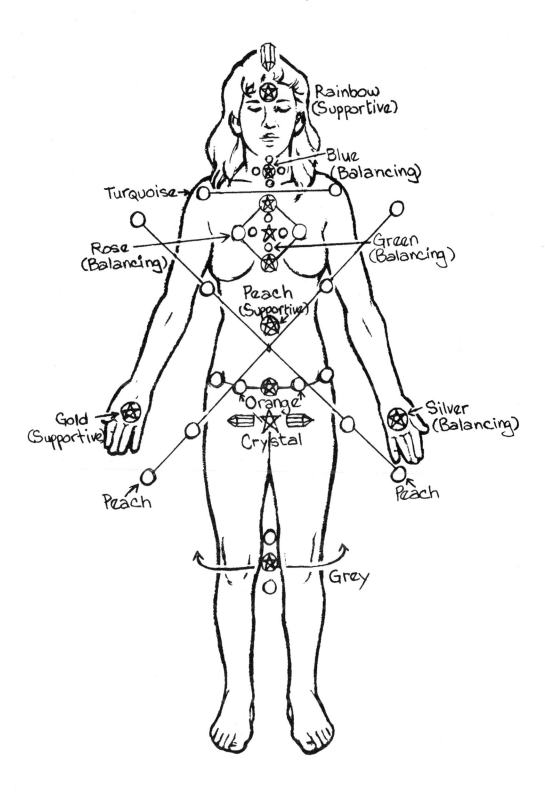

Sacral Center: Orange Ray Layout

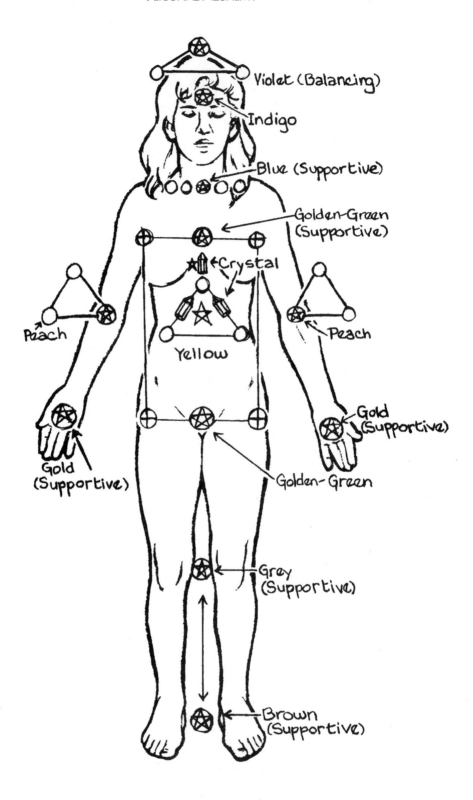

Solar Center: Yellow Ray Layout

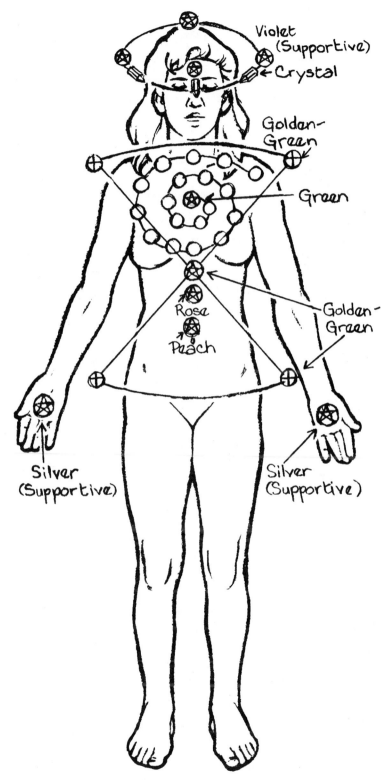

Heart Center: Green Ray Layout

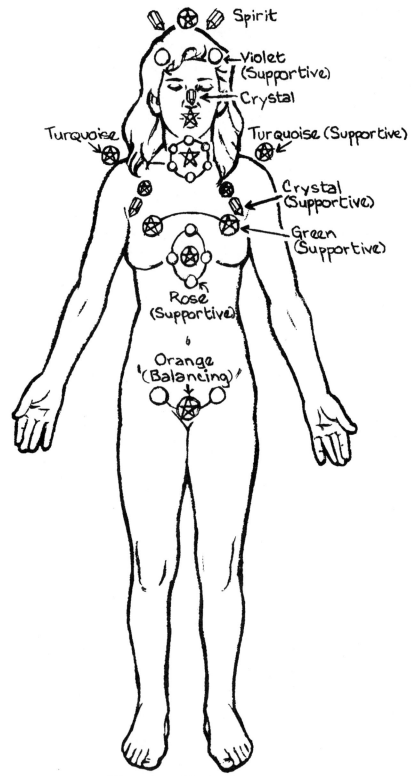

Throat Center: Blue Ray Layout

Heart Center—Green Ray

Green is the bridge between Mind and Spirit as it manifests in the body. Disorders of the Green Ray manifest as jealousy, envy, greed, arrogance, resistance to sharing and negativity. These have to do with holding on to Green Ray energies. Activate and open the heart center. Start with rose quartz, as almost everyone is positively responsive to this stone. Next, use the clearest possible green stone with a clear Green Ray. An emerald or dioptase crystal would be excellent. Malachite is also good, but you will have to support it with something more intense, such as a crystal, to amplify Green Ray energy in malachite.

If you have heart-area problems, such as ulcers, blood pressure and heart palpitations, this has to do with giving out too much Green Ray and not taking enough back in. Open the heart area with clear, healing greens. Start with gentle energy stones, like the green quartz, fluorite or peridot. Try aventurine to ground and support the energies. Move Green Ray in an expanding spiral. Place green stones all over the body so that all aspects and points begin to vibrate with needed energy. This helps begin to get in the flow of receiving. Rose quartz, chrysocolla and turquoise can also work beautifully with Green Ray. Try adding silver, as well, for greater receptivity.

Exercises

- How would you center an overly expansive flow of Green Ray energies?
- How would you stimulate positive lifeforce for healing magick?
- How would you release negativities and renew healing cycles?

Throat Center—Blue Ray

Disorders of this energy point arise from constriction issues which manifest as isolationism and passivity, possessiveness, and withdrawal. This is pooled Blue Ray, simply speaking. Activate a positive flow to balance this. Use Peach or Orange Ray with carnelian, amber, citrine and/or rhodochrosite. All of these stones are very warm, energizing, activating and stimulating.

Place these stones on the throat and upper chest area. Pull some activating energies down and some up through the throat. At the same time you are activating positive Blue energy, soothe the insecurities which led to this imbalance. For this, use Blue Ray, Rose Ray and some Violet Ray. Blue lace agate, rhodonite or rose quartz would be excellent. These have soothing yet opening energies. The other way Blue Ray disorders appear in the throat center is with throat problems and constant respiratory infections. Sometimes that has to do with blocking, but many times it has to do with not receiving enough Blue. This seems particularly true if there is fever (or a feverish "pace") involved. This indicates there is just not enough of Blue Ray's cooling, expressive energies.

Begin by soothing the inflamed areas to allow the expression of Blue Ray energies. Use blue topaz, blue fluorite or blue lace agate. Lapis is also excellent for direct physical effects. Follow with a more crystalline blue or violet stone. You may also use Yellow or Golden-Green to rejuvenate, using amber and peridot again. Peridot is a natural antibiotic. Focus on all the tissues being soothed, with Blue Ray coming in to energize and cool. Focus on the completion of the healing with Green Ray and Rose Ray.

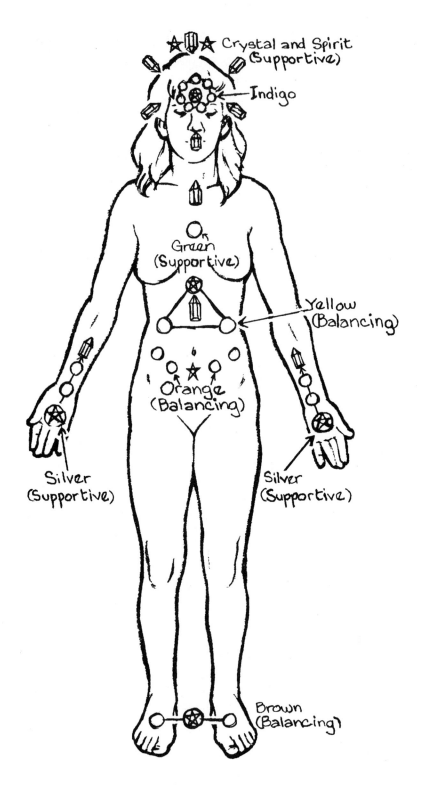

Brow Center: Indigo Ray Layout

Exercises

- How would you combat isolationism which manifests as reclusive behavior in relationship to others?
- How would you provide energies of dedication to Blue Ray?
- Which symbols would compliment and balance Blue Ray?

Brow Center—Indigo Ray

With the sixth center and the Indigo Ray, disorders can manifest as spiritual arrogance, constant irritability, conceit, totalitarianism, nervous stress, headaches and sinus problems. These are all indicative of things just not coming together; of not being together. There is also a sense of being about to "fly off the handle."

Activate the Indigo energy of synthesis by feeding it with Blue and Indigo stones, and balancing it with Gold and Yellow stones to keep energy moving. Finish with Green for deepest healing. Indigo and synthesis can also be worked with by visualizing and using the red, yellow and blue of indigo, bringing them in one at a time in a renewal and realignment. For this you can use azurite, lapis or sodalite. Lapis and sodalite are intense and supportive. Fluorite is also excellent for dealing with synthesis as it is linear and ordered about bringing the energies together harmoniously. With fluorite, it is a good idea to balance Indigo Ray with Golden Light to give warmth and overall tonic from dealing with the energies of synthesis.

Exercises

- What energy patterns or harmonic postures would demonstrate Indigo Ray?
- How would you bring focused, ordered energies into being before using Indigo for synthesis?
- What Rays or Lights prevent Spiritual arrogance?

Crown Center—Violet Ray

This point involves spiritual connection. When the energies of this point are out of balance, you get over-excitement and "bliss ninnies," or lowered resistance. Migraines can emerge from the crown center, too. Regardless of whether you consider this to be depletion or overabundance of Violet, activate the Violet Ray and let Spirit energies transform to their highest good. This is the time to bring out the rich, deep amethyst and sugilite. These will help you find out what is going on and why the pattern is occurring. Blue lace agate and celestite can work well here, too. You may find that celestite and fluorite can be a bit linear when used with Violet Ray. If you use these, balance them with Golden Ray.

If the body seems depleted by this imbalance in Violet Ray energies, use peridot and run Golden-Green Ray through it. This will give the natural cleansing and spiritual antibiotic which may be needed to reconnect proper Violet Ray flow. Aventurine is also good for this, as it is cleansing and supporting at the same time.

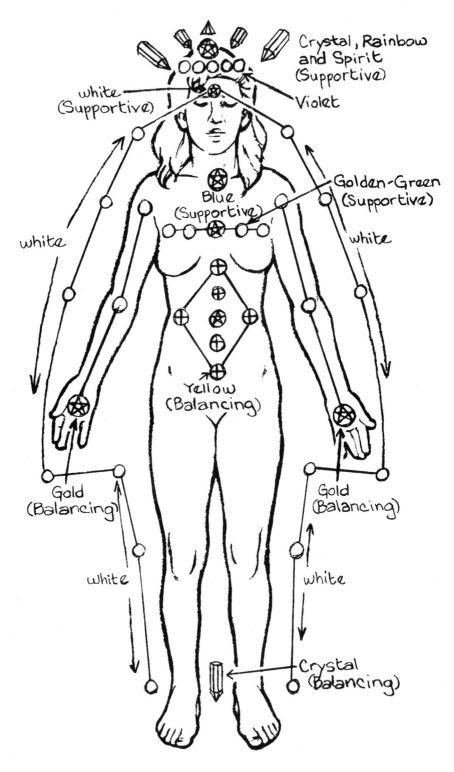

Crown Center: Violet Ray Layout

Exercises

- Which harmonics and symbols would you use to connect Spiritual Violet with the energies of Mind and Body?
- What would you use for an even more exalted experience of Spirit realms?
- If Orange Ray is too dissonant and "clashes" with Violet, how would you deal with a situation involving vitality loss due to Spiritual repression and discontent?

Part Two

Essential Energies of Vitality and Lifeforce

Red

Scarlet

Rose

Orange

Free will does not mean one will, but many wills conflicting in one man. Freedom cannot be conceived simply.

—Flannery O'Connor

Shamana: Earth Journey

Begin by finding a quiet place within . . . prepare for an Earth Journey of Power and Renewal.

Feel the vibration of the earth . . . allow that vibration, the heartbeat of the Earth Mother, to rise up slowly into your body . . . your entire body is vibrating with the beat of Mother Earth. You are surrounded by this energy.

Feel the Earth connection . . . find your self in a cave, in a beautiful room with stalactites and stalagmites lit by crystals. Find an underground waterway . . . a beautiful little boat carries you into the quiet darkness . . . lulls and deepens . . . feel your self lulled into the very depths of your being . . . know your gentle spirit.

Far away you hear the sounds of a dance . . . chanting. Slowly the boat moves closer . . . you see a circle of women standing along the shoreline . . . waiting to greet you . . . join the dance of celebration.

Close to the campfire women circle . . . dance . . . chant . . . giving gifts of the dance . . . gifts of empowerment from the earth to you. Women's faces . . . the wisdom . . . the compassion . . . the power . . . receive. Feel your spirit fly free. Take note that the women are all here to empower you with an aspect found within your self.

Feel the energy build. Breathe in to receive . . . the dance is ancient and timeless . . . accept this energy as yours. An old woman rattles . . . summoning spirits . . . whispers woman-secrets . . . woman wisdom . . . Know this wisdom comes from your highest self. Still you feel the gentle steady heart beat of Mother Earth.

The Dance slows . . . the old woman steps in the center of the circle and whispers messages just for you. Time to consecrate the sacred circle . . . smell sage . . . drummer signals . . . the old woman rattles East, South, West, North . . . clarifies, purifies. Another woman smudges you with smoke and feathers you with the wing of a hawk. Purified, you are ready to enter the sacred circle formed to help you contact your power spirits. Allow power spirits to enter the cave slowly and stand at the outside of the circle of Women. Notice, are any of the spirits animal? . . . human? . . . living in this earthly plane? . . . in spirit? Consider the gifts of each of these spirit helpers. These are gifts of spirit you may use . . . power belonging to no one. The last power spirit enters . . . stands outside the circle.

You consider which spirits you need now in your life, and why you need them at this time . . . find the right power spirit . . . make the connection . . . invite the power spirit into the circle with you. Absorb what you need whenever you need . . . invite in as many as you need. Know that all of these come from within your highest dimension.

Time to bid farewell to power spirits. From time to time some will change . . . some will always be the same. Allow the spirits to return to their special place, thanking them.

Women sing gently in celebration . . . gifts of your empowerment. Women encircle you . . . look at each of their faces . . . which aspect is in each woman . . . see recognition . . . . acceptance . . . love. See beauty . . . wisdom . . . compassion in these women's faces.

Recognize these are already within you. Accept and honor your self. Honor the wisdom, honor the love.

As with power spirits, faces of these woman may change from time to time . . . some stay the same . . . some have messages . . . smiling faces . . . gentle faces . . . strong faces . . . women's faces.

Time to bid farewell. You may return to this place when you choose. This cave dwells within your heart . . . in joy . . . in peace . . . in harmony . . . in balance . . . in love.

Take all the time you need . . . let the image fade . . . know that the connection you have made with the earth was made long before you were even born onto this place and will not change. Take a reminder in the vibration, the heartbeat of Mother Earth.

Let the image fade . . . return to the present time and place . . . what you received is real . . . all you need is within you . . . you have but to look inside and step within that quiet place.

Be here now . . .

Chapter Eight

Red Ray: Lifeforce

Veni, Vidi, Vici
(I came, I saw, I conquered)
—Julius Caesar

The only thing we have to fear is fear itself.
—Franklin Delano Roosevelt

Red is associated with the root chakra or the first energy point, located at the base of the spine or on the pubic bone. Red Ray has to do with Life itself—essentially, its physical nature. Red reflects the energies in issues of survival and strength. It is the energy of thrust and primal drive—both conscious and unconscious.

Red involves both voluntary and involuntary systems of physical survival. Red energies are straight and direct, and can also be hot. The trick with Red Ray is to focus, connect, pace, and maintain a flow of breath. Breath is life, or "prana;" the essential vibration of being.

Elemental Alchemy	Fire and Earth
Key Issues	Sensation, regeneration, knowledge, structure
Stone Alchemy	Ruby, red coral, jasper
Cumulative Alchemy	Lifeforce

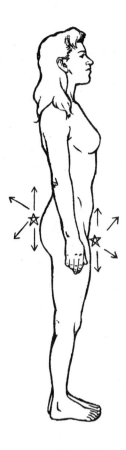

Red Ray Energy Centers

Red Ray Keys

Harmonic	Sound of **e** as in **she**
Alchemical Properties	Activation of essential Lifeforce
Sensory Key	Cinnamon
Symbols	Feathered arrow, drum, drop of blood
Personifications	Essential Warrior (Mars, Ares)
Runic	Sigel (Sowelu) or Tyr (Teiwaz)
Astrological Correlates	Aries, Aquarius
Major Arcana Key	The Emperor
Archangel	Samael (Mars)
Stone Alchemy	Ruby, red coral, jasper

Excessive Red Ray Energy Pattern

Depleted Red Ray Energy Pattern

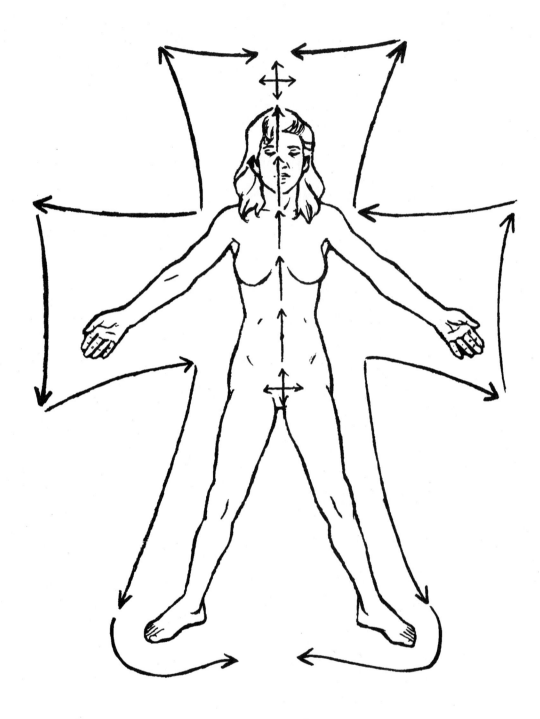

Harmonious Red Ray Energy Pattern

Harmonic

The harmonic key for Red Ray is the sound of long **e** as in **she**.

Vibrational Energies

The energies of Red Ray are direct, thrusting, fast-paced and physical. Focus on the bodily sensations and the total physical experience as the energies vibrate. Focus on the feel as well as the image of Red Ray.

Harmonic Breathing Pattern

The primary breathing pattern for Red Ray with the harmonic **e** is rapid, shallow breaths through the mouth. Rapid breaths activate and energize. Follow these with slow inhalations and a burst of exhalation. This will help align the Red Ray energies and prevent hyperventilation. Resume natural breathing as soon as possible.

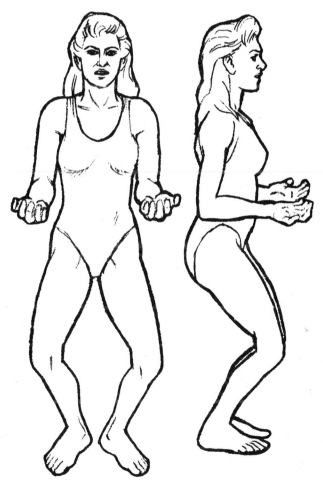

Red Ray Harmonic Postures

Suggested Harmonic Exercises, Chants, and Word Mantras

Using the words "heal" and "me," focus on strong healing energies flowing through the physical body. Concentrate on the energies of Red circulating as the bloodstream does, keeping the vital Lifeforce flowing.

Using the word "angry" (an-gree), focus on unblocking constricted anger. Amplify the experience by creating a beat—stamp the feet, clap hands, or beat a drum. It is also helpful to devise chants to specify and signal transformational changes.

For example: **Angry, angry**
                      Release me
                      Release me

Followed by: **Peace, peace**
                      Peace for me
                      Peace, peace
                      So mote it be

Additional Harmonics for Red Ray

Ecstasy	(Use for sexual focus)
Liberty, free	(Use for expression and release)
See, feel, be, me	(Use for secure self-image)

Alchemist's Note: Words and phrases found in literature, the arts, and in common language can also provide harmonic key chants and word mantras. Music by its lyrical and harmonic nature is a particularly good source.

For example:
                      See me
                      Feel me
                      Touch me
                      Heal me

                                —(From the rock opera "Tommy" by the Who)

This may be used for deep Body/Mind connection and healing. Concentrate on uplifting through the physical into spiritual realms.

Alchemical Properties

Red Ray activates the primal flow of essential lifeforce energies. Red unblocks all energies in a direct, physical manner.

Powers	Direct, focused, linear action
Activates	All catalysts, honor, independence motivation, strength, will power
Amplifies	All energy flow, physical love, regeneration, self-respect, service, trust, zeal

Balances	Yearning
Releases	Inferiority, martyrdom, procrastination, resistance
Realigns	Destructiveness, frustration, insecurity, rebellion, vengeance, violence

Sensory Key

The sensory key correlated with Red Ray is cinnamon.

Shared attributes of cinnamon and Red Ray:
Physical healing
Protection
Sexual drive
Intensification of energies
The element of Fire

Cinnamon is moderately expensive. It is available most often as a spice (either ground or in stick form) and as an oil. Cinnamon-scented candles or herbal mixtures are quite effective to amplify the Red Ray energies.

- Burn cinnamon in a hot fire to unblock intense energies of anger and frustration.
- Burn cinnamon in a slow fire to build the energies of sexual attraction.
- Smudge the environment with cinnamon to set up a shield of active protection.
- Light cinnamon candles to represent the active energies of love.
- Mix a few drops of cinnamon oil in a palm of massage oil for body work, root chakra healing, activating sexuality, and stimulating the circulation of the blood.
- Rub cinnamon oil on longer decorative sticks of cinnamon and display. This activates the sensory keys of sight and touch as well as smell.
- Combine cinnamon-flavored candies or mints with Red Ray harmonic breathing to create positive physical associations. (Finish the candy or mint first.)

Alchemist's Note: The smell of cinnamon, as well as its taste, has long been associated with holiday festivities. These pleasant associations can provide positive sensory and psychological keys for most of us. This alchemical association makes cinnamon a truly viable helper for Red Ray insecurity issues. Additionally, it creates an atmosphere of warmth and good feelings.

Symbols

Feathered arrow represents direction with guidance and support. The energies of Lifeforce guide our personal alchemy as surely as an arrow shot from the stars.

Drum represents the deep rhythm of essential energies. Each of us dances to a different drum, celebrating the same Lifeforce.

Drop of blood represents the essential fluid of Lifeforce. The alchemy of Lifeforce flows through each drop of our blood.

Personifications

Lifeforce

Red is the energy of the essential, mythic warrior. It is Mars, God of War, symbolic representation of Lifeforce. Red is the essential energy of structuring and restructuring life.

Musings

That which we sometimes mistake for power is, in truth, the uprush of repressed rage. That which we frequently fear as rage is the uprush of power striving to be expressed in truth.

The mythic warrior battles the forces of entropy, apathy, and greed. With weapons of Truth, the warrior of Spirit activates the Light in thought, in word, in deed.

Power runs through our being: hot, red, burning fires of Lifeforce, sacred fires from within the heart of planet earth—essential fires of warmth, preserving the hearths, homes, and hope of humankind.

Power runs through our being—with it, a call to the blood, a rhythm from spirit drums, awakening the champions of the world.

If there shall be "wars and rumors of war," then the Alchemists of the Aquarian Age shall restructure the elemental energies of War into structures for Peace.

Runic Correlates

Sigel (Sowelu) and Tyr (Teiwaz)

Shared aspects with Red Ray:
>Essential power
>Warrior Spirit

Sigel (Sowelu)

Sigel (Sowelu) distills the alchemy to amplify its purest essence. It is the direct energy of the sun. Self-transformation is a continuing process of self-distillation. Activate the forces of self-transformation with the rune Sigel (Sowelu).

Tyr (Teiwaz) forges the weapons of the spiritual warrior: drive, will, focus and detachment. Activate direction and structure in your self-transformation with the rune Tyr (Teiwaz).

Tyr (Teiwaz)

Together, Sigel (Sowelu) and Tyr (Teiwaz) create a force which is best tempered with the highest positive intentions and spiritual guidance from within.

Astrological Correlates

Solar Aries

Alchemy of Activation and Enhancement

>Shared aspects with Red Ray:
>
>| Physical Energy | Thrust |
>| --- | --- |
>| Drives | Determination |
>| Primal Force | Activation |
>
>(+ Gold Light = Essential Activator)

If you use the positive attribute of your sign (Aries)—the great driving power of Mars—by channeling it into decisive action and sustaining this action until your ideas bear fruit, you can be successful as a reformer and pioneer in just about any sphere of life.

—Sybil Leek

Lunar Aquarius

Alchemy of Receptivity and Reflection

Shared aspects with Red Ray:

Determination	Service
Loyalty	Courage
Activation	Universal force

(+ White Light = Zealous Transmitter)

As we move farther into the Age of Aquarius, lunar Aquarians will have a greater role to play in laying down the guidelines for a new Society . . .

—Sybil Leek

Major Tarot Arcana Key

The Emperor

Shared aspects with Red Ray:

Lifeforce	Power
Structure	Leadership
Courage	Activation

He is the paternal power, the driving force of humanity, the personification of the sun.

—F. D. Graves

Musings

You are, in Truth, the Creator of your own condition.
You are, in Effect, the Emperor of your life experience.

The structure of the future is built upon the power of the past; the courage of the present, and the activation of the Lifeforce Eternal.

Archangel

Angelic Dimension Key

Samael: Archangel of Mars
       Alchemy of Protection and Courage
          Day   Tuesday
          Times   6-7 AM
                          2-3 PM
                          10-11 PM

You gain strength, courage, and confidence by every experience in which you really stop to look fear in the face. You are able to say to yourself. "I lived through this horror. I can take the next thing that comes along." . . . You must do the thing you think you cannot do.

—Eleanor Roosevelt

Angelic Invocation

Samael, I call to thee for courage to face the tasks before me.

I call for the security of your protection in my life, and the certain foundation of faith.

Let highest good structure my service to the Light, and grant me freedom from fear.

Stone Alchemy

Alchemist's Note: Some stones are more effective placed specifically on set physical points; others can be placed all over the body. Red stones have a tendency to fit the specific point category—orange stones also, to a somewhat lesser degree—yellow stones to a slight degree. All in all, this seems to be most related to the combination of lower chakras, or energy points, and to the focus of Red, Orange and Yellow Rays. This seems linear because the lower chakra energies are structured and linear. Black stones are also often used on the root chakra because they help absorb and unblock energies which pool easily in that area. It is effective to follow the black stone absorbing process with a red stone. Red stones with black stones can be used together to balance each other.

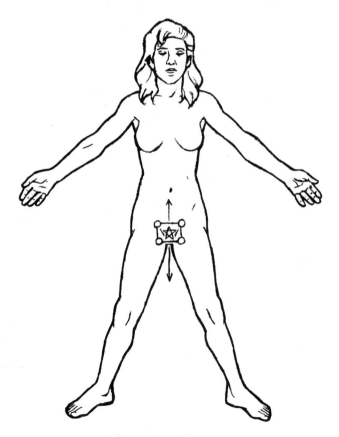

Red Ray Stone Placement

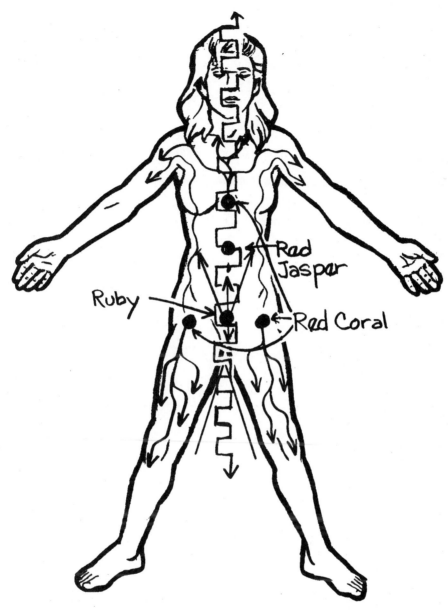

Ruby: ⟶
Red Coral: ⤴
Jasper: ⊓⊔⊓⊔⟶
(Bloodstone Jasper: ∿∿∿⟶)

Red Ray Stones Energy Patterns

Ruby: Divine Fire Stone
Element: Fire

The ruby is an expensive gemstone in a cut or faceted variety; this form has an intense vibration. A rough ruby can be used effectively as well, as its vibration is almost as intense as that of the cut stone. Because ruby itself is so intense, and especially so combined with focused Red Ray, a small piece goes a long way.

The ruby works by activating through the bloodstream for a whole body effect. Ruby is now successfully used for treating debilitating diseases in conjunction with visualization and holistic or alternative methods of healing, as well as with traditional medicine or modern medicine healing. These diseases require a lot of blood-building and renourishing of all the tissues.

Additionally, ruby can be used with Golden Light energies to activate the healing process. This will produce an intense effect, but not as intense as a combination of Red Ray with ruby, which is a bit like a laser.

Ruby is symbolic of love, compassion and devotion. It is a stone of divine fire. Avoid a ruby if the mood of the moment is too angry or too exhilarated. In that case, use a denser red stone, such as the jasper.

Alchemist's Note: Sometimes the combination of Red Ray intense stones on the heart with focused Red Rays can cause palpitations. Work up to these kinds of energy combinations slowly. Keep checking the energies. It is not the stone—it is not the Ray—it is not you— it is not any one of these elements; it is the combination. Soften your focus, breathe deeply, relax, and be aware. These things happen to tell us what needs our attention. A person who is quick to show palpitation needs to change the pace of their life. Suggest a medical checkup when palpitations seem more intense than those which occur after normal exercise or emotional release.

Red Coral: Shamanic Stone
Element: Water (with some Fire)

The next Red Ray stone is red coral, which can range from moderately expensive to relatively inexpensive, depending on how large a piece it is, or how fine. Red coral has a moderate vibration; steady and strong. Red coral represents structure, and also has to do with the root chakra.

Red coral is virtually a skeleton of life as a coral reef. Red coral is considered to be a Shamanic connector because it is grounded or rooted into the Earth, yet it reaches into Spirit through the symbolic consciousness of the ocean. Red coral symbolizes reaching from Earth into Spirit while remaining in balance.

Red coral acts as an effective tonic. Working with red coral is energizing for both brain and body, and opens the physical to higher consciousness.

Red coral is one of the five sacred Tibetan stones. It is also sacred to many Native American traditions and many other Nature (or aboriginal) traditions, as well.

The five Tibetan stones are:

Red coral	For life energy
Turquoise	For the sky and the sea
Crystal	For spirit life
Silver	For lunar, receptive energies
Gold	For solar, active energies

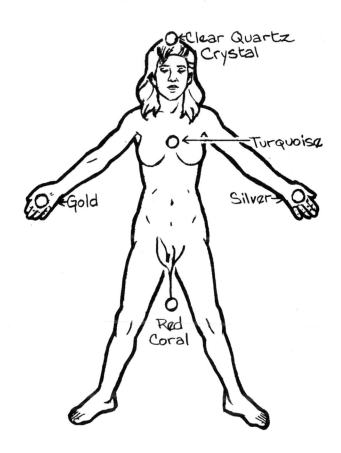

Five Tibetan Stones Placement

Just these five stones can be a balanced collection in themselves, when you consider all they include. If you want to start with just a few stones, these are good choices. I do suggest finding as fine a specimen of each as you can. "Fine" refers to purity or clarity, not size.

Red coral also works by activating and energizing the whole system with an earthy effect. It prevents lethargy and malnutrition because it stimulates the appetite. Do not wear red coral when trying to diet to lose weight; try the amethyst or smoky quartz instead.

Red coral works with Red Ray energy by moving its own energy from the root chakra into the heart gently, yet directly, with a kind of harmony. Red coral can also be used above a ruby to filter intense or direct energies.

Interestingly, the darker the red coral is, the more direct the energy seems. The lighter coral has a more diffuse energy, but the effect is still the same; it is only a difference in style. Coral has a Water element, which makes it good for everyone as a tonic.

Alchemist's Note: Other gifts from the sea, such as shells, can be used in relation to all these Rays. You can match them by color to the Rays whenever possible and use them as a focusing tool for your imagery and concentration. Shells have a structural effect, but it is rather subtle—like marble, which also has a gentle, structured effect. Use these subtle helpers when you want to support energies and create an environment conducive to healing.

Jasper: Protective Stone
Element: Earth (with some Fire)

Jasper is an inexpensive stone with a deep, earthy vibration. Jasper symbolizes some of the most vital energy aspects that reflect in Red Ray: the bedrock, the foundation, or the connection of humanity to earth. Important types here are the red jasper, the yellow jasper, and the green jasper (or bloodstone).

Jasper in combination with Red Ray can energize and stabilize at the same time. Jasper is not a spiritual stone, exactly; it is a physical, earth-energy stone. Jasper is considered to be a protective stone. It works well to give feelings of groundedness and security on all levels of Body, Mind and Spirit.

Alchemist's Note: Use jasper with Black Light, which is an absorbent Earth Light. These are excellent in combination when you wish to do Shamanic Earth journeys or any deep Nature work.

Jasper is an example of a stone whose color is not necessarily matched to the color of a Ray, but whose energy is. There are some subtle differences due to our expectations about color, to be sure. We can use our feelings and expectations about color to vary our alchemy with jasper. Red jasper can be for energizing the physical, yellow jasper for centering thought processes, and bloodstone for stabilizing the heart.

Alchemist's Note: In combination with Yellow Ray, yellow jasper helps organize thoughts and balance impulses along the nervous system. You can also use yellow jasper with Yellow Ray to support a higher vibration Yellow Ray gemstone.

Bloodstone Jasper: Protective Stone
Element: Earth (with some Fire)

Another form of jasper to use with the Red Ray on the root chakra is bloodstone. Generally speaking, bloodstone is dark green with red flecks. However, there are several different varieties of bloodstone.

Bloodstone is an inexpensive yet powerful, earthy stone. Bloodstone may be used directly on the root chakra with Red Ray energy. It may also be used on the heart with increased focus on the Green Ray. Bloodstone is effective for both Red and Green.

Bloodstone gives very direct strength through the physical. In other words, it works from the physical outward. Bloodstone can be excellent for anemia and for depleted energy. It has the activation of Red and the healing of Green.

Bloodstone is a good stone for protection, strength, and balance. It balances the feeling Green energy with the physical Red energy, uplifting and healing at the same time.

Alchemist's Note: Because bloodstone is both green and red, it can be wise to use it as a balance for Red Ray energies which may be too intense. Also, a tri-colored jasper with red, green, and yellow is an excellent, all-purpose healing stone for the Body/Mind connection.

Alternative Stone

A good Red Ray alternative stone is a red-orange agate. These are always in rock shops. Find one that "feels" very active and has "Red" intensity and vitality.

Chapter Nine

Scarlet Ray: Balance

For both men and women to look honestly at
romantic love is a heroic journey.

—Robert Johnson

Unity is plural and, at a minimum is two.

—Buckminster Fuller

The blended Rays, especially the newer ones, tend to work from the etheric into the physical bodies. Focus with increased imagery and/or sensory keys for multimodal, experiential healing magick.

Scarlet Ray is primarily Red with Blue and some Yellow in it. Scarlet Ray relates to the fundamental balance of ourselves. It is the balancing of all pattern energies: the Yin and the Yang, the receptive and the active, the female and the male. It is the balance of our personal pattern, the Self we are within.

Scarlet energies are gentle and rocking. The trick with Scarlet is to focus, quiet the mind, and observe within the Self. Use a "mindful" approach.

An effective placement or focus point for Scarlet Ray is just above the pubic bone in front, or just below the tail bone in back.

Elemental Alchemy	Fire with Water
Key Issues	Sensation, regeneration, intuition, healing
Stone Alchemy	Garnet, watermelon tourmaline, cinnabar
Cumulative Alchemy	Balance

Scarlet Ray Keys

Harmonic	Sound of **i** as in **ice**
Alchemical Properties	Balances Yin/Yang, receptivity/activity
Sensory Key	Cloves (If you are using cinnabar and Oriental meditation, try sandalwood)
Symbols	Seax (double-edged sword), scales of justice, Yin/Yang symbol
Personifications	Warrior/Adventurer, (Robin Hood)
Runic	Thorn (Thurisaz) or Beorc (Berkana)
Astrological Correlates	Scorpio, Libra
Major Arcana Key	The Lovers
Archangel	Gabriel (Moon)
Stone Alchemy	Garnet, watermelon tourmaline, cinnabar

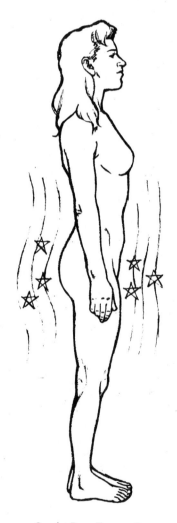

Scarlet Ray Energy Centers

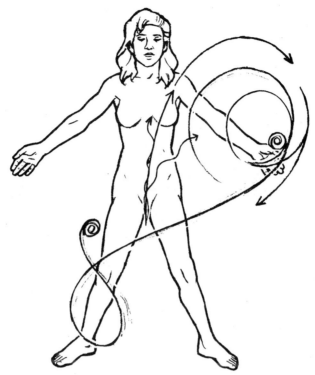

Imbalanced Scarlet Ray Energy Pattern

Harmonic

The harmonic key for Scarlet Ray is the sound of long i as in ice.

Vibrational Energies

The energies of Scarlet Ray are etheric, balancing and gently rocking. Focus on the area just outside the physical body.

Harmonic Breathing Pattern

The primary breathing pattern for Scarlet Ray is soft breaths in and out of the mouth, whispering the harmonic i. This has the additional benefit of expressing the personal I, strengthening one's self-awareness as an individual. Be sure to draw out the sound of i.

Suggested Harmonic Exercises, Chants, and Word Mantras

Using a blended approach of harmonics (as Scarlet is a blended Ray), combine keys to bridge physical with etheric realms.

For example: Red Ray   (Physical)   e
                 ScarletRay   (Etheric)   i

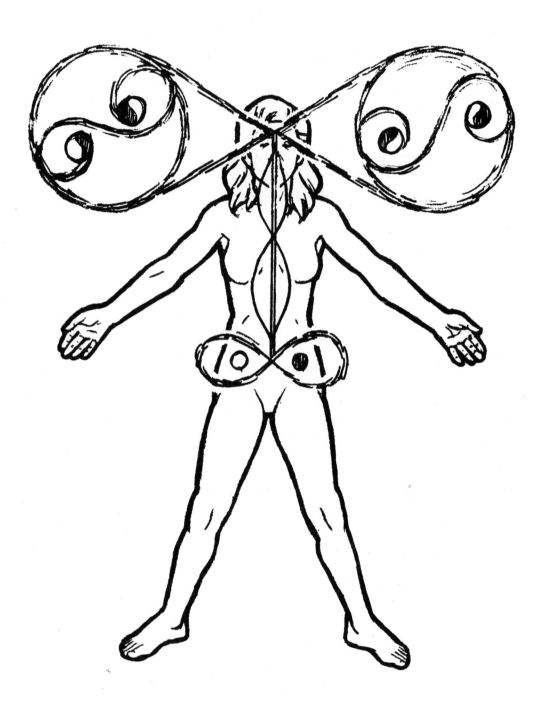

Harmonious Scarlet Ray Energy Pattern

Chant "I," "me," and "my." Bring the focus of energies in and out of physical and etheric realms to strengthen the Body/Mind connection and balance.

For deeper self-balance and self-identification, try combining harmonic keys with mirror work. Gaze in a full-length mirror if possible for full-body effect, or just a full-face reflection.

Focus on the left side of your body and chant "she."
Focus on the right side of your body and chant "he."
Focus on the center of your body and chant "me."
Follow by touching the heart and chanting "I."

For group work, link arms, focus on the circle of people and chant "we." Build the chant up to a crescendo, then soften slowly to a whisper.

This exercise may also be done by focusing only on the eyes. Chant combinations of "he," "she," "me," "I," and "my eyes."

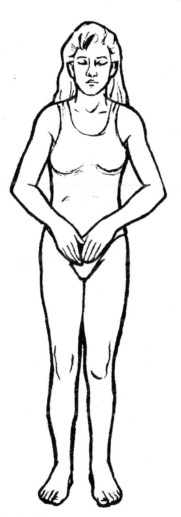

Scarlet Ray Harmonic Posture

Additional Harmonics for Scarlet Ray

I spy   (For focus and precision—select specific items in the environment to spy
                 and move energy toward)

I fly   (For expression or balance—imagine having perfectly balanced wings to
                 transport your self into the etheric realms)

Alchemical Properties

Scarlet Ray actively realigns imbalances in Yin/Yang energies and brings a balanced flow
of receptivity and activation, input and output in an emotional and etheric manner.

Powers   Indirect, etherically focused, slightly diffuse, lemniscate action

Activates   Androgynous balance, relationships

Amplifies   Communication, honor, integrity, perception

Balances   Idealism, independence, loyalty, soul consciousness, synthesis, confusion,
                 hate, jealousy, lack of self-respect, rebellion, stubbornness, superiority

Releases   Vacillation, indecision

Realigns   Arrogance, ego disorders, extremes, behavior, imbalance, perfectionism

Sensory Key

The sensory key correlated with Scarlet Ray is that of cloves.

> Shared attributes of cloves and Scarlet Ray:
> Sexual balance and expectations
> Balance of positive and negative energies
> Physical attraction
> The element of Fire

Clove is relatively inexpensive. It is available most often as a spice, either ground or
in whole form, and as an oil. Clove oil may be added to scent either candles or herbal mixtures effectively.

- Sprinkle cloves in cider or tea to dispel negativities and create positive energies.
- Burn cloves to activate Scarlet Ray energies of sexual balance. This is also good
  when working with sex role expectations. Focus on the sweet smell of cloves to
  evoke the female energies, either physical or etheric. Focus on the spicy scent of
  cloves to evoke the male energies.
- Burn ground clove as an incense, or throw cloves on a fire. Focus on the sensory
  experience. Next, meditate on the many dimensions of Yin/Yang balance: personal, interpersonal, societal, global and universal.

- Use clove-scented oil (just a few drops) in massage oil to awaken sexuality and release inhibitions. Smudging the environment with cloves will have a similar effect when dealing with Scarlet Ray issues of sexuality.
- Use cloves with Tantric Yoga to deepen the experience of sexual relationships.
- Mix cinnamon with cloves to unblock repressed sexuality. Focus on Red Ray energies for more physical issues. Focus on Scarlet Ray for more mental/spiritual issues.
- Carry cloves in a pouch. Breathe in the scent when feeling out of balance. Focus on realigning the active/receptive flow of energies within the Self or the environment.

Symbols

Double-edged sword represents the activation of change in alchemical balance. When both sides of the blade on the sword of Self are equally sharp, we no longer have the need to cut or separate.

Justice scales represent the eternal balancing of universal alchemy. The alchemy of balance is guided by the ruthless compassion of Source.

Yin/Yang symbol represents the eternal dynamic balance with the each and the All of us. Yin/Yang is not just a static symbol, but an ever-turning wheel. Yin/Yang is not just a wheel, but a constantly spiraling sphere.

Personifications

Balance

Scarlet is the energy of the Warrior/Adventurer. It is Robin Hood challenging wealth and redistributing the balance of power in Albion, England. It is Robin of the Greenwood holding the old ways of magick when they were threatened. Scarlet is the loyal opposition.

Musings

The warrior adventurer wears the scarlet ribbons of Truth,
The brilliant plumes of many birds,
The jewelled sword of a revolutionary spirit, and
The broad-brimmed hat of a cavalier.

The warrior adventurer also wears the ragged robes of a beggar,
The sandalwood beads of a holy man,
The shoes of a fisherman, and
The mark of Spirit at his brow.

Balance is the brass pendulum of a universal clock. Each swing marks the cycles of day and night and the times of darkness and light with measured perfection.

From within, the Yin has sung the melody of all the songs the Yang sang outwardly.
From within, the Yin receives and the Yang activates the balance of androgyny.
From within, the Yin together with the Yang become One in perfect Harmony.

Runic Correlates

Thorn (Thurisaz) and Beorc (Berkana)

Shared aspects with Scarlet Ray:
    Catharsis
    Chaos
    Balance

Thorn (Thurisaz) reflects the image of inner-Self. Self-transformation requires knowledge of all that is hidden or imbalanced within. Activate truthful self-reflection with Thorn (Thurisaz).

Thorn (Thurisaz)

Beorc (Berkana)

Beorc (Berkana) activates development of personal alchemy through the catalyst of change. Balance of Self in all dimensions requires movement of personal catharsis. Together, these runes create a cycle of growth blended with patience and preparation.

Astrological Correlates

Solar Scorpio

Alchemy of Activation and Enhancement

    Shared aspects with Scarlet Ray:

Sexuality	Androgyny
Balance	Socialization
Distribution	Karmic patterns

        (+ Brown Light = Centered Balance)

Part of the secret of Scorpio . . . is the simplicity with which he accepts the merger of the material and the Spiritual.

—Grant Lewi

Lunar Libra

Alchemy of Receptivity and Reflection

    Shared aspects with Scarlet Ray:

Balance	Decisiveness
Socialization	Judgment
Communication	

        (+ Gray Light = Devotion Seeker)

These people always try to understand the other person's point of view, but the instincts of self-preservation saves many Moon in Libra people from making mistakes in judgment.

—Sybil Leek

Major Arcana Key

The Lovers

Shared aspects with Scarlet Ray:

Balance	Union
Relationships	Sexuality
Yin/Yang	Androgyny

Learning that other people are real, that they have feelings, is to gain a sense of responsibility, but it is also a loss—for you can no longer give your feelings, your actions, your words free reign.

—Ellen Cannon Reed

Musings

The marriage of self-consciousness with sub-consciousness is a union blessed by the Divine source of Super-consciousness.

In balanced relationships, sexuality reflects the androgyny of divine union, with no concealments of self to Self.

Neither me, nor he, nor she—but we.
Neither we, nor she, nor he—but me and thee.
Or me and Thee?
But Thee is me and he, and she; and we is me.

Archangel

Angelic Dimension Key

Gabriel: Archangel of the Moon
      Alchemy of Balance and Cycles of Transformation
          Day   Monday
          Times   5-6 AM
                       1-2 PM
                       9-10 PM

The Phoenix riddle hath more wit
By us, we two being one, are it.
So to one neutral thing both sexes fit
We die and rise the same, and prove
Mysterious by this love.

                               —John Donne

Angelic Invocation

Gabriel, whisper to me of the moon and her many faces.

Speak to me of the balance which comes from cycles of change, ever-moving in relationship to the light of Self-understanding.

Gabriel, bring the light of balance into my being that I may, in turn, reflect that balance by being one with the Light.

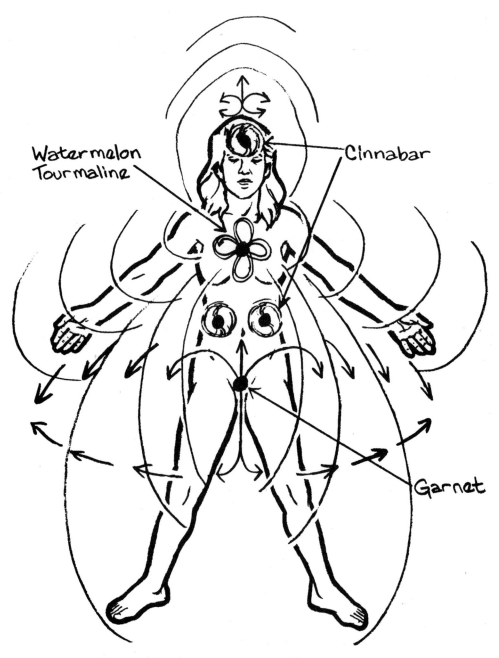

Watermelon
Tourmaline

Cinnabar

Garnet

Garnet: Cinnabar:

Watermelon Tourmaline:

Scarlet Ray Stone Energy Patterns

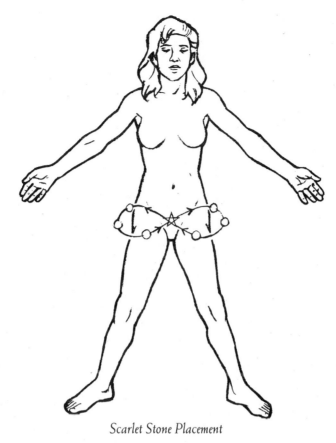

Scarlet Stone Placement

Stone Alchemy

Garnet: Primal Stone
Element: Air and Earth

Garnet can be moderate to expensive, depending on how large a piece, how fine, and how it is faceted. Garnet has a very high vibration, yet is less intense than the ruby. Garnet has a bit more Blue Ray in it than in the ruby. This gives garnet a deeper kind of spiritual fire. This fire is somewhat like the Eastern Kundalini or primal transformative energies, yet definitely more gentle than the intense kundalini fire.

Garnet can be used for Red Ray as well as Scarlet. This blend is suggested for healing anger due to grief or trauma. Use garnet with Scarlet Ray to heal anger a little more gently. Garnet with Red Ray or ruby with Scarlet Ray can be too intense to use for long periods of time. For a quick, direct release or stimulation of blocked energies, experiment with these together for the desired effect. Remember: watch, pace, and be compassionate—to your Self or others. Physically, garnet works well on the generative system and the reproductive organs. Garnet also works well with issues of sexual drive and sex role expectations. Garnet may be used for preventing feelings of insecurity and depression relating to sexual issues, and also helps get rid of judgmental negativism.

Garnet is excellent for easing pain in combination with focused energies and imagery. This is because the blue of garnet can be used to absorb the pain, and the red to activate the healing and restructuring. Garnet is very good for spiritual vision, meditation or shamanic journey work. Garnet allows you to reach into Spirit levels, while keeping the energies of your body in focus and balance. This can help prevent "spacy side effects."

Alchemist's Note: Garnet works especially well through the Mind/Body connection. When using a garnet, use more focus on the etheric, or mental. Let the energies flow more freely. You might want to think in terms of the Body as Earth and the Mind as Air. Approaching with the garnet from the Mind/Body shows that you enter from the etheric into the physical, as you do with many blended energies. This may help you key in a useful correlation of blending mental and physical effects. Work with it, experiment, and remember that divisions—even Mind, Body and Spirit—are arbitrary.

Watermelon Tourmaline: Balance Stone
Element: Air

Watermelon tourmaline is green and pink together. It has a moderate to very high expense, depending on size and clarity. Size seems to have no effect on intensity; clarity does, to some extent. Watermelon tourmaline has a high vibration and is similar to the garnet in the way it works, but it is even more gentle. Watermelon tourmaline can be used directly on the heart without worring about intensity.

The watermelon tourmaline—indeed, all tourmaline—has electrical system energy. Watermelon tourmaline balances our basic input and outgo. This is very like Yin/Yang in the sense of active/receptive energies. Watermelon tourmaline can be used to focus all qualities of Scarlet Ray. Since watermelon tourmaline has a balance all its own, with the green gentle-receptive and the pink gentle-active, it is a great overall stone.

An alchemical "trick" is to focus through the pink in watermelon tourmaline to activate, then finish with the green to heal and balance. This also works the other way around: heal with the green, then activate continuing healing with the pink. The watermelon tourmaline has the added benefit of stimulating our own imagery work in its blend of colors and energy. It has the green energy of expansion and the rose-pink energy of harmony.

All tourmaline has a moderate but strong vibration which balances healing and rejuvenation within any process. Particularly with Scarlet Ray, a tourmaline motivates to action and balances out the transformation processes in our lives.

Specifically, green tourmaline works on the physical through the central nervous system. Pink tourmaline can also be used with Scarlet Ray for a gentle emotional effect; it works a little more in the heart area. This is why watermelon, with its pink and green together, can produce such a wonderful overall effect. Regardless of the color itself, the shade of that color, the combination or number of colors, or the size—tourmaline reflects a balanced energy.

Alchemist's Note: Tourmaline can be a profound, yet gentle, catalyst. If you want to start with just one stone, this could well be the one to choose.

Cinnabar: Meditative Stone
Element: Earth with some Water

Cinnabar is not exactly a stone, but an ore from a mercury process. Cinnabar is usually moderately inexpensive to expensive. Cinnabar is generally found carved into beads or medallions, usually with an Oriental motif.

Caution: mercury content can be toxic on people's skin. It is advisable to put cinnabar over clothes. When working on someone else, put a sheet between stone and skin.

Cinnabar is best used as a meditative focusing tool. It is the Great Evaluator; inscrutable and very Oriental. Cinnabar with Scarlet Ray helps us observe personal, societal, and universal Yin/Yang balance. This is very effective with the quiet mind, Oriental types of meditation. Cinnabar can also be used with Yellow Ray because of its qualities of stillness, focus, balance and order.

Alchemist's Note: Small statues or carved eggs made of cinnabar are excellent meditation tools. Visualize Red as Yang, Blue as Yin. Bring it to balance with Yellow just a bit for order. That is an effective meditation and color energy blend for Scarlet and for cinnabar.

Alternative Stone

A good alternative stone for Scarlet Ray is a single clear, very pale lavender amethyst crystal point, preferably tiny for increased focus. If you can find a double-terminated one, it is a superb tool for Scarlet Ray as well as Violet and the Sky Lights.

Chapter Ten

Rose Ray: Temperance

Were I Pygmalion or God,
I would make you exactly as you are in all dimensions.
—Walter Benton

Let it be noted that . . . "the Magick is in the Rose." Antediluvian,
secret Societies to date incorporated the Rose as being symbolic of the
Magick contained in their teachings. In all philosophies, all religions,
the Rose is revered.

—Stardragon

Rose Ray is primarily Red, with Violet and some Blue. Rose has to do with emotional
growth, and also relates to our connection to others. Rose energies affect physical
compromises and bring moderation into our lives. Rose is the Ray of temperance.

A great deal of Rose Ray work is happening as people connect with each other and
share energies for unity of Mind, Body and Spirit. Rose reflects the unity of harmonious
blending. Rose stones and Rose Ray combine to give an uplifting energy of balance and
harmony. The trick with Rose Ray is to take the time to connect with these higher aspects
of love and harmony.

Elemental Alchemy	Air and Water
Key Issues	Perception, communication, intuition, healing
Stone Alchemy	Alexandrite, rose quartz, rhodonite
Cumulative Alchemy	Temperance

Rose Ray Keys

Harmonic	Sound of **y** as in **why**
Alchemical Properties	Harmonic, communication, moderation
Sensory Key	Floral (very sweet)
Symbols	Wreath, links in a chain, full-blown rose
Personifications	Active Healer (Mother Teresa)
Runic	Os (Ansuz)
Astrological Correlates	Libra, Taurus
Major Arcana Key	Temperance
Archangel	Anael (Venus)
Stone Alchemy	Alexandrite, rose quartz and rhodonite

Harmonic

The harmonic key for Rose Ray is the sound of long **y** as in **why**.

Vibrational Energies

The energies for Rose Ray are etheric, heart-centered, circular and outwardly reaching. Focus on the emotional experience reflecting throughout the Body/Mind connection.

Rose Ray Energy Centers

Harmonic Breathing Pattern

The primary breathing pattern for Rose Ray is short breaths which stop quickly on the sound of **y** (as in **why**). Breathe in through the nose to be receptive to the peaceful Rose energies, and exhale out of the mouth to activate Rose Ray. Make the exhalation short and breathy to leave a full supply of air (prana) in the body at all times.

Suggested Harmonic Exercises, Chants, and Word Mantras

Focus on the etheric areas just outside the heart center. Breathe to expand energy outward and inward, as well. It is helpful to image Rose Ray spiralling in and out, from physical to etheric and back.

For emotional release, chant combinations of:
> I try   I sigh

For more spiritual connection to the highest energies of Universal love, chant combinations of:
> I love   Try love
> My love   Thy love
> High love

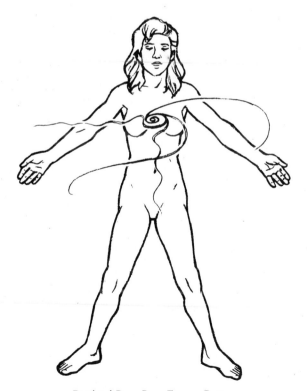

Depleted Rose Ray Energy Pattern

Harmonious Rose Ray Energy Pattern

Additional Harmonic Mantras for Rose Ray

Smile   (For tenderness and communication)
Higher Love   (For Spiritual attunement, empowerment
Higher Light   and communication)

Focus by breathing out the harmonic of **y** and **i**.

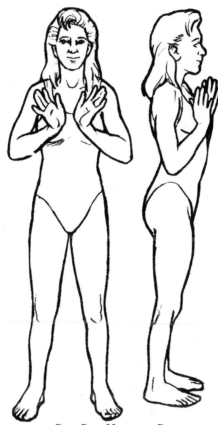

Rose Ray Harmonic Posture

Alchemical Properties

Rose Ray catalysts harmonious flow with energies of communication, moderation and temperance. Rose removes obstacles to unity in a mental, etheric, and spiritual manner.

Powers	Indirect, etherically focused, slightly diffuse yet circular action
Activates	Humility, love, security, self-respect, serenity, temperance, tenderness
Amplifies	Androgynous balance, compassion, expansion, harmony, mercy, peace, relationships, responsiveness, sensitivity, understanding
Balances	Devotion, energy flow, psychic abilities, responsibility, sharing, sincerity, trust, unity, will power, arrogance, authoritarianism, cruelty, vanity, destructiveness, imbalance, irritability, judgmentalism, revenge, violence

| Releases | Anxiety, criticism, insecurity, jealousy, greed, stubbornness, yearning |
| Realigns | Cowardice, hate, lack of self-respect |

Sensory Key

The sensory key correlated with Rose Ray is that of rose. A floral blend highlighted by Rose may also be used.

Shared attributes of rose and Rose Ray:
Love
Growth
Fertility
Communication
The element of Water

Rose is inexpensive as an incense, moderately expensive either fresh or dried, and very expensive as an essential oil. Rose oil, however, is often sold in combination with other oils, such as jojoba. Rose geranium oil is an excellent substitute as a sensory key. Rose-scented candles and herbal mixtures are available and quite useful to activate Rose Ray energies.

- Float fresh rose petals in a bowl of clear water. Breathe the fragrance and focus on activating the flow of Rose Ray energies of love.
- Sprinkle fresh rose petals on your bed sheets to activate the receptive energies of sexual love. Burning rose incense or rose-scented candles will have a similar, if somewhat less interesting, effect. Rose-scented massage oil combined with the healing touch of Rose Ray energies will open a relationship to new dimensions of tenderness, communication, and love.
- Use rose ceremonially to activate physical, mental, or spiritual energies of fertility.
- Place a full-blown rose on a Full moon altar in celebration of the growth of love, personally as well as universally.
- Use a rosebud to symbolize new beginnings in a relationship, or other cycles of growth and self-transformation.
- Cast roses into moving bodies of water, such as rivers or oceans, to symbolize the emotional flow of Rose Ray energies in your life.
- Use the scent of rose whenever you want to energize tender, heartfelt connections in any relationship.
- Add ginger to rose to spice up a love.

Symbols

Wreath represents the circular shape of harmony and unity. Whether the Sun or the Son, we honor the wheel (Yule) that brings the returning power of Light.

Links in a chain represent the connections of heart and mind. The circle is forged by the fire of Source which burns within the circle of our Self.

Full-blown rose represents the nurturance of universal love. With moderation in all things for our personal alchemy, we reflect the harmonious oneness of Universal Alchemy.

Personifications

Temperance

Rose is the energy of the Active Healer. It is Mother Teresa working to bring healing and compassion to the untouchables—the pariahs—the cast-offs of India. Rose is the energy in her fervent prayer, "Lord, make me an instrument of thy peace . . . " Rose is the temperance and moderation of solving life's problems, one at a time, with the fullest alchemical power of love.

Musings

Rose is the strength of the Healer reflecting the full force of the Light.
In Temperance, the power of Love becomes the catalyst of Light.
Love is the catalyst which activates the alchemy of transformation.
Love of the Self brings temperance to the love of self.

Only in activating the ability to receive healing from our Self are we able to catalyst the self-healing of others. Love unfolds from within the heart of the healer as the petals of a Universal Rose. Love freely shared is never wasted, so long as it is neither given, nor received with expectations. Temperance freely practiced is never binding, so long as it is lovingly upheld without judgment, but with Self-Judgment.

Runic Correlate

Os (Ansuz)

Shared aspects with Rose Ray:
>   Benevolence   Communication
>   Balance   The element of Air

Os (Ansuz)

Os (Ansuz) signals the presence of great gifts and sacred knowledge. Self-knowledge is obtained at the highest dimensions when it is supported by spiritual wisdom. Activate communication from the highest aspects of your Self with the rune Os (Ansuz). The alchemy of the rune Os (Ansuz) is best accessed when the focus is receiving with grace from Source.

Astrological Correlates

Solar Libra

Alchemy of Activation and Enhancement

>   Shared aspects with Rose Ray:
>   Temperance   Balance
>   Unity   Harmony
>   Socialization   Communication
>   (+ White Light = Harmony Medium)

Librans pursue education, and enjoy being known as meditators in the universe . . . they have the ability to bring diverse people together in a spirit of cooperation.

—Betty Lundsted

Lunar Taurus

Alchemy of Receptivity and Reflection

>   Shared aspects with Rose Ray:
>   Harmony   Growth
>   Groundedness   Moderation
>   Communication
>   (+ Gold Light = Harmony Activator)

You're likely to be popular because, demanding little of yourself, you also demand little of others and are the most agreeable of companions. You are not likely to be ardent in human relations; you take what comes, especially if it isn't too much trouble.

—Grant Lewi

Major Tarot Arcana Key

Temperance

Shared aspects with Rose Ray:

Moderation	Unity
Healing	Growth
Universal Love	Love
Priorities	

14 Temperance 14

Musings

That I may conceive—I can achieve, in deed.
And access to excess frailties breed;
Engendering human greed.
Then from Delphi, long since past, I take my simple creed.
"Moderation in all Things."
Or "Nothing in Excess" (the sign did read, in deed!)

In releasing ourselves from the expectations of others, we find ourselves left with the expectations of our self. In releasing the expectations of our self, we find the Self. In finding the Self, we realize expectations.

Archangel

Angelic Dimension Key

Anael: Archangel of Venus
      Alchemy of Relationships, Harmony and Love
            Day   Friday
            Times   1-2 AM
                             9-10 AM
                             5-6 PM

Harmony is pure love, for love is complete agreement.
                                                    —Lope de Vega

Angelic Invocation

I send love upward from my heart, Anael, light of Harmony, illuminator of hope.

Let me be in harmony with the heart of the Universe.

Let the strength of highest love temper my needs and unify my consciousness with the one true Source of all Harmony.

Stone Alchemy

The stones chosen for Rose Ray are the alexandrite, rose quartz and rhodonite. There are many effective points on which to place these stones. Rose Ray stones work well on the spine just above mid-shoulder blades, or just above the heart area, about mid-sternum in the front. Rose Ray and rose stones, though, tend to get a bit lost in the lower chakra areas, so try them on the upper chakras for maximum effects. Rose stones also work well on the crown of the head.

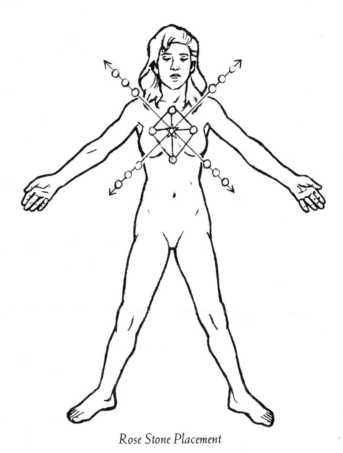

Rose Stone Placement

Alexandrite: Transformative Stone
Element: Air (with some Spirit)

Natural alexandrites are rare and very expensive. Fortunately, manufactured ones are made from corundum, a natural energy element. These alexandrites have been processed so they have qualities which are similar enough to the natural ones to have a good effect.

Both natural and manufactured alexandrites have the ability to change color, which is their most exciting property. This change moves from red-violet into a blue, if manufactured; and into blue-green, if natural.

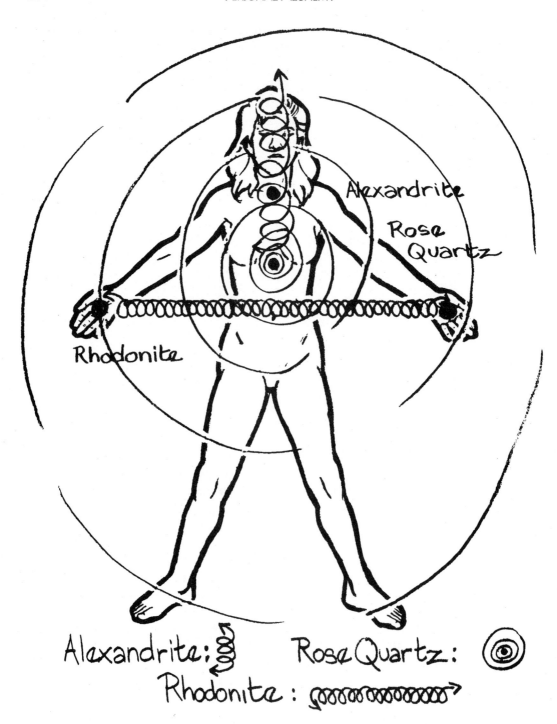

Rose Ray Stone Energy Patterns

The change of color in alexandrite is representative of transformation energies. Because the alexandrite transforms gently and continuously, it relates to the balancing and the compromises which help transform us in much the same manner. It reflects the constancy of transformation; the certainty of change.

Alexandrite's energy moves from etheric to physical. Alexandrite can have a uniting effect when used in romantic relationships. With focus and imagery, alexandrite can build personal harmony from which everything else benefits.

Alchemist's Note: A combination of alexandrite and Red Ray is useful for Tantric Yoga. Alexandrite with Scarlet Ray works to create a more gentle transformation and communication. Both combinations have an effective Tantric energy which brings harmony through sexual relationships. Since alexandrite also has an energy of connectedness, this can strengthen a relationship which is already solid. It can also bind a relationship which may really need to be over and can drag things out.

A watermelon tourmaline reflects a similar energy to alexandrite. Use it interchangeably and/or to support the energy. A rubellite can also be a useful alternative. Have these stones do double duty. We all need to do this at times, but especially when we're just starting to collect stones, so be creative.

Rose Quartz: Harmony Stone
Element: Air and Earth

The next stone is one of the best overall stones. Rose quartz is inexpensive and is easily obtained. It is quite gentle but effective in its vibration, like the power of love.

Rose quartz has the magnetism of quartz and the tenderness of the Rose Ray. This combination is quite good for heart-related disorders. These disorders can be physical, having to do with circulation, pacing, and palpitations of the heart; or psychological, involving the classic broken heart, closed heart, or too-tender heart of those who have been exploited.

Rose quartz works to awaken or reawaken the consciousness of love, and builds strength within that consciousness and the power it can have in our lives. Rose quartz enhances love and the childlike spirit. Rose quartz can be placed anywhere on the body or close by. Keep it in the environment and let it radiate its gentle, powerful energy.

Alchemist's Note: When you are working with love energies through rose quartz, you might find that the clearer the stone is, the more it reflects the spiritual energies of love. The more opaque rose quartz reflects friendship energies—like that of community love. Experiment for your self.

Rhodonite: Physical Stone
Element: Earth

Rhodonite is an inexpensive, all-purpose pink stone with black veins. It has an earthy, dense energy good for stabilizing the whole body. Rhodonite emanates and vibrates soothing energy outward.

If rhodonite is worn or carried for a long time, it can provide ongoing stabilization for minor palpitations or for an overstressed pace due to nervousness and tension. (I stress "minor" here. Remember, there is really no substitute for rest and relaxation.)

When working with rhodonite, place it directly on the heart area and focus on slowing the pace. Focus on moderation, gentleness and love. Rhodonite also soothes broken hearts, grounding the torn, scattered energy and stabilizing the flow of healing. The black in rhodonite can absorb the negativity of many a traumatic experience, while the rose-pink reopens the heart energies gently.

Rhodonite can also be used for Scarlet Ray, since it is a balancing, stabilizing stone on its own. Rhodonite won't have quite as intense an effect as garnet or watermelon tourmaline.

Alchemist's Note: You can use rhodonite with Red Ray to begin, instead of moving directly into ruby or even into red jasper. Rhodonite can gently move the energy of the root chakra. The black in the rhodonite can relate well to unblocking, and the pink can gently filter the flow. These stones can be used in a lot of different ways. Experiments, of course, lead to discoveries—that's alchemy.

Alternative Stone

An inexpensive alternative stone for Rose Ray is pink coral. Pink coral is gently supportive and can enhance the Rose Ray energies of love, caring and connecting.

Chapter Eleven

Orange Ray: Vitality

Personal power decides who can or cannot profit by a revelation.

—Carlos Castaneda

Orange Ray relates to the second energy point, which is the sacral or splenic chakra. Orange Ray blends the essential lifeforce of Red with the mental energies of Yellow. Orange gives us self-control, creativity and enthusiasm. Orange is activating, yet contains more control than the essential, active energy of Red.

Orange Ray is excellent for overall good health. It helps the digestive system by keeping the functions going effectively. Use Orange Ray for physical or emotional indigestion. Sometimes we do have to digest things psychologically. Often, psychological indigestion is the cause of physical indigestion.

Elemental Alchemy	Fire and Air
Key Issues	Health, vitality, self-control, creativity
Stone Alchemy	Amber, carnelian, fire agate
Cumulative Alchemy	Vitality

Orange Ray Keys

Harmonic	Sound of short **e** or **eh**
Alchemical Properties	Vitality, self-control, creativity
Sensory Key	Ginger
Symbols	Flame, control panel, cauldron
Personifications	Creative Muse (White Goddess)
Runic	Ur (Uruz)
Astrological Correlates	Leo, Gemini
Major Arcana Key	Strength
Archangel	Michael (Sun)
Stone Alchemy	Amber, carnelian, fire agate

217

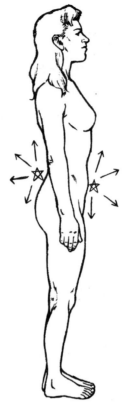

Orange Ray Energy Centers

Harmonic

The harmonic key for Orange Ray is the sound of short **e** or **eh** as in **bet**.

Vibrational Energies

The energy of Orange Ray is a mechanical, automatic, churning, processing flow that connects physical to mental realms. Focus on the active process as the energies move throughout the body, digesting and sorting what is needed to bring vitality and creativity to the entire system.

Harmonic Breathing Pattern

The primary breathing pattern for Orange Ray is in through the nose and out through the mouth with a steady, automatic pace. These breaths are measured to almost match inhalation with exhalation. Place slightly more emphasis on the inhalation to activate the vitality of Orange Ray. Exhale with the harmonic of short **e**.

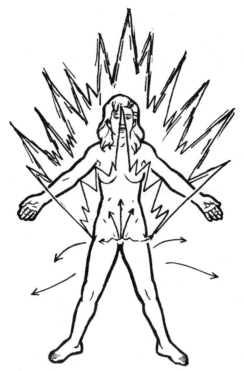

Excess Orange Ray Energy Pattern

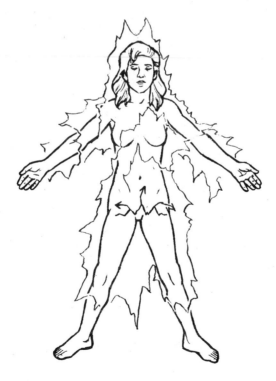

Depleted Orange Ray Energy Pattern

Harmonious Orange Ray Energy Pattern

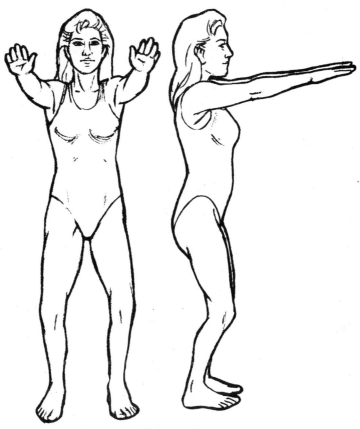

Orange Ray Harmonic Posture

Suggested Harmonic Exercises, Chants, and Word Mantras

For a vitality "tune-up" to keep all systems digesting mentally as well as physically, try a measured breath with the harmonic key.

For example: Breathe in to the sound of **eh**
Breathe out to the sound of **he**

For extra release of difficult-to-digest issues, stress the exhalation and emphasize the sound of **h**.

For example: Inhale to the sound of **eh**
Exhale to the sound of **neh**

Additional Harmonic Mantras

Steady (reinforces the involuntary systems of digestion, combining mental and physical)

Steh dee . . .
Steh = orange **eh**   dee = Red **e**

Good, better, best, success	(Use for motivation)
Digest, process	(Use to strengthen balance flow)
Manifest, bless	(Use for healing and magick)

Alchemical Properties

Orange Ray controls the vital flow of Body/Mind energies. Orange unblocks obstacles to the process of self-transformation in a primarily physical, emotional and mental manner.

Powers	Direct, focused, invigorating process action
Activates	Action analysis, confidence, courage, creativity, vitality
Amplifies	Determination, implementation, inspiration, intellect, mental discrimination, motivation, prosperity, rejuvenation, release
Balances	Dedication, memory work, security
Releases	Conceit, cynicism, desolation, deviousness, fear, indifference, laziness
Realigns	Anger, cruelty, ignorance, inferiority, superiority

Sensory Key

The sensory key correlated with Orange Ray is ginger.

> Shared attributes of ginger and Orange Ray:
> Activation of energies
> Vitality
> Power
> Success

Ginger is moderately inexpensive. It is generally available as a spice, either ground or in root form; less often as an oil. Oriental groceries or health food stores are the best source for fresh ginger root. Crystallized ginger, often preserved in sugar, is sometimes available and is very special.

- Bury a ginger root at the base of a tree to tap into the vital energies of the Earth. Allow it to remain for at least one natural cycle of earth, moon, or sun—i.e., 24 hours, 28 days, or the time between an Equinox and a Solstice. When the cycle has passed, remove the root from the ground. Slice off only as much as you need to flavor food for a ceremonial feast. As you eat the ginger-flavored food, focus on activating your own vital energies and partaking of the vitality of the Earth. Return the remaining ginger root to the ground with ceremonial awareness. Focus on empowering the creative force of your life and the life of the planet. Leave the root until the next cycle you have chosen has passed, or until the need arises.

- Burn ginger to activate Orange Ray vitality in the environment, to generate creativity and inspiration, or to set goals and empower success.
- Bury ginger in the ground to help manifest your successes, goals, inspirations and creative ideals.
- Sprinkle a bit of ginger, either fresh or dried, on yogurt or ice cream. Eat slowly to soothe physical or psychological indigestion.
- Use ginger as a meditative as well as a sensory key. Combine with Orange Ray to balance the flow of the Body/Mind processes. This brings vitality where it is needed throughout the system.
- Use ginger sprinkled in a candle flame to empower any purpose. Be sure its a positive need or this "hot" mixture can backfire.

Symbols

Flame represents the vital alchemy of the Body/Mind connection. The eternal flame of creation burns brightly when energized by fuel from Body and Mind.

Control panel represents the involuntary (or invisible) systems that regulate our vital life processes. We pilot the processes of our own transformation, and thereby create the product of Self.

Cauldron represents the Source of all inspiration and creativity. In the creation of our Self, we are sustained by the transformational alchemy of wisdom.

Personifications

Vitality

Orange is the energy of the Creative Muse. It is the White Goddess bringing forth the vitality of enthusiasm and inspiration. Orange is the energy that fuels the ongoing internal processes of life and encourages the manifestations of vision.

Musings

The processes of self-transformation are regulated by the inner fires of Self-Creation. The processes of world transformation are regulated by the inner fires of Self-Creation.

Creativity is a magical alchemy blended from freedom of spirit, faith in the self, and the forces of self-destiny. Those experiences and opportunities we agree upon voluntarily catalyst the involuntary alchemy of growth for the good of all. Vitality is the celebration of vital life processes in harmonious flow with the Body, Mind and Spirit system. Inspiration is the breath of the Muse, fanning the flames of Creativity.

Runic Correlate

UR (Uruz)

Shared aspects with Orange Ray:
Potency
Courage
Strength

UR (Uruz)

UR/Uruz processes the development of strength in self through the retrieval of that which is essential, and the rejection of that which is nonessential. Strength is obtained from the efficient use of all elements in your personal alchemy. Activate the strength of Self-discrimination without Self-recrimination using the rune UR/Uruz. The alchemy of UR/Uruz is maximized with courage, faith and self-conviction.

Astrological Correlates

Solar Leo

Alchemy of Activation and Enhancement

Shared aspects with Orange Ray:
    Vitality   Activation
    Control   Relationships
    Creativity
    (+ Gold Light = Creative Activator)

It's important for Leos to learn Self-approval, for that is the key to the proper use of their energy . . . Idealism is very much a part of Leos— they can radiate enthusiasm for new causes and new ideas which they have a basic respect for.

—Betty Lundsted

Lunar Gemini

Alchemy of Receptivity and Reflection

Shared aspects with Orange Ray:
    Self-determination   Relationships
    Control   Psychological processes
    (+ Gold Light = Peaceful Activator)

Being articulate, loving to have your words applauded, you go to the limit of your capacity and will not stop going till you have extracted the maximum from life according to your tastes and your abilities.

—Grant Lewi

Major Tarot Arcana Key

Strength

Shared aspects with Orange Ray:
    Self-determination   Achievements
    Self-control   Vitality
    Health   Inspiration
    Cooperation

The astonishing power inherent within each of us may be aroused and brought into full awareness only through agencies of harmony and compassion.

—R. J. Stewart

Musings

In creativity, I find strength.
I feel the spear point of inspiration with Self-determination as its shaft.
I feel vital, awake—alive.
I feel imperious. The strength of the lion.
The lion roars—(a British lion by the sound of it).
Raj. Raj. Raj.
(Hmmm, perhaps a bit more time with Rose Ray to temper those Western Imperialistic Tendencies.)

I feel the fires of Vitality and Health flowing golden Orange, grandiose and glorious.
I feel I could conquer universes (or perhaps a week of laundry).

Archangel

Angelic Dimension Key

Michael: Archangel of the Sun
    Alchemy of Activation, Motivation, and Achievement
        Days   Sunday, Thursday
        Times   4-5 AM
                    12-1 PM
                    8-9 PM

If happiness is activity in accordance with excellence, it is reasonable that it be in accordance with the highest excellence.

—Aristotle

Angelic Invocation

Michael, light of lights, strength of the Sun, and manifestation of divine fire, I ask for the vital flow of right action and creativity to course through my being.

I call for the guidance of truth and the activation of faith to motivate my path and empower my achievements.

Stone Alchemy

Orange Ray helps us receive, absorb, process and release energies in a way that creates, but does not consume, our Self. Orange Ray is excellent for all self-transformational processes. The trick with Orange Ray is to balance the breathing. Too shallow breaths are insufficient for Orange, and too fast-paced breaths scatter the energy. Deep, even breaths alternating between mouth and nose work well with orange energies.

    The stones chosen here for use with Orange Ray are amber, carnelian and fire agate. The placement of stones for Orange Ray is in the small of the back; or in front, about three inches below the navel.

Amber: Magnetic Stone
Element: Earth with Fire

Alchemist's Note: Of course, amber is not a stone at all, but petrified resin from ancient trees. Amber has transformed to become a bridge between the Stone or Mineral World and the Plant World. Because of this, amber has great potential for use in many kinds of bridges in our own lives. Amber helps rebuild bridges to ancient memories, providing us with information as we recall our connection to Nature.

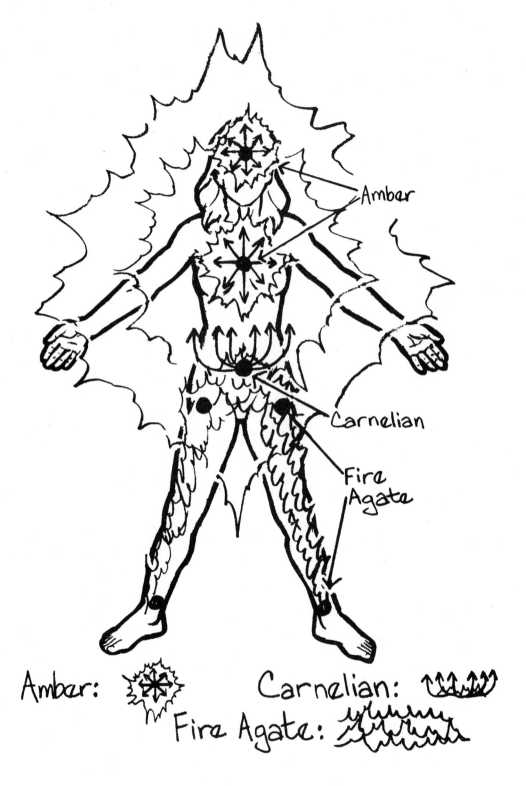

Orange Ray Stones Energy Pattern

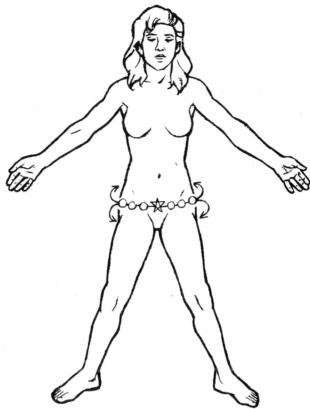

Orange Ray Stone Placement

Amber is of moderate to expensive price, depending on size and cut or polish. It is relatively inexpensive in the rough state, and just as effective.

Amber has a strong vibration with a diffuse magnetic or electrical effect. Its energy spreads like honey, with a gentle insistence. Amber works on the whole physical system through the auric, etheric bodies; bridging the physical and the etheric (the Body and the Mind) with a radiant, glowing energy. Amber purifies the system. It cleanses by spreading throughout the Mind, Body and Spirit, changing the flow and recharging the energies.

Amber gets rid of negative psychic energies and emotional issues, as well. It also activates and soothes, allowing us to receive the positive. Amber creates a holistic overall digestive system when used in combination with Orange Ray energies. In combination with Orange Ray, amber is like an electrical tonic that effectively clears out mental toxins and gets the creative juices flowing at the same time.

The darker ambers can also be used with the Red Ray as useful filters. For example, to activate Red Ray energy to move upward, use a darker amber on the root chakra. In this way the energy will move up slowly and spread vital magnetism to "recharge the batteries" without "blowing the fuses." When using amber for root chakra issues, it is helpful to unblock or absorb first—perhaps with a black stone. Then follow with amber for an overall healing tonic.

The darker red amber energies appear to be more physical and affect the lower chakras more directly. The more orange amber connects Physical and Mental together simultaneously and is a clearer bridge. The clearest golden-orange ambers are good to inspire creativity. Yellow amber, which is definitely lighter, is very powerful in its magnetic vibration. It relates more directly to the mental processes. Yellow amber is also very good for the kinds of headaches issuing from mental exhaustion.

Amber in all forms or colors is helpful for muscle cramps. With Orange Ray, amber manages to warm and unblock resistances which cause muscle cramps; it works by soothing and reactivating the muscles gently. If you have to choose one amber to start, try the golden-orange variety. Some people find the inclusions in amber to affect the energies. This has not been the case for me, but see what you discover for your self.

Alchemist's Note: You can also use yellow amber with Yellow Ray or Golden Light. Yellow is more structured; Gold is a stronger activator, particularly with increased focus. When using amber for mental stresses, it is best not to strain, as this will only complicate the problem. Breathe, and allow an amber glow to wash through your entire body and mind. Let your mind rest and receive.

I have a piece of blue amber. Held in a natural light, it produces a translucent kind of bluish-green. At another angle, it is golden. When I get a "writer's brain cramp," I tend to use my blue amber. It soothes, un-cramps, and gets those "muscles" of the brain (because sometimes I think the brain is a muscle) functioning again. When your energies seem too electric, amber helps reduce your "voltage."

Carnelian: Action Stone
Element: Earth and Fire

Carnelian is an excellent all-purpose stone which can have a whole-body effect when placed on the lower chakra points. Carnelian, particularly the translucent orange forms, reflects the Orange Ray most purely. Carnelian has a somewhat slower vibration than the Orange Ray, but it has the same functional vitality. The blend of carnelian and Orange Ray is the blend of the energies of Earth and Fire. Carnelian is Orange Ray most clearly.

Carnelian is inexpensive and easily obtainable. Even the finest pieces are not expensive. Carnelian has a moderate, friendly vibration. If intensity becomes an issue with carnelian, it is probably because it has been used at the wrong time, or for too long a time or by someone who is sensitive to it.

To use carnelian with Red Ray, try the darker, almost red shades. These darker carnelians are used successfully for treating anemia and other physical blood disorders. Carnelian can rebalance the whole system, help digest negativities, and reactivate the building of healthy blood cells. Additionally, carnelian is great for the tissues and the skin because it works through the circulatory system. Carnelian with Orange Ray vitalizes and nourishes; it is a tonic for vitality. With Orange Ray energies, carnelian can be wonderful with the poor circulation that comes from sitting or spending a long time in one position. This is done using gentle breathing and focusing on the recirculation of blood flow and the movement of the physical and etheric bodies.

Carnelian is a stimulant that can energize, but it is not a substitute for rest. Carnelian can be good for giving that one little extra energy lift. Continued use of this could create a state of insomnia due to overexhaustion. When using carnelian with Orange Ray, set a time to stop, as Orange Ray has creative energies that do not always know when to quit. It also has a control panel for the Physical. Program that, as well. Set a time to allow flow and to stop.

As a psychological helper, carnelian has been thought effective in working with blood kin. Carnelian can help release the "tired blood" that sometimes occurs in family relationships. The way carnelian works with family relationships is to help clean out "bad scripts" or inappropriate patterns developed in the past. It helps us digest what we could not before.

Carnelian can be used for all kinds of families, because families can be made up of friends, too. That's kinship. Traditionally, carnelians were thought to relate only to blood kin. But, of course, kinship does not necessarily come from blood.

Alchemist's Note: When you are working with your own bad scripts or anyone else's, be gentle. A lot of these scripts came from childhood. However old the person is, or however old you are, that inner child still has the script. It is fine that you are using carnelian to help unblock the energy of negative script. Go ahead and focus Orange Ray gently. You will also want to support the heart and the emotional aspects of the heart. As the bad script energy comes up the body, you will focus to release this, but it could go into the heart and create emotional confusion about the scripts, particularly childhood ones. Remember, children want to love their families, no matter what; this makes them vulnerable. Of course this manifests etherically, but the effect is ultimately the same.

When you are working with bad scripts from childhood and Orange Ray energy to clear them, be sure to protect and support the emotional, vulnerable heart. You can do this with a bloodstone to stabilize the heart area. Rhodonite is another good choice, since it allows love to be less vulnerable. Rose quartz, in this case, could open the heart too much.

If you are concerned, just remember to be gentle. Go slowly, a bit at a time—rest—and repeat. Sometimes these processes take a while, and we always have time to be gentle. If we don't, we are not ready to work. Wait until there is the right amount of time to do active self-healing and self-transformational work on personal issues.

An issue that has to wait a bit will begin to work its own healing alchemy. This happens when you consciously decide to work on it, and set a date. It is a little like romance that way. Anticipation is very alchemical.

Carnelian has an very uplifting energy. Because carnelian is so purely Orange Ray, it is a bridge between the Mental of Yellow and the Physical of Red. All signs can use that as an image to focus and bring the connection of Body/Mind into their life.

Alchemist's Note: Peach-colored carnelians are quite gentle, and are useful for family issues or for people who need somewhat more tender energies. Try peach carnelian with a Fire sign, such as Sagittarius, or any Air sign who has too intense a reaction to the darker colors of carnelian. An added benefit of peach carnelian is that it can be used with Peach Ray. The darker and the more orange carnelians are so clearly Orange Ray, it is sometimes difficult to put the more blended Ray of Peach together with them. For example, try peach carnelian with Peach Ray (which is peace) on a Friday (which is ruled by Venus, which rules beauty and relationships) with someone you love.

Fire Agate: Courage Stone
Element: Fire and Earth

Fire agate is an inexpensive little stone with a powerful vibration. It is also an excellent sub-stitute for the more expensive alchemical opals. Fire agates have an appearance of molten fire. These agates reflect the Orange Ray intensely.

Fire agates are excellent for balancing body functions. They have long been known for their use with sugar disorders, such as diabetes or hypoglycemia. The combination of fire agate and Orange Ray can rebalance the internal physical processes. Fire agates are also good for courage and fortitude. A fire agate does more than just give us this psychologi-cally. With Orange Ray, it builds internal "intestinal" fortitude.

Alchemist's Note: You can also use fire agates with Red Ray if you are trying to "clear out the tubes" after releasing negative energies. With focused Red Ray, a fire agate can work to help recharge energies from the root chakra upward. This combination is very much the essential warrior.

I have a special fire agate I call General Pershing. I have recently acquired two rough rubies of the same size and similar shape. I have worked with them a bit and gotten to "know" them; I am considering calling them General Patton and General Montgomery. See how you can have fun with this? It deepens the experience and strengthens your alchemy.

Alternative Stone

An alternative stone for Orange Ray is amber-colored or orange-colored calcite. This cal-cite has an effect similar to an opaque carnelian or a rather dense piece of amber. When using orange calcite, focus on the Orange Ray a bit more, or use Red Ray instead.

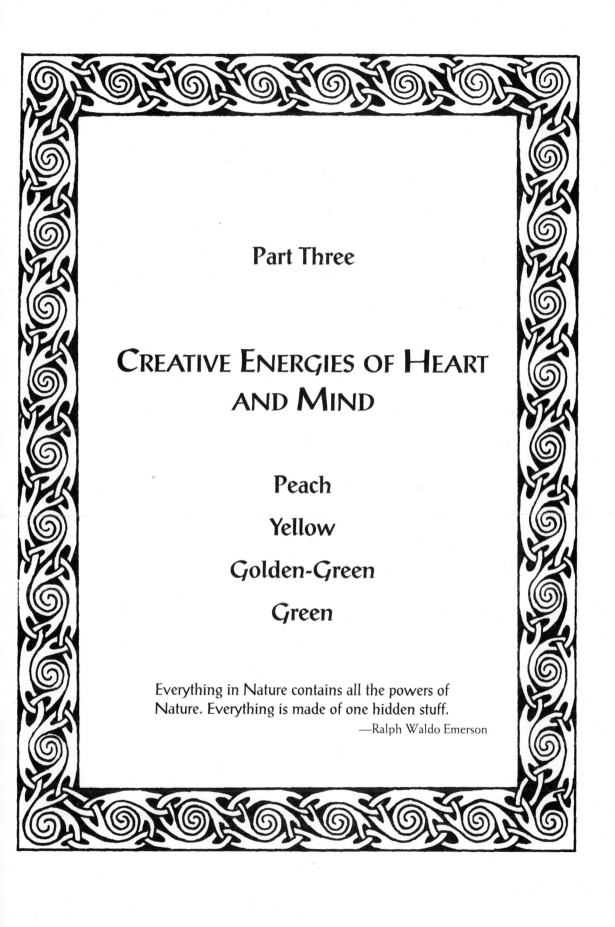

Part Three

CREATIVE ENERGIES OF HEART AND MIND

Peach

Yellow

Golden-Green

Green

Everything in Nature contains all the powers of
Nature. Everything is made of one hidden stuff.
—Ralph Waldo Emerson

Rain Flowers: Emergence and Exploration

Take a long, slow deep breath . . . let it flow through you. Gently let your breath clear away all the tensions of the day. Let the sound of rain cleanse and clear you. Breathe deeply again . . . slowly inhale . . . hold it for a minute . . . then slowly release.

Once more, take a long, slow, deep breath. As you breathe in, tense all the muscles in your body . . . hold your breath for just a moment . . . then gently release your breath and relax your muscles. Just let your body go . . . let your mind float freely. Breathe gently and naturally. Let your self step into a new image.

You are walking along a wild and deserted rocky sea coastline, and find your self caught in a rainstorm. Though the weather is mild and the rain is warm, you seek shelter among the rocks and boulders at the base of a cliff. You find a place where three great stones lean together, forming a shelter from the rainstorm.

Quickly, you slip in between the stones through an opening just large enough to let you in and still keep the weather out. As you settle your self, you find plenty of room to stretch out comfortably. Breathe deeply and feel the softness of the ground inside this stone sanctuary. Reach out and touch the cool dampness of the stones.

As your eyes adjust to the light, you see that the stones are covered with hundreds of carvings . . . wonderful and mysterious. From where you sit, you see countless spirals carved into the stones . . . runic symbols . . . some familiar and some new to you.

Some carvings seem crisp and fresh, as if carved recently. Some are so old that you find you must reach out and trace the patterns with your fingertips to make out what they are. Feel the gentle blanket of moss covering these ancient carvings.

Intrigued by your find, you move close to the stones for a better look. At the base of the largest stone just beside the opening you find an unusual carved pattern gently blanketed with deep green moss. Bending down near the carving and running your fingers over it delicately so as not to crumble the stone, you find a curving pattern of tiny shapes.

Beginning with a delicate little crescent, hardly more than a scratch in the stone, the shapes, one after another, are each somewhat wider and fuller than the one before. Midway in the pattern, you find a carving that is perfectly round and full . . . followed by more shapes slowly returning to a crescent shape and becoming smaller and smaller, until the last one is a tiny line etched in the stone, facing the opposite direction of the first crescent.

As you trace these shapes you realize that someone . . . perhaps some ancient wise woman . . . once sat here and carved these shapes to represent the cycles of the moon as it shone through the opening in the stones. Feel your self as this ancient woman.

Breathe deeply and know you have found a special place . . . a sacred place from ages past . . . feel the magic of this stone sanctuary around you . . . strong . . . safe . . . supportive.

Know that within this place, this womb of Mother Earth, you can renew your self . . . you are free to explore dimensions of your being . . . you are free to allow a rebirth of your self.

Breathe deeply . . . allow your self to go deeper than before . . . feel your self cleansed by the rainstorm and the ancient purity of this place. Feel this place as an entrance to Mother Earth . . . to your Mother-Self. Feel this place as a womb of your Woman-Self.

Feel your self merge with the stones, with the rain, with the ground. Feel your self descend below the surface of Mother Earth. Feel the vibration, the heartbeat of the earth beneath you. Feel the nourishment of the rain as it trickles down from above the ground. Feel the richness of the soil around you. Know that you are part of all these things . . . the rain, the stones, the sky, the soil . . . the ancient sanctuary that is your deepest self.

Breathe deeply, and feel your self respond and grow in this earth womb. Feel your self as a group of seeds nestled in the soil . . . nurtured and nourished . . . and grow.

Feel the anticipation . . . the promise of growth . . . feel each seed awaiting emergence. Feel the gentle pulling, the opening and gentle thrusting as each seed becomes a tiny sprout moving steadily to blossom as a beautiful flower . . . each seed a part of a beautiful garden.

One by one, each seed of your self . . . each sprout . . . reaches through the surface. Each tiny plant reaches out tenderly and is washed by the rain, until all have emerged. With special effort, each tiny plant blossoms. Feel each blossom unfold. Feel each flower open to the rain and turn its face skyward. Feel your self as each blossom, each wild rain flower, born anew of the earth . . . fresh and natural. Feel the many types of flowers that you are.

Take time to notice what sort of flowers have emerged. In what colors have you emerged? Which fragrances represent you in this garden of your self? Are these familiar? Are these new scents, new colors, new sensations?

Feel the strengths of these rain flowers. Are some of these blossoms strong and durable? Do they hold their faces up high to the rain? Do some of the blossoms bend sadly? Do some seem to dance and frolic?

Notice which of the rain flowers is a fleeting blossom, perhaps only blooming for a few days or even a few hours. Feel the delicacy of these blossoms, yet remember the strength it took for them to grow. Notice which flowers last longer, and may bloom for a full season of growth. Which kinds of flowers are those which are fleeting? Which kinds are those which last? Which parts of you are represented by these flowers?

Take time to consider these things.

Know that from time to time these kinds of flowers change. Some flowers blossom only once or twice in the garden of the Self. Some blossoms are always growing in your garden.

Take a few more moments to experience your self as a garden of rain flowers. Experience all the different textures, fragrances, shapes, and colors that are you as a garden.

Experience all the parts of your self as a beautiful garden of flowers kissed and nurtured by the earth and the rain. Appreciate all the parts of your self . . . each blossom, each part, however strong, however delicate, is a flower in the garden of the wholeness of your self. Each emerged from within you as the blossoms emerged from the earth . . . and each has a purpose and a function in your life.

Take another moment and experience which of these blossoms represent a part of your self that needs special attention just now. What does that blossom represent for you?

Find another blossom that represents a part of your self that has a special strength for you just now. What aspect does that blossom represent for you?

Know that in the garden are all the blossoms you need to nurture your own being.

Now breathe deeply, and rise above the blossoms . . . high enough so you can see the whole of your garden, yet still feel the petals of each flower and smell each fragrance. Take a few moments to do this . . . experience the whole of your self as a garden of rain flowers . . . fresh and new. What do you see?

Notice the shape of your garden. Notice which colors are most abundant . . . notice which are scarce or not represented. Balancing may be needed . . . decide for your self. Know that you are the gardener of your self, and may change the pattern as you feel the need.

Do you wish to add a particular blossom just now? It is your choice.

Do you feel that a particular blossom is not right for your garden just now? You may honor it for the part it has had in your garden, and ask it to return to the earth . . . transmuted to its highest good . . . to become soil for another blossom.

Take a few moments to make adjustments to your garden. Know that your garden will change on its own, as you grow and change.

Now the time has come to gather these blossoms of your self into a beautiful bouquet of being. Gently pick the flowers . . . gather special manifestations of your self.

Holding these flowers close to your heart, find your self again in your sanctuary of stone. The fragrance of the bouquet fills the air, and the colors of the flowers glow and reflect in the stones.

In the luminous glow, you notice a sharp rock on the ground . . . points sharp as a chisel. Placing your bouquet down gently, you carefully carve a tiny flower in one of the great stones. With that, you have recorded the growth of your self . . . and the wisdom represented in the blossom of the flower.

Know you may return to this stone sanctuary whenever you choose to grow, to nurture, to experience the garden of your self.

Begin to let your image fade. Slowly return to the present time and place.

Feel your self energized . . . renewed. Accept your self in all your parts . . . accept your self as a whole growing being.

Be here now. Be peaceful. Be content. Emerge into the present time and place renewed.

Chapter Twelve

Peach Ray: Peace

I will fight no more for ever.
—Chief Joseph (Nez Pierce)

Man must evolve for all human conflict a method which rejects revenge, aggression and retaliation. The foundation of such a method is love.
—Martin Luther King, Jr.

Peach Ray is primarily Yellow with Red and some Blue to it. Peach, generally speaking, represents peace. It is a complex ray quite active in its aspects. Peach seems to reflect an energy that is also receptive and reflective in its effect. That combination defines the action and energies of peace. Peach Ray involves active participation in peace, and it reflects the active aspects of communication and good will. Peach Ray is good for the energy of restructuring individual life and the life of the community peacefully. Peach has a lot to do with humor, which is a great catalyst for peace. It is difficult to hate what you can laugh at honestly.

The touch of Blue in Peach Ray moves it a bit closer to the spiritual energies of synthesis. Peach also stimulates Rose Ray and the heart. Peach Ray is similar to Rose, except it is more active. You can use Peach and Rose interchangeably, bearing in mind that Peach Ray has a more active vibration. These can be an excellent combination for actively opening to peace and love.

The trick with Peach Ray is to be both a receptor for it and an activator of it. Transmutation of nonpeaceful energies is best accomplished by first opening to the need for peace, then actively focusing on the right (and the rites) to awaken peace in one's life.

Elemental Alchemy	Air and Spirit
Key Issues	Perception, communication, right action, oneness
Stone Alchemy	Rhodochrosite, unikite
Cumulative Alchemy	Activation of peace

Peach Ray Energy Centers

Peach Ray Keys

Harmonic	Sound of **a** as in **sat**
Alchemical Properties	Activation of peace, reflective transformation
Sensory Key	Fruity
Symbols	Peace symbol, handprint, keystone arch
Personification	Receptive Resistor (Mahatma Gandhi)
Runic	Ethel (Othila)
Astrological Correlates	Sagittarius, Leo
Major Arcana Key	The Hierophant
Archangel	Anael (Venus)
Stone Alchemy	Rhodochrosite, unikite

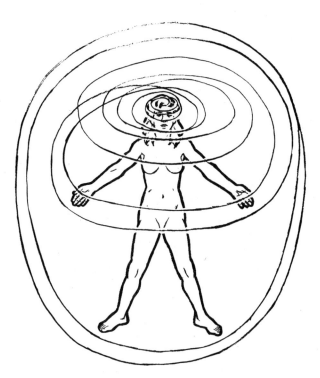

Harmonious Peach Ray Energy Pattern (Expansive)

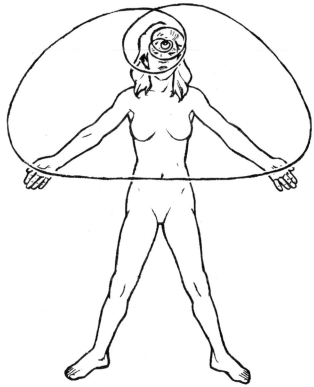

Harmonious Peach Ray Energy Pattern (Intrapersonal)

Harmonic

The harmonic key for Peach Ray is the sound of short **a** as in **sat** or **half**.

Vibrational Energies

The energies of Peach Ray are communicative, linking, harmonizing and activating peace through the etheric realm. Focus on the mental/emotional reaction to the energies of Peach Ray. It is useful to visualize a peace symbol moving just above the center of the body, from below the solar plexus into the heart area.

Harmonic Breathing Pattern

The primary breathing pattern for Peach Ray is inhaling slowly through the nose, exhaling partially through the nose, then completely exhaling with the harmonic **a** as in "aah." Draw the sound out and let it fade with the last part of the exhaled breath. This brings a peaceful, centered state of being to the entire Body/Mind system.

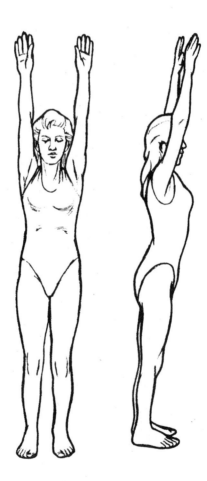

Peach Ray Harmonic Posture

Suggested Harmonic Exercises, Chants, and Word Mantras

To activate the energies of Peach (and peace), inhale and exhale first through the nose silently, then through the mouth with the harmonic **a**.

For example: inhale, exhale   (silent)
                inhale   **ah**
                exhale   **ha**

For an alchemical blend of energies, combine Peach Ray (short) **a** with Green Ray (long) **a**. Focus on the active expansion of peace and healing. Combine with chants or mantras.For example:

Activate   peace at last
Communicate   the circle is cast

Stress the long **a** and the short **a** for balance.

Follow with Peach harmonics, such as:

Dance, Dance, Dance
Peace has its chance

Alchemist's Note: For a deeper alchemical understanding of the power of harmonics, analyze the component elements of this famous "chant:"

All we are saying . . . is give peace a chance.
                                        —John Lennon

Break down by sounds; remember that:
    Red—**e**—physical lifeforce
    Green—**a**—healing expansion
    Peach—**å**—activated peace

Additionally, "all" has the sound of **aw**, which is the harmonic of Turquoise Ray. Turquoise represents dedication and service to a higher cause.

Also, "is" and "give" have the harmonic of short **i**, which correlates to Golden-Green Ray. Golden-Green represents rejuvenation, rebirth, and renewal.

Consider the powerful harmonic alchemy of that profoundly simple chant by John Lennon, and you may begin to realize how much universal alchemy works through the conscious and unconscious human mind.

Alchemical Properties

Peach Ray activates the energies of peace. Peach dispels strife and negativities in a primarily mental, etheric, spiritual manner.

Powers	Indirect, etherically focused, slightly diffuse, spreading action
Activates	Harmony, humor, openness, peace
Amplifies	Cleansings, confidence, synthesis, tenderness, unity
Balances	Intellect, justice, mercy, release, responsiveness, revelations, sensitivity, serenity, anger, bitterness, frustration, greed, vengeance
Releases	Depression, isolation, violence
Realigns	Disorganization, self-righteousness, vanity

Sensory Key

The sensory key correlated with Peach Ray is a fruity blend.

> Shared attributes of fruity blends and Peach Ray:
>   Primarily symbolic

Fruit is the result of a good harvest, both materially and mythically. Fruit symbolizes the attributes of sharing abundance, activation, celebration and wisdom. Peace is also the result of a good harvest, both personally and philosophically. Peach Ray is the ray of active peace. Peach Ray energies are those of communication, positive restructuring, good will, and humor. Thus the correlation of Peach Ray with fruit.

Fruity blends for scents, incense or potpourri mixtures are inexpensive and easily obtained. Fruit, either fresh or dried, is also quite effective for Peach Ray work.

Alchemist's Note: The choice of particular fruit, or a specific fruit scent highlighting a fruity blend, is up to the personal alchemist. So long as the sensory essence serves as a sensory key to activate Peach Ray work, any kind will do. If the essence overpowers the senses or seems artificial, the alchemy of Peach Ray energies will not be effective. The energies of Peach Ray are multidimensional and complex, reflecting personal, societal, global and universal elements. Working with Peach Ray requires complex thoughts and careful linking. Select your sensory keys for Peach Ray to best represent the dimensional aspect with which you are working most clearly.

- Use fruity, peach or citrus candles to activate fresh energies for communication and good will in the environment.
- Use an apple-scented blend to represent the wisdom of peace. Sprinkle with cinnamon, cloves or ginger to vitalize peace in your environment.

- Plant fruit trees to symbolize positive restructuring for transformation, both personal and planetarily.
- Burn dried citrus peelings to activate Peach Ray ceremonially.
- Bury peelings around trees and bushes to nourish the soil—and symbolically, the planet.
- Share seasonal fruit at Nature celebrations and festivals to manifest peace and communication within the circle, and to celebrate unity.
- Leave fruit out for animals and birds, particularly when their food supply is scarce because of winter or population density.

Symbols

Peace symbol represents the shared activation of peace. The rune of protection is reversed, transmuting the need for fear and activating the Circle of Peace and Light.

Handprint represents the mark of humanity and the reaching out to others. Peace extends an open hand, asking only to be held gently.

Keystone arch represents the essential part that each of us has in the Strength of the All of us. We carry the weight of Self-responsibility far more easily when we realize it is a burden shared with the strongest building blocks of the knowledge we have obtained on our own, and the wisdom we have gained together.

Personification

Peace

Peace is the energy of the Receptive Resistor. It is Mahatma Gandhi transmuting the power of violence into the greater power of nonviolence with the undaunted faith that "good always triumphs over evil." Peach is flower children placing blossoms in the barrels of loaded guns, reflecting Gandhi's teachings.

Musings

The fruits of harmony burst forth fully ripened in the warm sun of peace.
To wage war and plan for peace is to keep peace in the unmanifest future and war as a manifestation of the eternal present.
To wage peace and plan for war is the alchemical restructuring of both war and peace.
To visualize peace is to lay the foundations. To celebrate peace is to complete the structure.

To motivate peace is magick.
To activate peace is alchemy.

To fight against war is to feed the energies of war. This is the way to lose.
To fight for peace is to utilize the energies of war and peace. This is a way to "tie."
To receive the energies of war, but reflect only the energies of peace, is to win.

Runic Correlate

Ethel (Othila)

Shared aspects with Peach Ray:

Unity	Consolidation
Allegiance	Communication

Ethel (Othila)

Ethel (Othila) connects the self to all significant relationships and severs connections to the insignificant. The personal alchemist's must ultimately do the work that is solely their own, even when it seems most shared by others. Activate self-unity and the unity of positive relationships with the rune Ethel (Othila). The alchemy of Ethel (Othila) is detached attachment.

Astrological Correlates

Solar Sagittarius

Alchemy of Activation and Enhancement

Shared aspects with Peach Ray:

Unity	Communication
Friendship	Creativity
Activation	
(+ Gray Light = Friendly Peacemaker)	

Sagittarians are hopeful, happy, cheerful, and, like the archer, very direct. Ask a Sagittarian for advice and you'll get plenty—he will think of many original ways to help. Sagittarians have great intuitive powers.

—Ursula Lewis

Lunar Leo

Alchemy of Receptivity and Reflection

Shared aspects with Peach Ray:

Self-esteem	Friendship
Vitality	Communication
Activation	Leadership

(+ Silver Light = Vitality Receptor)

These people are very lovable and loving; they enjoy entering into any relationship where there is potential for growth either by understanding, appreciation, business deals, or affection. They will go more than halfway to make these things happen and will generally succeed.

—Sybil Leek

Major Tarot Arcana Key

The Hierophant

Shared aspects with Peach Ray:

Peace	Order
Right action	Structure
Illumination	Evolution

The Hierophant becomes the spring cleaner, making way for summer glory and autumn acceptance. Winter then becomes the womb of eternity for further growth.

—Eileen Connolly

Musings

Evolution is an active process. It may be observed and encouraged, but never fully structured, ordered, or understood—only accepted as the manifestation of Right Action.

Personal evolution illuminates Universal Evolution. It is not the teeming masses that will create an order of world peace—it is the teeming masses that will do it.

"So what is God to you?" said he, challenging me.
"Right Action," said I.
"Right On!" said he.
"Good-bye, and Peace," said he to me.
"Peace and Gods be with ye," said I. "Tee hee hee."
Peace is priceless. It has to be.

The Hierophant

Archangel

Angelic Dimension Key

Anael: Archangel of Venus
    Alchemy of Relationships, Love, and Harmony
        Days   Friday, Monday
        Times   1-2 AM
                     9-10 AM
                     5-6 PM

Relationship is a pervading and changing mystery. Brutal or lovely, the mystery waits for people wherever they go, whatever extreme they run to.

—Eudora Welty

Angelic Invocation

May my relationships with others reflect the purest peace of my relationship with highest self.

May I activate peaceful communication by my receptivity to your messages of active love and harmony.

Fair Anael, bringer of love and harmony, bring to me the peaceful wisdom of unity and the sacred knowledge of the relatedness of all life.

Stone Alchemy

The stones best representative of Peach Ray are the rhodochrosite and the unikite. The placement is just above the small of the back, or in the belly button. If that won't generate humor, I don't know what will. Peach stones are also effective on the heart chakra.

Rhodochrostite: Peacemaker Stone
Element: Earth (with some Spirit and Fire)

Rhodochrosite can be moderately expensive if cut or made into jewelry. It works quite effectively in raw form or slightly tumbled. It is what I call a "peacemaker stone." Rhodochrosite actively brings together the energies of Physical, Mental and Spiritual realms. Use Peach Ray with rhodochrosite to focus pure, direct peace energies. Place on the "third eye" area for a peaceful synthesis.

Rhodochrosite can be used to awaken the Body/Mind connection and the spiritual energies. This helps by building yet another bridge to spiritual awareness. Rhodochrosite can also be used with Rose Ray to activate love energies. For example, if someone is using rose quartz but just cannot seem to get "open," sometimes a Peach Ray stone could be more effective. It will activate, warm and energize. Experiment with Rose Ray and Rose Ray stones, and Peach Ray and Peach Ray stones in various combinations. The pattern we all share will benefit, no matter how they are put together. That's alchemy at its best.

Alchemist's Note: Peace and Peach are tricky, complex energies. Maybe that reflects why peace is so hard for us to grasp in the larger sense of the pattern. Peach energy may seem receptive at first, until you realize it is actively receiving energy. You may think it is absorbing, but

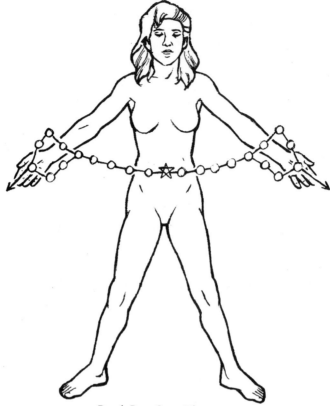

Peach Ray Stone Placement

it is transmuting. When Peach has done this, it transmits the energy into the pattern as peace. This happens regardless of the energy it received to start with. (I told you it was complex.) An increasing number of people are beginning to work with rhodochrosite, experimenting with its attunement energies. We haven't been working with it very long, so it is still not familiar to many people. Rhodochrosite seems to encourage a compassionate involvement in life, stimulating an awareness and a new kind of joy. It is just like peace.

Unikite: Healthful Peace Stone
Element: Suggests Earth (with some Fire)

The next Peach Ray stone is the unikite. This is a wonderful earthy stone, and very inexpensive. Unikite is peachy-pink with green markings. Unikite can also be used with Rose Ray and Green Ray as it has a bit of both, but its active energies more clearly suggest Peach Ray. Unikite has such a subtle effect, it can be blended in a variety of ways. Unikite activates, but it does not push.

Unikite reflects a healthful kind of Peach. The Green in it is very soothing to health, and the peachy-pink is very uplifting. The energy of unikite works by spreading energy diffusely outward. It is not energy as magnetic or electric as amber, but it spreads in a similar fashion.

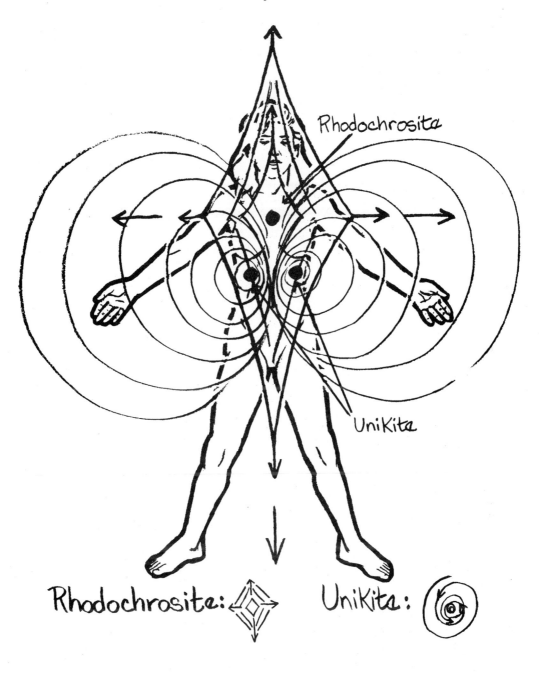

Rhodochrosite

UniKita

Rhodochrosite: UniKita:

Peach Ray Stone Energy Patterns

Alchemist's Note: I find it helpful to take unikite along on spiritual journeys. It is like holding a little bit of earth in your pocket. Unikite with Peach Ray is a good combination on which to move through consciousness. It has that peaceful, gentle vibration and that quality of transmutation that are necessary elements for any spiritual journey and deep meditative work.

Alternative Stone

An alternative stone for Peach Ray is orange moonstone. Moonstones come in many different colors; this one is almost a peachy kind of orange. Moonstone is also actively receptive and works well with the Peach Ray energy. With moonstone, you will have to focus harder to activate the transmutation and the transmittal of Peach Ray peace.

Chapter Thirteen

Yellow Ray: Intellect

The whole of science is nothing more than a refinement of everyday thinking.

—Albert Einstein

Yellow Ray is associated with the solar plexus energy center, the third chakra. Yellow Ray is basically intellectual, involving wisdom, philosophy, contemplation, organization and mental equilibrium. Yellow Ray helps in the organization of thoughts and the everyday orderedness of mind. Yellow is also excellent for sharpening perception by quieting the rhythms of the mind to allow illumination to enter. Because of its properties of focus and mental activity, Yellow is also effective for stimulating creativity.

The trick with Yellow Ray is to use a precise, structured pattern of breathing. It is also helpful to be ordered in the process you use for Yellow Ray alchemy. An analogy for this would be to have all the ingredients in a recipe on the kitchen counter before cooking.

Elemental Alchemy	Air and Fire
Key Issues	Perception, communication, sensation, regeneration
Stone Alchemy	Topaz, golden citrine, tigereye
Cumulative Alchemy	Intellectual illumination

Yellow Ray Keys

Harmonic	Sound of **ah** as in **father**
Alchemical Properties	Order, focus, illumination
Sensory Key	Sandalwood
Symbols	Obelisk, pagoda, maze
Personification	Teacher/Sage (Gautama Buddha)
Runic	Daeg (Dagaz) or Man (Mannaz)
Astrological Correlates	Virgo, Capricorn
Major Arcana Key	The Magician
Archangel	Raphael (Mercury)
Stone Alchemy	Topaz, golden citrine, tigereye

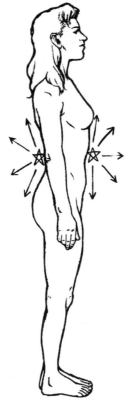

Yellow Ray Energy Centers

Harmonic

The harmonic key for Yellow Ray is the sound of short **ah** as in **father**.

Vibrational Energies

The energies of Yellow Ray are measured, ordered, and pointed in focus, moving from Mental into Physical and Spiritual. Focus on the organization of energies as they move through the Body/Mind system. Sort by type for greater observational detachment.

   For example:

That is a thought	Mental
That is a pain	Physical
That is a higher emotion	Spiritual

Harmonic Breathing Pattern

The primary breathing pattern for Yellow Ray is breathing in slowly and silently through the nose. Pause for a moment, holding the breath and focusing on stillness and order, then release slowly through the mouth with the harmonic **ah**. This brings the quiet mindfulness and focused perception of Yellow Ray.

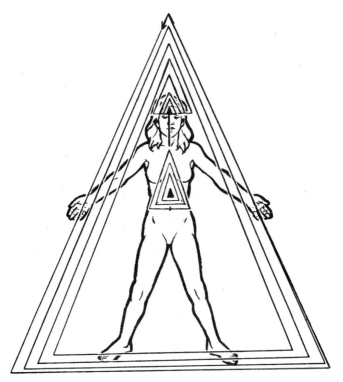

Excessive Yellow Ray Energy Pattern

Depleted Yellow Ray Energy Pattern

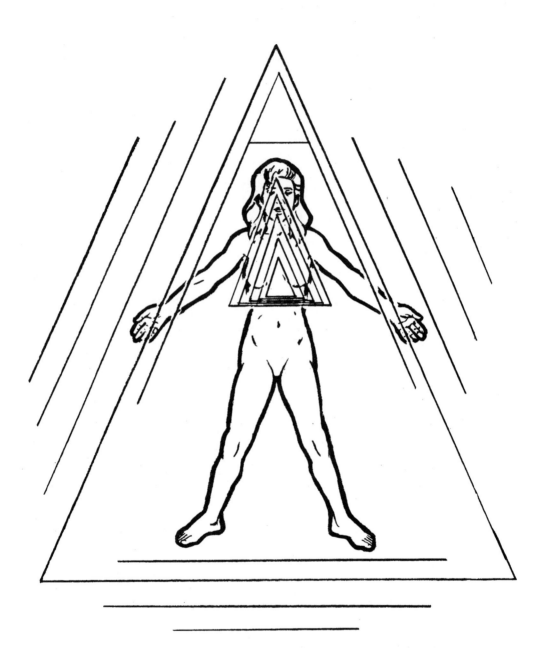

Harmonious Yellow Ray Energy Pattern

Suggested Harmonic Exercises, Chants, and Word Mantras

Using the word "Atman," which means the highest Source, focus on measuring your breath and chanting in ordered precision. This is excellent for Eastern void meditations and shamanic journey work.

For example:	inhale	**at**	(like **aht**)
	exhale	**man**	(like **mon**)

Use the word "all" for both Yellow and Turquoise Ray to energize dedicated focus and ordered service. A blend of **ah** for Yellow Ray and **o** for Blue Ray can create a serene state of conscious awareness. Combine and express with the words "ah so" for the best effect.

For example:	inhale	**ah**	(Yellow Ray order)
	exhale	**so**	(Blue Ray devotion)

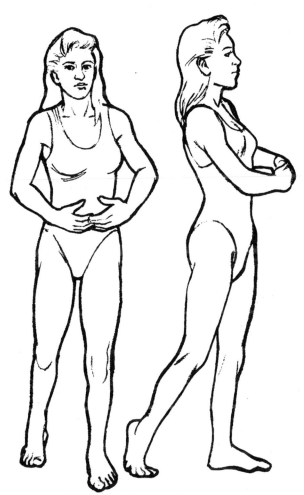

Yellow Ray Harmonic Posture

Additional Harmonic Mantras for Yellow Ray

Eureka	Use for stimulating brain activity. Combines the **e** of Red Ray (physical) with the **ah** of Yellow Ray (mental). Additionally vitalizes like Orange Ray in its alchemical harmonic blend.
Awake	Use for healing illumination. Combines the **a** of Green Ray (healing) with the **ah** of Yellow Ray (mental awareness).
La, La, La	Used as a rhythmic chant, helps focus the ordered realignment of mental process; brings organization and clarity to the Body/Mind system.

Alchemical Properties

Yellow Ray brings linear structure and organization to chaotic energies. Yellow focuses awareness, and activates intellect and illumination in a primarily mental manner.

Powers	Direct, focused, linear organization
Activates	Active intelligence, communication, illumination, intellect, mental discrimination, organization, perception
Amplifies	Active analysis, expression, memory work, sincerity
Balances	All catalysts, creativity, detachment, enthusiasm, expansion, hope, humor, vision, wisdom, anxiety, delusion, disorganization
Releases	Agitation, arrogance, ego disorders, expectations, intolerance, obsession, self-rejections
Realigns	Contempt, criticism, judgmentalism, laziness, negativities, stubbornness

Sensory Key

The sensory key correlated with Yellow Ray is sandalwood.

Shared attributes of sandalwood and Yellow Ray:
Meditative healing
Focus
Visualization, imagery
Awareness
Clarity
The Element of Air

Sandalwood is fairly inexpensive. It is available as an incense in powdered or solid form, and as an oil. Sandalwood-scented candles and herbal blends are also available. Sandalwood sticks, beads, fans and chips can be used, particularly if the scent can be amplified with sandalwood oil.

- Burn sandalwood for any activity requiring focused concentration.
- Burn a sandalwood-scented candle. Concentrate on visualizing and imaging your goals in an ordered manner. Hold your concentration precisely. Finish by blowing out the candle and saving it for the same purpose.
- Burn sandalwood chips or powder in a hot fire to release mental stresses and constrictions. Focus on the ordered flow of Yellow Ray reorganizing your energies for mental clarity.
- Light sandalwood incense. Breathe and focus on meditative consciousness. Maintain a mindful awareness by wearing sandalwood, as an oil or as beads.
- Use sandalwood beads as prayer or wish beads to focus Yellow Ray organization and healing structure.
- Rub sandalwood oil (dilute, if need be) on your temples and third eye area. Focus on Yellow Ray energies bringing clarity and perceptive awareness to the Body/Mind system through the neural pathways of the brain.

Symbols

Obelisk represents focused, linear ordered thought and deed that directs the evolution of our Self ever higher. Reaching upward unswayed by imbalance, we touch the highest dimensions of awareness.

Pagoda represents the studied balance of line and form we use to organize our perceptions of illumination. We create the structures of our Self with the materials of Nature and the designs of Spirit.

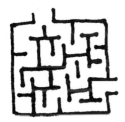

Maze represents the path, the progress and the process of our self-transformation. In traversing the twists, turns and blocks in the maze of transformation, we find the ordered perfection of our Self.

Personification

Intellect

Yellow is the energy of the Teacher/Sage. It is Gautama Buddha teaching focus, self-aware-ness and self-order. Yellow is the Buddha's energy as he told his students he was not a god, he was "just awake."

Musings

Order enters quietly,
Often unannounced;
Rarely having been invited,
Yet always welcomed.

The alchemist needs the hidden wisdom of the owl,
    The focused perception of the hawk,
        The idealism of the eagle,
            And the ego of the peacock.

Intellect is the key to the vault of wisdom that dwells inside the Mind.

Illumination brings Light to the Mind . . .
Sometimes like gentle moonbeams sparkling on a dark pool,
Sometimes like rays of sunlight streaming in through lace curtains,
Sometimes like dawn breaking through a cloudy sky,
Sometimes like a falling star,
And once in a while like a lightening strike.

Wisdom is invariably self-taught.

Runic Correlates

Daeg (Dagaz) and Man (Mannaz)

Shared aspects with Yellow Ray:
    Information   Study
    Facts   Self-knowledge

Daeg (Dagaz)

Daeg (Dagaz) illuminates the self through the focus of study and learning. Self-transformation is a course designed to result in the gain of the highest degrees of wisdom. Activate opportunities for wisdom to break through and empower your personal alchemy by using the rune Daeg (Dagaz).

Man (Mannaz)

Man (Mannaz) deepens self-information into self-knowledge through the processes of personal experience. Knowledge of the self is best gained without obstacles of self-expectations. Activate an attitude of openness and self-exploration with the rune Man (Mannaz).

Together, Daeg (Dagaz) and Man (Mannaz) create an alchemy of self-reflection with inner guidance, and bring focused support to the process of Self-transformation.

Astrological Correlates

Solar Virgo

Alchemy of Activation and Enhancement

Shared aspects with Yellow Ray:
Order	Organization
Intellect	Perception
Achievement	

(+ Gold Light = Active Organizer)

You can always be relied upon to improve on someone else's ideas since you're the perfectionist of the Zodiac . . . Lone periods of Self-analysis are essential to you if the positive qualities, which can lead to positions of responsibility and success in life, are to emerge.

—Sybil Leek

Lunar Capricorn

Alchemy of Receptivity and Reflection

Shared aspects with Yellow Ray:
Structure	Formulation, perception
Practicality	Focus

(+ Brown Light = Ordered Connector)

Some of the greatest leaders of the world have Moon in Capricorn, and owe their success to the image of success that always plays on their mind.

—Grant Lewi

Major Tarot Arcana Key

The Magician

Shared aspects with Yellow Ray:

Inventiveness	Experimental attitude
Perception	Organization
Information	Mental acuity
Innovation	

The Magician represents Man's will in union with the Divine achieving the knowledge and power to bring desired things into manifestation through conscious self-awareness.

—Eden Gray

Musings

To focus only on the wisdoms of the past or of the future is to be an archivist—or an opportunist. To blend the past and future wisdoms into the wisdom of the present is to be an alchemist.

Science is at its honorable best when it operates within the framework of Conscience. The personal alchemist is the transformer of self through experience, and thereby the transmitter of universal experience.

The five most powerful magickal gifts are Taste, Touch, Smell, Sight and Sound.

Archangel

Angelic Dimension Key

Raphael: Archangel of Mercury
      Alchemy of Inspiration, Intellect and Communication
          Days   Wednesday, Saturday
          Times   7-8 AM
                         3-4 PM
                         11-12 PM

Who shall be a light between truth and intellect?
                        —Dante

Angelic Invocation

Awaken me, oh Raphael, with messages of spirit and inspiration.

Illuminate me that I may communicate the wisdom of the ages to the willing vessel of my mind.

Alert me, oh Raphael, with timely perceptions from my senses that I may attain the focus needed for my work.

Inspire me, oh Raphael, to create a fragment of divine order within my life.

Stone Alchemy

The stones used here for Yellow Ray are topaz, golden citrine (or plain citrine) and tiger-eye. Traditionally, the placement for Yellow stones is on the spine at waist level, or right at the waist in front.

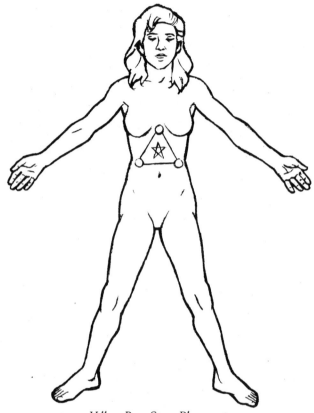

Yellow Ray Stone Placement

Topaz: Brain Stone
Element: Air

Topaz works by energizing the intellect and balancing the central nervous system. The golden-yellow topaz works on the nerve ends, and the blue topaz works more on the points of nerve origins in the brain. Both stones work well together as Yellow Ray stimulant and balancer.

Topaz stimulates focus, concentration and awareness. It is great for clarity and awakening our sensory perceptions. Topaz, particularly the warmer-colored varieties, can also combat lethargy and boredom. These are good for mental exhaustion from too much concentration.

Topaz is good for removing fears and defensive blocks we have in our lives. It removes the obstacles directly from the etheric, because these blocks are more psychological or mental in nature.

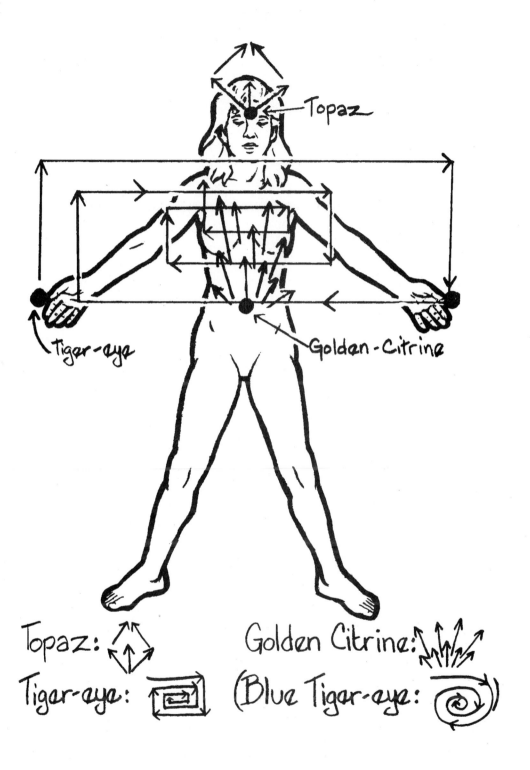

Yellow Ray Stone Energy Patterns

Alchemist's Note: Topaz is useful as a divination tool. Either use it as you would a crystal ball, or hold the topaz and let its energies clear your mind to receive. Blue topaz soothes along the neural pathways. You can also use·it in a structured way in correlation with Blue, Indigo or Violet Ray. Take the structured energy of topaz, mental and contemplative, and combine it with the spiritual Blue Ray. This clarifies higher processes within the brain. Remember, the brain is the organ of the Mind.

Blue topaz can be a good refresher. The blue seems to unblock obstacles to communication, opening the abilities of expression and calming the nerves at the same time. With an overuse of Yellow Ray mental activity energies, a little blue topaz balances and refocuses for expression. Blue topaz also represents the moon, as it has more receptivity than the yellow topaz. Yellow and blue topaz can be useful as Sun and Moon keys in combination.

Citrine: Organization Stone
Element: Air (with some Spirit)

The next Yellow Ray stone is the citrine, particularly the golden-yellow type. Some citrine is actually amethyst which has naturally evolved into golden citrine. Other citrine has been created artificially with heat. The created citrine retains strong energies, while natural citrine feels deeper and older in its energy.

Citrine can be very inexpensive to moderately priced, depending on the size and crystal structure. Citrine is a high-vibration crystal, and activates as a good overall system energizer and reorganizer.

Citrine has a good effect with issues of self-confidence or positive self-image. Citrine works etherically by removing psychological doubts and fears. With citrine, the healing work is done more in the ethers, and less in the physical. Of course, etheric affects the physical and vice versa. Mind and Body . . . Body and Mind . . . it is all the same, ultimately.

Citrine also works psychologically on emotional blocks by counteracting depression. Pooled or depressed energies can be counteracted with citrine and Yellow Ray. This combination works by stimulating focus and concentration on positive images.

Alchemist's Note: Try using a golden citrine in the left hand and a dark smoky quartz in the right at times to pull in the energy (citrine) and then to release (smoky quartz). This combination makes a wonderful energy cycle. .

Tigereye: Practical Stone
Element: Earth

The next stone for Yellow Ray is the tigereye. Tigereye can be used for Gold Light as well, with a denser effect. However, it fits well under Yellow because of its organized effect on Body, Mind and Spirit energies.

Tigereye is inexpensive and easily obtained. It has an earthy vibration of stability, organization and the strength of self-connectedness; not just a mental self-connectedness, but holistic well-being arising from feeling centered and grounded.

Tigereye combined with Gold Light and Yellow Ray can energize and activate physical healing in a practical fashion. This is especially important when the body is recovering from illness, surgery or physical trauma. Combined with positive energy, this activates self-healing, shifting the mindset away from illness toward healing. Tigereye is especially good as it does not tear the fragile, newly healing energies. Tigereye helps the physical body transform from sickness to health, from the tissue levels on.

A blue tigereye that has an additional, almost Indigo Ray effect is commonly called hawk's eye. It is good for serious focus and concentration. (The hawk, shamanically as "hawk medicine," has to do with focus and concentration.) Blue tigereye can be used with Yellow Ray or Gold Light, as well as with Indigo and Blue Ray.

Hawk's eye is a good all-purpose stone. The blue of it changes the vibration somewhat; instead of just focus and concentration, hawk's eye helps with the process of active imagery and creative visualization—the imagery processes by which we structure and synthesize our lives. This is more Indigo Ray in its energy and intent. Alternate Yellow and Indigo with tigereye or hawk's eye to help imagery and visualization.

Alchemist's Note: Tigereye can also be good for balancing sensory impulses. If you have too much going on and you need to get focused, tigereye is wonderful for that. Try using it to connect to physical, earth energies when you've been working with mental energies. It is good to balance spiritual work, too. For example, if you feel as though you are not connected to the earth, but want to retain mental concentration, use tigereye for that. It helps you stay attached and not detached from what you are doing.

Alternative Stone

A Yellow Ray alternative to consider adding to your collection is a yellow fluorite crystal. It is an organized mental, focus and meditative stone.

Chapter Fourteen

Golden-Green Ray: Renewal

Though leaves are many, the root is one.
—William Butler Yeats

Golden-Green Ray is primarily Green with some Yellow and a bit of Orange. Golden-Green represents rejuvenation, transformation, rebirth and metamorphosis; a growing, changing, releasing and renewing energy. Golden-Green Ray is the energy of natural healing and transformation.

The trick with Golden-Green is to focus on each breath as symbolic of the cycles of renewal. Each inhalation begins the cycle, bringing rejuvenation. Each exhalation is a release, bringing transformation.

Elemental Alchemy	Earth and Spirit
Key Issues	Knowledge, moderation, right action, oneness
Stone Alchemy	Peridot, serpentine, jade
Cumulative Alchemy	Metamorphic renewal

Golden-Green Ray Keys

Harmonic	Sound of i as in sit
Alchemical Properties	Renewal, transformation, rebirth
Sensory Key	Mixed herbal or minty
Symbols	Flower bud, spoked wheel, tiny green sprout
Personification	Transcendental naturalist (Thoreau or Emerson)
Runic	Ger (Jera)
Astrological Correlates	Gemini, Sagittarius
Major Arcana Key	Transformation (Death)
Archangel	Azrael (Pluto)
Stone Alchemy	Peridot, serpentine, jade

Golden-Green Ray Energy Centers

Harmonic

The harmonic key for Golden-Green Ray is the sound of short **i** as in **sit**.

Vibrational Energies

The energies of Golden-Green Ray are expansive, active, cycling and recycling through-out the Body, Mind and Spirit. Focus on the anabolic and catabolic systems of rejuvenation and renewal activating the physical cycles from the etheric realms.

Harmonic Breathing Pattern

The primary breathing pattern for Golden-Green Ray is measured, either in and out of the mouth or the nose. This emphasizes the balanced cycles of birth, transformation, rebirth and renewal.

| For example: | inhale (mouth) | chant harmonic of **i** as in **it** |
| | exhale (mouth) | chant harmonic of **i** as in **bit** |

Mouth breathing generally provides a more physical effect.

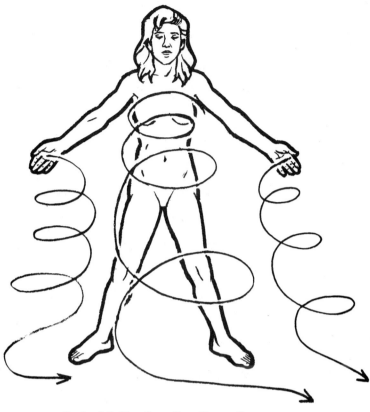

Depleted Golden-Green Ray Energy Pattern

Also: inhale (nose)   silent pause
                 exhale (nose)   silent pause

Follow with the harmonic **i** as an activator to connect with etheric realms.

Suggested Harmonic Exercises, Chants, and Word Mantras

For connecting to Spirit through the etheric realms, chant combinations of:

Gift   **Live**   **Spirit**   **Give**

For example: **Spirit gives the gifts**
                          The gift of Spirit lives

Also, make a simple mantra using harmonic breathing with the word "Spirit."

For example: inhale (mouth)   Spi . . . (short **i**)
                          exhale (mouth)   . . . rit

or chant the word "Spirit" and breathe naturally.

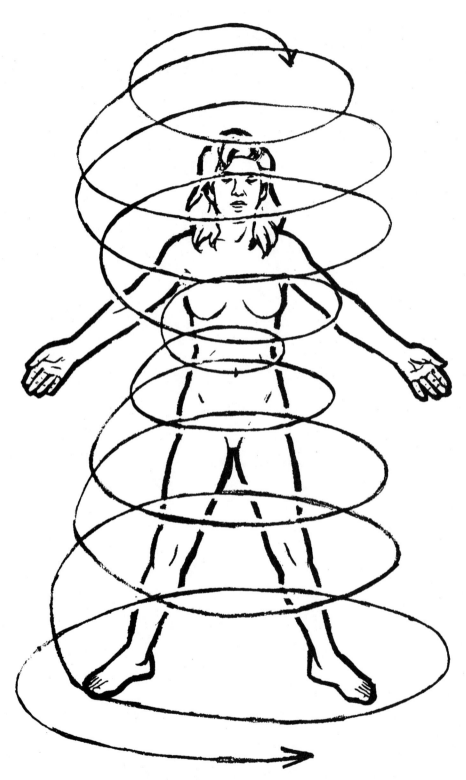

Harmonious Golden-Green Ray Energy Pattern

Additional Harmonic Mantras for Yellow Ray

Mists and Bliss	(For Spiritual, etheric work)
If, If, If	(For renewing possibilities)
Metamorphosis	(For activating the strongest energies of Golden-Green recycling)

For example:	inhale	Metamorpho . . .
	exhale	. . . sis

Stress the harmonic short **i** in "sis."

Invigorate   (For blending Green Ray long **a** healing expansion with Golden-Green Ray short **i** renewal)

For example:	inhale (mouth)	In vi go . . .
	exhale (mouth)	. . . rate

Additionally, the harmonic long **o** of Blue Ray brings an expressive energy element to catalyst the combination; invigorating the alchemy, we might say.

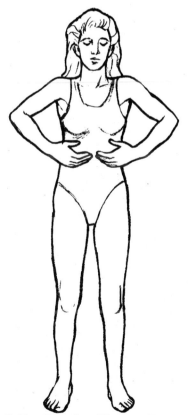

Golden-Green Ray Harmonic Posture

Alchemical Properties

Golden-Green Ray is a catalyst for renewal and transformation for all dimensions. Golden-Green attunes to the cycles of Nature in a holistic Mind, Body and Spirit manner.

Powers	Indirect, etherically focused, expansive, clearing action
Activates	Cleansings, memory work, regeneration, rejuvenation, release
Amplifies	Idealism
Balances	Implementation, vitality, conceit
Releases	Negativities, pessimism, regrets, revenge, fear, inferiority, self-righteousness
Realigns	Bitterness, confusion, delusion, deviousness, procrastination, yearning, psychic vampirism

Sensory Key

The sensory key correlated with Golden-Green Ray is a minty, herbal blend.

> Shared attributes of mint and Golden-Green Ray:
> Natural medicinal properties
> Rapid cycles of growth
> Purification, renewal, rejuvenation
> Healing transformation
> Activation

Herbal blends of mint are inexpensive and available in many forms. Most mint is sold as an herb, either fresh, dried, or packaged as a tea. Mint-scented incenses and candles are easy to obtain, as is oil of mint.

- Burn mint leaves to activate rapid cycles of growth and material prosperity.
- Burn mint-scented candles or incense to create a fresh atmosphere. Use it to signal times for renewal and recycling of stale energies.
- Plant a variety of mints—spearmint, peppermint, orange mint. Let your nurturing of this garden of mint reflect your active nurturing of your Self.
- Drink mint tea for an overall medicinal tonic effect in the Body/Mind system. This is particularly effective for healing digestive disorders, and can also be used with Orange Ray for this purpose.
- Crush mint leaves and rub on your hands, or use mint oil instead. Focus on the active rejuvenation energies of Golden-Green Ray flowing through your hands to specific points on the physical body.
- Use a mint-scented massage oil on the body to create a tingling effect. Focus on Golden-Green flowing through the physical and etheric realms.
- Chew fresh mint leaves to refresh the Body/Mind system.

Symbols

Flower bud represents the renewal cycles of Nature. The tender bud of the future pushes forth from within the growth of the past, signaling the metamorphosis of the eternal present.

Spoked wheel represents the turning wheel of life cycles supported by the strength of Spirit. Each turn of our self-transformation is accomplished by the internal strength and structured perfection of Truth.

Tiny sprout represents the balance of determination and fragility in personal transformation. Fed by the regenerating energies of Earth and Sun, we break through the limitations of expectation to the Light.

Personification

Renewal

Golden-Green is the energy of the Transcendental/Naturalist. It is Thoreau seeking the rejuvenation of Nature at Walden Pond. It is the joy of his heartfelt connection to Nature, as in his words, "Methinks my own soul must be a bright invisible green."

Musings

Metamorphosis is painlessly accomplished by butterflies, but not so by humankind.

	Meta	Morphe	Osis

Meta	Beyond, over, transcending, altered
Morphé	Form or shape
Osis	The condition, process, or state

Self-acceptance is the catalyst of self-rejuvenation.
No form of purification quite satisfies the purist.
Purification is most effective when combined with forgiveness of faith.
Self-transformation has its own schedule.
　　Rebirth, Renewal and Right Action
　　　　Form the healing triune
　　　　　　The holy trinity of Healing.

Runic Correlate

Ger (Jera)

Shared aspects with Golden-Green Ray:
　　Harvest　　　　Completion
　　Cycles　　　　Transformation

Ger (Jera)

Ger (Jera) renews the Self with natural cycles of endings and beginnings. No personal alchemy can be stagnant or inert so long as the Self continues to flow with the essential energies of change. Activate cycles of renewal and remove resistance to change with the rune Ger (Jera). The alchemy of Ger (Jera) is activated in the celebrations of Self and the harvests, the cycles, and the seasons of universal alchemy.

Astrological Correlates

Solar Gemini

Alchemy of Activation and Enhancement

　　Shared aspects with Golden-Green Ray:
　　　　Transformation　　　　Unity
　　　　Metamorphosis　　　　Balance
　　　　(+ White Light = Renewal Medium)

Geminis minimize or maximize any life situation based on the interests of the moment.

　　　　　　　　　　　　　　　　—Betty Lundsted

Lunar Sagittarius

Alchemy of Receptivity and Reflection

Shared aspects with Golden-Green Ray:
Activation   Renewal cycles
Communication   Self-healing
(+ Gold Light = Renewal Activator)

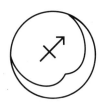

When you have learned the techniques of life-as-it-is, you will be able to make your image of yourself stand forth in the light and color of success for all to see as clearly as you see it yourself.

—Grant Lewi

Major Tarot Arcana Key

Death

Shared aspects with Golden-Green Ray:
Transformation   Renewal
Metamorphosis   Rebirth
Karmic patterns

She is the power of Death in Life and Life in Death, creatrix and destroyer of relative form . . . the terrible understanding that all existence, from wheeling stars to the merest atom, is subject to change and death.

—R. J. Stewart

Musings

A tiny blade of grass growing in the cracks of a concrete street contains more power than all the armaments built by humankind.

Nature is inexorable,
Transformation is inescapable,
Evolution is inestimable,
Death is invaluable.

Karmic patterns are patterns of personal choice for which we are to assume responsibility to fully understand the power of Choice itself.

Archangel

Angelic Dimension Key

Azrael: Archangel of Pluto
Alchemy of Metamorphosis, Transformation and Renewal
    Days   Thursday, Saturday
    Times   (None traditional)

(Alternate compatible times correlated with **Cassiel**)
    Day   Saturday
    Times   3-4 AM
                    11-12 AM
                    7-8 PM

P

Even a thought, even a possibility, can shatter us and transform us.
—Nietzsche

Angelic Invocation

I call on you, Azrael, to keep my faith strongest during the metamorphosis of my self.

Send your promises of renewal springing forth from cocoons of constraint that I may remember the promise of regeneration and rebirth.

Teach me, oh Azrael, to find a new beginning in every ending, and new life in the face of death.

Stone Alchemy

Alchemist's Note: Golden-Green is difficult to define by color as it is intensely involved with individual metamorphosis. Golden-Green includes "colors" such as tropical green, spring green, and pale sea-green. Golden-Green changes constantly. This is appropriate, since it is the Ray of renewal. Again, you are going to want to experiment with some of these newer blended Rays; they are more etheric and experimental. We are learning together; each person we work with is different. Even when we work specifically with ourselves, we find we are different from day to day, as well. Be flexible.

The stones for Golden-Green Ray are peridot, serpentine and jade. Placement for Golden-Green stones is about midpoint of the body, at the bottom of the rib cage in the front, or just above the waist on the spine.

Peridot: Antibiotic Stone
Element: Air

Peridot can be very expensive as a cut, faceted gemstone. These types have an extremely high vibration, but the rough or tumbled peridot also has a strong vibration.

Interestingly, peridot has a tranquilizing effect on the emotions while stimulating the mental; this makes it particularly good when working with psychological issues. Peridot makes our functions more conducive to clear thinking. When working with peridot, let go of the emotions gently, think clearly, and focus inward.

Physically, peridot is a cleansing stone that works directly on the body from the etheric. Peridot also stimulates proper heart rate while it works. This can be maximized when balanced with a red jasper to ground some of the more intense energies.

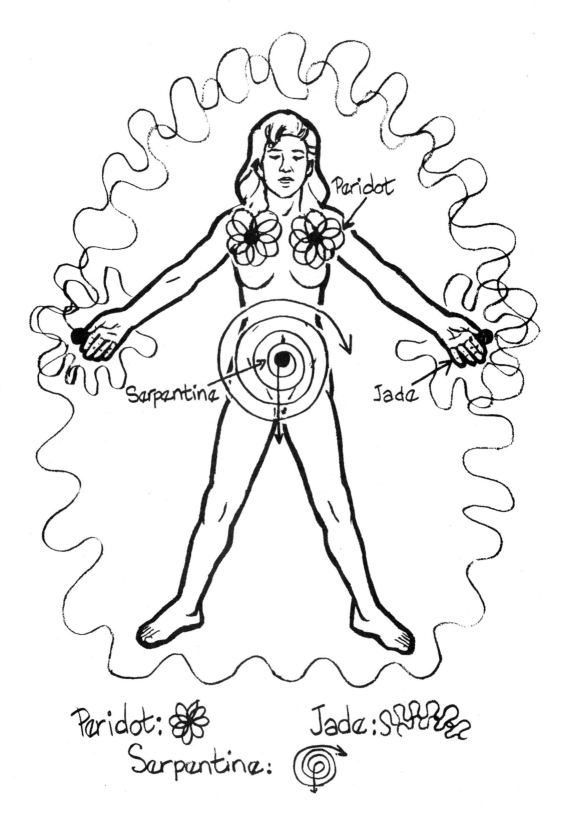

Golden-Green Ray Stone Energy Patterns

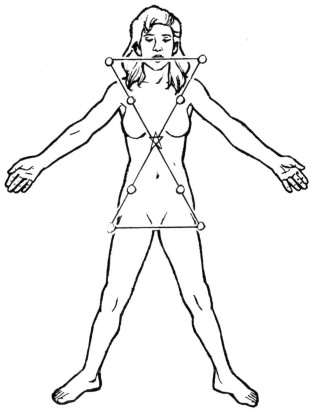

Golden-Green Ray Stone Placement

Peridot is an antibiotic stone that cleanses the Mind, Body and Spirit system from the physical to etheric and back again. It relates directly to the interstitial fluids of our bodies, keeping those essential "waters of life" clear and in balance.

Peridot helps with the function of the liver by assisting in the removal of toxins. It also cleanses the upper digestive tract and helps clear viruses and bacterial infections. Peridot is good for ulcers, too, as it stimulates clear thinking, removes the mental stress that can cause ulcers, and soothes with Golden-Green renewal energies, all at the same time.

Peridot is a good overall stone and can be placed anywhere. Use peridot with Yellow Ray to revitalize or refresh all aspects, and with Green Ray to help organize overly expansive energies to focus healing.

Peridot can be used for soothing over-stressed mental capacities without interfering with the thought processes. Peridot is a tranquilizer that affects the body but not the mind, allowing for calm, focused healing energies to flow.

Alchemist's Note: To me, a cut peridot can be too intense. If you have intense Green or Golden-Green energy, this seems strange because Green is supposed to be soothing, not intense. Work with cut peridot carefully. Try to balance it with amethyst or an indigo stone, preferably a denser amethyst, and work with the energies together.

Jade: Contemplative Stone
Element: Earth (with some Spirit and Air)

Jade ranges from moderately inexpensive to slightly expensive in price. Jade has a deep, earthy vibration that is excellent for the contemplative processes. It is good for strengthening the nervous system, which we tend to overload at times. Jade comes in many different colors, most of them with a rather mental effect. The yellow-green and the darker green jades have an effect much like Golden-Green Ray. It is rejuvenating, and it helps with release and renewal in the environmental, atmospheric energies.

Jade does not work directly on the body, but is more of an environment stone which works by sending out vibrations. It does not hurt to wear it or put it on the body, however, because jade helps bring awareness and focus to the renewal energies it exudes.

Jade is not a receptive stone; it just does not absorb. What jade does, though, is activate and radiate a steady, gentle energy. As it radiates harmonious energy into the environment, it works subtly from the etheric.

Jade is oriental and meditative in that respect. It works gently but persistently. There are not going to be dramatic results with jade, but a steady constant effect instead.

Alchemist's Note: Jade works well with Yellow Ray to organize and renew thoughts. If you have a piece of jade, breathe in and absorb. The jade does not absorb—you do. Darker green jades generally have the same qualities as lighter ones. With dark green, the emphasis is on physical healing. Yellow-green, lighter jades have a more mental effect. The darker green jades are often used in the environment for abundance, inner strength and good luck. The dark jade infuses the energy field in a more physical way, whereas the yellow or yellow-green jade comes in more through imagery. It is a subtle difference, but it is there.

Serpentine: Centering Stone
Element: Earth

Serpentine is relatively inexpensive and can work a lot like jade. If jade is expensive or hard to get, serpentine can do about the same job. However, serpentine does more than just radiate etherically. It can affect the physical directly and be used effectively for overall healing and rejuvenation. It is an excellent stone for grounding and focus.

Serpentine has long been considered protective. Often fetishes and figurines (little totem animals) are carved out of serpentine, because the stone's vibration enhances the ability of the spirit animal or the fetish to protect the person.

Alternative Stone

An alternative stone for Golden-Green Ray work is green quartz. It has a wonderful, luminous quality about it and a reputation as the friendliest of all the Green healer stones. It is an excellent stone to have.

Another alternative is the kyanite. Use kyanite to receive renewed energies, then release impurities into smoky or black tourmalinated quartz.

Chapter Fifteen

Green Ray: Expansion

Conquer with Love.
—Twylah Nitsch

To be alone is life.
To think alone is death.
—Stardragon

To fear love is to fear life—and to fear life is to be three parts dead.
—Bertrand Russell

Green Ray correlates with the fourth chakra, or the heart energy point. Green is the blending point between the lower (active) chakras and the upper (receptive) chakras. The attributes of Green Ray involve health, expansion, abundance and harmony. Green Ray reflects restorative, healing, growing energy. It is different from Golden-Green in that Golden-Green Ray is new growth, while Green Ray is continuing growth, ever green and eternal.

Green Ray radiates outward from us when we connect through our heart-felt attunements. Green connects through the heart to Body, Mind and Spirit. Green is a powerful healing Ray; if you choose to work with just one ray, Green Ray is the one to choose. Green is all-purpose, and affects all the aspects harmoniously, with ever-expanding energy; it is Mother Nature energy. The trick with Green Ray is to match its expansive energies before focusing it on one area specifically.

Elemental Alchemy	Water and Earth
Key Issues	Intuition, healing, knowledge, moderation
Stone Alchemy	Emerald, malachite, aventurine
Cumulative Alchemy	Healing Expansion

Green Ray Keys

Harmonic	Sound of **a** as in **say**
Alchemical Properties	Healing, expansion of heart and mind
Sensory Key	Bayberry
Symbols	Heart, evergreen tree, money sign
Personification	Creator/Nurturer (Mother Nature)
Runic	Feoh (Fehu)
Astrological Correlates	Taurus, Cancer
Major Arcana Key	The Empress
Archangel	Sachiel (Jupiter)
Stone Alchemy	Emerald, malachite, aventurine

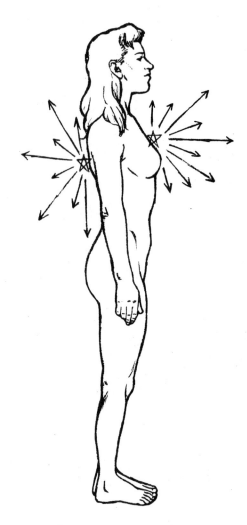

Green Ray Energy Centers

Blocked Green Ray Energy Pattern

Over-Extended Green Ray Energy Pattern (Martyr Pattern)

Harmonious Green Ray Energy Pattern

Harmonic

The harmonic key for Green Ray is the sound of long **a** as in **say**.

Vibrational Energies

The energies of Green Ray are expanding, circling, spiraling flows of healing, love, heart-felt connections, and abundance. Focus on the center of the heart area and experience the physical, mental and spiritual emotions which arise as the Green Ray energies move throughout your entire being.

Harmonic Breathing Pattern

The primary breathing pattern for Green Ray is deep breaths inhaled through the nose silently until the chest area is expanded fully. This is followed by a direct, steady release of breath, exhaled from the mouth with the strong sound of the harmonic (long) **a**. Finish by pulling in the tummy to expel any remaining breath. Make this breathing pattern deep and dramatic for expansion.

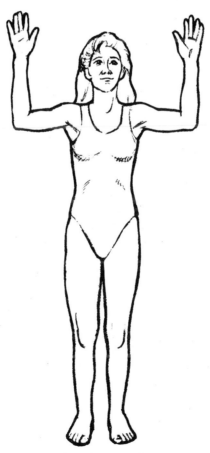

Green Ray Harmonic Posture

Suggested Harmonic Exercises, Chants, and Word Mantras

Use the deep breathing method described for Green Ray combined with appropriate chants.
For example:
>   Pain away
>   Healing stay

This combines the (short) **a** of Peach for etheric communication and also the (long) **e** of Red for physical connection. Emphasize the (long) **a** of Green Ray for active healing. Other chants may be devised to best utilize the expansive energies of Green Ray.

For example:

Heart awake	or:	Love's mistake
Sorrow break		Bindings break
Goodness make		Sadness slake
Evil take		Gladness stake

Also:

Chances take	or:	Activate
Monies make		Fortune's gate
Fortune's stake		Lady Fate
Fears break		Communicate

Additional Harmonic Mantras for Green Ray

>   Communicate   Activate

Combine with specifics to expand the energies.

For example:
>   Healing, Healing, Activate

combines (long) **e** of Red, physical, with the (long) **a** of Green, expansive healing.

Or:
>   Love, Love, Communicate

phonetically-harmonically translates as **Lahve, Lahve, Cahmunicate.**

This combines the precision of the Yellow Ray harmonic **ah** with the Green Ray (long) **a**. Additionally, this brings in the Violet Ray harmonic of (short) **u** or (long) **u** as in **oo**. Violet Ray represents the higher spiritual aspects.

Finally:
>   **I claim the flame of Love**

Repeat as a chant for personal and universal energies of love.

Alchemical Properties

Green Ray catalysts positive expansion for all healing issues of transformation. Green activates healing by connecting the heart and mind in a primarily physical, emotional manner.

Powers	Direct, focused, expansive, spiraling action
Activates	Energy flow, enthusiasm, expansion, hope, prosperity, sharing, responsiveness
Amplifies	Active intelligence, courage, dedication, independence
Balances	Androgynous balance, communication, compassion, expression, gratitude, integrity, love, peace, regeneration, relationships, tenderness, remorse, understanding, desolation, isolation, obsession, possessiveness, rejection
Releases	Authoritarianism, cruelty, destructiveness, dissatisfaction, hate, judgmentalism, perfectionism, psychic vampirism, totalitarianism
Realigns	Greed, jealousy, pessimism, resistance

Sensory Key

The sensory key correlated with Green Ray is bayberry.

Shared attributes of bayberry and Green Ray:
Prosperity
Luck
Abundance
Growth
The element of Earth

Bayberry is inexpensive and easily obtained in a variety of forms. Bayberry is most often found as an incense, oil, or scent for candles and herbal blends. Fresh or dried bayberry is found less often. However, the deep connection of bayberry to the energies of sharing and abundance, as well as its solid association with the color of deep, rich green, ensure its effectiveness for Green Ray work.

- Rub bayberry oil on a dollar bill (or a larger denomination). Focus Green Ray energies of abundance and prosperity surrounding the money. Expand the Green Ray energies to include your Self, your home, your circle of friends, and your community. Focus on the balanced distribution of abundance for the good of all. Then either burn the money to activate fast luck, or bury the money in the Earth to activate a slower, steadier growth of abundance.
- Mix a few drops of bayberry in a massage oil. As you rub this oil into the body, focus the Green Ray energies of healing expanding outward from the heart area. Focus on the abundant growth of a healthy Body/Mind system. This is particularly helpful in changing the energies from sickness to health.

- Smudge the environment with bayberry incense, or burn bayberry-scented candles to create an atmosphere of harmony and well-being.
- Collect small cuttings of evergreen (i.e., cedar, juniper, pine). Scent with bayberry oil. Charge with Green Ray energies. Place in a small pouch, then carry or wear over the heart area for ongoing harmony and healing.

Symbols

Heart represents the connection of love which brings harmony in our life and temperance to our alchemy. From the Source of all Being to the center of our Self reaches the healing heart strings of universal love.

Evergreen tree represents the eternal presence of growth, expansion and abundance. In the cold indifference of winter, the evergreen tree continues to grow, nourished by the love of Nature.

Money sign represents the prosperity, abundance and business which flourishes with the guidance of heart and mind. Our prosperity expands in exponential proportion to what we lovingly share, and in limited relationship to what we keep.

Personification

Expansion

Green is the energy of the Creator/Nurturer. It is Mother Nature providing all the resources necessary for life. Green is the expansive energy of abundance, and the healing energy of heartfelt sharing.

Musings

Expansion without harmony is chaos.
Expansion with harmony is order.

Abundance is self-perpetuating when it is activated as well as it is accepted.

To speak of love with a sleeping heart is to dream.
To speak of love with an awakened heart is to touch the divine.

The communication of love can never be a part-time job.

> *More kindness will do nothing less*
> *Than save every sleeping one*
> *And night walking one of us.*
> *My life belongs to the world.*
> *I will do what I can.*
>
> —James Dickey

Runic Correlate

Feoh (Fehu)

Shared aspects with Green Ray:

Growth	Abundance
Prosperity	The element of Earth

Feoh (Fehu)

Feoh (Fehu) bestows abundance and growth to the endeavors of the personal alchemist. Success and failure are both products of the process of self-development, since the energies are equally abundant, regardless of how they are utilized. Activate positive growth with positive intentions and the rune Feoh (Fehu). The alchemy of Feoh (Fehu) has no limitations or deprivations, other than those you impose on your Self.

Astrological Correlates

Solar Taurus

Alchemy of Activation and Enhancement

Shared aspects with Green Ray:

Heart-centered	Harmony
Communication	Self-healing
Expansion	

(+ Brown Light = Grounded Healer)

Once you know a person, no one will be a more faithful friend, especially in times of need . . . You'll be faithful to your friends, but always with the proviso that they return the same amount of fidelity. Your practical nature exerts itself even in romantic affairs.

—Sybil Leek

Lunar Cancer

Alchemy of Receptivity and Reflection

Shared aspects with Green Ray:
Relationships	Loyalty
Familial love	Self-healing
Nurturance	

(+ Black Light = Healing Seeker)

You exclude a desire to be understood, to be loved—also, to understand, and to love, if you have objectified your approach, which you must do if you are to be happy or successful.

—Grant Lewi

Major Tarot Arcana Key

The Empress

Shared aspects with Green Ray:
Abundance	Growth
Expansion	Healing
Nurturance	Love
Harmony	

Experience the throb of Divinity in every growing thing. Learn to listen to the constant cry of mankind reaching out to touch it's destiny . . . True love is being in perfect harmony with the Universal heartbeat.

—Eileen Connolly

Musings

In You, there are no limitations—only Expansion.
In You, there are no separations—only Harmony.
In You, there are no rejections—only Nurturance.

The Empress

3 3

©R. Good 1989

In You, there are no deprivations—only Abundance.
In You, there are no stagnations—only Growth.
In You, there are no afflictions—only Healing.
In You, there are no manifestations which are not born of Love.

Archangel

Angelic Dimension Key

Sachiel: Archangel of Jupiter
      Alchemy of Expansion, Success, and Prosperity
         Days   Thursday, Sunday
         Times   12-1 AM
                  8-9 AM
                  4-5 PM

24

Life shrinks or expands in proportion to one's courage.

—Anais Nin

Angelic Invocation

Sachiel, light of abundance, shine your brightest wisdom through my folly, and teach me the powers of success.

Sachiel, light of abundance, send your strength into my life and expand my horizons to meet my needs.

Sachiel, light of abundance, let the powers of success enter purely through my heart that I may not fall prey to greed.

Stone Alchemy

The stones for Green Ray are emerald, malachite and aventurine. The green stones have often been called the "healer" stones. Traditionally, the placement for Green Ray stones has been right over the heart in the front or in the back. Green stones can be put safely anywhere, regardless of how intense a vibration they carry, because Green Ray is such an all-purpose healing Ray.

Alchemist's Note: You can also use rose-pink stones in the heart chakra area with the Green Ray. These balance and harmonize with each other very well. Also, if you are working with the heart areas and you want to have a softer effect at first, start with rose quartz and Rose Ray. Bring Green Ray in with the rose later. Sometimes the expansive energy of green almost sweeps us off our feet when we first connect with it. Rose Ray or rose quartz is a more gentle introduction.

Emerald: Healer Stone
Element: Air and Earth (some with Spirit)

Emerald can be expensive if it is a faceted, cut gemstone. The raw or tumbled form also carries a high vibration and can be obtained for amazingly small prices at times. Even a very tiny emerald, or a rather opaque one, has a good overall effect which connects well to the Green Ray energy. As with all gemstones, the more opaque the stone, the more physical the effect; the clearer the stone, the more Spirit-related the effect.

Emeralds are used for direct, focused healing. Their energy is an overall healer for the vital organ functions. Simply carrying a small piece of emerald can help overall balance. Emeralds keep all the systems on GO, so to speak.

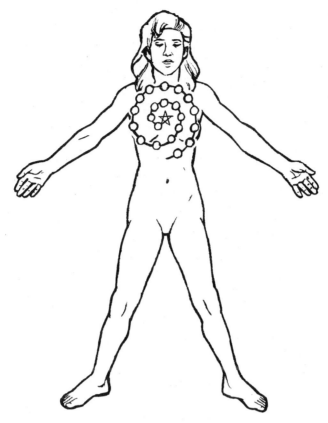

Green Ray Stone Placment

Emerald is good for balancing the heart rate in a quiet and not too intense manner. Emerald soothes energies of nervous tension and realigns the vibration of physical and etheric bodies. Again, the more crystalline or clear the emerald, the more it will help with the etheric. The more dense or opaque the emerald, the more it will help with the physical. This is a subtle difference, but an alchemical one.

Emerald is also excellent for tired eyes or tired mental capacities because it is very soothing. Place an emerald in a glass of water and focus on or gaze through its beautiful color. Bring Green Ray energy in through the heart and spread throughout the body.

The energy of Green Ray and emerald brings abundance and well-being . . . Physical, Mental and Spiritual. Some people like to put an emerald in a glass of pure water, let it sit through the day, remove the stone, and then drink. That can be done for several days, each time consciously bringing in Green Ray abundance and healing.

Alchemist's Note: If you have a very clear emerald, let the sun shine through it. Sunlight clears Green Ray and focuses it purely. Then you can focus it on your self, your plants, your environment, your planet. Emeralds are just wonderful to have around. Do not let the fact that they can be high-priced gemstones scare you off.

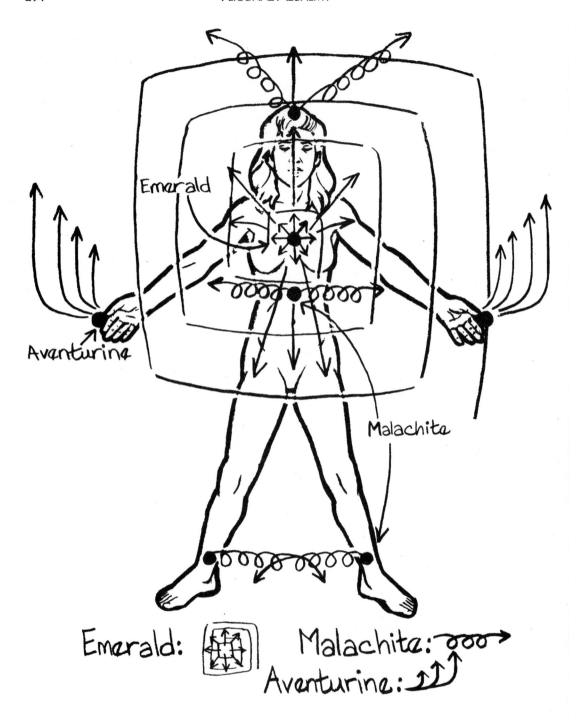

Green Ray Stone Energy Patterns

If you wish to have the high vibration of a clear emerald, like a gemstone—but you don't want to deal with the price—look for a dioptase crystal. Dioptase crystals are a wonderful kind of "bottle green" and carry a similar vibration to emerald. These are usually small, but their energy reflects all the best aspects of Green Ray. Dioptase has an element of Earth, because it relates to copper. Dioptase also has Air and Spirit, because of its crystalline structures.

Malachite: Strength Stone
Element: Earth

Malachite can be relatively inexpensive to moderately expensive, if it is cut and set in jewelry. The slightly polished pieces are quite good. Raw malachite has an earthy vibration which directly brings the healing Green Ray energy into the physical.

All malachite has a strong and steady vibration. Whether polished or rough, it is superb over all. Malachite can be put all over the body for general well-being. It is a lot like peridot or the golden purifying stones, such as amber and citrine. This is because malachite cleanses and balances for the good of all.

Malachite takes a little longer to work because of its slightly denser vibration. Malachite reflects the energies of strength, particularly in times of transition.

Traditionally, malachite has been used for eye disorders. It can also be used to soothe not just the physical eyes, but the psycho-physical, third eye area (even though that is traditionally a brow chakra energy). Malachite on the brow chakra helps restore balance and healing synthesis throughout the entire being.

Malachite can have a slightly negative effect for some, due to its basic transformative nature. Malachite will definitely make a difference and effect a change. Oftentimes it seems malachite is ahead in vibrating to the forthcoming changes. If there is a negative reaction or resistance to malachite, look at the possibility that the resistance is actually to change. To be more receptive to change in your life, use Silver Light and/or the metal silver with malachite. When change is impending, activate by using malachite with Gold Light or the metal gold.

Alchemist's Note: Malachite works by directly affecting the physical. Again, it takes a little longer, because it has a slow but steady vibration. You can put malachite right on the points you want balanced. Malachite has wonderful black veins, lines and swirls in it. The black in malachite can absorb, and the green can heal. In and of itself, malachite can be an all-purpose stone for deep physical renewal and healing. If you have just a little bit of emerald or one small dioptase crystal in combination with malachite, the effect is solid. Pull in the highest aspects of Green Ray, then let the malachite "earth it," or bring it into the Physical. Malachite works effectively with crystal or supported with some of the bluer stones for a more spiritual effect.

Aventurine: Good Luck Stone
Element: Earth

Aventurine is an inexpensive stone with an earthy vibration, stabilizing to the heart area. It brings emotional balance and tranquility, much as jade does, by emanating energy which radiates outward.

Aventurine works slowly but very steadily. It is nice to carry or use as a touchstone. Aventurine affects the personal environment, the physical environment, and the expanding environment around us all.

Traditionally, aventurine is reputed to be good for luck. Aventurine vibrates well with the money energy aspects of Green Ray. It is used along with Green Ray energy for manifesting prosperity.

Alternative Stone

An alternative stone to use for Green Ray is the moss agate, sometimes called the tree agate. Moss agate vibrates with energies like a dense emerald. This is particularly so with the deep, rich green moss agates. These are healing and quite energizing.

Chrysophase is also an excellent Green, as well as Golden-Green Ray stone. Chrysophase vibrates in a manner similar to a rough or tumbled peridot, and is a stone of rejuvenation.

Part Four

SPIRITUAL ENERGIES OF SERVICE AND DEVOTION

Turquoise   **Blue**

Indigo   **Violet**

Something that appeared not-self has become self.
Something that was thought to be other—has become
intimate; something which seemed to be out there
has become in here.

—Ken Wilber

Rain Flowers: Expansion and Empowerment

Take a long, slow, deep breath. Let your breath flow through you, gently sweeping away all the tensions in your body. As you become more aware of your breathing, take time to notice the natural pauses between breaths. Stretch out these pauses.

Breathe in . . . pause . . . hold in . . .

Breathe out . . . pause . . . release.

Slowly allow the pauses to become longer . . . notice the rhythm of your breathing begin to slow and steady. Feel yourself deepen and relax. Take one more long deep breath, and stretch your body like a cat. Hold it for a moment . . . feel the pause . . . now gently release your breath and relax your muscles.

Allow your self to step into a healing image.

You are sitting inside a massive rock formation of three great stones leaning together to form a sanctuary from a rainstorm. Feel the deep vibration of these stones as you sit surrounded and protected by their presence. This is an ancient place . . . the stones are covered with carvings and symbols, magickal and mysterious. Take a moment to look around your image. Do you notice any new symbols on the stones?

Breathe deeply. Make your image real. Feel the rainstorm all around you . . . feel your self snug and secure. As you sit in this stone sanctuary you hold a beautiful bouquet of rain flowers . . . each blossom representing an aspect of your self.

Take a moment to enjoy the bouquet . . . catch the fragrance of the blossoms as they perfume the air around you. Feel the cool, velvet softness of the petals. Absorb the vibrancy of their colors. Enjoy all the aspects of your self represented in this bouquet of flowers.

Breathe deeply and absorb all that you need from this bouquet of flowers, for the time has come to release them to their highest good . . . to expand all your aspects to their greatest healing capacities.

Just as all things change . . . all things flow and move . . . so you too can begin to trust the creator of flow and change within your self. Trust the creator of your own life streams.

Outside the stone sanctuary the rain falls steadily, causing great rivulets of water to run across the ground . . . moving and changing the landscape slowly as the water makes its way back to its source . . . the sea.

Breathe deeply, and pick the blossoms from your bouquet one at a time, and reach through the opening and place each one face up to the sky . . . notice how beautiful the colors shine and glisten with raindrops.

Slowly, the rainwater begins to lift each blossom . . . the lighter, smaller blossoms first, then the sturdier flowers. The rainwater sweeps them gently away, until only one remains to be released from your bouquet.

Which blossom is the last to be released for you? What aspect does that blossom represent? Take a moment to consider its meaning for you.

Know that by releasing these blossoms you are releasing aspects of your self and allowing them to move and change naturally. You are detaching your self from these things which are merely reflections of your deepest self . . . your truest being . . . your highest spirit.

You are like the rainwater which carries these blossoms . . . the aspects of your self which you create are blossoms floating in your life stream. You are the water . . . flowing, swirling, raging, nourishing . . . changing the landscape around you.

Breathe deeply, and place the last blossom on the ground. As this blossom is lifted by the rainwater streaming along the ground, feel your self become the water. Feel your self as constant movement . . . flowing energy . . . liquid ever-moving to a deeper source. Feel your self moving swiftly over the earth, around rocks and stones. Feel the roots of trees and plants reach out to you for nurturance.

You are a crystal stream purified by your own path . . . clarified by flowing around and over all obstacles. Feel your self deepen and expand as you join with other streams. These, too, are parts of your self.

Dance and sway in your course as you move in tune with the land around you. Feel the certainty, the insistence of your path as you move steadily toward your deepest source . . . your self. Feel your pace quicken as you reach the edge of the land.

Breathe deeply, and let your self cascade down into a beautiful waterfall . . . feel your self splashing into the pool below. Take a few moments to experience the gentle swirling of the pool below the waterfall. Notice the freshness and newness of this pool . . . constantly renewing and changing, cycling.

Breathe deeply, and begin to feel a slower, steadier rhythm as you are pulled gently onward . . . feel its gentle insistence . . . its patient persistence . . . as it moves away from the pool . . . away from the rapid pace of the waterfall.

Pace your self more slowly and widen . . . become a great, slow-moving river . . . inexorable, constant, peaceful . . . steadily rolling towards the sea to the source . . . feel your self bend and curve as you move on in the course of your own choosing to the source of your self. Feel your self expand and change as you fan out into a delta.

Feel the rhythm of the river replaced by the ebb and flow of the shallow tidal pools . . . experience the quietness of the shallows. Blend gently with the seawater as it kisses the mouth of the river. Feel your vibration change as you become part of the sea . . . let your natural tides carry you out with your natural rhythm. Do you sweep out dramatically, pulling waves from the shoreline? Or do you creep out slowly, barely aware of the change within you?

Breathe deeply, and consider that this too is a reflection of your self. For water, whether tiny streams or great tidal surges, represents your emotions . . . your personal tides of life. Take time to consider the pace of your own ebb and flow . . . your own life stream.

Know that just as water takes the strength of a cascading waterfall as well as the patience of a tidal pool to reach the sea . . . so too does the flow of your emotions help you reach the source of your self.

Even as storms may rage around you, the flow of your life stream continues courageously towards the source of your highest self . . . the deep source of being.

Breathe deeply, and feel your self expand into a great ocean . . . vast, powerful, deep . . . feel your self as the depths of Mother Ocean . . . only your surface is skimmed by even the greatest storms. Beneath your surface the certainty, the strength of impenetrable depths known only to your deepest self . . . feel the power of that deep ocean strength within you . . . this is your source of Being.

Feel your self as waves sweeping back and forth . . . ebb and flow reflecting your life rhythms. Feel your self as tiny waves lapping gently at the shoreline. Feel your self as great breakers crashing onto rocky beaches. Feel your self as deep ocean waves, miles high, with only the peaks and troughs showing in the surface.

Know that the relationship of sea to land is but another reflection of your self to your emotions. As the shape of your life changes . . . so too does the shape of your personal landscape. Let your emotions be in balance with your life . . . know that you may choose these for your self.

You may be gentle waves caressing gentle shorelines. You may be great crashing waves rushing to meet the rocky places in your life. You may wish to let only tiny ripples in the surface reflect your deeper undercurrents, just as the tiniest raindrops becomes a part of Mother Ocean.

So too are you and all your emotions a part of your self. Let each emotion be respected for the part it plays in the wholeness of your being. For you are a part of all things . . . and all things are a part of you. Flow together . . . peacefully. Breathe deeply, and honor the wisdom your emotions bring you. Let them flow more freely in your life as the waters flow to Mother Ocean.

Trust that you will flow in balance . . . trust the strength of your emotion to carry you onward in the path of self, as you trust the rivers to flow to the sea. It is this flow which gives the gift of power to your highest self. Receive . . . return . . . flow.

Breathe deeply, and let your image change . . . let the waters fade away. Find your self walking once again along a rocky seacoast. The storms have passed and you are renewed by the cleansing of the land around you. As you glance toward the sea, your eyes catch bright flashes of color on the water.

Looking closer, you see lovely flowers floating gently on the waves . . . a beautiful collection of blossoms tenderly rocked and caressed by Mother Ocean.

Breathe deeply, and feel attuned with your self as a beautiful reflection of nature . . . know that you may return to experience this flow whenever you choose.

Begin to let your image fade away . . . return to the present time renewed, attuned.

Chapter Sixteen

Turquoise Ray: Dedication

Never mellow.
—Linda Ellerbee

The real political, revolutionary act
is to enable someone to see something
he has not been able to see before.
—Marilyn Ferguson

Turquoise Ray is primarily Blue with some Green and a little bit of Yellow in it. Turquoise Ray energies reflect the energies of dedication. This not quite like the Blue Ray energy of devotion, as Turquoise Ray is more active and more oriented to self-determination, or to service through the use of self-determination. It involves dedication to the higher aspects of the Self; the cause of higher Self. Turquoise Ray reflects unity, zeal, and the sharing of Earth, Sky and Spirit energies. Turquoise is a cosmic Ray, yet it has an earthy intent that gives purpose to our spiritual journey.

The trick with Turquoise Ray is to enhance positive self-image and develop self-confidence in one's potential abilities to serve a higher cause—the Universal Self.

Elemental Alchemy	Water and Fire
Key Issues	Intuition, healing, sensation, regeneration
Stone Alchemy	Aquamarine, turquoise, chrysocolla
Cumulative Alchemy	Active Dedication

Turquoise Ray Keys

Harmonic	Sound of aw as in draw
Alchemical Properties	Activates dedication, spiritual service
Sensory Key	Bay laurel
Symbols	Shield (badge), staff, sword
Personification	Revolutionary Humanist (Thomas Jefferson)
Runic	Eoh (Eihwaz)
Astrological Correlates	Aquarius, Aries
Major Arcana Key	The Hanged Man
Archangel	Sachiel (Jupiter), Asariel (Neptune)
Stone Alchemy	Aquamarine, turquoise, chrysocolla

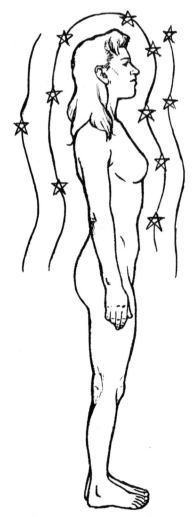

Turquoise Ray Energy Centers

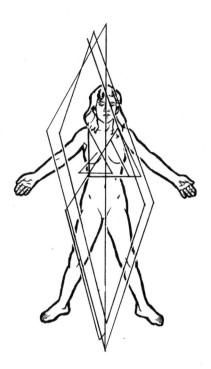

Blocked Turquoise Ray Energy Pattern

Expansive Truquoise Ray Energy Pattern (Spiritual Service Pattern)

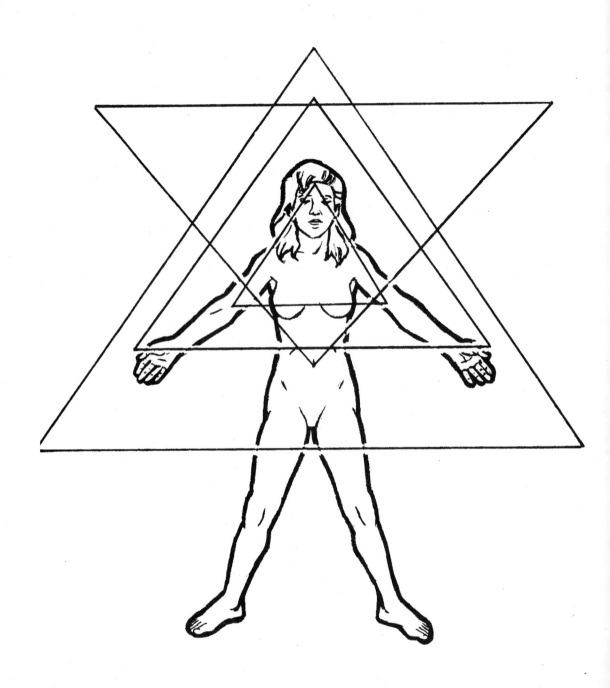

Harmonious Turquoise Ray Energy Pattern

Harmonic

The harmonic key for Turquoise Ray is the sound of long **aw** as in **draw**.

Vibrational Energies

The energies of Turquoise Ray are etheric, quick-paced, zealous and enthusiastic. Focus on the experience of connecting the Self to the service of highest cause.

Harmonic Breathing Pattern

The primary breathing pattern for Turquoise Ray is to inhale slowly through the nose and exhale immediately from the mouth. Pause for a moment, then follow with the harmonic **ah**. Focus on creating an activated enthusiasm and an expression of dedication and attunement.

Suggested Harmonic Exercises, Chants, and Word Mantras

Using the breathing pattern described above, change the harmonic **aw** to the word mantra "Awe." Express with devotion. The word "awesome" is also quite effective if you can relate it to the highest service and resist the comparison to surf lingo. If it helps, visualize higher service or dedication to the highest causes as being much like riding an awesome wave.

Turquoise Ray Harmonic Posture

Combine with the Scarlet Ray harmonic of long i and/or the Rose Ray harmonic of long y for greater etheric balance and communication.

For example, chant:
>   High Law
>   My Law
>   Thy Law
>   High Law

Add: **One Law of Love**

This brings in the Violet Ray harmonic of short u for greater spirituality.

Additional Harmonic Mantras for Turquoise Ray

Combine:
>   **Ought**   **bought**   **caught**   **sought**

For example: **What I sought**
                    Cannot be bought

Or: **I'll not be caught**
                    In shoulds or oughts

Alchemical Properties

Turquoise Ray activates self-purpose, resolve and dedication in service to highest spiritual energies. Turquoise catalysts zealous participation in a primarily emotional, mental, etheric and spiritual manner.

Powers	Indirect, etherically focused, linear, enthusiastic action
Activates	Dedication, determination, integrity, service, zeal
Amplifies	Openness, sharing, vitality, will-power
Balances	Inspiration, mental discrimination, prosperity, self-respect, strength, temperance, cowardice, criticism, depression, deviousness, dissatisfaction, ego disorders, ignorance, indifference, laziness, negativities, procrastination, regrets, separateness, totalitarianism
Releases	Bitterness, extremes
Realigns	Authoritarianism, desolation, expectations, martyrdom, power-seeking

Sensory Key

The sensory key correlated with Turquoise Ray is bay laurel.

Shared attributes of bay laurel and Turquoise Ray:
Courage
Purification
Dedication
Strength
The element of Fire

Bay laurel is relatively inexpensive, particularly when purchased as a loose herb in health food stores. Fresh bay laurel is also available.

- Create a wreath (from fresh bay laurel, if possible) or from dried bay laurel leaves. Display in your environment to symbolize the circular path of dedication and harmonious service to a higher cause.
- Burn bay laurel in a hot fire to activate the zealous energies of Turquoise Ray.
- Burn bay laurel leaves in a slow fire or on charcoal for a more ceremonial approach to self-determination and dedication. Focus on the spiritual enthusiasm of Turquoise Ray energies flowing into your entire being.
- Smudge your home with bay laurel for cleansing and purification of the environment. Finish by ceremonially smudging your self.
- Carry bay laurel leaves in a pouch made of turquoise fabric for continuous focus on all aspects of higher service.
- Carry bay laurel leaves near your heart to activate courage and strength in your life.
- Make small bundles of bay laurel and tie with turquoise thread. Share with others to honor their acts of dedication, strength or courage.
- Make a tea from bay laurel leaves. Strain and store in an airtight jar. Use a few drops of the bay laurel liquid in clear water for ceremonies of purification.
- Scatter bay laurel to the four winds to symbolize dedication to, and gratitude for, the higher energies of Spirit in your life. Call forth personal deities.

Symbols

Shield (or badge) represents openly declared dedication to the service of highest cause. The shields of service gleam only when polished from the inside, and tarnish quickly when the external and artificial is applied.

Staff represents the enthusiastic connection of Earth and Spirit supporting the journey of self-transformation. We take our personal measure to determine the universal measure of our worth to the service of Truth.

Sword represents the power of our ideals as expressed by our dedicated service to the highest causes of transformation. That which is used in the service of Truth is a weapon to some and a magickal tool to others.

Personification

Active Dedication

Turquoise is the energy of the Revolutionary Humanist; it is Thomas Jefferson writing the Declaration of Independence. Turquoise is the energy of Jefferson's zealous dedication to the higher service of human rights in his words, "We hold these Truths to be Self-evident . . . that all mankind is created equal."

Musings

Mellow in your manner if you must, but never mellow inside your mind.

Fight for freedom fearlessly; without force, but with faith.

Spiritual service does not require Self-deprivation, but demands Self-determination.

A revolution of self-enlightenment hastens the evolution of truth.

> *You're only as old as the last time you changed your mind.*
> —Timothy Leary

Runic Correlate

Eoh (Ehwaz)

Shared aspects with Turquoise Ray:
    Service   Preparation
    Readiness   Growth
    The element of Fire

Eoh (Ehwaz)

Eoh (Ehwaz) empowers the alchemy of self-transformation with highest energies of idealism. The power for your personal alchemy is abundant and freely accessible for the service of Self-evolution. Activate highest dimensions of service with dedication to truth using the rune Eoh (Ehwaz). The alchemy of Eoh (Ehwaz) is a formula which can never be patented nor hidden from service for the good of all.

Astrological Correlates

Solar Aquarius

Alchemy of Activation and Enhancement

    Shared aspects with Turquoise Ray
        Service   Self-determinism
        Asceticism   Idealism
        Universal devotion
        (+ Gold Light = Dedicated Activator)

Aquarians seek to improve the lives of their fellow men, and their power comes through the intellect . . . they are detached, impersonal and believe in justice for all. Because of their detachment, they may have difficulty forming close personal relationships and should recognize that they were born to function impersonally.

—Ursula Lewis

Lunar Aries

Alchemy of Receptivity and Reflection

Shared aspects with Turquoise Ray:

Enthusiasm	Activator
Transmitter	Self-determinism
Manifestor	

(+ White Light = Zealous Transmitter)

Your message to yourself is: Be strong, be forceful, be independent, be brave . . . This is one of the positions in which the Moon can be strong enough to take the dominance of the nature away from the Sun and cause you to actually become in the outer world what you imagine yourself to be.

—Grant Lewi

Major Tarot Arcana Key

The Hanged Man

Shared aspects with Turquoise Ray:

Individuality	Spiritual service
Uniqueness	Choice
Flexibility	Acceptance
Wisdom	

He is reversed as an image in a pool is reversed but, though inverted, he sees the same as others, only from another vantage.

—F. D. Graves

Musings

The freer the choice, the greater the levels of responsibility. Acceptance of responsibility to self is the first step on the path of true Spiritual Service.

Universality is best understood through the exploration of individuality. What you experience as upright and straight is sure to be perceived by someone else as upside down and crooked.

Archangel

Angelic Dimension Key

Sachiel: Archangel of Jupiter
Asariel: Archangel of Neptune
    Alchemy of Success, Vision, and Spiritual Evolution
    Sachiel
        Days   Thursday, Saturday
        Times   12-1 AM
                        8-9 AM
                        4-5 PM
    Asariel
        Days   Monday, Saturday
        Times   (None traditional)

4   *And for the support of this declaration with a firm reliance on divine providence, we mutually pledge to each other our lives, our fortunes, and our sacred honor.*

—Thomas Jefferson

Additional compatible times correlate with:

Auriel
Day	Monday
Times	2-3 AM
	10-11 AM
	6-7 PM

Gabriel
Day	Monday
Times	5-6 AM
	1-2 PM
	9-10 PM

Angelic Invocation

Sachiel of good fortune, and Asariel of clear vision, I call on your combined powers to grace my life work with the honor of Spiritual service.

Sachiel of expansion in Truth, and Asariel of evolution in Spirit, strengthen the transformation of my self with the opportunity to serve the forces of highest truth with dedication and resolution.

Stone Alchemy

The stones we will use to reflect Turquoise Ray are the aquamarine, the turquoise itself, and the chrysocolla. Placement is flexible as Turquoise is a blended Blue and Green Ray. Start by trying it just above or below the heart, either in front or back. It is also effective if you place Turquoise Ray stones on the solar plexus or the sacral chakra to soothe and balance Orange and Yellow energy.

Aquamarine: Purity Stone
Element: Air (with some Spirit)

Aquamarine can be expensive if you want a gemstone-quality faceted cut, but the tumbled pieces are quite effective. Sometimes you can find a nice little crystal which works beautifully. Gemstone aquamarine is high in vibration and intense in effect. It brings clarity of vision to our spiritual, creative and artistic natures. Aquamarine cleanses etherically, which then reflects onto the physical.

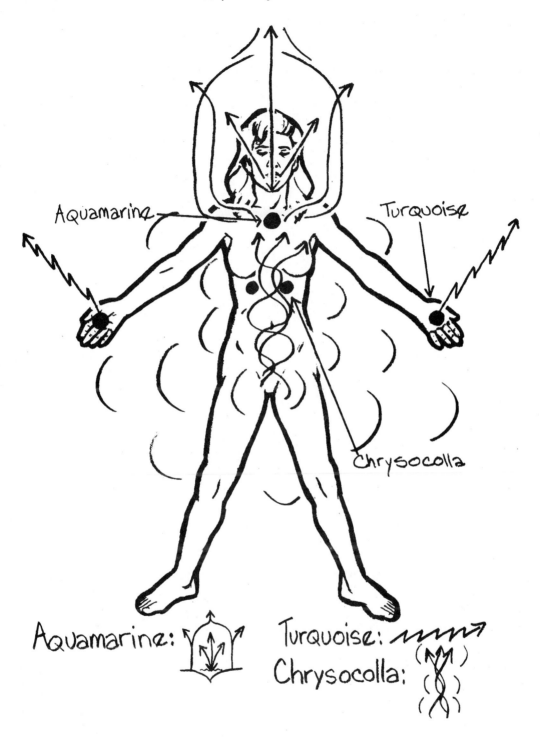

Aquamarine

Turquoise

Chrysocolla

Aquamarine: Turquoise: Chrysocolla:

Turquoise Ray Stone Energy Patterns

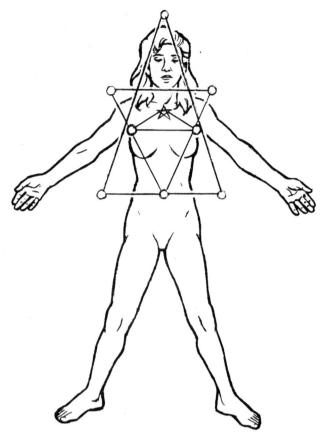

Turqoise Ray Stone Placement

Aquamarine does not deal directly with the earth or with the physical body; you will have to bring the energies down. Aquamarine with Turquoise Ray etherically clears expressive blocks in Mind, Body and Spirit.

Alchemist's Note: Aquamarine is best used on the spiritual, higher chakras, up with the Sky Lights and the more spiritual, devotional rays. If you put aquamarine with the lower chakras, it may not be effective. However, you can focus etheric healing through the stone onto the lower chakras, if you want.

Aquamarine has a natural, spiritual purity that can heal us and balance our energies. I think of my aquamarine gemstone as a nun who lives a sequestered life. She has a great spiritual connection, but I have to get what she says and bring it home with me.

Turquoise: Sacred Earth Stone
Element: Earth

Turquoise can be moderately expensive to very expensive, depending on how large, how polished, or how fine a piece you require. Turquoise has an extremely powerful earth vibration, steady and slow, so you may be fooled at first and think it does not have any intensity. Indeed, it does; it just shows a bit differently. Turquoise is sacred to many cultures because it represents the Sky, the Sea and the Universe.

Turquoise has a hot and cool alchemical combination; a receptivity and activity together in balance. This makes turquoise useful for balancing physical as well as etheric or psychic polarities. Turquoise works by steadying the vibrations within and around you, then by realigning the energy gently but effectively. Turquoise may well be the greatest overall healing stone.

Alchemist's Note: Turquoise is attuned to the Earth and to the Sky, which makes it very shamanic. It has certainly been the choice of aboriginal cultures for a long time. For maximum potency, combine turquoise with red coral to create the shamanic living tree connector energies.

When you are deciding on your turquoise, there are different shades of color and inclusions to consider. For instance, if a turquoise has a little more green in it, then it is going to have a more earthy vibration. The bluer turquoises relate more to Air and Spirit. With silver veins or metallic inclusions, turquoise tends to be a little more receptive. If turquoise has a lot of black lines in the matrix, then it is more protective.

If you use a turquoise with Silver Light it can increase your receptivity, attuning you to the Earth and Sky energies at the same time. This is important if you are doing any sort of shamanic journeying.

Chrysocolla: Resolution Stone
Element: Earth (with some Air)

Chrysocolla can be relatively inexpensive. It doesn't take a large piece for it to work, because it has the high vibration of crystal along with the earthy vibration of stone. Chrysocolla can balance like turquoise, but the crystal in it makes it a bit more spiritual. If you use chrysocolla with Crystal Light energy, you are going to find it is a good overall refresher and enhancer.

Chrysocolla falls between the aquamarine and the turquoise in the way it operates. It works etherically to calm and give courage, then needs to be brought into the physical. Chrysocolla is also inspirational to look at. It is very soothing with its blues, greens, turquoises, crystals and whites.

Alternative Stone

Another alternative stone you might want to add to your collection is the amazonite. It is a blue-green stone which works a bit like a subtle turquoise.

Chapter Seventeen

Blue Ray: Expression

Personal will brings you to a place where you can empty . . .
so spiritual energies can move through you—not of you.

—Oh Shinnah Fastwolf

Blue Ray is aligned with the fifth energy point (the throat chakra) and promotes spiritual uplifting. Notice that as you move into the Greens and the Blues things become more interchangeable. Energies are not as specific as they are lower down in the root chakra, sacral, or solar areas. When you get into Blue, energy begins to move upward quickly. Energy starts in Red, and moves through Orange and Yellow. When it gets to Green, it expands, circles around the heart, and then moves up through Blue. Once it has touched the Blue, it starts moving really fast. Be clear.

Blue Ray helps you express your entire being. It is an inspirational Ray; the Ray of devotion—not just devotion in the sense of martyrdom, but devotion to an ideal or a way of being. Blue is idealism and the expression of personal will in concert with universal will.

Blue has a lot to do with self-expression on all levels and attuning that expression with Mind, Body and Spirit. Blue Ray can be exhilarating and crystalline when it comes through purely. When you have no blocks in the lower chakras and reach Blue Ray, you can have a sense of exhilaration expressing heart-felt devotion and moving into the Spiritual upper-energy areas. Enjoy it. The traditional chakra placement for Blue Ray is either between the shoulder blades on the spine, or in the hollow where the collar bones meet in front.

The trick with Blue Ray is to express its energies by communicating your sensations, thoughts, and emotions. If it is difficult to express these in words at first, try using sounds to communicate.

Elemental Alchemy	Water and Spirit
Key Issues	Intuition, healing, right action, oneness
Stone Alchemy	Celestite, sodalite, blue lace agate
Cumulative Alchemy	Expressed Devotion

Blue Ray Keys

Harmonic	Sound of **o** as in **boat**
Alchemical Properties	Devotion, expression of will
Sensory Key	Thyme (tranquility)
Symbols	Musical note, grail, wave
Personification	Spiritual Poet/Bard (Krishnamurti or Talesin)
Runic	Wyn (Wunjo)
Astrological Correlates	Cancer, Scorpio
Major Arcana Key	The Chariot
Archangel	Asariel (Neptune)
Stone Alchemy	Celestite, sodalite, blue lace agate

Harmonic

The harmonic key for Blue Ray is the sound of long **o** as in **boat**.

Vibrational Energies

The energies of Blue Ray are spiritual and expressive, yet ordered, reflecting devotion and will. Focus on the experience of Blue Ray energies as expressed in the Body, Mind and Spirit realms of your being. Feel the holistic combination of Blue Ray energies connecting all aspects from physical into etheric.

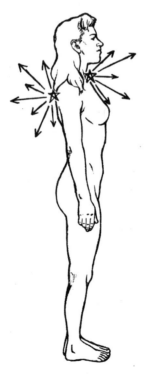

Blue Ray Energy Centers

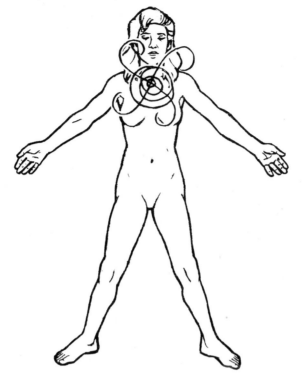

Blocked Blue Ray Energy Pattern

Excessive Blue Ray Energy Pattern

Harmonious Blue Ray Energy Pattern

Harmonic Breathing Pattern

The primary breathing pattern for Blue Ray is silent, devoted breathing in and out of the nose. Pause for a moment, then speak the harmonic o from deep in the throat. Make the harmonic an expression of Self, a statement of personal will.

Suggested Harmonic Exercises, Chants, and Word Mantras

Breathe quietly through the nose for a few moments, omitting the harmonic (long) o. When you feel centered, softly chant appropriate word mantras. Focus on expressing your devotion to the will of your highest self and spirit helpers.

For example: **The angels spoke**
                      My will to evoke

Or: **Angels invoke**
                      Thy will I spoke

Or: **Spirits' stroke**
                      Devotion evoke

A simple mantra which is effective for Blue Ray is the word "Hope." This reflects the expression of personal as well as universal alchemy.

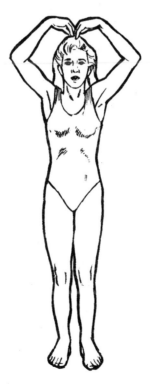

Blue Ray Harmonic Posture

Additional Harmonic Mantras for Blue Ray

Open, How	(Use for activating flow of spiritual energies)
Throat	(Use for healing and expression of will)
Devotion	(Use for connecting physical (harmonic **e**) with Spiritual (harmonic **o**); stress the harmonic (long) **o** for activation)

Alchemical Properties

Blue Ray catalysts the energies of self-will and spiritual devotion. Blue expresses the centered connection of Body, Mind and Spirit in a primarily emotional/spiritual manner.

Powers	Direct, focused, uplifting, expressive action
Activates	Compassion, detachment, expression, mercy, sensitivity, sincerity, trust, understanding, wisdom
Amplifies	Creativity, justice, loyalty, psychic abilities, responsibility, security
Balances	Action analysis, confidence, determination, humility, illumination, openness, organization, rejuvenation, insecurity, intolerance, perfectionism, resistance
Releases	Anger, cowardice, ignorance, irritability, lack of self-respect, rebellion, vanity
Realigns	Anxiety, depression, indifference, possessiveness, separateness, self-rejection

Sensory Key

The sensory key correlated with Blue Ray is thyme.

Shared attributes of thyme and Blue Ray:
Psychism
Etheric flow
Clarity
Inspiration
The element of Water

Thyme is inexpensive and readily available. Thyme is most often sold as an herb or spice, either fresh or dried. Thyme plants may also be found at nurseries carrying herbal selections.

- Burn thyme in a shallow dish. Fan the flame to create an abundance of smoke. Focus on the patterns created as the smoke rises. Express thoughts, images, emotions and physical sensations as they rise into awareness, regardless of how seemingly unrelated they might be. When the smoke ceases, make notes about your experience. (It is helpful to have taped your comments, if need be.) Review the material for significant emotional statements or psychic revelations. After you have done this several times, you may find that merely the scent of thyme will activate expression of your deepest thoughts, feelings and wisdoms.

- Burning thyme is effective for clearing the environment of static or obstacles which block the natural flow of etheric energies.

- Burn thyme to activate Blue Ray energies of inspiration. Try not speaking or making notes. Instead, use a blue marker to express your ideas on paper in swirling lines. This activates the free flow of expressive energies and opens the self to recurring inspiration. Thyme is excellent for "courting the Muse" and stimulating the ability to activate inspiration.

Symbols

Music notes represent the harmonic expression of devotion in our lives. The music of devotion played on the instrument of free will drowns the dissonant sounds of forced will.

Grail represents the sacred source of healing wisdom. Drink from the celestial contents of the grail to speak with the voice and the will of the Great Mother Goddess.

Wave represents the tidal ebb and flow of transformative energies. To wait in faith at ebb tide is to be carried gently inward by the first waves of Truth and transformation as they flow into your life.

Personification

Devotion

Blue is the energy of the Spiritual Poet/Bard. It is Krishnamurti expressing devotion to the unstructured perfection of the universe, and to the power of "freedom from the known."

Blue is Talesin crossing the seas to Ireland, bringing the old wisdoms of the Celts. It is the expression of the ancient wisdoms in Talesin's poetry, stories and songs. It is the gift of the Bard heard down through the ages.

Musings

There's simply no sense in trying to be something that you're not. Accept who you truly are—then be that, in Truth. Express your self, inside out. Free will is an active alchemy, endlessly brewing.

Runic Correlate

Wyn (Wunjo)

Shared aspects with Blue Ray:
>   Self-will   Achievement
>   Spiritual gain   The element of Spirit

Wyn (Wunjo)

Wyn (Wunjo) brings spiritual, joyful tones to the music of Self-expression. Self-transformation is a solitary achievement borne of Spirit and will in perfect harmony. Activate Self-expression and self-determination with gladness and the rune Wyn (Wunjo). The alchemy of Wyn (Wunjo) is catalyzed by joy.

Astrological Correlates

Solar Cancer

Alchemy of Activation and Enhancement

>   Shared aspects with Blue Ray:
>   Devotion   Intuition
>   Self-expression   Spiritual nurturance
>   Will
>   (+ Silver Light = Devoted Receptor)

Cancerians respond better to feelings than to words. If you want them to respond to you or to a situation, ask them how they feel about it rather than what they think.

—Betty Lundsted

Lunar Scorpio

Alchemy of Receptivity and Reflection

>Shared aspects with Blue Ray:
>   Karmic patterns   Experiential learning
>   Personal expression   Spiritual devotion
>   Privacy
>   (+ Black Light = Devotion Seeker)

Moon in Scorpio people carry many scars on their psyche. They are very clever at hiding their true feelings, but it is necessary for them to develop optimistic points of view.

—Sybil Leek

Major Tarot Arcana Key

The Chariot

Shared aspects with Blue Ray:
>   Expression   Will
>   Spirituality   Idealism
>   Communication   Devotion

The Chariot is a major symbol of divine power in motion; it is a vessel, vehicle or enabling form carrying the force of spiritual or essential being.

—R. J. Stewart

Musings

In most of humankind there still exists a battle of wills, the will expressed by the nature it believes it should have.

The Spiritual path requires that its followers be devoted to idealism, but not indentured to it.

Communication with Divine Will is best accomplished by the active expression of Self-will in accordance with the Light.

The Charioteer accepts either/or as a duality which creates the whole through the interactive dynamics of the spiritual forces.

Archangel

Angelic Dimension Key

Asariel: Archangel of Neptune
    Alchemy of Spiritual Expression, Conscientiousness and Vision
        Days   Monday, Saturday
        Times   (No traditional times)

Additional compatible times correlate with **Auriel:**

Day   Monday
Times   2-3 AM
                10-11 AM
                6-7 PM

In a word, to let the spiritual, unbidden and unconscious, grow up through the common. This is to be my symphony.

—Wm. Henry Channing

Angelic Invocation

Asariel of the mystic realms, I long to explore the dimensions of spiritual wisdoms and express my devotion to the sacred flow of Universal knowing.

Asariel of the manifest realms, I long to experience my will and thy will as one will in the highest form.

Teach me your powers of perfect expression that I may summon the strength of Spirit.

Stone Alchemy

Alchemist's Note: If you put Blue stones on the root chakra, you may not get the full effect of the stone itself or of the energies it represents. Still, it can serve to balance Red Ray energy. Blue stones are effective as balancers either on the Orange Ray second chakra area or on the Yellow Ray area up a little higher. Experiment with this. If you want to work with Blue Ray purely, try its traditional placement until you get a feel for it.

Celestite: Intellectual Stone
Element: Air and Spirit

Celestite is a crystalline structure usually sold in the form of geodes or small pieces of a geode. It can be expensive if you get the kind which comes from Madagascar. Some comes from Mexico and is moderate in price. Mexican celestite is more gray, but has a similar vibration and works beautifully.

A large amount of celestite is not required because it is a high vibration stone. It works with Blue Ray as well as Indigo Ray; you can interchange these clearly. Celestite seems to have a mental effect—at least it appears that way at first, because it tends to work a lot through imagery. Yet what is actually happening is that it is working through the etheric and physical body simultaneously and reflecting in the mind as imagery. Celestite is a very alchemical stone; experiment with it.

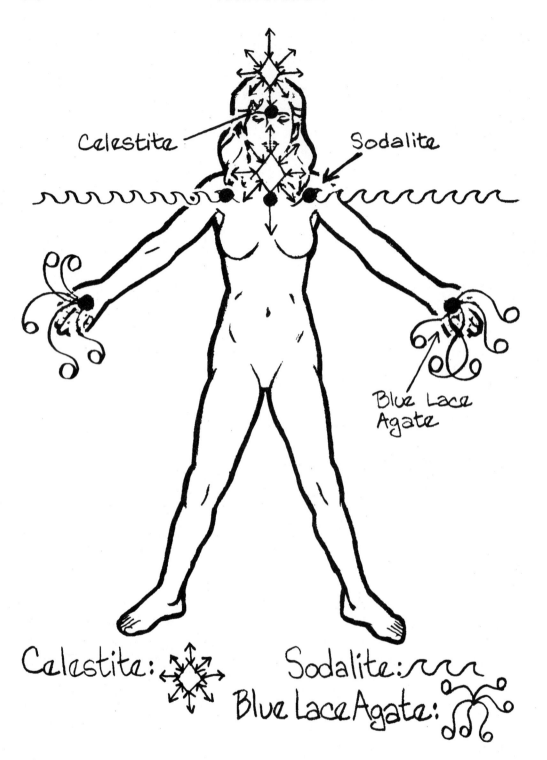

Blue Ray Stone Energy Patterns

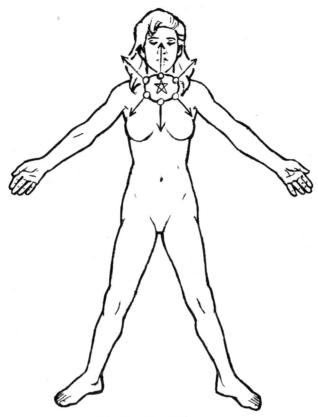

Blue Ray Stone Placement

Celestite is extremely effective for migraines and other sorts of constrictive disorders related to blocked flow from too much mental energy. When working with celestite, it is as though you are receding from outside your self clearly. That is why it is good for imagery and personal mirror work.

Use celestite for your own journey or healing work. Celestite is a good dreamstone, but better as an imagery meditation stone, as its energy is a bit more fixed. You can get a clear effect combining meditation with it. Celestite is good when actively trying to visualize or create.

Alchemist's Note: I feel celestite needs to be used on the upper chakras, or just above the crown of the head in the etheric bodies, or outside of the body somehow, because it tends to work best when it has free access to the higher energies. This is not a value judgment; it has more to do with vibrational frequencies. When you weave these higher vibration energies, if it feels giddy or you feel you are "flowing away," say so. Always get feedback from your self and the people you work with or you are not really able to catalyst the healing process. If you have decided beforehand how it is going to be (or they have), then there is no room for growth.

Celestite is very much a pathway stone. The blue helps us express some of our devotional energies and can translate them back to us. If you can, hold celestite a bit away from the body and have it work inward so it is not bound by the physical energies.

Substitute for Celestite

Celestite is difficult to obtain, but an excellent substitute is a fluorite crystal, especially the bluer shades. This is particularly so with the lighter, clearer fluorite crystals. These can work in a similar fashion to celestite, although you may find it has a more dreamlike or spiritual effect because the fluorite has a different vibration.

For instance, if you wanted to use it meditatively, you might find you have fallen asleep and are doing dream work instead of active imagery. Still, it can be very effective.

If you have a headache and you try to use a fluorite, it is best to focus on the healing energy coming in to you. Fluorite is often linear in the way it works. You might find it is not opening, but constricting further.

Sodalite: Supportive Stone
Element: Earth

Sodalite is an inexpensive, beautiful blue stone with several variations in color. It ranges from a fairly light blue with a lot of white in it to a deep, dark blue—almost an indigo. Sodalite can be used with Indigo Ray, as well, by focusing on the energies synthesizing (coming together).

Sodalite works a lot like malachite—directly and steadily. Some people feel sodalite is best used to support a higher vibration blue stone, but I feel sodalite has a lot of uses of its own. If nothing else, it is a great balancer when working with the active energies of the lower energy centers. Sodalite has a steady, balancing effect all its own.

The deep, pure blues of sodalite serve as a soothing agent for focusing energy. Use sodalite in creative healing visualizations. It soothes, relaxes and helps you get into the quiet place where healings can occur.

Sodalite has a true physical effect, as well. If you wear sodalite at the neck, it helps the thyroid. Sodalite keeps your "idle" set right, so to speak. It is especially good if you wear sodalite all day or night as a necklace, because it works slowly but steadily. Sodalite is a good overall stone.

Alchemist's Note: The darker sodalite works best with Indigo Ray; use it to support some of the more expensive Indigo Ray stones. If you want, you can use sodalite in large chunks, or get it untumbled and just have it in the environment. Sodalite can be soothing to look at. Of course, it is all part of the Mind, Body and Spirit connection. What soothes you affects all aspects of your Self.

Blue Lace Agate: Sensory Stone
Element: Earth (with some Air and Spirit)

Blue lace agate is inexpensive and quite pretty. It has a subtle, earthy vibration with a touch of Spirit. It is not really so much blue as lavender, yet it is called blue lace agate.

Blue lace agate works by opening sensory channels throughout the body so you can express your self. In this way, blue lace agate can attune to the Blue Ray of expression. It helps to increase the flow of input, association, integration and output which defines our expressive dance with our lives.

Blue lace also works to balance the thyroid, but more spiritually than the sodalite. You may have to work with blue lace agates somewhat harder to focus the Ray energies. Blue lace is excellent to balance lower chakra energies, although not quite as strong as the sodalite.

Blue lace agate is a wonderful overall stone. You can put it anywhere on the body you wish. However, it is most effective used a little higher up or out from the body.

It is useful to use blue lace agate with Rose Ray, as well. Blue lace has the tender, gentle kind of Rose Ray energy found in the rose quartz or rhodonite. Focus on blue lace agate bringing in a more spiritual awareness of love. You can use blue lace agate with Violet Ray, as well. If you are doing a lot of spiritual work, blue lace agate can serve to earth some of the spiritual energies.

Alternative Stone

If you want another Blue Ray stone, a good addition would be blue chalcedony. If you know what chalcedony is, you know that is almost like saying, "Go get a blue rock." Chalcedony is a root stone for many other stones. You can sometimes find chalcedony in geode form. It is usually the blue which surrounds crystal or amethyst geodes, but once in a while you can find a geode which is solidly blue. Those are especially effective with Blue Ray. If it has a little bit of crystal in it, that's nice to amplify the energies.

Chapter Eighteen

Indigo Ray: Synthesis

The first and wisest of them all professed to know this only,
that nothing he knew.

—John Milton

Indigo is also a blended Ray, yet it has been actively used longer than the newer blended Rays. Indigo correlates with the sixth energy point, the brow chakra. Indigo is called a synthesis Ray because it blends the primary Rays of Red, Yellow and Blue in perfect balance. Some say the energies of Black and White are also present in Indigo.

The Indigo Ray energies are those of synthesis at the deepest level. Indigo energies have to do with ceremony and ritual, unity of Mind, Body and Spirit, and upwardly spiraling enlightenment.

Indigo Ray is often used with magick as it opens deep levels for spiritual journey, ritual, and ceremonial work. The trick with Indigo Ray is to breathe deeply, focus on the third eye area, and chant the sound of **om** repeatedly.

Alchemist's Note: As we move into the sixth and seventh chakras, the process becomes a little bit different. For instance, in the sixth chakra, which has to do with the Indigo Ray of synthesis, we do not look at whether the Ray is being pulled or whether it is depleted, we look at how the process of synthesis is actually occurring. In the seventh (crown) energy center, which deals with the Violet Ray, we look to see if spiritual connection and flow is in balance. It is a little bit different than before.

Elemental Alchemy	Earth and Air
Key Issues	Knowledge, moderation, perception, communication
Stone Alchemy	Sapphire, azurite, lapis
Cumulative Alchemy	Synthesis

Indigo Ray Keys

Harmonic	Sound of **om** as in **home**
Alchemical Properties	Wisdom, synthesis of all energies
Sensory Key	Jasmine (Deep temple incense)
Symbols	Equilateral cross, sailor's knot, Egyptian eye
Personification	Prophet/Oracle (Edgar Cayce)
Runic	Lagu (Laguz)
Astrological Correlates	Capricorn, Pisces
Major Arcana Key	Judgment
Archangel	Cassiel (Saturn)
Stone Alchemy	Sapphire, azurite, lapis

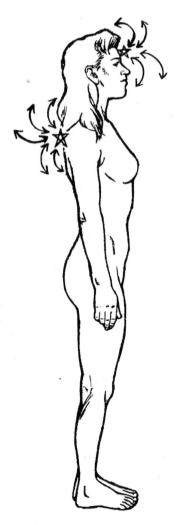

Indigo Ray Energy Centers

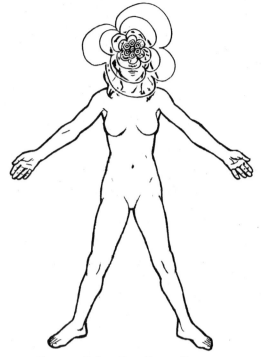

Excessive Indigo Ray Energy Pattern

Depleted Indigo Ray Energy Pattern

Harmonious Indigo Ray Energy Pattern

Harmonic

The harmonic key for Indigo Ray is the sound of **om** (or **ohm**) as in **home**.

Vibrational Energies

The energies of Indigo Ray are sacred, spiritual, synthesizing, harmonizing, and consolidating for all aspects of your being. Focus on the long **o** to activate the harmonic blend of all aspects coming from deep within the physical. Finish with a balanced vibrating of the **m** to bring Spirit into connection with the Body/Mind system. The harmonic **om** is the all-purpose harmonic.

Harmonic Breathing Pattern

The primary breathing pattern for Indigo Ray is deep, silent inhalations and exhalations through the nose. Pause for a moment, then follow with a deep, silent inhalation through the mouth. Pause, then exhale slowly while chanting the harmonic **om**. These breath patterns may be alternated as you chant. Find the pattern which suits you best, so long as the breaths are deep and sacred.

Suggested Harmonic Exercises, Chants, and Word Mantras

The classic harmonic chant for Indigo Ray is:

	om	mani	padme	hum
(phonetically:)				
	ohmm	mahnay	pahd may	hum

This is repeated many times, often accompanied by rocking gently while sitting cross-legged on the floor. Additionally, focusing on the third eye area—the point of synthesis—amplifies the energies of Indigo Ray.

Roughly speaking, "om mani padme hum" translates as:

om	The All, Atman, unmanifest, Spirit
mani	The Jewel or Crystal
padme	The Lotus, unfolding flowering Self
hum	The Heart

Alchemist's Note: Since there are several interpretations of the alchemical meaning for this combination, I defer gladly to that special spirit Ram Dass (Richard Alpert) for his clarity of definition for "om mani padme hum."

> *So, on one level what it means is the entire universe is just like a pure jewel or crystal right in the heart or center of the lotus flower, which is me, and it is manifest, it comes forth in light, in manifest light, in my own heart.*
>
> —Ram Dass, in *The Only Dance There Is*

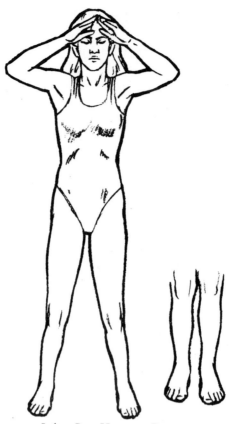

Indigo Ray Harmonic Postures

The trick with this chant is to allow its repetition to build a vibrational frequency which, in turn, connects you to the energies of universal vibration, consciousness and frequency. It's the synthesis of self to Self.

Additional Harmonic Mantras for Indigo Ray

Breathe deeply and chant repeatedly:

| Be | here | now | (thanks again, Ram Dass) |
| In | the | moment | (emphasize **o**) |

Use this for deep level centering and personal synthesis.

An effective Indigo harmonic mantra is the repeated use of the word "home," stressing the (long) **o**. Use when feeling displaced or scattered, as well as for deep shamanic journey work. An extension of the energies created by the mantra "home" can be made by combining additional appropriate words or phrases.

For example, chant the following, stressing the harmonic **om**:

Sea is foam
Earth is loam
I may roam
But Spirit is home

Finally, combine the harmonics of Red, Blue and Yellow to actively synthesize all aspects of your being.

For example:
    Start with long **e** for Red (Physical)
    Add an **ah** for Yellow (Mental)
    Follow with long **o** for Blue (Spiritual)

Chant:
        Eee   aaah   oh

Finish by extending the long **o** into **om** (Indigo) for synthesis and spiritual serenity.

Alchemical Properties

Indigo Ray actively synthesizes the strongest vibrational energies of Body, Mind and Spirit. Indigo brings the alchemical elements of wisdom together in a primarily mental, etheric, spiritual manner.

Powers	Indirect, focused, multi-dimensionally centering action
Activates	Implementation, inspiration, psychic abilities, synthesis, unity, vision
Amplifies	All catalysts, devotion, gratitude, organization, revelations, serenity, soul consciousness, wisdom
Balances	Active intelligence, courage, honor, motivation, perception, service, zeal, anger, expectations, extremes, vacillation
Releases	Confusion, contempt, delusion, disorganization, frustration, imbalance, power-seeking, separateness, superiority
Realigns	Conceit, irritability, regrets, remorse, totalitarianism

Sensory Key

The sensory key correlated with Indigo Ray is jasmine.

Shared attributes of jasmine and Indigo Ray:
      Spirituality
      Ceremony, ritual, magick
      Prophecy
      Unity
      Love
      The element of Water

Jasmine is inexpensive and available in a variety of forms, such as incense, herbs, oils, teas and scented candles. Several varieties of jasmine plants, each with the distinctive jasmine flowers, can easily be cultivated in your garden.

- Rub jasmine oil on your third eye area, wrists, temples, and ankles. Breathe deeply to absorb the scent into the etheric energies surrounding your body. Focus on the synthesis of Indigo Ray pulling deeply spiritual energies toward the center of your being. Feel any scattered energies flowing inward from your wrists, ankles, and temples, moving toward your third eye area—the point of centering and personal synthesis.
- Burn jasmine incense or jasmine-scented candles to awaken to soul-level connections in a loving relationship.
- Burn jasmine in a ceremonial or ritual circle to activate deepest spiritual synthesis. Place burning jasmine in each of the cardinal directions: South, West, North and East. Sit in the middle of this circle of jasmine. Focus on Indigo Ray energies flowing toward the center of the circle, into the center of your Self. Continue to focus on the jasmine and the Indigo Ray energies until you feel all aspects of your Self blend into a unity of being. From this state of centered synthesis, you may activate self-transformation and healing using the highest energies of love and divine prophecy to guide your choices and your changes.

Symbols

Equilateral cross represents knowledge spreading outward to the world from the center of Self to reach the universal dimension of wisdom. When the information we reach for comes together with the knowledge of our Self, then the cross of struggle becomes the wheel of wisdom.

Sailor's knot represents the synthesis of wisdom we have collected to secure our lives to truth. With the strength of our bodies and the flexibility of our minds, we connect to the purpose of our rituals, the catalysts of our ceremonies, and the magick of our personal alchemy.

Egyptian eye represents the rituals and ceremonies of sacred knowledge. In visions we find the synthesis of Mind, Body and Spirit, and the unity of knowing.

Personifications

Inner Wisdom

Indigo is the color of the Prophet/Oracle. It is Edgar Cayce reaching through dimensions of matter, time, and space to bring healing and knowledge. Indigo is the synthesis of action, reception, and reflection which led Cayce to research the processes of enlightenment for the good of all.

Musings

A dream never fades, but can be neglected or misplaced.

The structure and function of fantasy is to bridge the dimensions of your Self.

The spiritual celebrations you share with others are no more or less than elements for the creation of your personal ceremonies.

The experience of the alchemist holding the energy of the elements is that of an actor holding character in a play—it is the experience of empathetic detachment.

Runic Correlate

Lagu (Laguz)

Shared aspects with Indigo Ray:

Inner wisdom	Ceremony
Ritual	Magick
Mystery	The element of Earth

Lagu (Laguz)

Lagu (Laguz) synthesizes the elements of personal alchemy with the inner flow of wisdom and vision. When we gather together all the aspects, elements and information about our transformation, we access a dimension of Self beyond our initial estimate. Activate attunement to the flow of your personal transformation with the rune Lagu (Laguz). The alchemy of Lagu (Laguz) is best guided by the lessons of inner council.

Astrological Correlates

Solar Capricorn

Alchemy of Activation and Enhancement

> Shared aspects with Indigo Ray:
> Organization   Synthesis
> Psyche   Ordered wisdom
> Will
> (+ Black Light = Ordered Connector)

A Capricorn needs his belief in a higher power because once he has reached a goal and has no other place to go, he must fall back on himself.

—Ursula Lewis

Lunar Pisces

Alchemy of Receptivity and Reflection

> Shared aspects with Indigo Ray:
> Karmic patterns   Personal synthesis
> Occult wisdom   Psyche
> Transformation
> (+ White Light = Synthesis Medium)

Many (lunar) Pisceans feel the world in which they live is so ill adjusted that they want to reject it, but guidance will teach them that this is part of their karmic experience, and then they adjust philosophically.

—Sybil Leek

Major Tarot Arcana Key

Judgment

Shared aspects with Indigo Ray:
> Synthesis   Integration
> Wisdom   Psychism
> Ceremony   Ritual
> Metaphysical mastery

. . . Knitting together through some mysterious process of the intuition the experiences and insights gained from each stage of the journey, and magically blending these to form the beginnings of a new and larger personality.

—Juliet Sharman-Burke and Liz Green

Musings

When the individual self can grasp the concept of the Universal Self, it activates the fire of Spirit and warms the heart of the Metaphysical Masters.

The magical teacher within awakens as quickly or as slowly as his pupil, the Self, does.

Through ritual and ceremony from the heart, we evolve our selves, and thereby, the world around us. This process of shared evolution will continue to be in process unless we confuse "elevate" with "evolve."

Archangel

Angelic Dimension Key

Cassiel: Archangel of Saturn
> Alchemy of Synthesis, Integration, Karmic patterns and Ritual
>
> | | |
> |---|---|
> | Days | Saturday, Monday |
> | Times | 3-4 AM |
> | | 11-12 AM |
> | | 7-8 PM |

♄

Physics tries to discover the pattern of events which controls the phenomena we observe. But we can never know what this pattern means or how it originates, or even if some Superior intelligence were to tell us, we should find the explanation unintelligible.

—Sir James Hopwood Jeans

Angelic Invocation

Weave for me, oh Cassiel, keeper of the Karmic patterns. Weave for me a fabric strong and fine.

Bring wisdom together in me, oh Cassiel, keeper of the sacred threads. Bring wisdom together, yet unbound, free within the oneness of the weaving.

Weave a ceremony of synthesis and bring the ritual tools of trust and clear mind.

Stone Alchemy

Alchemist's Note: A powerful way to do deep rebalancing and restructuring of your Self is to use any of the Indigo stones, focus on the Red Ray, the Yellow Ray, and the Blue Ray coming in. Bring in Black and White Lights for balance. Finish by focusing on Indigo Ray.

Sapphire: Laser Stone
Element: Air

Sapphires can be very expensive if you want a high-quality faceted gemstone. I find the vibration of the sapphire is so intense that a tiny, tumbled rough-cut piece is more than adequate. The star sapphire, with its little white inclusions, can represent the bursting of energy and synthesis in our lives. Sometimes star sapphires are not quite as expensive.

All sapphire works by emitting a direct laser beam of energy which quickly and dramatically creates purification on all levels. Sapphire works by connecting us with the earth plane, then to the abstract (or spiritual plane), then back again. Psychically, sapphire can work by helping to release emotional blocks that can cause mental stress and disorders

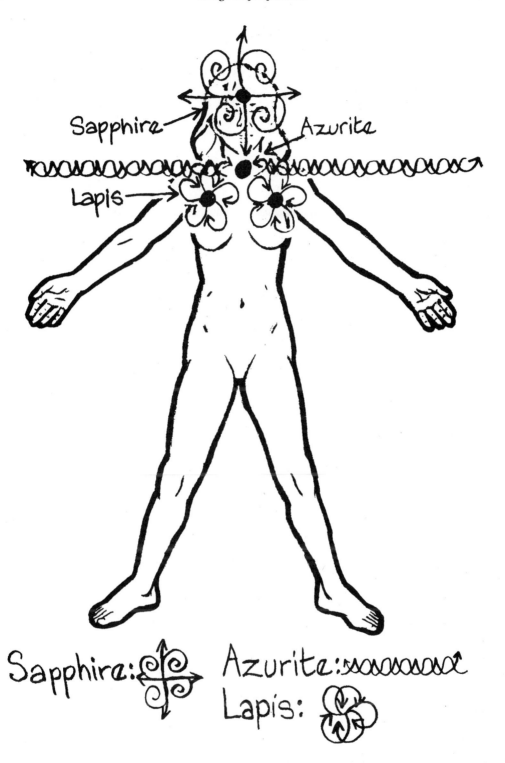

Indigo Ray Stone Energy Patterns

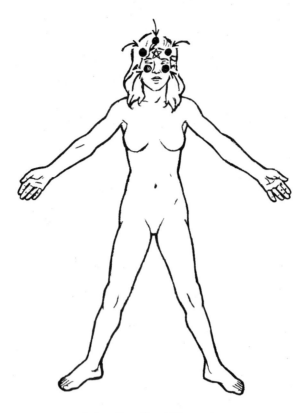

Indigo Ray Stone Placement

which, in turn, cause us to become physically ill. Indigo Ray with sapphire can synthesize energies for deepest healing and personal transformation.

The lighter blue sapphires are used for expressive disorders, and the golden sapphires correlate well with Blue Ray, as they have an active spiritual contact. I feel golden sapphires are best used if they are balanced with denser stones, such as the sodalite or blue lace agate.

The dark indigo sapphires are best attuned to shamanic journey, ritual, ceremonial and magickal work. Sapphire is used in high ceremony or ritual to develop a clairvoyant and direct channel to spiritual wisdom. Dark sapphires are attuned to the divine.

Alchemist's Note: Sapphire with Indigo Ray lets us become spiritual bridges and helps us become clear so Light can flow through and across ourselves.

Azurite: Truth Stone
Element: Air and Earth (with Spirit)

Azurite can be moderately expensive if you have it polished or cabochon cut. A cabochon cut is a stone which is flat on one side and smooth or rounded on the other.

Azurite has a powerful spiritual effect which works dramatically. It is a little slower than a sapphire, but the effect is much the same. Indeed, I find azurite to be a bit deeper in its energies. The physical effects can be profound for healing when azurite is used with spiritual awareness. With the sapphire, you will know immediately that it is working, while azurite can take you unaware. Azurite works subtly yet powerfully; be ready when you work with it.

Azurite usually occurs with some green malachite in it. Generally, the more green malachite, the more earthy the vibration of the azurite piece. If you are just starting to work with azurite, or you do not really want to work with the intensity of Indigo, you might look for azurite which has more malachite in it to start. Azurite with more Indigo is often intensely dramatic and spiritual in its effect.

Alchemist's Note: Azurite is deeply metamorphic in its energies. You may think it is moving from Green Ray malachite into Indigo Ray azurite, but my favorite "stone Gypsies" tell me azurite is actually moving into malachite. In other words, Indigo returns to Green, synthesis returns to heartfelt levels, or Mind connects back to Heart for healing. Use this natural alchemy combined with Indigo Ray for accessing the deepest wisdom and bringing it into practical application. Earth spiritual energies with azurite.

Azurite is excellent for intuition, clairvoyance, deep meditation, and reaching the deepest levels of truth and wisdom. Personal synthesis cannot occur when we are blocking truth or personal wisdom. Azurite, as other Indigo stones, relieves those blocks, giving a direct channel to truth. Sometimes that is a little heavy to take in all at once—be gentle.

Azurite increases receptivity to all kinds of wisdom. If you are using it when you want to study or learn, but you do not want such a deep spiritual effect, balance it with red jasper. You could also use some of your Green stones, such as malachite, to keep the energies earthed.

Azurite is a deep, ceremonial stone. I advise you to obtain one if you are working magick, ceremony or ritual. The effects of azurite can be intense with ceremonial work. It calls forth some deep, dramatic alchemy.

Alchemist's Note: Also use azurite in combination with another crystal or a little bit of fluorite to induce dream states. Don't worry if you fall asleep or "go into the void" a few times before you have dream recall—that's natural.

Lapis: Penetration Stone
Element: Earth (with some Spirit)

Lapis can also be used with Blue Ray, but because of its intensity I placed it here with Indigo. Indigo Ray is more intense than Blue Ray. Indigo energies swirl rapidly, and lapis works directly, making lapis and Indigo an ideal alchemical combination.

Lapis can be moderately expensive, but you don't need much. Its energy is subtle, but has a powerful vibration. Lapis can be a lot like azurite, except it works more directly on the physical, penetrating blocks. You don't have to help lapis much at all, just add a little awareness and focus.

Lapis opens the abilities for the deepest aspects of expression and self-transformation. The expressive energy of lapis attunes to the Blue Ray, and the deep transformative qualities reflect Indigo Ray synthesis.

Lapis is one of those stones which can be used anywhere, but it is most effective physically in the upper chakras. Place lapis on the throat, brow, crown, or just above the head. Lapis with Indigo Ray can be used meditatively to instill devotion and inspiration. This will be an active, almost regal, energy. The flecks of gold you find in lapis indicate it is not sodalite and also remind us how active the stone itself is.

Alchemist's Note: Attune to even higher spiritual energies by pulling Violet Ray through a lapis. The lapis tends to spread energies out and let Spirit penetrate into the physical. This can be used for very profound healing. For this alchemy, focus on Violet Ray and let the lapis earth the energies into the physical.

Lapis is also good for balancing the ego needs from the lower, active chakras. To use lapis specifically for ego disorders, put it on the upper chakras and pull the energies through to the lower. If you put lapis on the lower chakras, it may create tension you do not want.

Lapis is probably best worn at the throat. It is also good if you can hold a small piece at the throat chakra or on the brow and meditate with it. Physically, lapis clears and opens a spiritual channel to higher energies. Lapis is good for helping you work with your spirit guides and communicate in a real physical way. Lapis earths Spirit and opens to Spirit at the same time.

Alternative Stones

Indigo Ray stones are often rather expensive. For an alternative, you might try a very dark amethyst or possibly a clear quartz crystal. You could also use sodalite, but you will have to work with its energies. Focus on the color of sodalite in order to bring the Indigo Ray directly in.

Chapter Nineteen

Violet Ray: Spirituality

As he brews, so shall he drink.
—Ben Johnson

Every man is his own doctor of divinity in the last resort.
—Robert Louis Stevenson

Violet Ray is correlated with the crown chakra or the seventh energy point on the body. Sometimes Violet Ray is called "purple" or "purple-violet." The traditional placement is at the top of the forehead, crown of the head, or base of the skull. Some traditions place Violet a little above the head. Since Violet is so ultimately representative of the connection of humankind to Spirit, I feel that touching the physical is important with Violet.

Violet blends the physical energy of Red with the spiritual energy of Blue in perfect balance, working to transform us on the highest spiritual and karmic levels. It gives us an awareness of karma—the ultimate choices we have in life. Karma is choice. Violet is the Ray of highest transmutation.

The trick with Violet Ray is to focus on its energies spiraling downward into the physical.

Elemental Alchemy	Spirit and Water
Key Issues	Right action, oneness
Stone Alchemy	Amethyst, fluorite, sugalite
Cumulative Alchemy	Evolved Spirituality

Violet Ray Keys

Harmonic	Sound of **u** as in **sun**
Alchemical Properties	Spiritual growth and connection
Sensory Key	Lavender, lilac
Symbols	Lotus blossom, temple, star (five or six points)
Personification	Magician/Alchemist (Merlin)
Runic	Ken (Kano)
Astrological Correlates	Pisces, Virgo
Major Arcana Key	Justice
Archangel	Auriel (Uranus)
Stone Alchemy	Amethyst, fluorite, sugalite

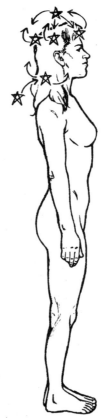

Violet Ray Energy Centers

Alchemist's Note: When working with Violet Ray in a spiritual, ceremonial manner, remember that Violet Ray is already an extremely Spiritual, powerful, high vibration energy. To connect with Violet ceremonially is to tap the strongest transmuting energies of Source. However, it is important to remember that Violet is still connected to the physical body. To reach into the highest Spiritual energies with Violet and not get lost or "blissy," there must be a balancing with other, more physical energies. The physical body cannot be neglected—particularly when using Violet.

As a balance, Yellow Ray can be useful to give order to the experience of Violet for a somewhat centered, grounded individual. In some people, this combination can create a Spiritual yet dogmatic state of being—a kind of religious imperialism. This creates judgmental elitism or separatism.

Green Ray can be useful to connect the Spiritual experience of Violet with the heartfelt energies of healing love. However, the expansive energy of Green Ray can create a sincerely Spiritual, yet overly giving state of being—a kind of Healer/Martyr. This creates physical debasement or depletion.

Red Ray can give structure to the Spiritual experience of Violet Ray. On the other hand, the driving energies of Red Ray can create an actively Spiritual, yet raging state of being—a kind of Crusader/Evangelist, creating emotional disconnection or arrogance.

To create an alchemical blend to catalyst the most effective energies and experience of Violet, combine Violet Ray with:

- Red Ray—to keep physical lifeforce activating and receiving as it should. This gives direction to the driving force of Red Ray.

- Green Ray—to keep the emotional, expansive energies circulating in a harmonious fashion. This brings healing balance to the selfless, sharing energies of Green.

- Yellow Ray—to give order to the Spiritual experience so that it may find application in your life. This gives purpose to the organizing energies of Yellow.

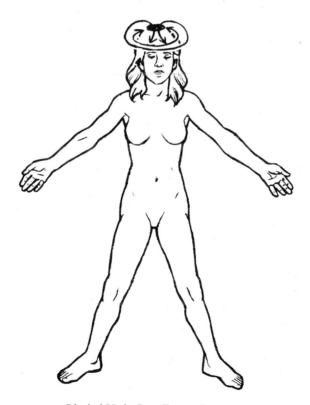

Blocked Violet Ray Energy Pattern

Harmonious Violet Ray Energy Pattern (Expansive)

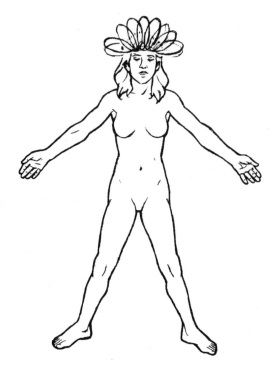

Harmonious Violet Ray Energy Pattern (Intrapersonal)

Note that direction, healing balance, and purpose arise from the connection to Violet Ray. This is one reason that Violet is important in connection to the physical and mental energies. Violet is the link to Source and to Body/Mind well-being—Violet is the channel.

Harmonic

The harmonic key for Violet Ray is twofold. Primarily, it is the short sound of u as in **sun**. At a higher vibration, the harmonic for Violet becomes the sound of oo as in **moon**. These may be used interchangeably, or by beginning with u and uplifting into oo.

Vibrational Energies

The energies of Violet Ray are uplifting—sometimes intense, sometimes sedate, spiritual, cosmic and universal. Focus on the connection to Spirit as a crown of light resting on your head. Focus on the energies of highest love and light uplifting humankind in its evolution into Spirit.

Harmonic Breathing Pattern

The primary breathing pattern for Violet Ray is sedate, spiritual and sacred. Breathe slowly in and out of the nose, pausing after each inhalation and exhalation. Observe the energies of Spirit found in those brief pauses of breath. Breathe silently for a time, then add the harmonic (short) u after the exhalation. Continue with the harmonic u, then scale up slowly to the harmonic oo.

For example: Breathe—then chant u u u u u
                      Breathe—then chant u u u u oo oo
                      Breathe—then chant only oo oo oo for a time
                      Breathe—then chant u u u u oo oo o oo oo

This connects the element of Spirit, which is primarily your Self, to the realm of Spirit, which is the Self.

Alchemist's Note: If moving directly into the Violet Ray harmonic makes you a bit "blissy," try activating from a more physical harmonic vibration.

For example, begin by slowly chanting the vowel sounds, stressing the long sound of each one: a, e, i, o, u . . .

When you come to u, skip the short harmonic u and move directly into oo. Thus you have a, e, i, o, oo oo oo (stressed).

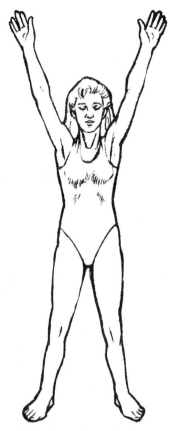

Violet Ray Harmonic Posture

Suggested Harmonic Exercises, Chants, and Word Mantras

Using quiet, sacred breathing, chant softly:

> **The Sun**
> **The Son**
> **The One**
> **The Sum**

Increase your volume as you feel Violet Ray spiritual energies flowing and increasing in frequency. Center and ground your self by slowly reducing the volume of your chart. Combine the dual harmonics of Violet by chanting:

> **You, the one**
> **The one, You**
> **Truth, the one**
> **The one Truth**

Bring in the highest vibrations of the Violet Ray by chanting combinations using some of these words:

> **croon**   **moon**   **soon**   **tune**   **lume**

For example:

> **Croon the tune**
> **Of Lady Moon**

Or:

> **The Light, the Lume**
> **The Sun, the Moon**

Finally, a simple but effective mantra can be created using both harmonics of Violet. For example, chant:

at	**one**	**ment**	(stress **u** as in **un**)
at	**tune**	**ment**	(stress **u** as in **oon**)

Use for all aspects of Spiritual work, meditation, and healing to connect with the All.

Alchemical Properties

Violet Ray connects the physical to the spiritual realms to ensure the flow of the highest energies of healing and universal alchemy. Violet catalysts spiritual evolution in a primarily mental, etheric and spiritual manner.

Powers	Direct, focused, evolutionary spiritual action
Activates	Devotion, gratitude, idealism, justice, responsibility, revelations, soul consciousness
Amplifies	Detachment, humility, temperance, vision
Balances	Contempt, martyrdom, pessimism, power-seeking, procrastination
Releases	Remorse, self-righteousness, vengeance
Realigns	Agitation, intolerance, obsession

Sensory Key

The sensory key correlated with Violet Ray is lavender (or lilac).

Shared attributes of lavender and Violet Ray:
> Highest Spiritual energies
> Love
> Spiritual connection
> Spiritual protection
> Multi-dimensional linking
> Highest energies of choice
> The element of Spirit

Lavender is inexpensive and can be obtained in several forms such as herbs, oils, incenses and scented candles.

- Fill a clear bowl with lavender flowers. Place in the environment where it can be seen and smelled easily. Focus on Violet Ray energies connecting with the lavender buds. This reflects the energies of Spirit connecting to the body. Focus on the bowl of lavender as a collector of energies and a connection to the many dimensions of consciousness, awareness and wisdom.

- Use the Violet Ray energies of lavender to activate a regal, masterly attitude.

- Burn lavender specifically to summon the highest levels of personal choice. Acknowledge your right to choose your path, and accept with honor the responsibility of that choice. Be certain that you remember to live in gratitude.

Symbols

Lotus blossom represents the multifaceted aspects of Self unfolding within the highest dimension of Spirit. We are the thousand-petalled blossoms, opening to the Light, drifting on the currents of Spiritual flow.

Temple represents the holy place within our Self where our personal connection to Spirit is honored. Sacred structures exist so long as the winds of change can blow through their open doors.

Star (five or six points) represents the limitless multiplicity of spiritual energies. While our traditions may differ in direction, like points on a star, our connection to Spirit forms a core which has no differences.

Personification

Transformation

Violet is the energy of the Magician/Alchemist. It is Merlin, the ancient wizard of Western consciousness, casting masterly spells with the power of Spirit realms. Violet is the alchemical fantasy of Merlin manifesting in fact in modern times, reflecting wisdom in dreams, ceremony, ritual and magick.

Musings

If religion is the opiate of the masses, then dogma is its poison.

Spirit has no rules, only choices.

The flow of Spirit is activated by the catalyst of personal choice.

You can't ever lose faith once you have found it.

Runic Correlate

Ken (Kano)

Shared aspects with Violet Ray:
    Spiritual guidance
    Fate
    Opportunities for spiritual growth
    The element of Spirit

Ken (Kano)

Ken (Kano) opens us to the highest Spiritual dimensions of Self-transformation, and awakens new realms within our being. The personal alchemist learns to recognize the realms of Spirit and to approach them with a blend of honor, humility and gratitude. Activate your personal connection to the power of Spirit with Ken (Kano). The alchemy of Ken (Kano) is in approaching Spirit with self-honor, self-humility, and self-gratitude.

Astrological Correlates

Solar Pisces

Alchemy of Activation and Enhancement

    Shared aspects with Violet Ray:

Spiritual evolution	Self-knowledge
Transformation	Transmutation
Magick	

        (+ Silver Light = Spiritual Receptor)

Let Pisces follow his heart, his conscience, his inner desire for Service, self-realization and self-knowledge . . . and he is the happiest, most useful of mortals, living comfortably with deep spiritual truths that give him an almost mystic grip on other people and on the reins of his own life.

—Grant Lewi

Lunar Virgo

Alchemy of Receptivity and Reflection

Shared aspects with Violet Ray:
Divine order	Purity
Precision	Ritual
Asceticism	

(+ Brown Light = Grounded Spiritualist)

With the moon in this position, Virgo people are very conscious of keeping fit and enjoy admiration for body fitness . . . When they become obsessed, they can be very irritating, especially when they insist that everyone should follow the same exercises and diets they have taken up.

—Sybil Leek

Major Tarot Arcana Key

Justice

Shared aspects with Violet Ray:
Spiritual connection	Universal alchemy
Karmic patterns	Highest self

The wheel of Justice is the highest boundary or limiting pattern of energy known within human consciousness; beyond this pattern we leave transpersonal awareness and approach the transhuman.

—R. J. Stewart

Musings

It is difficult to have a clear and private connection to Spirit if you're living your life on a spiritual party line.

Accept the gift of Spiritual Self-determination. It is a gift which grows in proportion to the amount you value and accept it—in truth.

That which seriously impedes your spiritual progress can be a challenge to be met and mastered with the pure forces of love. That which impedes can be something to be excused, something to be avoided, or something to hide behind.

Patterns of choice are reflected in the mirror of the Highest Self. The elements of Universal Alchemy are discovered in the personal, alchemical elements of the Self.

Archangel

Angelic Dimension Key

Auriel (Uriel): Archangel of Uranus
　　　Alchemy of Universal order
　　　　　Days:　　　　　Monday, Wednesday
　　　　　Times　　　　　2-3 AM
　　　　　　　　　　　　10-11 AM
　　　　　　　　　　　　6-7 PM

I am nothing; I see all; the currents of the Universal Being circulate through me; I am part and parcel of God.

—Ralph Waldo Emerson

Angelic Invocation

I glimpse your magick in the cycles of nature, Auriel, electric being of Spiritual light. I see the hem of your robes in the ebb and flow of each tide. I glimpse your wonder working in every transformation of my life.

I call for the power of your faith in the ordered Spiritual beauty of the divine.

I see the order of Universal alchemy in the elements of my self-transformation.

Stone Alchemy

The stones for Violet Ray are amethyst, fluorite and sugilite (also called royal azule). The traditional placement for Violet stones is on all the upper chakra areas around the head, on the shoulders, and on the crown (right at the top just touching the head).

Amethyst: Source Stone
Element: Air (some with Earth, some with Spirit)

Gemstone-cut amethyst is moderately expensive. You can obtain inexpensive tumbled stones or individual amethyst crystals. My personal choice is to use either individual crystal points or rough, untumbled crystal. I have found that since amethyst crystals seem to have a higher vibration than cut gemstone amethysts, there is no sense in spending the money for cut gemstones. Again, this is a matter of choice.

Amethyst is a potent painkiller, useful for physical as well as psychological pain. If you are using amethyst for physical pain (such as burns) or to soothe ulcer pains, the more dense amethyst is most helpful to bring in healing energies. Amethyst is quite good for burns when focused with Green, Blue, Indigo or Violet Rays.

Amethyst is generally thought to be good for insomnia and stress-related disorders, with the exception of insomnia caused by grief or traumatic loss. In those cases, Violet Ray amethyst energy may be too heavy and depressing; try using fluorite or blue lace agate instead. If you feel you need to work with amethyst's spiritual connection to get in touch with the karmic aspects of loss or trauma, take time to balance the heart energies with rose quartz or blue lace agate.

Amethyst helps heal addictions, such as alcohol. It breaks the cycle of dependency by putting us in tune with the choices we are making and the awareness of our pattern. This is particularly so when used purely with Violet Ray.

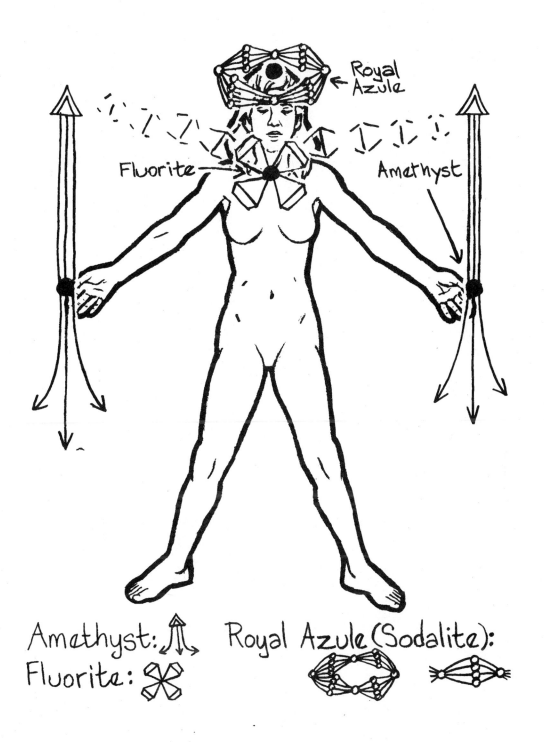

Violet Ray Stone Energy Patterns

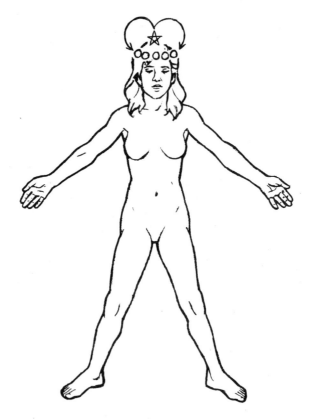

Violet Ray Stone Placment

Alchemist's Note: Amethyst is transformative in nature, working from the Spiritual into the physical, and opening channels to truth, higher service, and the highest sources of Being. Amethyst with Violet Ray connects you with the All. It is quite effective to use for mental disorders, as long as there is a lot of balance and love.

Fluorite: Catalyst Stone
Element: Air and Spirit

Fluorites are relatively inexpensive. They all have a high vibration, which is more intense with separate crystals. Fluorite crystals look like little pyramids set on top of each other. Whatever the vibration—spiritual, mental or physical—it will be enhanced by fluorite in a direct, linear fashion.

Fluorite is a catalyst for spiritual growth, cosmic connection, and physical regeneration. It takes some work to bring its energies down to the physical. Use lots of focus and imagery with fluorite, and bring in Earth Lights and Green Ray to ground it.

Alchemists Note: All fluorite can vibrate well with spiritual Violet Ray energy. I find that lavender and violet fluorites are slightly more attuned to Violet Ray; this may simply be because the color is so powerful that it draws us into the Ray. Generally speaking, the darker fluorites can be used for Indigo Ray, as well, while the light blue fluorites are great with Blue Ray.

Green fluorite is more physical in the way it works. The indigo and the blue are more spiritual and mental; yellow fluorite is mental and philosophical. Because of the focused nature of fluorite, the color has a much more intense effect, as fluorite works mentally, connecting spiritual to psychic energies.

Fluorite is an excellent dreamstone. It lifts your spirits and puts you in a position to receive, whether you are doing traditional or imagery dream work. When you need to work things out psychically and you have not had time to meditate, take some fluorite to bed with you and let it dream. Sleep on it, so to speak.

Fluorite can be useful for dream work by enhancing our natural abilities to listen to our intuition and to develop psychic abilities. Sometimes this work has to come through in dreams, because we tend to get busy during the day. The darker the fluorite, usually the more depth to its spiritual energy. The lighter fluorite is a little difficult to contact. See if you can get a darker fluorite to start, and work from Indigo into Violet.

Alchemists Note: Fluorite is a map maker in the sense that it uses linear energies to get to spiritual planes. It is almost as though fluorites are little ladders. You can use that as an image to help you work with fluorite. Fluorite is also good to support the healing work of other stones. Place the supporting fluorite just outside the body boundaries, and focus the spiritual and etheric energies in through the fluorite to the other stones.

Sugilite/Royal Azule: Mastery Stone
Element: Earth (with some Spirit)

Royal azule is a new alchemical stone element in the sense that we have not been working with it long. It is very potent, even in small amounts; this is good since royal azule can be expensive. Royal azule works quite effectively, particularly if you place it either on your third eye or a little bit higher. Royal azule works to help us access what we call the Akashic records, or the DNA codes. These records or codes are the basic maps, the blueprints of our lives; the blueprints of our soul's journey.

Royal azule is truly a mastery stone. When you have the awareness of what your patterns are, then you are indeed master of your life. Royal azule provides an opportunity for us to get in touch with our past-life wisdoms or past-pattern experiences. When we can see what we are doing again (and again), it allows us the opportunity to choose new paths.

We need to work with royal azule a while before we can decide how it is helping us. As we move into greater awareness, we are certainly going to be able to access far more in our own codes than we ever thought possible. Royal azule will continue to be a good helper as we expand brain potential.

Royal azule is good to use with Gold Light. This activates choice of change and understanding of pattern transformations made on a high level. With Silver Light, royal azule vibrates more with the reincarnation or past-life wisdom experiences. Experiment with royal azule; test its alchemy in your own work.

Royal azule works on a physical and spiritual level at the same time, creating pathways to wisdom for us on earth. If you use royal azule with Green Ray, it can become your helper on the earth walk. With Indigo Ray, royal azule puts you in touch with your inner counsel, or spirit guides. Use it when you need to "meet with the council."

Alternative Stone

If you want another stone to use with Violet Ray, you can always use a clear crystal point. Clarity of crystals is not always an issue with me. However, crystals for Violet Ray should have a single point and be very clear, since you want precision as you start to work with these kinds of flowing spiritual energies.

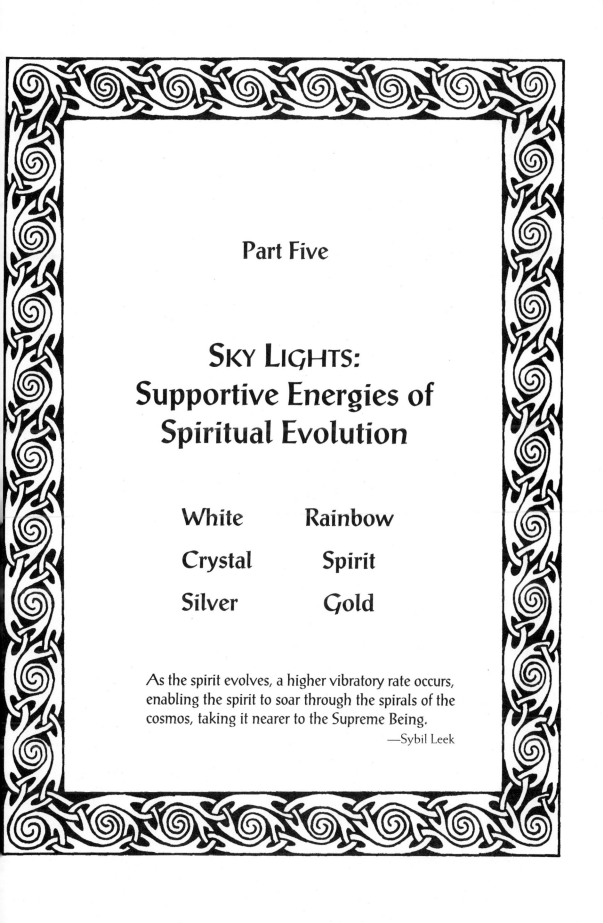

Part Five

SKY LIGHTS:
Supportive Energies of
Spiritual Evolution

White	Rainbow
Crystal	Spirit
Silver	Gold

As the spirit evolves, a higher vibratory rate occurs,
enabling the spirit to soar through the spirals of the
cosmos, taking it nearer to the Supreme Being.

—Sybil Leek

Moon Dancing: Full Moon Renewal

Take a long, slow, deep breath. Hold it for a few moments . . . . now gently treat your self to a long stretch, just like a cat. Feel each muscle tighten and release . . . let your breathing find its own gentle rhythm. Let your body relax.

Find a quiet place within your self. Breathe deeply and bring your awareness inside. You are going to journey to a full moon celebration. On the journey, you will feel your self grow in power and wisdom, and you will rejoice in the fullness of your life path.

Breathe deeply, and step into an image of your self walking on a silver ribbon of a path in the midst of a dark, ancient forest. Moonlight trickles down through the leaves and branches of the trees, giving just enough light for you to see your way clearly.

Night birds call to each other from far away. There is a slight rustling in the underbrush as some tiny night creature scurries home, hoping to avoid the watchful eyes of the great horned owl gliding noiselessly through the shadows of the forest.

Breathe deeply and feel the damp coolness of this peaceful forest. Feel connected to the earth as you walk . . . with each step you feel more serene and powerful.

Dancing faerie lights encircle you, coaxing you onward. There is gaiety in their companionship. Several of them dart forward as if to show you the way. As you look in the direction they have flown, you glimpse a small clearing in the forest just ahead.

A few more steps, and you find your self at the edge of a lovely moonlit meadow encircled by the great, dark forest. At the center of this meadow stands a large gnarled tree. Its branches spread out freely, in a wide circle, and sweep low to the ground as though weighted heavily by the moonlight shining on the leaves. This is a special place . . . a natural place of reverence and beauty.

Take a long, slow deep breath. Make this image real. Feel the power and presence in such a place as this.

Stand for a few moments, and watch the wind and moonlight weave patterns of light and shadows through the branches of the tree and across the clearing. Even now, as you stand quietly absorbing the beauty of this place, you notice that the moon grows fuller and brighter in the sky. Breathe deeply, and feel the power growing within you as well.

When you are ready, walk slowly around the circle of the meadow. Walk clockwise around the perimeter . . . pace off this special place as your very own. As you come abreast of the great tree in the center, you hear the silver sound of a young maiden's laughter from deep in the forest. There is a quicksilver flash of light, and the young huntress dashes by you, swiftly crossing the meadow and disappearing behind the great tree. Though you wish to dash after her, you steady your pace and continue walking the perimeter of this sacred space. Faerie lights twinkle from inside the branches of the tree. Rising up in a little cloud of sparkles, they return to encircle you and guide your steps.

You make your way slowly around the great tree. You watch carefully but see no more sign of the silver-clad huntress . . . just an occasional shimmer of light which seems to drop from the moonlight on the leaves.

Breathe slowly and gently. Allow your self time to finish your circle. As you complete this circle, you notice that the moon rides still higher and brighter in the sky. Now its light is great enough that you can more clearly see all the beauty around you. You take a deep breath, and slowly begin to approach the tree.

A single faerie light gleams deep in the roots, beckoning you. As you draw nearer, you see an extremely old and weathered chest half hidden by the roots. You reach down, and with a great effort you manage to lift the massive lid of the chest. As you do this, the moon breaks full and bright from behind a cloud, and casts its beam of light onto your find. Sparkles and shimmers of light dance out from inside the chest. Colors, like rainbows in the night, seem to surround you. Looking closer, you see that the chest is filled with jewels, crystals, beads, charms, and chalices. Robes of gossamer silks and satin, lustrous and beautiful, shine in the light of the moon. An ornate mirror, deep in the chest, reflects your surprise. Startled, you laugh, then merrily begin to dig deeper into the chest for more treasures. Breathe deeply and enjoy the find. It is for your pleasure.

When you have discovered all the beautiful objects in the chest, take time to select those articles most beautiful and special with which to array your self. Enjoy the feel of the fine materials, the sparkle of the jewels, and the power of the sacred objects known only to you which you have found in this chest. Take note of these objects. Have you found pieces which are magical talismans for you?

What symbols have you found on your jewels or decorating your robes? What colors have you chosen? How do they make you feel? Breathe deeply and remember. Make this real for your self . . . it comes from your inner wisdom.

You place the ornate mirror against the tree, and gaze at your reflection. How beautiful and powerful you are, sparkling and shimmering in the light of the full moon. You step fully out into the clearing, and dance about filled with energy.

Refreshed by your dance in the moonlight, you decide to make a small circle of stones just the right size for your self alone.

Thirteen stones . . . one for each of the moons of the year. Take all the time you need to gather the stones. You do not need to decide, for the stones themselves seem to catch your attention with a twinkle or a cool, smooth reflection of moonlight as they lie peacefully in the grass.

You finish your small circle of stones and stand inside it, feeling special and sacred. You turn to face the full moon as it completes its rising in the East. For a moment, you stand quietly and bathe in its beautiful light.

You take an especially long, deep breath, and reach one hand as high as you can toward the moon. Slowly, carefully, you bring your hand down and across, making the sign of a star. For a moment, the star you have drawn blazes in a silver blue light in the East, then gently fades into the night. From the East, you turn right to the South, then West, then North. Each time you make the sign of the star, it hangs shimmering in the air for a few moments before fading away.

Take your time to make this circle and draw your stars. Each time feel the energy deepen and the power build within you. You are creating Sacred space . . . a circle within a circle.

When you have returned to face the East once again, you notice visitors coming into the clearing to share this sacred time with you. You welcome these visitors as warm and familiar companions of your life journey. Perhaps someone will come who you have not seen in a great while. Perhaps someone who no longer walks the earth plane. Perhaps someone very special. Remember that this is a sacred space created between the worlds, and you are able to greet these friends and guides as you can not always do in the world of everyday. They are here to remind you of your special place in the universe. They have come to help you remember the fullness of your power, and to celebrate the strength of your love and wisdom in your life journey.

Take a few moments to greet them and feel the warmth of their caring and support. Perhaps you will be surprised to find someone from history has come to celebrate with you. Greet the visitors with honor, and celebrate your good fortune to have guides of such Power. Remember them, as they may have special places within your life's work.

Your friends join hands and stand just outside your little circle of stones, sending you love and power. Breathe deeply and absorb these gifts. As you release your breath, your circle of friends smiles and vanishes slowly. You are alone once again in your sacred space. You feel blessed and empowered.

Again you notice the faerie lights begin to dance around the great tree. As you watch, a silver glow spreads around the trunk of the tree, up through the branches, into the leaves and out into the moonbeams shining down from the sky. As you watch, enthralled by the light, a beautiful woman steps, seemingly out of the tree itself, and stands, bathed in moonlight, just in front of you.

Her beauty is subtle and luminous like the full moon at the height of its glory. Her face is serene, compassionate, and gentle. In her eyes you see both the vitality of youth and the wisdom of age. Her robes, falling softly around her feet, are much like the ones you have chosen for your self. On her bosom, a star, encircled in silver, gleams in the moonlight. In her hands she holds a beautiful silver bowl filled with water.

As you stand entranced, she dips her fingers in the water and touches your forehead. In a voice deep as midnight, yet light as silver bells, she says:

> Bless you, for you are my child. Know that you are blessed for you have called me, not unto you, but from within you. For I have been with you always, and am ever more so when you celebrate the beauty and fullness of your life. Know that in celebrating the gifts in your life, you are creating them thus. Remember this, for it is a great and sacred mystery. And now my child, I will teach you to call me from within your very being.

She reaches into the folds of her robes and brings out a lovely crystal. She places it in your hands, and bids you hold it up so that the moonlight may cascade down through it.

As you do so, you feel the cool, gentle moonbeams caress your head and face. Moonlight flows down over your body, slowly filling you with a power of deep and abiding strength.

As the moonlight shining through the crystal reaches your feet and spreads out on the ground, you feel a completeness, a fullness of spirit. The beautiful lady says to you:

> *Celebrate this feeling, and remember to carry it with you at all times. For though I am the Goddess of the full moon, I am within you at all times.*

She spreads her arms as if to embrace you. You open your arms to receive the embrace, and breathe deeply to savor the moment of joy. As you do so, the beautiful lady transforms into a gentle beam of light which swirls once around you, then slowly enters your heart. For just a moment, you feel all your empty spaces filled with joy . . . love . . . nurturing . . . power . . . fullness of spirit.

Breathe deeply and celebrate this beautiful feeling. Take a few moments to celebrate all the joy and beauty in your life. And it will be just so. Celebrate your being.

When you are ready, shift your focus to the beautiful light within your heart, and let your self return to the present time and place. Know that you may come back to your image whenever you need. It is one of your sacred spaces, and like the Goddess of beauty and abundance, it dwells within you all the time.

Return peacefully. Energized, refreshed.

Be here now and be content.

Sky Light Keys: Overview

The outer energies are often called "Lights" or "colors." They are less focused than Rays and more like glowing Lights. I call them Lights, because that seems gentle. Lights have a more etheric vibration than Rays.

Some of these Lights are sensed in the upper energy areas of the body, the upper etheric, or the upper aura. These are more Spirit-oriented; I call these Sky Lights. They are White, Rainbow, Crystal, Spirit, Silver and Gold.

Harmonics

The harmonic key for the Sky Lights is the sound of **m** as in **me**. This harmonic is higher pitched and far more variable than the deep **m** of the Indigo harmonic **om**.

Vibrational Energies

The energies of Sky Lights are lighter, veiled, spiritual, diffuse, swirling, upper etheric, upper body sensations. Focus on the specific properties of each Sky Light to activate its energies. Combine with active imagery and personal concepts of each Light. Amplify with variations on the Sky Light harmonic **m** as in **me**. Humming produces several tonal changes to create a "match" for these diffuse energies. These are best individually selected, but here are some suggestions:

White	Dense vibration	Deep-toned hum
Rainbow	Multifaceted vibration	Scaled hum
Crystal	Precision vibration	Clear tonal hum
Spirit	Intangible vibration	Silent, inner hum
Silver	Receptive vibration	Inhalation hum
Gold	Activation vibration	Exhalation hum

Harmonic Breathing Pattern

The primary breathing pattern for Sky Lights is gentle, airy breaths sweeping in and out of the nose silently. Pause after each exhalation to reform the mental image and physical sensation of each Sky Light's primary energy attributes. Generally, these attributes are:

White	Protective, transmitting medium
Rainbow	Balancing, organizing distribution
Crystal	Focused clarity, amplification
Spirit	Empowering, intangible, source connection
Silver	Receptive, reflective nurturance
Gold	Activating, energizing inspiration

Suggested Harmonic Exercises, Chants, and Mantras

Using appropriate chants and mantras devised to focus these diffuse energies to their specific purpose is helpful. Accompany all mantras with variations of the harmonic **m**.

Emphasize by humming each **m**. This is particularly helpful when you have chosen the correlating hum to activate each Light for your own alchemy. Let the samples in each section catalyst your own creations.

Sensory

Sensory keys for the Sky Lights are, in general, interchangeable:
Frankincense
Myrrh
Vanilla
Almond

Symbols

White	Pyramid, clouds, feather
Rainbow	Rainbow, solar system, beribboned maypole
Crystal	Quartz point, crystal ball, wand
Spirit	Eight-point star, wings, crown
Silver	Moon, female symbol, basket
Gold	Sun, male symbol, rocket (fireworks)

Personifications

White	Receptive healer	*(Mother Mary)*
Rainbow	Active expresser	*(Georgia O'Keefe)*
Crystal	Guardian angel	*(Personal)*
Spirit	Christ/Avatar	*(Jesus/Buddha)*
Silver	Counselor/Queen	*(Guinevere)*
Gold	Provider/King	*(Arthur)*

Stone Alchemy

White	Milky quartz, white agate
Rainbow	Rainbow crystal, abalone shell
Crystal	Clear quartz crystal, double-terminated crystal
Spirit	Clustered quartz crystal
Silver	Silver, moonstone
Gold	Gold, rutile quartz

Chapter Twenty

White Light: Healing

Even the greatest sorts of spiritual teachings must be adapted
to the culture of the people they are presented to
if they are to really connect with their whole psyches.

—Charles Tart

White is the reflected Light with the properties of all the traditional Rays as well as the blended ones. White Light is a protective, centering energy, the medium through which all light and positive energies can pass. White Light is a channel for transmitting all kinds of healing energies. To send a healing Ray, send White Light with the specific Ray energy in it. White Light is the wrapping, or the transportation medium, of all positive energies.

The trick with White Light is to weave it like a veil surrounding whoever or whatever you wish to transmit positive energies toward.

Alchemist's Note: White Light is effective at all times. It is advisable to surround all your healing transformation work with White Light because it amplifies gently, strengthens, and gives support to the highest aspects of the Light. White Light work is the work of personal, planetary, and universal healing.

Elemental Alchemy	Spirit and Air
Key Issues	Right action, oneness, perception, communication
Stone Alchemy	Milky quartz, white agate
Cumulative Alchemy	Healing Medium (or channel)

White Light Keys

Harmonic	Sound of **m** (dense vibration, deep-toned hum)
Alchemical Properties	Transmitted medium for healing energies
Sensory Keys	Interchangeable (use vanilla to start)
Symbols	Pyramid, clouds, feather
Personification	Receptive Healer
Runic	Eolh (Algiz)
Astrological Correlates	Gemini, Aries
Major Arcana Key	The High Priestess
Archangel	All dimensions
Stone Alchemy	Milky quartz, white agate

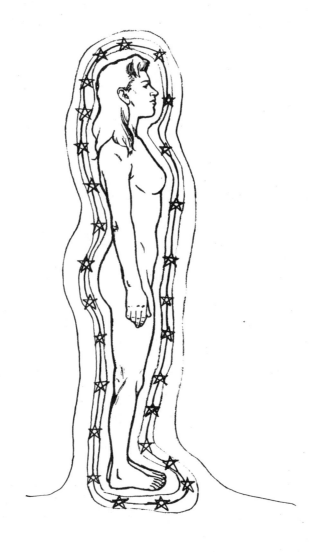

White Light Energy Centers

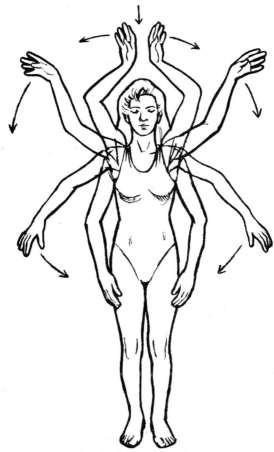

White Light Harmonic Posture

Harmonic

Dense vibration, deep-toned hum.

Creamy, dreamy light revealing,
Protective medium of healing.
Shield of goodness and warm feelings,
Surrounding me from floor to ceiling.

Amplify with sweeping movements to activate the veil of White Light.

Alchemical Properties

White Light is a diffuse medium for the transmittal of positive energies, communication, healing and protection. White provides a channel for releasing negativities by infusing positive energies in a primarily mental, etheric, spiritual manner.

Depleted White Light Energy Pattern

Powers   Supportive, diffuse, environmental, filtering action
Activates   All healing and positive alchemy filters for energy flow
Amplifies   Dispersal of other Ray-Light energies, protection
Balances   Diffuse, scattered energies and toxic buildup
Releases   Negativities
Realigns   Proper flow of positive, essential energies

Sensory Key

(Interchangeable)
The sensory key suggested with White Light is vanilla.

Shared attributes of vanilla and White Light:
       Healing
       Purification
       Protection
       Intuition
       Love
       The element of Spirit

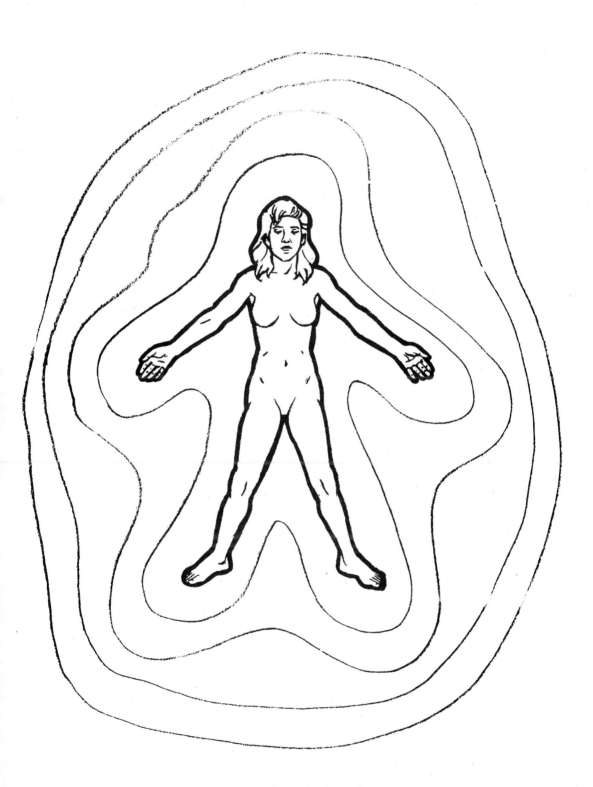

Harmonious White Light Energy Pattern

Vanilla is inexpensive and readily available as incense, herb oils, extracts, scented candles, et cetera. The predominance of vanilla as a flavoring in foods points to an interesting shared preference. Vanilla is especially evocative of the gentle healing aspects of the Lady. Use vanilla alone or with other sensory keys for a foundational element to all positive transformational alchemy.

- Use a vanilla-scented candle for the Lady (or Goddess), and a cinnamon or spicy candle for the Lord (or God). In combination, this brings strength to the Lady (female aspects, receptivity) and focus to the Lord (male aspects, activation).

- White Light is most effective when it is received and activated in balance. To practice this alchemy, place vanilla oil or scent on both your wrists. Sniff your left wrist, then image White Light entering and healing your Body/Mind system. Breathe and receive. Breathe again to release residue or tension. Sniff your right wrist, then image White Light flowing forth from within. Breathe deeply, and send White Light outward to strengthen loved ones, and for specific personal, societal, and planetary issues. Follow with specific color Rays or Lights for intensive, transformational alchemy.

Symbols

Pyramid represents the sacred, etheric energies which transmit all energies to and from spiritual realms. From a solid base of personal alchemy, we can touch the pinnacle of Self-transformation.

Clouds represent the nurturing forms of healing light which carry the sustenance of positive energies. In order to see the silver lining of each dark cloud, we must first look for the healings in each storm of transformation we encounter.

Feather represents the transmittal of positive healing energies. Like the feather, our intentions must float lightly on the energies of Spirit, yet be strong enough to carry the weight of our needs for protection.

Personification

Healing

White is the energy of the Receptive Healer. It is the Virgin Mary, patroness of all healing, and holy Mother of God. White is the energy of Grace transmitted with highest blessings.

Musings

That which we weave in our fantasy strengthens the fabric of our reality.

The sending of White Light is the purest expression of good intentions and a primary catalyst for the alchemy of all healing transformations.

A shield of White Light is only protective in proportion to the amount of light one radiates from within. White Light is illuminated by all colors and elements but is supercharged with the energies of Spirit.

Runic Correlate

Eolh (Algiz)

Shared aspects with White Light:

Protection	Shield
Etheric medium	Assistance
The element of Spirit	

Eolh (Algiz)

Eolh (Algiz) protects the transmittal of spiritual energies and provides an opening for highest Light to illuminate self-transformation. The process of self-development can leave the alchemist feeling tender and covered with "new skin." Activate a healing medium in which to grow your self with the rune Eolh (Algiz). The alchemies of Eolh (Algiz) must remain positive.

Astrological Correlates

Solar Gemini

Gemini people are restless, nosy, news gathers—valuable and very versatile. They are eager to know too much too fast.

—Ursula Lewis

Lunar Aries

For instance, a Moon in Aries type can talk about big plans, and invoke a lot of enthusiasm for these plans, but when called on to deliver more details, he falls apart.

—Sybil Leek

White Light and Aries work with issues of protection, filtering, and communication. Overall, each elemental group of signs has a correlating alchemy in relation to White Light.

Fire signs	Filtering medium
Water signs	Balancing structure
Earth signs	Transmittal medium
Air signs	Communication medium

Major Tarot Arcana Key

The High Priestess

Shared aspects with White Light:

Experiential wisdom	Spiritual medium
Intuition	Protection
Transmutation	Transmittal of Elemental Energies

She is the link between the seen and the unseen.

—Eden Gray

She is the door to the temple.

—F. D. Graves

Musings

White light is woven from the pure energies of all that is Spirit in Nature. White light is formed from the ethers of all that is Goodness and human kindness. Even in the simple process of sending white veils of light for healing and protection, we have become the high priestess, for we have chosen to take action. White Light and good intentions from the heart create a purely magickal, healing alchemy.

For what purpose do we attain experiential wisdom?
In order to know when to use it—or when not to, more likely.

The more we know, the less we understand.
The less we understand, the more we rely on faith.
The more we rely on faith, the less we need to know.
The less we need to know, the more we begin to understand.

Archangel

Angelic Dimension Key

All

Alchemy of Healing, Highest Light Work and Magick, Transmittal of Right Action

We are healed of suffering only by experiencing it to the full.

—Marcel Proust

Angelic Invocation

I call upon the highest angelic beings of light to send their help in this healing magick.

I call upon my highest Self to receive the purity of the Light—perfection—and to guide me in the healing actions I must take for the task before me.

Let me be a vessel for this, an instrument of the highest healing light.

Make my thoughts and my intentions clear. Make, I pray, my actions right.

Stone Alchemy

Any white stone works well for White Light energies. The stones chosen specifically for White Light are the milky (or opaque) quartz and the white agate.

Placement of white stones is above each shoulder, above the top of the head, or on the outside edge of an ankle. This places White Light healing around all the other energies. White Light is a gentle facilitator for all rays and lights, as well as a purifier and a protective shield.

Milky Quartz: Transmitter Stone
Element: Earth, Air and Spirit

This quartz can be in opaque crystal points or a piece of quartzy-looking stone. Opaque quartz symbolizes strength and reflects the foundation shield of White Light energy. White Light has been thought to be amorphous, but it is actually a foundation energy. White supports us from the etheric and back again. In much the same way as Red Ray or Black Ray connects to Earth, White Light serves as a foundation connecting all other transformation work.

Opaque, milky quartz is inexpensive because many people are interested in clarity of crystals. This is not one of those times when clarity is important. In this case, the denser white quartz vibrates best with the White Light. This particular quartz blends the Spirit in crystal with the denser vibration of Earth. This also represents what White Light energy does; it is a Spirit and Earth connector and can be shamanic in its work.

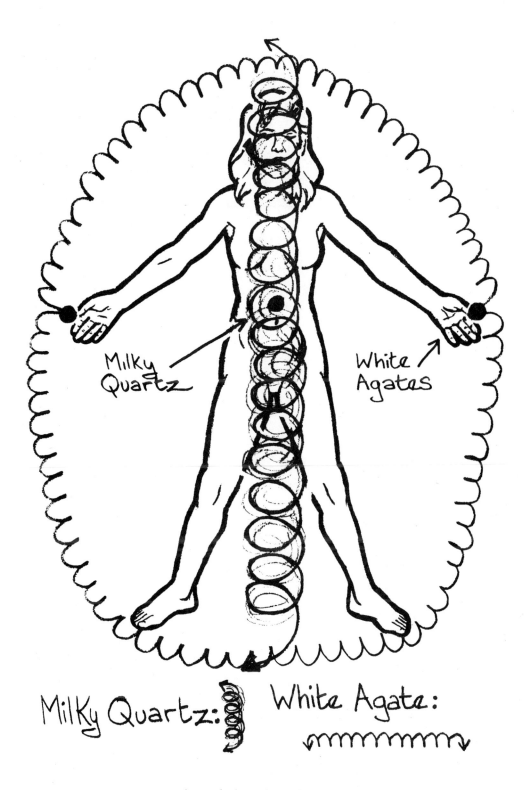

White Light Stone Energy Patterns

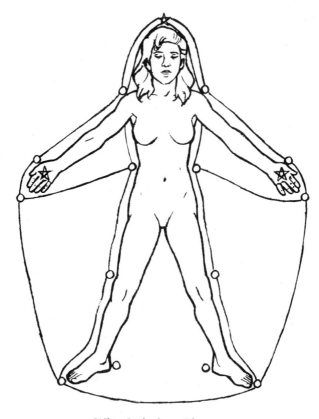

White Light Stone Placement

White Agate: Receptive Medium Stone
Element: Earth (with some Spirit)

The next of the white stones is white agate, or white chalcedony. If a stone seems milky, yet translucent, as though it could be reached through . . . that represents White Light. All white agates have an earthy vibration which can protect, support, and provide the needed foundation from which to work. They suggest lunar, receptive energies and earth energies in balance. This is a good energy alchemy for receiving and transmitting.

Alternative Stone

Another white stone to use for White Light is white calcite, particularly if you can get a crystal. These calcite crystals are shaped like little rectangles which have been twisted a bit. These are called "refracted crystals," which is very metaphysical considering that our personal light reflects, and refracts, the Universal Light.

Chapter Twenty-one

Rainbow Light: Blending

We shall never understand one another
until we reduce the language to seven words.
—Kahlil Gibran

Rainbow Light reflects the balanced and ordered blending of all the Rays. This happens either as Rays enter from Spirit coming into the body, or as they come out of the physical, returning to Spirit for transmutation. Rainbow Light realigns all energies in harmonious balance. Imagine putting light through a prism—this produces the spectrum or rainbow effect.

Rainbow Light is used as a focus for calling in any specific Ray energy. This is because all energies are contained in Rainbow Light. This is true of the newer blended Rays, as well as the traditional ones. Rainbow Light is used to help in transmuting, releasing or rejuvenating any energy.

The trick with Rainbow Light is to sweep it up from the ground, widely arch it over the body, then return to the ground or the other side—just like a rainbow.

Alchemist's Note: Imagine the energies being pulled into Rainbow Light. Focus on your specific intent. When the energy transmutes and you feel it become part of the balanced whole again, then pull in what you need. It is nice to send out a little Rainbow energy for the Highest Universal Good. Send a rainbow of peace.

Elemental Alchemy	Fire and Spirit
Key Issues	Sensation, regeneration, right action, oneness
Stone Alchemy	Rainbow crystal, abalone
Cumulative Alchemy	Ordered Blending

Rainbow Light Keys

Harmonic	Sound of **m** (multifaceted vibration, scaled hum)
Alchemical Properties	Ordered distribution of energies
Sensory Keys	Interchangeable (almond to start)
Symbols	Rainbow, solar system, beribboned maypole
Personification	Active Expresser
Runic	Peord (Perth) or Daeg (Dagaz)
Astrological Correlates	All signs
Major Arcana Key	Wheel of Fortune
Archangel	Cassiel (Saturn), Auriel (Uranus)
Stone Alchemy	Rainbow crystal, abalone

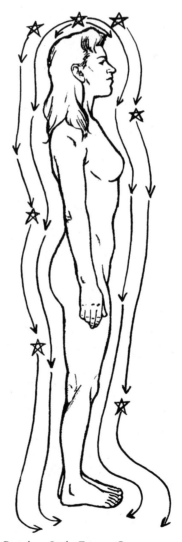

Rainbow Light Energy Centers

Harmonious Rainbow Light Energy Pattern (Expansive)

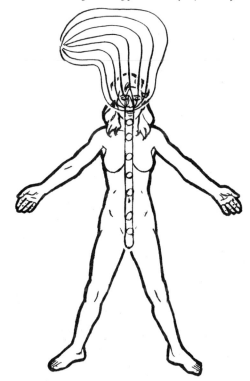

Harmonious Rainbow Light Energy Pattern (Intrapersonal)

Harmonic

Multifaceted vibration, scaled hum.

Mesmerizing melodies
Of multicolored energies,
Dimensional frequencies,
The myth, the miracle, the mystery be.

Amplify by imaging each Ray color moving into a perfect rainbow arching over the physical body and through the etheric.

Rainbow Light Harmonic Postures

Alchemical Properties

Rainbow Light blends, orders and distributes the proper flow and supply of the Ray energies. Rainbow redirects energies in a primarily physical, etheric, spiritual manner.

Powers	Supportive, direct, ordered, sorting action
Activates	Ordered distribution of all Ray energies
Amplifies	Organization, transformation
Balances	Distribution of all essential energies
Releases	Surplus of Ray energies
Realigns	Proper flow of essential energies

Sensory Key

(Interchangeable)
The sensory key suggested with Rainbow Light is almond.

Shared attributes of almond and Rainbow Light:
>Distribution
>Balance
>Fortune
>Healing
>Love

Almond is relatively inexpensive and is available as oil, flavors, extracts, tea and nuts.

- Throw unshelled almonds in a blazing fire. Focus on the many colors in the flames and on those which emerge in your imagery. Focus on the warmth of the fire. Close your eyes and transmute the warmth into pure light. Receive what you need, then distribute pure light to issues and individuals in your life. Note the colors that emerge; these are clues to what specific Rays are also needed.

- Ceremonially light a candle oiled with almond. Next, send rainbows of light arching through the dimensions, connecting your self to people and places you love. Remember that rainbows are not binding energies, but reflections of the highest energies of light in harmonious order.

- Redistribute imbalances in energy with a quiet cup of almond tea and this simple focusing exercise:

  Imagine that you are sitting on a large rock in the center of a misty meadow. Slowly, the light begins to peek through the mists as fragments of rainbow. Breathe deeply and release slowly. Blow away the mists gently and quietly. Continue to breathe and release until the mists have dispersed and a perfect rainbow arches over your head. Experience being on the rock, in the meadow, under the arching Rainbow Light. Breathe, and file the image for your alchemy.

Symbols

Rainbow represents the sacred spectrum illuminated by the highest Light and reflecting the precision of Universal Alchemy. Between all banded lines of division lie the blended elements of multidimensional energies, and the vibrational frequencies of the All.

Solar system (galaxy) represents the variety of forms orbiting with constant, ordered perfection around the Source of all Light. We move with precision according to the changing patterns of our personal transformations.

Beribboned maypole represents the celebration of Nature's elemental energies connecting all life to the activator of life. We weave our lives free-form, holding the silken ribbons of our Lady's robes.

Personifications

Blending

Rainbow is the energy of the Artist/Expresser. It is Georgia O'Keefe painting flowers with all of Nature's colors. Rainbow is the filtering energy of the desert which gave clarity of vision to O'Keefe's creations.

Musings

Pan-dimensional pathways are paved with platinum and crystal jewels of rainbow hues.

How convenient to communicate with color, and how very real to relate to one another with rainbows.

So with the macrocosm.
As with the microcosm, so mote it be.
As above, so below, as above
So mote it be.
As below, so above, as below
So manifest be in Light with Thee.

Creatrix mater mother She.
Iris, rainbow blessed be.

The Rainbow represents perfection harmoniously distributed by the Light.

Runic Correlates

Peord (Perth) or Daeg (Dagaz)

Shared aspects with Rainbow Light:
    Order   Distribution
    Initiation   Fate
    Chances for growth
    The element of Fire

Peord (Perth) initiates the personal alchemist according to the transformational rituals of Spirit. All initiation is self-initiation guided by divine order. Activate the sequences of experience leading to self-initiation with Peord (Perth).

Peord (Perth)

Daeg (Dagaz) distributes the energies equitably for the processes of self-transformation. Self-acceptance requires an objective judgment of personal needs as separate from wants or expectations. Activate the harmonious flow of essential energies with faith and Daeg (Dagaz).

Daeg (Dagaz)

    Together, Peord (Perth) and Daeg (Dagaz) open the alchemist to receiving the most potent elements for self-fulfillment and spiritual advancement.

Astrological Correlates

Solar/Lunar: All signs

Rainbow Light works well with Aquarius and Virgo for issues of organizing sacred wisdom. Astrological signs correlate with Rainbow Light according to their element.

Fire signs   Energy organizer

Everything, including exercise and dietary habits, should be done in moderation so that the person doesn't exhaust what he has.

—Stephen Arroyo

Water signs   Structured blending

There may be a fear of emotional involvements because they question whether or not they can survive the ordeal if the relationships don't work out.

—Betty Lundgren

Earth signs   Practical distribution

They indicate how much material security we have, how determined we are . . . how we weather the storms in life.

—Betty Lundgren

Air signs   Ordered communication

The life of the air sign people leads to their finding the most comfortable modes of expression in art, words, and abstract thought.

—Stephen Arroyo

Major Tarot Arcana Key

Wheel of Fortune

Shared aspects with Rainbow Light:
Divine order   Experiential learning
Synchronicity   Energy distribution

Amidst all the pain of living, we still receive the blessings of this path, the consistency that keeps us whole.

—Ellen Cannon Reed

Musings

The sun pierces the clouds to create a rainbow of light. In the same way, we must pierce through the clouds of self-doubt to let the rainbow of our Self shine through.

A rainbow of healing peace can illuminate the darkest times.

It is possible to stop a rainbow emerging from a crystalline prism. One needs only to block the light. It is also possible to stop the balanced emergence of the self in the same way, but only for a little while. So why bother?

Archangel

Angelic Dimension Keys

Cassiel: Archangel of Saturn
> Alchemy of Divine Order, Distribution of Power, and Universal Flow
>> Days   Saturday, Monday
>> Times   3-4 AM
>>   11-12 AM
>>   7-8 PM

Auriel: Archangel of Uranus
> Alchemy of Divine Order, Distribution of Power, and Universal Flow
>> Days   Monday, Wednesday
>> Times   2-3 AM
>>   10-11 AM
>>   6-7 PM

♄

Nothing in the world is single.
All things by a law divine.
In one Spirit meet and mingle.

—Percy Shelly

⛢

Angelic Invocation

Cassiel, I call upon your powers of balance to create the order needed in this time of confusion and Spiritual dis-ease.

Auriel, I call upon your divine inspiration to create the fair solution to the situations I find before me.

I call upon the force of balanced power as it is reflected in the actions of Divine order and in my receptivity to Universal Flow.

Stone Alchemy

The stones chosen here for Rainbow Light are crystals which have rainbow inclusions in them and also abalone, or mother of pearl. Placement for the rainbow stones is above the White Light stones at the top of the head. Rainbow Light stones also can be used alone about four to six inches above the head.

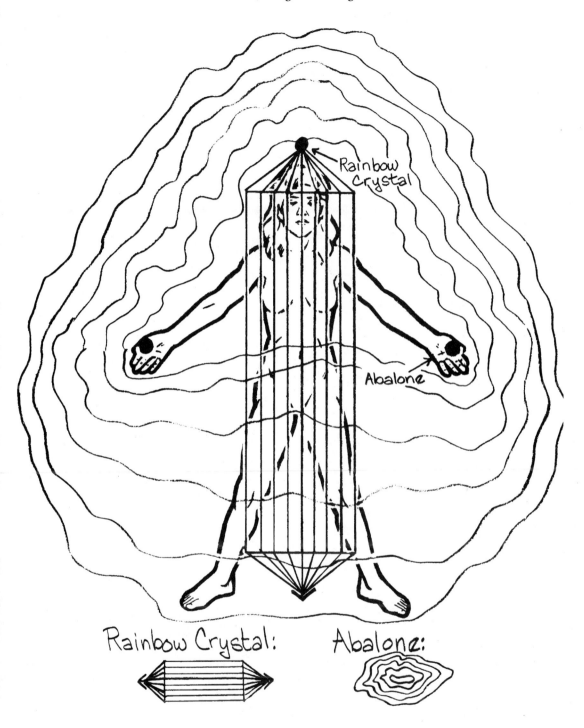

Rainbow Light Stone Energy Patterns

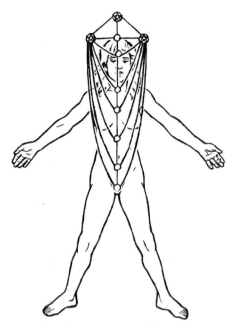

Rainbow Light Stone Placement

Rainbow Crystals: Order Stone
Element: Spirit and Air

Crystals with rainbow inclusions are also called rainbow crystals and sometimes rainbow quartz. They are not expensive, but may take time to locate. These crystals have a high spiritual vibration. Rainbow crystals can be used to balance from the spiritual, to the etheric, to the physical and back through the whole Being because Rainbow Light contains all energies in balance.

    The rainbow crystal, regardless of clarity, is excellent for healing. It is the rainbow that is most important for this particular stone, not the clarity. Some stones are surprisingly filled with rainbows, despite the fact they are dense or opaque; take time to look. The rainbow is the key factor as it reflects the energies to align and balance.

Abalone Shell: Filter Stone
Element: Water and Earth

Abalone shells and mother of pearl are inexpensive and have a subtle but powerful vibration. These work like coral, forming a foundation from and through which all energies flow. Visualize energies flowing into the shell, being transmuted and balanced, then flowing back into the body. Abalone shell serves as a tidal balancer, like the ocean. It helps with personal ebb and flow. To balance the energies of Mind, Body and Spirit, use abalone shells along with rainbow crystal; the crystal represents Spirit, and the shell symbolizes matter, or Earth.

Alternative Stone

An alternative for the Rainbow Light stone is peacock ore, also called bornite. It has a dark, intense, rainbow color. Amplify with crystals to deepen the energies.

Chapter Twenty-two

Crystal Light: Clarity

My visionary anger cleansing my sight.
—Adrienne Rich

Crystal Light represents White Light processed upward through Rainbow Light. As light moves up, it goes through White, breaks into the spectrum, then moves back up and out through Crystal. Also, if light is coming in, Crystal Light represents the protection of highest Self and Spirit.

Crystal Light is a dimensional link to inner guidance. The trick with Crystal Light is to focus on perfection. A single, clear note or tone such as a chime is most helpful.

Elemental Alchemy	Spirit and Fire
Key Issues	Right action, oneness, sensation, regeneration
Stone Alchemy	Clear quartz crystal, double-terminated crystal
Cumulative Alchemy	Amplified Clarity

Crystal Light Keys

Harmonic	Sound of m (precision vibration, clear, tonal hum)
Alchemical Properties	Clarity, focus, amplification
Sensory Keys	Interchangeable (myrrh to start)
Symbols	Quartz point, crystal ball, wand
Personification	Guardian Angel
Runic	Tyr (Teiwaz)
Astrological Correlates	All signs
Major Arcana Key	The World
Archangel	All dimensions
Stone Alchemy	Clear quartz crystal, double-terminated crystal

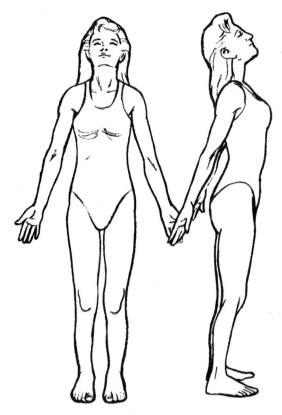

Crystal Light Harmonic Posture

Harmonic

Precision vibration, clear tonal hum.

Mystic, magic alchemy
Illuminating clarity
Perfection manifest I see
Purely connecting me to Thee.

Amplify by imaging a perfect crystalline shape encasing the physical from the etheric.

Alchemical Properties

Crystal Light amplifies clarity and focuses the flow of highest spiritual energies. Crystal purifies all dimensions of the Body/Mind system in a physical, etheric, spiritual manner.

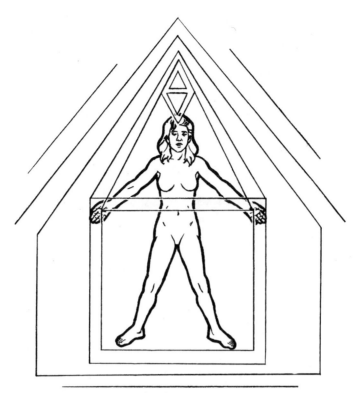

Harmonious Crystal Light Energy Pattern (Expansive)

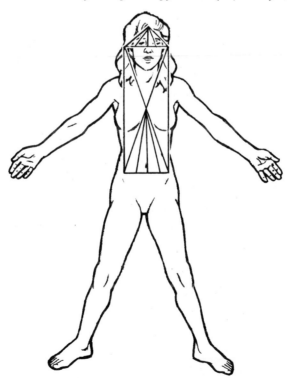

Harmonious Crystal Light Energy Pattern (Intrapersonal)

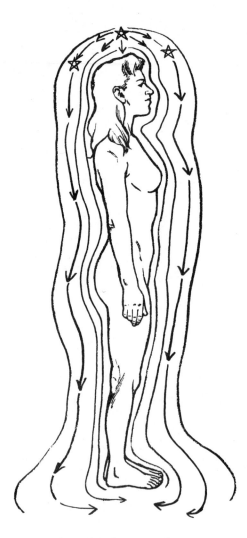

Crystal Light Energy Centers

Powers	Supportive, direct, almost intangible, clearing and amplification action
Activates	Clarity for transformation
Amplifies	All Ray and Light energies
Balances	Inadequate flow of essential energies
Releases	Energy blocks
Realigns	Focused flow of all energies

Sensory Key

(Interchangeable)
The sensory key suggested with Crystal Light is myrrh.

> Shared attributes of myrrh and Crystal Light:
> Clarity
> Purification
> Exorcism
> Healing
> Spirituality
> The element of Spirit

Myrrh is moderately inexpensive and is available as oil, incense, and in herb form. Myrrh is a highly sacred herb, long associated with ceremonial work. In combination with Crystal Light, myrrh catalysts personal clarity through spiritual illumination.

- Burn myrrh as an incense. Light one pale candle in an otherwise dark room. Sit facing the candle. Close your eyes and focus on the reflection of the candle flame dancing across the screen of your closed eyelids. Next, shift your focus and your screen to your third eye area. Open your eyes and gaze at the candle flame. In your mind's eye, see a clear crystal point emerge from within the center of the flame, pointing toward Spirit. Focus on the flame and your crystal image. Reflect on your life. Ask for clarity from the highest dimensions of Truth. Clarify your intentions. Clarify your Self.

- Burn myrrh incense. Focus on Crystal Light forming into a perfect sphere, a crystal ball of light. Focus with your inner vision. Use the crystal ball of your mind's eye for divination and meditation.

Symbols

Quartz crystal point represents the geometric perfection of clarity enabling Truth to be seen and Vision to be activated. The structured perfection of Truth is constructed in the constant clarification of our lives.

Crystal ball represents the quest for clarity, divined from within the reflection of our Self. Within the sphere of our self lie the spheres of the Self, revealed only when the clouds of self-doubt disperse.

Wand represents the ceremonial, ritual activation of clarity through the use of Highest Magick. We sweep our tiny wands across the boundless night sky, casting forth fragments of Light, awakening the stars.

Personification

Clarity

Crystal is the energy of our Guardian Angel and Spirit guides. It is the gentle attunement to angelic realms and the guidance from within ourselves as individuals. Crystal is the precision of cosmic attunement.

Musings

The mind of Spirit holds the map to multidimensional linking.
Everything is a mnemonic for self and spirit. And self and spirit are one.

The wisdoms we find,
Within one mind,
Are never found without it.

Clarity requires a narrow focus with a wide-angle lens.

It is not necessary for you to seek after perfection, only to accept it as you find it within your Self.

Gods are only as strong as the power with which we invest them.

—Stardragon

Runic Correlate

Tyr (Teiwaz)

Shared aspects with Crystal Light:

Knowledge   Truth
Understanding   Spiritual judgment
The element of Spirit

Tyr (Teiwaz)

Tyr (Teiwaz) empowers the personal alchemist with the essential energies of truth and clarity. The path to fullest self-transformation is illuminated by the light of personal clarity and the fires of personal truth. Activate clarity for all your transformational processes with the convictions of the Spiritual warrior and the rune Tyr (Teiwaz). The alchemy of Tyr (Teiwaz) is sharpened with the addition of focus, awareness and inner silence.

Astrological Correlates

Solar/Lunar: All Signs

Crystal Light works well with Pisces and Scorpio for issues of self-awareness and spiritual clarity. In general, astrological signs, grouped by elements, have specific effects when used with Crystal Light.

Fire signs   Clarity catalyst

Lots of fire also symbolizes high ideals . . . with a sense of humor they are then able to put themselves into perspective and will pick ideals that can be lived.

—Betty Lundgren

Water signs   Precision enhancer

They are therefore happiest when their fluidity is channeled and given form by someone else.

—Stephen Arroyo

Earth signs   Illumination catalyst

The earth element tends to be cautious, premeditative, rather conventional . . .

—Stephen Arroyo

Air signs   Perceptive structurer

These people are generally curious; they read a lot or study subjects on their own.

—Betty Lundgren

Major Tarot Arcana Key

The World

Shared aspects with Crystal Light:

Fortune	Spiritual clarity
Purity	Empowerment
Connections	Universal flow

If we knew how to realize our potential, we would find that we are in touch with the Universe.

—R. J. Stewart

Musings

Can we requisition clarity, or must we earn it for our selves? I wonder. Clarity cannot simply be ordered. It emerges according to our own "orders."

Can we request a more useful gift from Spirit than the pure gift of clarity? Can we request a more useful gift from our Self?

Can we ask for no less than a clearer path?
A clearer path to Self?
A clearer path to Spirit?
Or a clarity of Self?
And a clear connection to the personal empowerment of Spirit?

Can we ask for this gift of clarity, no less, no more; or shall we just accept it when it comes, and be grateful? Will we know then that we have chosen to give our Selves what we were "cleared" to receive from the start?

Archangel

Angelic Dimension Keys

All

Alchemy of Clarity, Illumination, Perception, Spiritual precision

Hold every moment sacred. Give each clarity and meaning, each the weight of their awareness ,each its true and due fulfillment.

—Thomas Mann

Angelic Invocation

I call for the crystal clarity of angelic realm.

I call for the crystalline purity of Spirit's light to illuminate my journey and clarify my purpose.

I call upon my Self to be awake, aware, and alert to the messages of Spirit and the meanings of this life experience.

Stone Alchemy

Placement for Crystal Light stones is between the feet and also about six to twelve inches above the head. Stones suggested here for the Crystal Light are very clear quartz crystals (in this case, clarity is important) and double-terminated crystals.

Alchemist's Note: You might want to move Crystal Light energy slowly upward with a crystal. As you do, draw the energies in carefully. Physically, you can place a Crystal Light stone on affected areas as you go along. It is helpful to balance the crystals, if you have several. Put one at the foot; one at the head. I move another crystal up and down the body for a

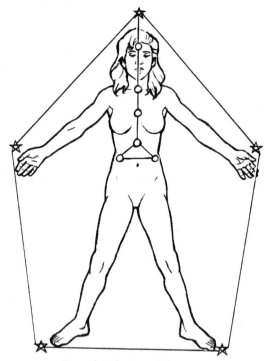

Crystal Light Stone Placement

direct connection with Crystal Light. If you have just one, surround the body in light first and then work with the crystal.

When working with Crystal Light, you are working beyond any sort of division, so you can affect the world. Be careful when working this way, because what you work with comes through you. Stay clear, like the crystal. When you have worked with pure Crystal Light, be sure you follow with an earthy stone such as sodalite, malachite, or granite.

Clear Quartz Crystal: Perfection Stone
Element: Spirit

For Crystal Light, use the most perfect crystal, regardless of size. A symmetry of form and clarity reflects Crystal Light. Dense crystals with a clear, perfect point can also be used. In fact, that is often a good way to start.

Bringing the Crystal Light down through the clear point into the denser crystal vibration is like bringing light from Spirit to Earth. Clear quartz and Crystal Light together help activate the evolution of psychic cosmic energies, not only in the personal mind, but in the Mind of Humankind.

Alchemist's Note: Use crystals which you have charged with Crystal Light energy for charging other high vibration crystals and stones. Clear quartz crystal, of course, can be inexpensively or unreasonably priced, depending on where you buy it and on the size. Size really does not make any difference in working with a crystal. Some of the most potent crystals I have come across have been tiny, almost fragments.

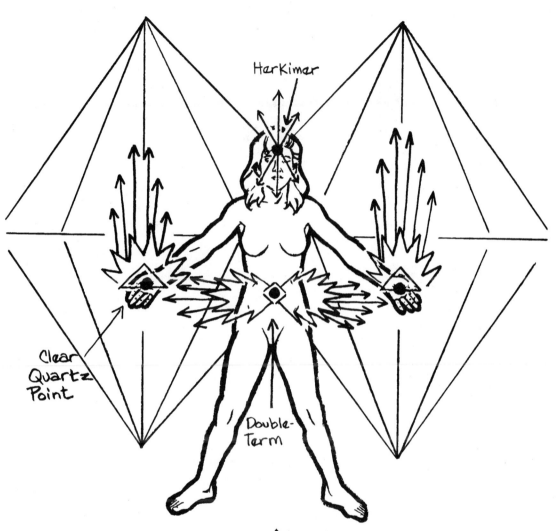

Crystal Light Stone Energy Patterns

Double-terminated Crystal: Direction Stone
Element: Spirit

Double-terminated crystals are moderately inexpensive but more difficult to find. Look for stones that are pointed on both ends, as though they grew on their side. The energy flows from side to side, moving energy in a direct, balanced manner. It is best to use a double-term with another one-point clear crystal or rainbow quartz so the energy in the double-term can flow back and forth, then activate through or be received from the single-pointed crystal. Work with these a while to see how they flow together.

The double-terminated crystal is usually placed on the body at blockage points. Double-terms rotate the energy back and forth, breaking up specific blocks. If these are psychological blocks place the stones outside the body, or decide where the pain is manifested physically, even though it is psychological in origin. Work symbolically with lots of imagery, by putting the double term directly on the body. In this way, the body can be the vehicle for breaking up psychological blocks. Since Body and Mind are ultimately inseparable, this is an effective deep-level method for healing.

Double-terminated crystals are excellent for dealing with congestions and infections by breaking them up before they can really get started. (Focus, common sense, rest and Vitamin C are also helpful!) Double-terminated crystals are also excellent to keep the highest energies flowing when doing spiritual work.

Alchemist's Note: Be careful when you are working with double-terminated crystals and Crystal Light together, because you can get fatigued. This combination can drain you if you do not ground your self on a regular basis. Keep the flow moving through the body into the earth; transmute and ground with earth energies or Earth Light stones.

Alternative Stone

Another stone which can be used for Crystal Light is the Herkimer diamond. This is a clear, usually double-terminated stone, with a few little black specks in it. It is a high vibration Spirit stone and a dreamstone of intense degree.

Alchemist's Note: Since Herkimer is such an intense dreamstone, you may not have the awareness you had with the crystal point or double-term with the Herkimer. Herkimer diamonds let things work themselves out on a high plane, and you may simply not see any of it. I suggest that if you are going to work with a Herkimer, that you go ahead and do the dream work for a while until you can get comfortable with it.

Herkimer can be difficult to wear, although I occasionally do. If you do wear it, make sure you are in a balanced place. It is not really a good idea to operate machinery if you are the kind of person who is affected by crystals intensely. Interestingly enough, I have a Herkimer diamond and a little double-terminated quartz that I can wear together. When they are separate they can be difficult to wear, because each has such intense energy. That's alchemy—it's personal.

Chapter Twenty-three

Spirit Light: Source

The most beautiful thing we can experience is the mysterious.
It is the source of all true art and science.

—Albert Einstein

Alchemist's Note: Since Crystal and Spirit Lights seem similar when attempting to describe them, let me clarify a bit. When receiving input, such as images or physical sensations, you are working with Crystal Light. When the energy shifts to a higher vibration, you "become the Light of Spirit" or the Light moves "through you," or you "tap Source directly." That is Spirit Light. Later, you may create your own images to describe the experience. At the time, though, you are the Light. Celebrate it.

Crystal Light can be conceived, or felt. Spirit Light has all vibrations in such perfect harmony that it frequently transcends sensory perception—at least at this point in the evolution of Humankind's abilities.

Questions and prayers of serious ceremonial intent and Light work of the purest intent are best sent up to Spirit Light. Answers, advice or visions which come in response to Spirit Light work often manifest in Crystal Light as guides, visions, or illuminations.

Spirit Light goes beyond vision and form. It may not even be appropriate to say that it is purely spiritual, because it is not devotional or religious; it is just there. It is absolute purity. There may not be realization of contact with Spirit Light until afterward. Often questions such as "Why did I do that?" or "How did that happen?" in regard to spiritual work indicate a clear connection to Spirit Light.

The trick with Spirit Light is to give up the need to receive something immediately tangible or concrete, and to give over to the intangible realms of Spirit.
Because Spirit Light and Crystal Light are so similar, do not be confused and try to divide them. Simply work with the best possible attitude and let the stones themselves speak with Spirit and Crystal Light energies.

Elemental Alchemy	Spirit
Key Issues	Right action, empowerment, transcendence
Stone Alchemy	Clear quartz crystal clusters
Cumulative Alchemy	Power from Source

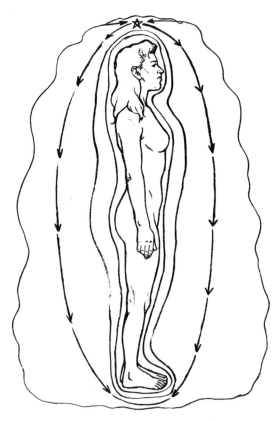

Spirit Light Energy Centers

Spirit Light Keys

Harmonic	Sound of **m** (intangible vibration, silent inner hum)
Alchemical Properties	Empowerment, transformation, healing
Sensory Key	Interchangeable (frankincense to start)
Symbols	Eight-point star, wings, crown
Personification	Christ/Avatar
Runic	Gyfu (Gebo)
Astrological Correlates	All signs
Major Arcana Keys	Self/The Star, Self/The Fool
Archangel	All dimensions
Stone Alchemy	Clear quartz crystal clusters

Spirit Light Harmonic Posture

Harmonic

Intangible vibration, silent, inner hum.

The might of Atman,
Creatrix of Love,
Source of the All, divinities plan,
Maker of manna, from heavens above,
Mother of gods, woman and man,
The first, the last, the middle, the Sum.

Amplify by whispering or silently chanting your mantra while humming softly.

Alchemical Properties

Spirit Light empowers the intangible energies of right action. Spirit transmutes all dimensions of energy to their highest good in a primarily etheric, spiritual manner.

Harmonious Spirit Light Energy Pattern (Expansive)

Powers   Supportive, direct yet intangible transformative action
Activates   Spiritual evolution
Amplifies   Spiritual connection
Balances   Limitations to personal power
Releases   Inappropriate choice (Karmic level)
Realigns   Right action, choice (Karmic level)

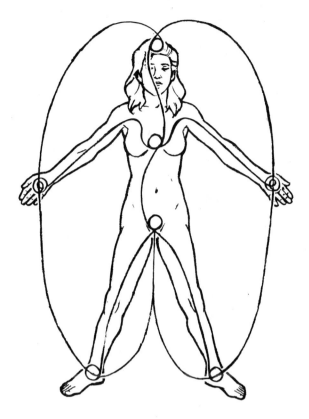

Harmonious Spirit Light Energy Pattern (Intrapersonal)

Sensory Key

(Interchangeable)
The sensory key suggested with Spirit Light is frankincense.

Shared attributes of frankincense and Spirit Light:
>   Spirituality
>   Magick
>   Protection
>   Transformation
>   Purification
>   The element of Spirit

Frankincense is moderately inexpensive and ost often available as incense, oil, or in herb form. The primary effect of Spirit Light with frankincense is the purification of the etheric bodies, allowing the flow of highest spiritual energies to move freely, unblocked by Body/Mind limitations. Frankincense and Spirit Light create a catalyst for ceremonial purification leading to personal transformation.

- Burn frankincense in generous quantities. Breathe, and focus inward. Continue until you reach your deepest place of inner silence. Focus only on the scent of frankincense and the profound stillness of your inner being. If thoughts or distractions arise, refocus on the frankincense and breathe to dispel disturbances to your inner silence. Breathe deeply, and release any residue of tension or negativities. Release your Self to the totality of your inner silence. Listen without expectation; open to the experience of Source. Take all the time you need to receive from the light of Spirit and the pure power of Source. When you have finished, slowly allow each of your breaths to become gentle infusions of Spirit. Breathe in and receive. Celebrate the eternity of Source.

Symbols

Eight-point star represents the transformation festivals of Nature which connect the elemental energies of Earth to Source. The highest energies of Spirit lie within the center of the great star and are reflected at each point of transformation in our lives.

Personal religious symbol represents the sacred preservation of highest wisdoms by the organization of shared or solitary religious observations. Only symbols which are freely chosen can reflect the truth of free choice.

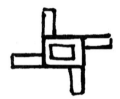

Wings represent the purest dimensions of energy guiding our flight toward Source. If we attempt flight toward the highest energies of Truth with waxen wings of self-deception, we will surely fare no better than Icarus in his quest to touch the Sun.

Personification

Blending

Spirit is the energy of the Christ/Avatar. It is the world without end, the place of no form spoken of by teachers of the Highest Light, such as Jesus of Nazareth and Gautama Buddha. Spirit is the Source of all Light—of all energies—of all power. Spirit is its own alchemy.

Musings

Beyond the beyond
Within the within

When one is a vortex
And another an upward spiral of Light
They shall dance only briefly.

> *We must allow Great Spirit's energy to move through us. In the medicine path, allowing is a byword. The only way to allow things to move through us is to be empty.*
>
> —Oh Shinnah

> *Follow your Bliss.*
>
> —Joseph Campbell

> *We have only to believe.*
>
> —Teilhard de Chardin

> *The idea of psychic objectivity is by no means a new discovery. It is, in fact, one of the earliest and most universal acquisitions of humanity: It is nothing less than the conviction as to the concrete existence of a Spirit World.*
>
> —Carl Jung

Runic Correlate

Gyfu (Gebo)

Shared aspects with Spirit Light:
Source   self/Self
Unity   Spiritual gifts
The element of Spirit

Gyfu (Gebo)

Gyfu (Gebo) unifies directly through the profound gifts and perfect experiences from within the Spirit realm. In its highest dimensions the alchemy of Spirit holds all elements for self-transformation. Activate and access the fullest dimensions of power with gratitude, and the rune *Gyfu (Gebo)*. The alchemy of *Gyfu (Gebo)* is that it must be recognized for its power and received as a gift. *Gyfu—Gebo—*gift. Power is a gift.

Astrological Correlates

Solar/Lunar: All Signs

Spirit Light works well with Capricorn and Pisces for issues of Karmic structure, choice, and duty. Each of the elemental groups of signs works differently with Spirit Light.

Fire signs　　　　　Physical transformation

They feel themselves to be channels for "life" . . .

—Betty Lundgren

Water signs　　　　　Emotional transformation

The water signs are in touch with their feelings . . . with the oneness of all creation and are able to help others by means of an empathetic responsiveness to the feelings of fellow beings.

—Stephen Arroyo

Earth signs　　　　　Behavioral transformation

These people are self-sufficient and that can be both good and bad.

—Betty Lundgren

Air signs　　　　　Mental transformation

These are the writers and reporters, the people who work well with constant change.

—Betty Lundgren

Major Tarot Arcana Key

The Star

Shared aspects with Spirit Light:

Joy	Transcendence
Spiritual inspiration	Universal harmony

Realization of the infinite, which is no realizition at all, is the first step toward enlightenment.

—F. D. Graves

Musings

Personal joy is the celebration of the individual experience. Universal joy is the celebration of infinite experience. When the individual and the infinite become one, just for a moment—that is transcendence. In that place of transcendence, one can find joy.

It would be a lot more helpful and easier to manifest if the deepest sorts of spiritual inspiration could be more specific!

Transcendence of Self is a purely internal process. It is the process of reaching the Source of your self.

Spirit defies definition, yet is given so many—and all correct, except in their exclusivity, which is not possible within Spirit. If you can conceive of the sum total of all that is, was, and ever shall be in this eternal present we call life, you can touch Spirit lightly.

Archangel

Angelic Dimension Keys

All

Alchemy of Source, Creatrix, Highest Power, Love, and Transformation

The most beautiful thing we can experience is the mysterious. It is the Source of all true art and science.

—Albert Einstein

Angelic Invocation

I call upon the angelic realms to send forth—through me and from within me—the highest power of love.

Let it be that this transformation, this healing, this magick, shall be the Work of the Source directly.

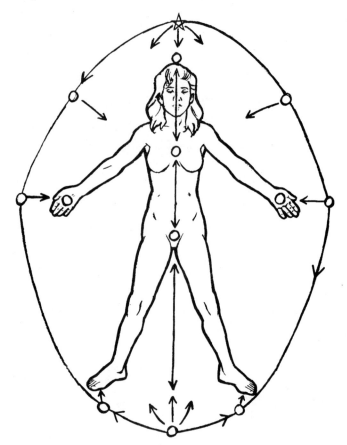

Spirit Light Stone Placement

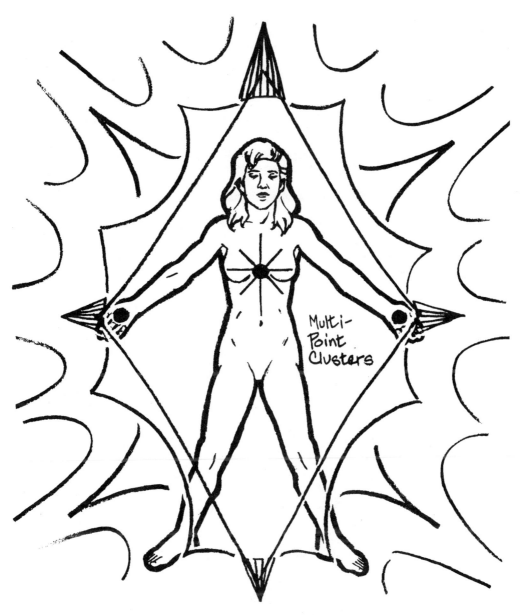

Multipoint Cluster
Clear Quartz Crystal:

Four-Point
Clear Quartz:

Double Terms (a pair):

Spirit Light Stone Energy Patterns

Stone Alchemy

Clear Quartz Crystal Clusters: Sacred Four Council Stones
Element: Spirit

Clusters of clear quartz crystals are effective for Spirit Light. I find these clusters need to have at least four points, in keeping with the Sacred Fours: the Four Archangels, the Four Winds, the Four Seasons and the Four of Synthesis.

If you have two of them (two separate stones), twin-point crystals can be used with Spirit Light. These are sacred partner stones.

Alternative Stone

A pair of very clear double-terminated quartz crystals.

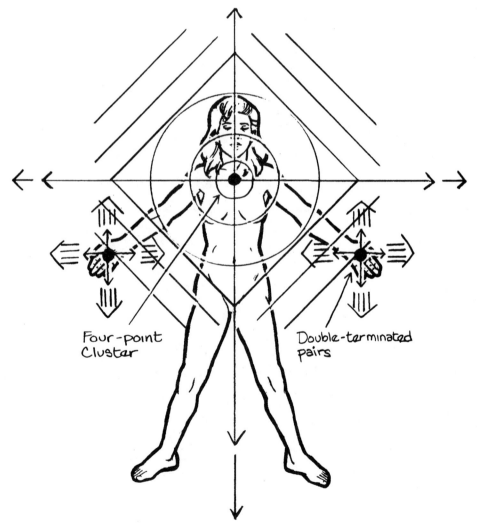

Spirit Light Stone Energy Patterns

Chapter Twenty-four

Silver Light: Receptivity

I am the daughter of earth and water,
And the nursling of the sky.
I pan through the pores of the ocean and shores,
I change, but I cannot die.

—Percy Shelley

Silver is the energy of receptivity. Silver relates to the moon energies: the lunar, female, or Yin energies. It is the energy of serenity and inner peace. The trick with Silver Light is to "encapsulate" and emulate the moon cycles. Let the energies "wax," building up to the fullness of receptivity. Let the energies "wane," releasing any obstacles to balanced receptivity.

Alchemist's Note: You may already be attuned to the lunar cycles and sensitive to Silver Light energies. If so, Silver becomes more than a Ray energy for you. In this case, finish your work with Silver energies by weaving a fresh veil of White or Rainbow Light around you. This is done because being too receptive makes it difficult to filter out the "static" of everyday living.

Elemental Alchemy	Water and Air
Key Issues	Intuition, healing, perception, communication
Stone Alchemy	Silver, moonstone
Cumulative Alchemy	Intuitive Receptivity

Silver Light Keys

Harmonic	Sound of **m** (receptivity vibration, inhalation hum)
Alchemical Properties	Receptivity, reflection
Sensory Keys	Interchangeable (vanilla to start)
Symbols	Moon, female symbol, basket
Personification	Counselor/Queen
Runic	Is (Isa) or Lagu (Laguz)
Astrological Correlates	Cancer, Pisces
Major Arcana Key	The Moon
Archangel	Gabriel (Moon)
Stone Alchemy	Silver, moonstone

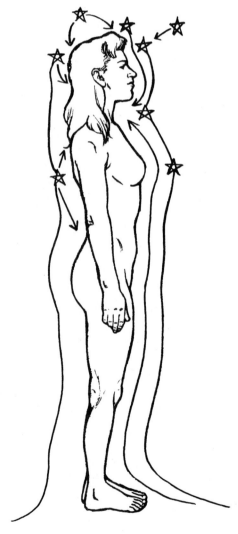

Silver Light Energy Centers

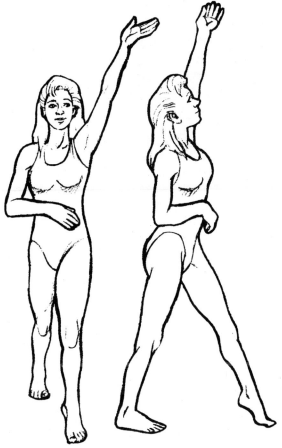

Silver Light Harmonic Posture

Harmonic

Receptive, breathy vibration; inhalation hum.

Lovely, lunar energy,
Moon maiden, mother and grandmother be.
Sends the wisdom receptively,
Communications from Mother to me.

Amplify by listening quietly; focus inward to activate receptivity.

Alchemical Properties

Silver Light catalysts the input or reception of energies. Silver receives and reflects intuitive transformation in a primarily physical, etheric, spiritual manner.

Overused Silver Light Energy Pattern (Tangled Receptivity)

Powers	Supportive, direct, tangible receptive action
Activates	Receptivity, inner knowing, absorbent qualities of all Rays and Lights
Amplifies	Flow of input for all Rays and Lights
Balances	Surplus of activity, output
Releases	Intuitive blocks
Realigns	All dimensions of awareness, receptivity

Harmonious Silver Light Energy Pattern

Sensory Key

(Interchangeable)
The sensory key suggested with Silver Light is vanilla.

     Shared attributes of vanilla and Silver Light:
          Intuition
          Yin
          Receptivity
          Relationships
          Love
          The element of Water

This alchemy is similar to that of vanilla and White Light in that it catalysts deep, intuitive wisdom and personal transformations due to a greater level of personal receptivity. The primary difference in this alchemy is that Silver gives it a more physical effect on the Body/Mind system. Silver and White in combination with vanilla create a powerful alchemy for healing transformation.

- Light a vanilla-scented candle. Hold a piece of silver metal so the light of the candle reflects and sends sparks of light from the face of the metal. Breathe, and focus on the play of Silver Light. Focus on the energy of Silver Light gathering in the reflections from the silver piece.

    Close your eyes and imagine silver flashes of light illuminating your self-image. Steady the flashes to create a shimmering mirror of Silver Light.

    In your mind's eye, focus on the reflection of your Self in the silver mirror of inner vision. Observe your Self with detachment and positive regard.

    Be open to what you experience—reflecting upon your Self. Decide, with detachment and positive regard, on the transformations necessary in your Self—in your personal alchemy. Stay open to guidance from within the Yin of your being.

Symbols

Moon represents the reflective aspects of light and the deepest dimensions of inner knowing. Illumination is often received when we emerge from the darkest shadows of introspection.

Female Symbol represents the creative, receptive energies which sustain growth with constant, conscious nurturing. The silver cord of Source runs unbroken through the chaos of the void, bringing sustenance for our growth and self-transformation.

Basket represents the receptive vessel of self-awareness and the receptacle of wisdom that is the highest Self. The strongest basket is woven from flexible fibers in order to insure its receptivity to changes in the load being carried.

Personification

Receptivity

Silver is the energy of the Counselor/Queen. It is Guinevere preserving Excalibur, symbolic sword of power. Silver is the receptive catalyst which brings power into the circle and counsels the steady wisdom of Nature.

Musings

The Yin
Illuminates the question
And reflects the answer
From within.

At the crossroads they gathered
In the depths of night.
Hidden by shadows of the moon
They gathered—seeking the light.

Runic Correlates

Is (Isa) and Lagu (Laguz)

Shared aspects with Silver Light:

Inner wisdom	Journey work
Secrets	Mystery
Inner guidance	
The element of Water	

I

Is (Isa)

Is (Isa) presents a situation in your transformational processes which requires deep and silent self-reflection. That which is viewed as non-action or an obstacle by others is seen as an opportunity for experience and growth by the personal alchemist. Activate personal dimensions of receptivity and remove self-limitations with the rune Is (Isa).

Lagu (Laguz) reveals the inner meanings of your personal alchemy and the flow of your transformational processes. Changes in the process of self-transformation are provided to redirect and reconnect with the spiraling path of universal alchemy. Activate and access the flow of universal alchemical wisdom with increased receptivity and the rune Lagu (Laguz).

ʰ

Lagu (Laguz)

Together, Is (Isa) and Lagu (Laguz) catalyst deep inner work best combined with routine, mundane tasks to keep you grounded.

Astrological Correlates

Solar Cancer

With so much ability to absorb all the people you meet, you should use great discrimination in choosing your close associates . . . You tend to take on their problems, although you're better at sympathizing than at offering solutions.

—Sybil Leek

Lunar Pisces

You are unhappy only when you violate, in action, thought, word, some truth that is essential to you, or when you realize you have acted counter to the dictates of your own self-taught wisdom.

—Grant Lewi

Silver Light is most effective with Pisces for issues of impulsivity, impatience, focus and planning. Each of the signs, grouped by elements, also has an effect with Silver Light.

Fire signs	Balances overactivation
Water signs	Psychic connector
Earth signs	Enhances awareness
Air signs	Focuses receptivity

Major Tarot Arcana Key

The Moon

Shared aspects with Silver Light:

Receptivity	Intuition
Emotionality	The Yin
Psyche	Inner Self
Self-reflection	

The Moon represents hidden and mysterious realms of consciousness that seem both powerful and close, yet distant and inaccessible.

—R. J. Stewart

Musings

Moon Dancer/me, inner Self, I ask you: shall I be ever-receptive to my inner flow, open to the songs of the muses and the laughter of the lords of light? Or shall the still, quiet voices of spirit within be drowned in the noises of the mundane?

Moon Dancer/me, outer Self, I ask you: when was the last time we danced with the Moon together?

Inner Self/Outer Self—Moon Dancer/Me. Be Free.

Archangel

Angelic Dimension Keys

Gabriel: Archangel of the Moon

  Alchemy of Psychism, Intuition, and Receptivity

Day	Monday
Times	5-6 AM
	1-2 PM
	9-10 PM

One in whom persuasion and belief
Had ripened into faith, and faith become
A passionate intuition.

　　　　　　　　　　　—William Wordsworth

Angelic Invocation

Gabriel, angelic light of the Moon and all the realms of inner Self, I call for stronger powers of intuition that I may be more open to receiving clearer guidance from within the realms of Self and Spirit. (And Gabriel, blow your horn at me if you have to, from time to time.)

Stone Alchemy

Stones chosen here for Silver Light are silver itself, and also the moonstone. (Regardless of the color of moonstone, its action is like Silver Light. It is receptive; absorbent.)

Placement for Silver Light stones can be anywhere that needs to be more open and receiving, either in life generally, or to specific Ray energies. Silver works like White Light in that it is a receptive medium for transmitting energies inward.

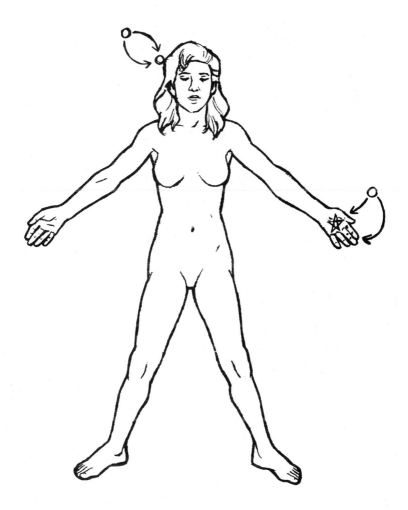

Silver Light Stone Placement

Silver Light Stone Energy Patterns

Alchemist's Note: For pulling in Silver Light directly to open the psychic receptive channels, place a Silver energy stone on the right side of the head. Now, most people feel that the left hand is the receptive hand, right? Remember, the brain controls the opposite side; the right brain controls the left side. So put the Silver energy stone on the right side of the head to activate the receptivity of your body. Don't get hung up on this left and right business; I know it is easy to say one thing is for one, and another is for another. Remember, we can receive and transmit throughout our physical, etheric and spiritual bodies. It is nice sometimes to have a system to help tune in directly.

Silver (The Metal): Lunar Stone
Element: Earth

Silver can be moderately expensive. However, all that is needed is a little charm, a couple of links of silver chain, or a silver dime. The metal silver symbolizes the receptive aspects of Mind, Body and Spirit. Silver opens all levels to awareness. Silver brings serenity, receptivity, intuition and emotional stability.

Moonstone: Absorbent Stone
Element: Water

Moonstone can be moderately priced in polished, gemstone jewelry, and inexpensive if tumbled or raw. Moonstone has a gentle, deep vibration, effective for all forms of receptive, intuitive healing.

Finest gemstone-quality moonstone is effective for releasing deep, etheric traumas and negativity. This is because all moonstone is so absorbent. Since moonstone is meditative, absorbent and receptive, it will need to be cleaned frequently. Moonstone takes in a lot and it holds onto it.

Alchemist's Note: Whatever Ray or Light is run through moonstone is softened and gentled by the process. Also, moonstone works to clear energies when you have worked with several Rays, Lights and stones. I use moonstone to clear my psychic, sensory or etheric receptors in much the same way a wine taster uses bread to clear the palate between sips.

Alternative Stone

A Silver Light alternative stone is white selenite. Sometimes this comes in a form called a "selenite sword." This is a long, thin, crystalline structure which can also be used as a wand. These are rare, fragile, and very special. These can also be used for White, Crystal, and Spirit Lights.

Chapter Twenty-five

Gold Light: Activation

There is no god higher than truth.
—Mahatma Gandhi

God is a verb.
—Buckminster Fuller

Silver is the receptive Light; Gold, of course, is the active Light. Gold energizes and stimulates all other energies. Whereas Silver is receptive and brings in energies, Gold catalysts them and gets them activated, moving around and outward. Gold Light is a "psychic vitamin." It works from within the etheric, transmuting negativity and energizing. Gold is Yang, the god force.

The trick with Gold Light is to activate it by breathing rapidly through the mouth. Balance or deactivate Gold Light by breathing slowly through the nose. If you are already an activator, Gold becomes like a Ray energy for you. Use extra thought, focus, and balance when activating energies.

Elemental Alchemy	Earth and Fire
Key Issues	Knowledge, moderation, sensation, regeneration
Stone Alchemy	Gold, rutile quartz
Cumulative Alchemy	Practical Activation

Gold Light Keys

Harmonic	Sound of **m** (activation vibration, exhalation hum)
Alchemical Properties	Grounded energizer, activator
Sensory Keys	Interchangeable (almond to start)
Symbols	Sun, male symbol, rocket (fireworks)
Personification	Provider/King
Runic	Man (Mannaz) or Wyn (Wunjo)
Astrological Correlates	Aries, Leo
Major Arcana Key	The Sun
Archangel	Michael (Sun)
Stone Alchemy	Gold, rutile quartz

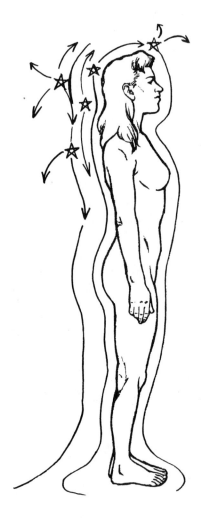

Gold Light Energy Centers

Harmonious Gold Light Energy Pattern (Expansive)

Harmonious Gold Light Energy Pattern (Intrapersonal)

Harmonic

Activation vibration; exhalation hum.

The strength of solar energy
And manifestor of destiny
Great Sun, activate thy might for me
Dis Pater, all father to mankind be.

Amplify by sweeping both arms wide to gather energies. Finish by placing both hands on the solar plexus.

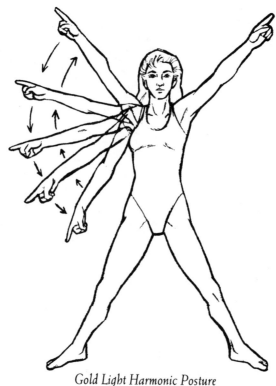

Gold Light Harmonic Posture

Alchemical Properties

Gold Light activates the flow of both focused and diffuse energies. Gold energizes transformation in a primarily physical, etheric, spiritual manner.

Powers	Supportive, subtle yet direct, activating and centering action
Activates	All Ray and Light energies
Amplifies	Grounded transformation energies and filters
Balances	Surpluses of receptivity, input, oversensitivity
Releases	Energy blocks
Realigns	Input/output flow of all energies

Sensory Key

(Interchangeable)
The sensory key suggested with Gold Light is almond.

Shared attributes of almond and Gold Light:
Prosperity
Abundance
Materialism
Activation
Organization
The element of Spirit

The alchemy of almond and Gold catalysts success in a practical, grounded manner. Almond and Gold create a catalyst for successful manifestation of prosperity. This is particularly true if the energies of sharing are already part of your personal alchemy.

- Rub almond extract or oil on a talisman, amulet, symbolic spiritual jewelry, et cetera. Focus on the energies of the sun and the activation of light manifesting on earth in the work of many spiritual people, such as your Self.
- Mix almond scent or extract into almond oil. Focus on Gold Light energies supercharging the mixture for an all-purpose activator oil.
- Anoint your third eye, crown chakra, solar plexus, palms of your hands and soles of your feet with almond oil. Focus on strengthening the connection of Spirit to self and to earth.
- Throw almonds in a hot, golden fire as a shamanic, ceremonial offering. Release Gold Light energies into the ethers, activating planetary abundance.
- Focus on the scent of almond. Close your eyes and imagine weaving a veil of Gold Light around your self, your home, and your community. Visualize the golden veil shimmering with pure energy, reflecting the full light of the sun. Shoot either Ray colors or Lights across the golden veil to activate specific intentions. For example, Golden-Green across the golden veil of light activates powerful healing transformation, while Rose across Gold activates communication.

Symbols

Sun represents the source of warmth and light. It ensures the survival of many dimensions of life in this solar system. Just as the full moon reflects the full sun, so does the balancing transformation of our Self reflect the transformational balance of the Self.

Male symbol represents the generative activation energies which catalyst growth through direct, focused action. That which we infuse directly into the activation of our self is often diffused indirectly by the activation of Self.

Rocket (fireworks) represents the upward thrust of elemental energies in the activation of our personal alchemy. It takes the strongest forces of faith and the purest elements of light to launch us on our journey to the farthest star.

Personification

Activity

Gold is the energy of the Provider/King. It is Arthur of Britain actively seeking to unite and empower the land and the people. Gold is the catalyst element of the circle, the unity symbolized by the creation of the Round Table.

Musings

You can't just go out and join a cause in order to avoid your own.

The activation of self is the empowering element of personal alchemy.

Fortunately, we can count on change being constant.

I am of the opinion that it does not matter what gods are acclaimed to be . . . so much as how active is their alchemy.

> *Live, because of the sun,*
> *The dream, the excitable gift.*
> —Anne Sexton

> *We are stardust*
> *We are golden*
> *And we've got to get ourselves*
> *Back to the garden.*
> —Joni Mitchell

Runic Correlates

Man (Mannaz) and Wyn (Wunjo)

Shared aspects with Gold Light:

Self-activation   Self-determination
Achievement   Practicality
The element of Fire

Man (Mannaz)

Man (Mannaz) activates all dimensions of personal alchemy in a practical, useful manner. Self-transformation needs the ever-present catalyst of positive self-motivation to keep the elemental energies of change flowing freely. Activate and manifest all dimensions of your personal alchemy with practical methodology and the rune Man (Mannaz).

Wyn (Wunjo) activates the highest energies of Spirit through the actions of your personal transformation toward the light. The truest activation of spiritual power is catalysted by self-recognition, self-acceptance and self-responsibility.

Wyn (Wunjo)

Together, Man (Mannaz) and Wyn (Wunjo) support deeds and actions rather than words and thoughts. Self-activate your alchemy.

Astrological Correlates

Solar Aries

Aries are always in a hurry, rushing into the future looking to accomplish something—and they don't always know what that mysterious "something" is.

—Betty Lundgren

Lunar Leo

To live up to the level of your inner picture is a lifetime job requiring energy, courage and a considerable sense of the drama of existence.

—Grant Lewi

Gold Light and Leo work well with issues of motivation and activation of goals. In addition, all signs work with Gold Light according to their elements.

Fire signs	Enhancement catalyst
Water signs	Expression activator
Earth signs	Empowerment activator
Air signs	Structural activator

Major Tarot Arcana Key

The Sun

Shared aspects with Gold Light:

Activation	Achievements
Physicality	The Yang
Success	Outer Self
Self-expression	

> *It is a card of growth, infinite truth, and the ineffable goodness of the universe surrounding man's tiny island.*

—F. D. Graves

Musings

That which is the son to some, is the Sun to others. Both are the purest activation of light.

There is a feeling of glory in the golden light of the Sun. This is true whether the Sun is setting or dawning. There is energy for honorable achievements, the pleasure of personal success, and simple fun.

Lord of Light, bold activation
Child of Light, gentle expression
Lady of Light, creative nurturer

Archangel

Angelic Dimension Key

Michael: Archangel of the Sun

    Alchemy of Motivation, Activation and Achievement

        Days   Sunday, Thursday

        Times   4-5 AM

                       12-1 PM

                       8-9 PM

I think that, as life is action and passion, it is required of a man that he shoud share the passion and action of his time at peril of being judged not to have lived.

—Oliver Wendell Holmes

Angelic Invocation

Michael, golden angel of the Sun, I call for the strongest inspiration of my Spirit and the motivation of the highest Light.

I call for help in bringing into manifestation that which I have undertaken to create for my self.

I ask for the catalyst of Golden Light to activate and empower my work.

Stone Alchemy

The stones chosen for Gold Light are gold itself, and the rutile or rutilated quartz. Placement for Gold Light stones is on the left side of the head to work with the right side of the body. This stimulates the physical, active, ordered Self.

Gold Light can be used anywhere, as it is an all-purpose activator. It is effective at the base of the spine, on the root chakra point, or on the crown chakra.

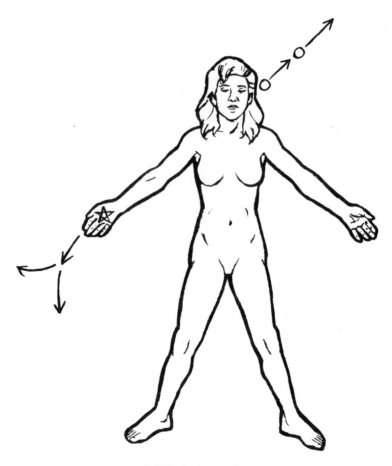

Gold Light Stone Placement

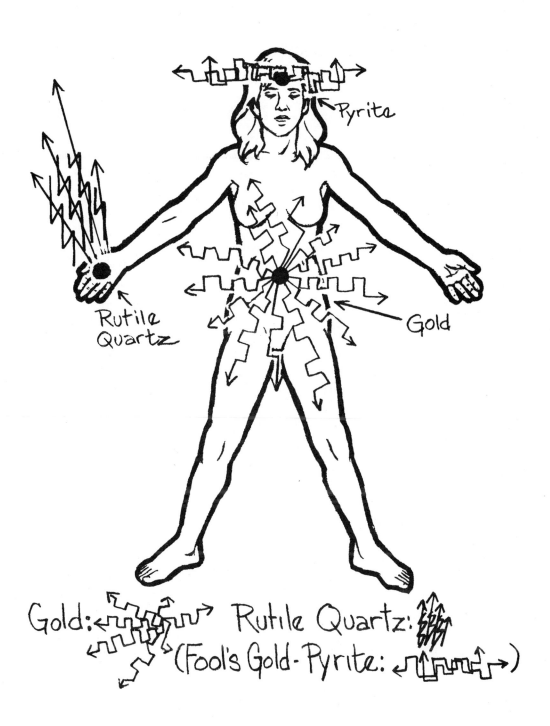

Gold Light Stone Energy Patterns

Alchemist's Note: Generally speaking, set stones in silver to be more receptive to their energies. Set stones in gold to activate their energies outward.

Gold (The Metal): Solar Stone
Element: Earth

Gold is an active catalyst in and of itself, and it also activates whatever stone is used with it. The metal gold can be rather expensive, but only a small amount is needed to work effectively. Gold has a dense, earthy vibration with a strong, active energy. Gold can be used for an ongoing tonic effect or a specific purpose.

Rutile Quartz (Rutilated): Activator Stone
Element: Air and Water

Rutile quartz is quartz with little gold fibers or inclusions. Structurally, the fibers are more closely related to iron; however, they are gold-colored and active within the quartz medium. Ironically, rutile quartz is often more effective for Gold Light work than pieces of the metal gold. Experiment with this for your self.

Rutile quartz is a transmitter of active healing light. It aids the physical by rebuilding healthy cells and tissues. It works a little bit like the ruby does in the bloodstream, except that Golden Light permeates not just the bloodstream, but the etheric stream of life, as well.

Alchemist's Note: I find that rutile quartz is effective with tourmalinated quartz, which has little inclusions of tourmaline in the form of black needles or green needles. The Green and Black absorb, and the Gold activates.

You might focus first on the tourmalinated quartz and then on the rutile. Watch how the energy moves. This makes a powerful combination which can be effective for all aspects of Body, Mind and Spirit.

Alternative Stone

An alternative to use with Gold Light is pyrite, which is sometimes called "fool's gold." Pyrite has a strong energy of its own; it is not a poor substitute or a lesser kind of anything. Pyrite is an activator which works a little more subtly than gold, and with a denser vibration. This is particularly so of pyrite crystals, which are little cubes. These crystals are good for activating all-purpose healing and enhancement in Gold Light energies.

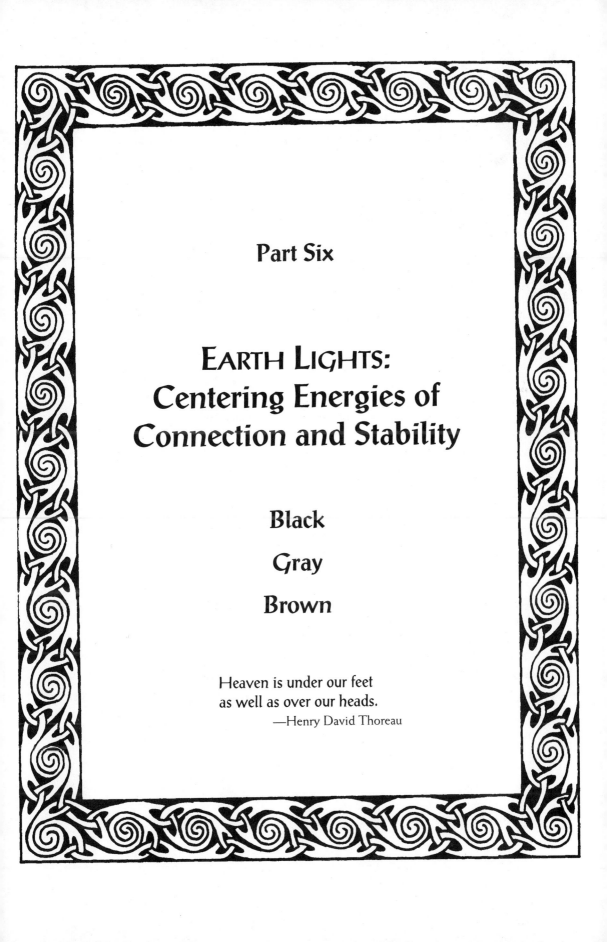

Part Six

EARTH LIGHTS:
Centering Energies of Connection and Stability

Black

Gray

Brown

Heaven is under our feet
as well as over our heads.
—Henry David Thoreau

Moon Dancing: Dark Moon Release

Breathe deeply, and slowly release your breath. Gently allow your muscles to relax. Breathe again, and find a quiet place within your self. You are going on a journey of release and renewal. Breathe slowly and quietly, and allow the rhythm of your breath to quiet your spirit. Let your breath breathe for you. Focus your awareness on the release of each breath. Note how it makes you feel: calm . . . serene . . . clear . . . deeply relaxed.

Breathe, and allow your self to go deeper. Let your body go . . . release.

Step into an image of a special, private place, deep in the darkness of an ancient forest. Find your self walking along a cool, smooth path through this deep forest. The only light comes from the few stars twinkling down through the leaves of the trees, and from the tiny silver crescent of a waning moon as it makes its final appearance before the dark of the moon.

Although it is dark, your step is sure as you make your way through the forest. Tiny faerie lights, like fireflies, flicker through the trees, and you know that you have companions on this journey. Breathe deeply, and walk on through the forest. The rich smell of earth calms you. You feel more and more connected to this place with each step. Release your cares as you continue on this path.

Just ahead in the dim light you see that the path leads to a large group of rocks and boulders. A tiny trickle of water glistens as it makes its way down the tallest rock and softly falls into a smooth, still pool of water.

Breathe deeply, and draw closer. Step carefully and slowly onto the rocks. As you reach out a hand to steady your self, you feel the cool dampness of the moss-covered stones. Gently, you make your way over the rocks and find a place to sit where you can gaze into the pool of water.

So dark and still is the pool of water that it shines like a polished mirror. As you gaze into the pool, you see the reflection of starlight twinkling on the water, and the silver shimmer of a crescent moon. As you watch this frail moon reflected in the pool, you notice that, even now, it is becoming smaller and dimmer. The time for the dark of the moon is near; a time of great release and rebirth. Breathe deeply, and consider all the aspects in your life and in your self you want to release. Imagine them dropping into the dark pool of water and fading slowly away . . . waning into the void like the reflection of the moon on the surface of the pool.

Take time now to consider that before rebirth and renewal there must be release. Notice which aspects are most difficult for you to release. Some things take more than one cycle of the moon to release . . . be gentle with your self and release what you can.

Breathe deeply. As you gaze into the dark pool of water you see that the moon has become little more than a shadow of itself. Reach gently into the water and watch the ripples, like the moon, fade away, carrying all you have released.

Breathe deeply, and sit in the quiet stillness of this dark and private place. You have done well, and are now cleared to begin another part of this journey of release and renewal.

The faerie lights have come again. Gently fluttering around you, they draw your attention away from the dark pool of water. You watch as they dance across the surface and gather on the other side of the pool.

In the glow of the faerie lights you can make out a structure you had not seen before. There, on the other side of the pool, stands the ruins of an ancient temple. Columns, now covered with moss and bramble, lie broken and askew on the steps leading to the temple entrance.

You can just make out the doorway, marked by great standing columns, and from within the temple you see a dim light, almost imperceptible, glowing faintly.

You begin to make your way carefully around the pool and over the rocks toward the temple. You step slowly over the broken columns covered with dark vines. The fragrance of night-blooming jasmine drifts by on the wind as you pause to catch your breath.

Breathe deeply, and begin to make your way up the steps of this ancient temple. Stones, soft with dampness and age, crumble as you move closer to the doorway. Although the night is dark, you focus on your steps and the tiny light glowing within the temple.

From above you a great white owl calls softly, spreads her wings, and glides away into the night. Breathe deeply, and know that this is a sign of great power and great spirit.

Empowered by this sign, you take the last step into the temple. As you step inside you feel the resonance deepen, the vibrations around you shift to a slower pace. A strangely calming smell of weathered stones and musty dampness fills the room in which you find your self.

At the far end of the room is a stone altar. Carved on the sides are runic symbols, barely visible in the pale light of a single tallow candle burning in a niche just above the top of the altar stone. Breathe deeply and approach the altar slowly.

As you come closer, you notice a dark corridor behind the altar. As you ponder where the corridor leads, you hear the owl once again. A cold wind blows through the temple, causing the candle flame to flicker and dance.

From deep in the darkness of the corridor, you hear the sound of slow, gentle footsteps approaching, and the sound of something tapping on the stone floor. As the tapping draws nearer, you hear the rustle of long robes. You feel a deep abiding peace as you wait for the visitor to emerge.

Faerie lights come to welcome the visitor, and dance down the corridor to light the way. As you breathe deeply in anticipation, an ancient woman emerges from the darkness. She is wearing long robes of black and purple cloth trimmed in silver, once grand, now faded with age. At her throat is a silver amulet of the crescent moon with points up, which, though tarnished, gives off a luster of well-worn metal.

Her face is lined and ravaged by time; her hands are bent and gnarled as they hold a massive wooden staff, smooth from years of giving support. The sound of the staff on the stone floor echoes through the temple. As she draws nearer, you see in her face the gentle beauty of her eyes . . . soft, loving, and compassionate with wisdom. You feel a comfort and an acceptance in her presence you have only glimpsed before. This is the wisest aspect of the Goddess, this is the crone . . . there is nothing that She has not seen or known. To her, you bring the depths of your soul you need to release. She has known you for all time, to her you can give all that limits you, all that holds you back from your path, all those negativities which keep you from being clear with your self.

Breathe deeply, and feel the gentle pull of her presence and her strength.

She bids you take a seat on a stone nearby and she sits across from you . . . staring deeply into your eyes with perfect acceptance.

You reach inside your memories to find all you need to release. Some things come quickly, some are familiar, some are surprises, for you have already shed many aspects into the dark pool of the waning moon. But this woman, this crone, ancient and wise, asks that you reach even deeper into the private places where negativity is stored . . . and even guarded for its familiarity. This aspect of the Goddess asks that you step back from your self and observe with detachment and acceptance . . . only then can you know what holds you back, what keeps you from being clear.

Breathe deeply, and let her help you release in the depths of your being all that limits you unnecessarily. Take all the time you need to be with this great-grandmother of wisdom.

When you have released all you can, breathe deeply and feel the change in your being. Know that in the darkest aspects of release are the gentle sparks of clarity and renewal. The woman speaks in a voice of timeless quality:

> *You have done well.*

She rises from her seat and moves close to you. Reaching out one ancient hand, she touches your forehead gently. You notice she is wearing a beautiful ring with an ancient symbol engraved on it. From now on, this will be a private symbol for you to use whenever you need to release that which limits you . . . be it anger, fear, negativity, or any of the many mortal frailties which impede progress.

She turns to leave, but you call for her to stay a bit longer. There is comfort in her presence.

She smiles, her eyes deep with mystery, and speaks to you again with timeless resonance:

> *As death must become birth, so must the time for release become renewal. Even now the new moon quickens in the womb of the sky and the young huntress, Diana, strains to be born. Come again, my friend, when the time is right and the moon glows once again dim in the sky. Until then, remember that the same seeds which make wheat also make chaff . . . and you will come again to separate your self from that which is chaff for you. Spend a quiet moment alone here and consider what you have learned.*

Having spoken, she turns and makes her way down the corridor. You strain to see her as she fades into the darkness . . . the sound of the staff on the stone floor echoes in your ears long after she has gone.

A sudden gust of wind snuffs the candle flame, leaving you in darkness. As you try to orient yourself, the gentle sound of a maiden's laughter rings through the temple, and silver light flashes around you. You turn quickly toward the entrance in time to see a young maiden running lightly down the temple steps, bow in hand, quiver of arrows strapped on her back. Her clothes are gossamer and free-flowing behind her veils in the wind as she runs.

She pauses at the foot of the temple steps, faerie lights dancing merrily in the silver glow surrounding her. As she turns to face you, a tiny crescent moon on a silver band twinkles on her forehead. And in her youthful, maiden face, are eyes of ageless wisdom. She speaks once more:

> What is your heart's desire, my friend? The hunt is beginning again. Come follow me, we'll catch your dreams and celebrate our prowess as the moon grows sleek and fat in the sky. Whisper to me, and I'll help you stalk your wishes as we grow in strength and power.

Her silver laughter rings through the forest and she is gone . . . a silver flash among the great, dark trees.

As you stand alone in the dark stillness at the top of the temple steps, your eyes catch a gentle glimmer of light almost hidden from view among the rocks and brambles at the base of the steps. Moving slowly back down the temple steps, you see that the glimmer comes from the light of a tiny crescent moon reflecting in the dark smoothness of your pool. Directly above you in the sky, a new moon grows brighter and stronger. The cycle has begun once more . . . you have renewed your own cycle of life.

You can see your way once more to your smooth, cool path . . . silver in the light of the new moon above.

Breathe deeply, and gently let your image begin to fade away. Know that you may return to this image whenever you need . . . it is yours for all time.

Return now to this time and place . . . refreshed, renewed, and energized.

Be here now. Alert, awake, aware.

Earth Light Keys: Overview

Harmonics

The harmonic key for all Earth Lights is the sound of short o as in **mom**. This harmonic is moderately deep in pitch, but not as much as the harmonic long o of Blue Ray or the harmonic **om** of Indigo. Variations of this harmonic are best sung or chanted with a sedate, grounded energy.

Vibrational Energies

The energies of Earth Lights are denser in frequency than those of Sky Lights. Earth Lights are diffuse, pulling energies that manifest as a grounding flow. These relate most to the lower etheric and lower physical areas of the body. Focus on the experience of an energy field which provides a constant current for centering and balance, as well as transmuting typical negativities. Activate with variations of the harmonic short o. Some samples of these are:

Black	Deep vibration	Low-pitched short o
Gray	Moving vibration	Melodic short o
Brown	Centered vibration	Soft-spoken short o

Harmonic Breathing Pattern

The primary breathing pattern for Earth Lights combines deep inhalations and extended exhalations through the mouth. This mouth-breathing helps center and connect the physical to the grounded frequency of Earth. Pause after each exhalation to reform mental images and physical sensations for each Earth Light's primary attributes. Generally, these attributes are:

Black	Filtering transmuter of negativities
Gray	Balancing stabilizer for flexibility
Brown	Grounding connector to Earth energies

Suggested Harmonic Exercises, Chants, Mantras

Design chants and mantras appropriate to the specific purpose of your Earth Light alchemy. Amplify and focus these diffuse energies by singing or grounding out variations on the harmonic short o. This becomes far more effective when you have keyed in a personal, specific tone for each of the Earth Lights used.

Experiment with the harmonic short o to find what activates the energies best for your work. The individual samples may provide guidelines for devising supportive mantras and chants using several variations of the harmonic short o. When using such chants and mantras, stress all aspects of the harmonic o to focus the Lights with greater precision.

Sensory Keys

Sensory keys used with the Earth Lights are interchangeable:
  Patchouli
  Sage
  Woodsy

Symbols

Black	Theta symbol, footprint, candle
Gray	Spiral, road sign X, river
Brown	Tree with roots, shell, seedpod

Personifications

Black	Shaman/Medicine Teacher	*(Herne)*
Gray	Dancer/Athlete	*(Greek Olympian)*
Brown	Earth Reverend	*(St. Francis)*

Stone Alchemy

Black	Apache tear, snowflake obsidian
Gray	Granite, hematite
Brown	Smoky quartz, petrified wood

Chapter Twenty-six

Black Light: Release

Yea though I walk through the valley of the shadow,
I will fear no evil, for Thou art with me.

—Twenty-third Psalm

Black Light is used for grounding and to absorb and transmute heavy negativity. Black Light is not negative in and of itself; it is receptive and highly absorbent.

Alchemist's Note: There are many superstitions about the color black, Black Light, Black energy—things like that. I think they stem from the idea that if white is good, then black must be a problem. It simply is not that way. Black is a part, and a balance, of all the Rays and Lights around us. However, if Black is a problem for you, don't use it. Just use Gray or Brown. Remember, we all have our own preferences and that is what makes us unique. That is personal alchemy.

Black Light is a shielding, protective Light that absorbs and filters natural negativities found in the environment. It is helpful to visualize Black Light as a long, black cape sweeping away everyday negativities. For more bothersome negativities, focus more intensely on Black Light to transmute with Mother Earth absorbing energies. Follow Black Light work with White and Spirit Lights for the Highest Good.

The trick with Black Light is to focus on its energies seeping into the ground after it has absorbed whatever negativities were present. Mother Earth knows how to deal with such negativities—She turns them into fertilizer for new growth.

Elemental Alchemy	Spirit and Earth
Key Issues	Right action, oneness, knowledge, moderation
Stone Alchemy	Apache tear, snowflake obsidian
Cumulative Alchemy	Transmutation by release

Black Light Keys

Harmonic	Sound of o (deep vibration, low-pitched short o)
Alchemical Properties	Grounded transmutation of energies, release
Sensory Key	Interchangeable (try patchouli to start)
Symbols	Theta symbol, footprint, candle
Personification	Shaman/Medicine Teacher
Runic	Haegl (Hagalaz)
Astrological Correlates	Capricorn, Cancer
Major Arcana Key	The Tower
Archangel	Azrael (Pluto)
Stone Alchemy	Apache tear, snowflake obsidian

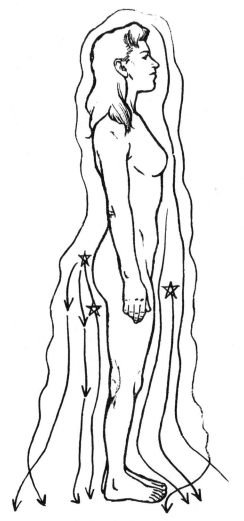

Black Light Energy Pattern

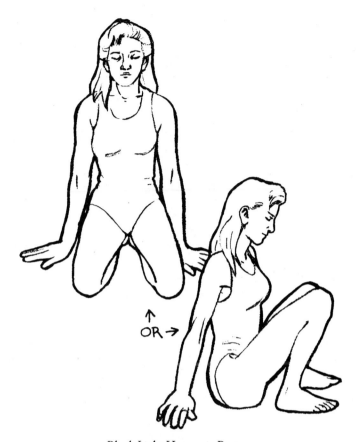

Black Light Harmonic Postures

Harmonic

Sound of (short) o—deep vibration, low-pitched tone.

Often seen, but never known,
Let the seeds of growth be sown,
Stopping sadness and fears forlorn,
Seeking light to be reborn.

Or:

Darkness flowing all around,
Rooted veil from sky to ground,
Covering silence, stops the sound,
Transmutation, most profound.

Amplify by visualizing negativities transmuted into new, positive opportunities and lessons for growth.

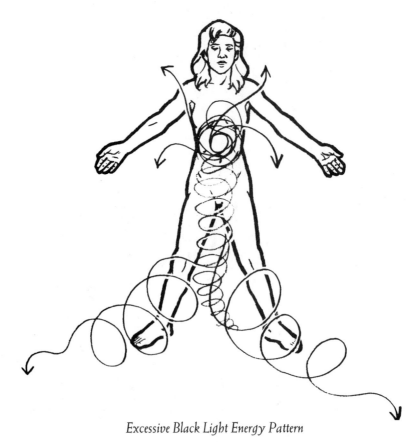

Excessive Black Light Energy Pattern

Alchemical Properties

Black Ray filters negativities, provides for release, and absorbs blocked energies. Black strengthens and supports the spiritual, transformational processes of seeking the highest light in a primarily physical, etheric manner.

Powers	Supportive, indirect, intangible clearing, grounding action
Activates	Grounded transmutation, releasing action of all Rays and Lights energies
Amplifies	Strength of all Rays and Lights, seeking of Light
Balances	Blissy, disconnected, scattered energies of all Rays and Lights
Releases	Negativities, surpluses of energies, toxic buildup
Realigns	Spiritual, evolutionary energies for transformation into Light

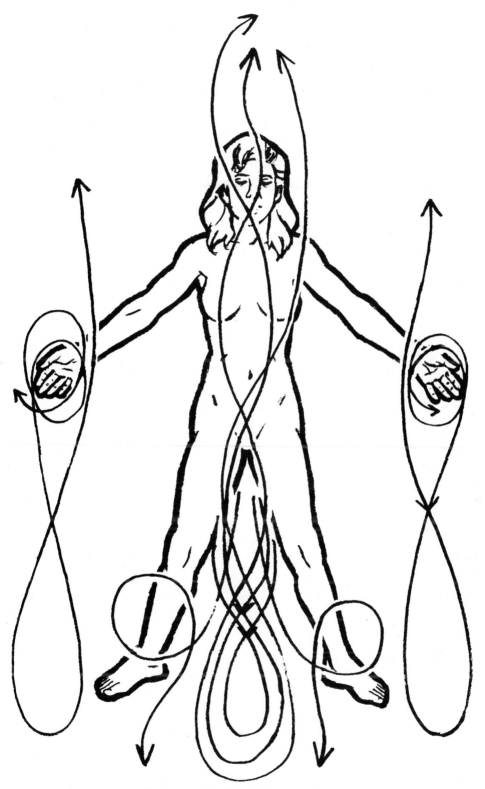

Harmonious Black Light Energy Pattern

Sensory Key

(Interchangeable)
The sensory key suggested with Black Light is patchouli.

> Shared attributes of patchouli and Black Light:
> Connectedness
> Fertility
> Purification
> Release
> Highest energies of choice
> The element of Earth

Patchouli is inexpensive and most often available as oil or incense. It is also available in herb form.

- Patchouli oil rubbed on black gauze or muslin makes an excellent "dust" rag for cleaning sacred spaces such as altars.
- Rub patchouli on parchment. Write or draw symbols to represent aspects of your Self which you want purified, manifested or released. Focus on these aspects entering the dimensions of earth, transmuting to the next cycle for the good of all.
- Burn patchouli incense to create a clearing smoke of transformation. Imagine the smoke spiraling downward toward the earth for transmutation.
- To release the obstacles of fear and superstition in your self, burn a black candle and patchouli incense. Focus on the positive powers of the planet earth energies supporting your personal alchemy and your personal transformation.

  Focus on obstacles to your positive growth into the light.

  Focus on these obstacles as they manifest within your personal environment.

  Focus on these obstacles as they manifest within your personal alchemy.

  Focus within. Find your personal obstacles to power and growth.

  Honor the lessons these obstacles have brought to your self-development.

  Honor, then release the obstacles.

Symbols

Theta symbol represents the Earth with its own alchemical blend of elemental energies. We honor the elemental energies of the Earth with symbols which catalyst our deepest alchemical connections to it.

Footprint represents the mark of humankind and other species dwelling on the planet. As we strive to honor the Earth and tread lightly across her surface, we notice the footprints of others who have come before us to lead the way to the wisdom of Nature.

Candle represents the seeking of light to dispel the dark. Inside the darkest cavern, even the smallest flame casts a wide circle of Light.

Personification

Release

Black is the energy of the Shaman/Medicine Teacher. It is Herne of the deep forest seeking the Light of Truth through solitary communion with Nature. Black is the energy which transmutes all obstacles to Nature's Wisdom, and connects us to the Earth.

Musings

What we fight, we empower.
What we fear, we feed.

Surrender is a hard habit to break. Use in moderation with that of the mundane, and freely with that of Spirit.

Anger is initially most effective, yet ultimately completely the reverse.
Release the need for anger, then release need.

There is no such thing as bad alchemy without bad intentions as its strongest elements.

Runic Correlate

Haegl (Hagalaz)

Shared aspects with Black Light:

    Transmutation   Fate

    Change   Disruption

    The element of Spirit

Haegl (Hagalaz)

Haegl (Hagalaz) prevents alchemy and Self-transformation from becoming stagnant due to negativities or resistance to change. Stormy situations and erratic emotions are signals for the personal alchemist to get out of the way of personal choice and change. Activate clearing for change with ceremonial release and the rune Haegl (Hagalaz). The alchemy of Haegl (Hagalaz) is only fully appreciated with the full release of personal fear.

Astrological Correlates

Solar Capricorn

Sometimes you're considered introverted or self-centered, but this is a defense mechanism to protect your own interests.

                        —Sybil Leek

Lunar Cancer

Forget yourself, your emotions, your reactions; harness your instincts to other peoples' problems or to creative work in business, science or the arts.

                        —Grant Lewi

Black Light works best with Capricorn for issues of judgment, self-determination and spiritual focus. All signs relate to Black Light according to their elemental nature.

Fire signs	Balanced transmutation
Water signs	Regulated release
Earth signs	Power connector
Air signs	Psychic clarity

Major Tarot Arcana Key

The Tower

Shared aspects with Black Light:

Purification	Release
Transmutation	Transformation
Shamanic healing	Spiritual seeking

The Divine fire that destroys only what is evil and purifies and refines what is good.

—Eden Gray

Musings

Black is seeking the light primarily through the release of all impurities. As such, it is a powerful Light to work with when one knows the difference between being pure and being a purist.

If you're not sure what your impurities are, just use Black Light in ceremony with the tower card. You'll find out quickly!

Shamanic Self-transformation (deep earth-centered self-healing) with Black Light can be like flying into a fluffy white cloud only to find a thunderhead within. The deepest healings of Self are invariably done while "flying by the seat of our pants" in the midst of such a storm.

Archangel

Angelic Dimension Key

Azrael: Archangel of Pluto
Alchemy of Life Cycles and Transformation
Days   Thursday, Saturday
Times   (No traditional times)

Alternate compatible times correlate with **Cassiel**:
Days   Saturday, Monday
Times   3-4 AM
                    11-12 AM
                    7-8 PM

♇

Emotion is the chief source of all becoming conscious. There can be no transforming of darkness into light and of apathy into movement without emotion.

—Carl Jung

Angelic Invocation

Azrael, angel of transformation, help me to not fear the shadows of my self, but to embrace them and disperse them with the light of release and purification.

Azrael, if I should feel the need to conquer rather than embrace these shadows of my Self, let me conquer them purely with love.

Stone Alchemy

The stones I have chosen for Black Light are Apache tear, which is a translucent obsidian, and snowflake obsidian, which has little white dots and is more opaque.

Placement of Black stones is below the tail bone, under the point at which Red stones are placed for use with the root chakra. When using a Black stone as an alternative to a Red stone, put the Black stone directly on the root chakra. Another placement for these stones is at mid-thigh between the legs. This helps you pull blocked energies downward.

Apache Tear: Mystery Stone
Element: Earth (with some Spirit)

Apache tear is an easily obtainable, inexpensive, translucent form of obsidian. These stones look opaque until held up to the light, then their translucence can be seen. Apache tears are symbolic of the shadow aspect of our own negativities, fears and doubts. Sometimes things look dark, but when we hold them up to the Light we find clarity.

Apache tears are excellent for releasing mental, emotional and spiritual blocks. They work on the etheric by drawing energy outward from the physical for transmutation with Earth energies.

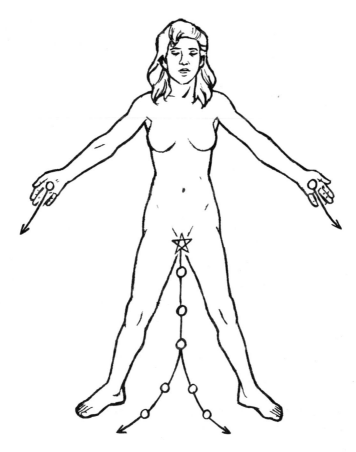

Black Light Stone Placement

Snowflake Obsidian: Grounding Stone
Element: Earth

Snowflake obsidian is opaque with little white flecks on a black background. It can be used for grounding energies and releasing physical pain, illness and negativities. It is advisable to use snowflake obsidian (or other forms of obsidian) on the root chakra when a Red stone might be too activating or intense. Snowflake obsidian allows for release in a gentle, grounded manner.

Alchemist's Note: Apache tear is a little more spiritual and etheric in the way it works than the snowflake obsidian, which is earthy. Both obsidians are good for cleaning out the physical intestinal system and not allowing energies to pool negatively.

You can also use obsidian to draw out viruses and toxins. Just let them flow into the stone, then let Black Light absorb the negativity and carry it away to transmute it for Highest Good. Sometimes negativities have to spiral down and out to reach through, ultimately, to Spirit.

Alternative Stone

Another stone to use for Black Light is black polished limestone. This stone is also good for Red Ray use. If this stone has a fossil in it, this helps connect it to ancient Earth energies.

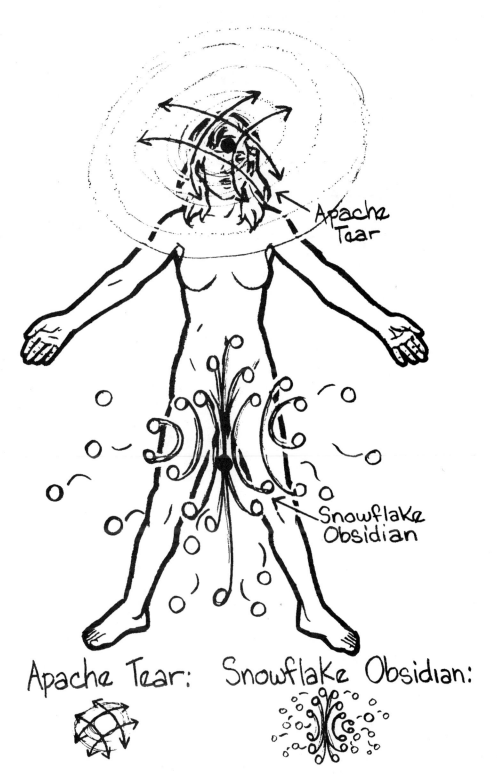

Apache Tear

Snowflake Obsidian

Apache Tear: Snowflake Obsidian:

Black Light Stone Energy Patterns

Chapter Twenty-seven

Gray Light: Flexibility

He is invited to great things who receives small things greatly.

—Flavius

Gray Light is an earth connector energy which has to do with flexibility—not just muscular, but emotional flexibility. Gray represents our balance in connection to Earth energies; it is how we are dancing on the surface of the earth. Gray also represents the balance of positive and negative, active/receptive, male/female, Yin/Yang, and so forth. Gray Light is gentle in this balancing. It helps in the way we move on our earth walk; on our path.

The trick with Gray Light is to focus it below the root chakra, especially in and around the legs. Visualize Gray Light as like the leg warmers dancers often wear to keep their muscles warm and flexible.

Elemental Alchemy	Air and Earth
Key Issues	Perception, communication, knowledge, moderation
Stone Alchemy	Granite, hematite
Cumulative Alchemy	Flexible Balance

Gray Light Keys

Harmonic	Sound of o (moving vibration; melodic, short o)
Alchemical Properties	Stability, flexibility, balance
Sensory Key	Interchangeable (try sage to start)
Symbols	Spiral, road sign X, river
Personification	Dancer/Athlete
Runic	Nyd (Nauthiz)
Astrological Correlates	Sagittarius, Libra
Major Arcana Key	The Hermit
Archangel	Raphael (Mercury)
Stone Alchemy	Granite, hematite

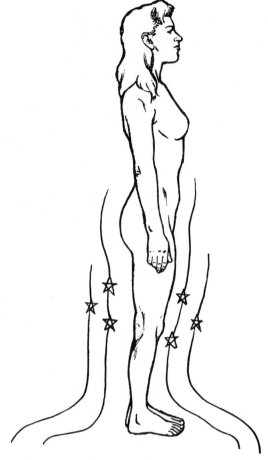

Gray Light Energy Centers

Harmonic

Sound of short o—moving vibration, melodic short o.

Stomping, clomping, moving free,
Grounded flexibility.
Open friendship, loving touch,
Our connections offer much.

Or:

Dancing, prancing 'til the morn,
Over, under and beyond.
To the dance we each are sworn,
In all the worlds, tout le monde.

Amplify by stretching your legs, bending your knees, and moving lithely, flexibly
across the floor.

Gray Light Harmonic Posture

Alchemical Properties

Gray Light enhances flexibility in the Body/Mind system. Gray balances and stabilizes the flow of positive and negative energies in a primarily physical, mental, etheric manner.

Powers	Supportive, indirect, maneuverable centering action
Activates	Flexibility, friendliness, centered awareness
Amplifies	Stability, balance, communication
Balances	Disorientation, rigidity
Releases	Imbalances in proper flow of centering, grounding energies
Realigns	Balanced, flexible connection to centered self-awareness

Harmonious Gray Light Energy Pattern

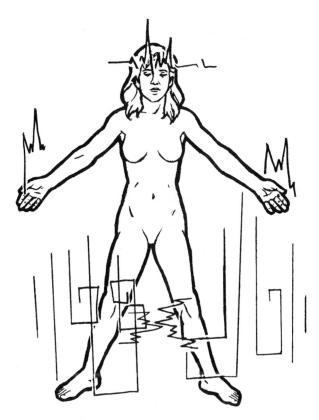

Depleted Gray Light Energy Pattern

Sensory Key

(Interchangeable)
The sensory key suggested with Gray Light is sage.

Shared attributes of sage and Gray Light:
Connection
Protection
Balance
Purification
The element of Air

Sage is inexpensive and is most often available in herbal or smudge stick form. It is also available as an oil.

- Sage and Gray Light combine to form an etheric "blanket" or cocoon when used in smudging. Focus on the Gray Light infusing the smoke with amplified clearing energies. Focus on the sage smoke weaving a blanket of protection, a cocoon in which to grow and change. Focus on Gray Light and remember, the process of growth requires flexibility. Let the weave on your etheric blanket be open, loose and flexible. Let an open mind and flexible nature be your surest protection.

- Burn sage and focus on Gray Light as a veil blowing in a gentle breeze. Play music which makes you feel light on your feet, and dance. Imagine the veils of Gray Light brushing your body as you dance. Dance lightly to the music of your self-transformation.

- Place a few drops of sage oil on a votive candle and light it ceremonially. Focus on the light of the candle flame and ask for balance in your self. Focus on the smoke from the candle, and ask for purification in your transformation. Focus on the scent of the candle and ask for flexibility throughout your Body/Mind system.

Symbols

Spiral represents the path of evolution into the Light which circles round from self—to self—to Self and Source. When we recognize that the spiral path to Source carries us ever upward, we lose our fear of sliding downward.

Road sign X represents the crossroads of choice, either personal and conscious, or universal and "unconscious." Choices, often seen as obstacles are, in fact, the marks of our progress in directing the journey of our Self.

River represents the flow of energies moving in direct attunement to the deeper forces of Nature. The oceans of consciousness and wisdom are fed by the free-flowing rivers of knowledge and truth.

Personification

Flexibility

Gray is the energy of the Dancer/Athlete. It is the Greek Olympian celebrating the fullness of human physical agility, balance and flexibility. Gray is the energy of the Dancer moving lightly, yet remaining ever-connected to the Earth.

Musings

Self-limitation is contagious.

Your flexibility loosens the knots (and the nots) of others, as well as your own.

Stretch outward to reach within.

Lighten up—it's enlightening.

Bend your knees once in a while. It brings you closer to earth.

> *Let it be.*
> —The Beatles

Runic Correlate

Nyd (Nauthiz)

Shared aspects with Gray Light:
   Stamina   Endurance
   Persistence   Resolve
   The element of Earth

Nyd (Nauthiz)

Nyd (Nauthiz) stabilizes personal alchemy with flexible maintenance of the homeostatic status quo. The personal alchemist requires stamina, balance and connected flexibility when dancing in the dimensional frequencies of elemental energies. Activate focused balance with a friendly nature and Nyd (Nauthiz). The alchemy of Nyd (Nauthiz) is in reserving elements of personal power while sharing elements of universal power.

Astrological Correlates

Solar Sagittarius

There's always an element of sincerity in your desire to help friends in a practical way, and you offer much more than sympathy. Many of you are the natural teachers of spiritual and material affairs, being able to combine both with ease.

> —Sybil Leek

Lunar Libra

This position gives a peculiar sweetness to the nature, a curious charm to the speech and manner, and allows the best of the inner-Self to shine before the world, which is brightened and made happier by it.

—Grant Lewi

Gray Light works well with Libra for issues of sharing, communication, flexibility, service and self-esteem. All signs correlate with Gray Light according to their basic elements.

Fire signs   Balanced aggression
Water signs   Assertive focus
Earth signs   Flexibility catalyst
Air signs   Communication enhancer

Major Tarot Arcana Key

The Hermit

Shared aspects with Gray Light:
Flexibility   Detached observation
Spiritual solitude   Self-clarification
Centeredness

However clever the intellect, however warm the heart, however strong the sense of identity, the vicissitudes of life would shatter us if we were unable to find somewhere within the patience and prudence of the Hermit, who teaches us how to endure and wait in silence.

—Juliet Sharman-Burke and Liz Green

Musings

The hermit knows when to pack it in, move onward, or when to abide. This is because the hermit is sensitive to the changes in all the energies, and is flexible enough to flow with these changes as they come and go.

The sensitivities of the hermit require the solitude of Self-reflection and the centeredness of Self-clarification.

The Hermit

Archangel

Angelic Dimension Key

Raphael: Archangel of Mercury

Alchemy of Creativity, Communication, Expression, and Healing

Days	Wednesday, Saturday
Times	7-8 AM
	3-4 PM
	11-12 PM

. . . lucidity of thought, clearness and propriety of language, freedom from prejudice and freedom from stiffness, openness of mind, amiability of manners.

—Matthew Arnold

Angelic Invocation

Raphael, angelic light of communication, teach me the skills of self-expression that I may find expression in the service of the healing light.

Raphael, bring balance to my work and creativity to my craft. Let healing light express itself through me.

Stone Alchemy

Stones I have selected for Gray Light are granite and hematite. Placement for Gray stones to increase flexibility is either below the base of the spine or between the knees.

Alchemist's Note: The back of the knees is my favorite place to put a Gray stone. This symbolizes the ability to bend and be flexible while maintaining our sacred connection to Mother Earth/Mother Nature energies.

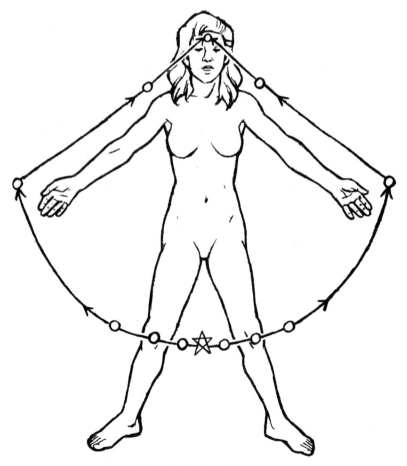

Gray Light Stone Placement

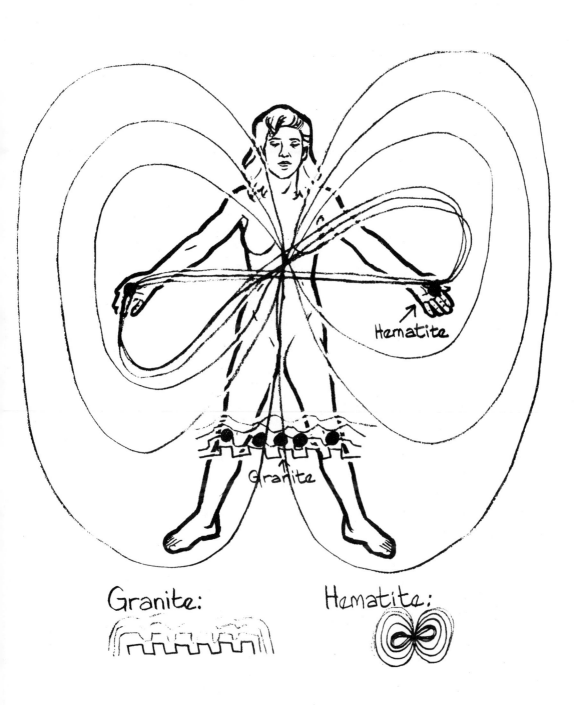

Gray Light Stone Energy Patterns

Granite: Foundation Stone
Element: Earth

Granite is an inexpensive, easily obtainable stone. It has a strong, deep, earthy vibration. Granite is a supportive stone which is useful on the root chakra for issues of structure. Granite stabilizes and relieves frustration, helping personal flexibility by strengthening the sense of security.

Alchemist's Note: Granite is a solid protective stone. Very shiny granite has some element of Spirit. It is nice to have around the house or in the garden.

Hematite: Guidance Stone
Element: Earth (with some Fire)

Hematite is moderately inexpensive and easily obtainable. It is a magnetic stone with an earthy vibration. Hematite is excellent to open the Physical to Spirit; it has a way of bridging the two.

Hematite also opens personal channels to healing from within the self and the Earth. This has to do with the earth connection of using that energy for our personal flow and connection and healing. Hematite works receptively like the metal silver, but not as dramatically.

Alchemist's Note: Silver Light may be used with hematite for a more lunar, receptive energy. Hematite itself is more earth-receptive. Experiment with this. It doesn't open psychic channels as much as it opens awareness channels in the physical, and increases sensory perceptive skills.

Hematite is excellent as a brain stimulant and blood builder. You can use hematite with Red Ray to help Red Ray stones, such as jasper or even ruby. I like to use garnet together with hematite or granite; this is a friendly combination for issues of Yin/Yang balance.

Alternative Stone

A Gray Light alternative stone is a gray crazy lace agate. Crazy lace agates of any color have a friendly, supportive energy that correlates well with Gray Light flexibility. A gray stone helps focus Gray Light more clearly.

Chapter Twenty-eight

Brown Light: Connection

The lands wait for those who can discern their rhythms.
—Vine Deloria

Brown Light is the energy of the planet Earth connecting us to Mother Nature. Brown Light is Nature's way of staying attuned to life in the environment and rooted to the ground.

The trick with Brown Light is to let its energies form like little roots. If you form large roots, like tap roots, you may find yourself too grounded. While forming tap roots may be necessary at times, smaller spreading roots are effective most of the time. Try grass roots, or those air roots that connect ivy as it runs over and climbs around whatever it can.

Alchemist's Note: When we tap into Brown Light, we connect with the woodland devic energies; the Tolkien middle-earth type of nature consciousness. (Did you ever wonder why some of the little people are called Brownies? Hmmm . . .)

Elemental Alchemy	Earth and Water
Key Issues	Knowledge, moderation, intuition, healing
Stone Alchemy	Smoky quartz, petrified wood
Cumulative Alchemy	Devic Connection

Brown Light Keys

Harmonic	Sound of o (centered vibration, soft-spoken short o)
Alchemical Properties	Nature energies, connection, centering
Sensory Key	Interchangeable (woodsy to start)
Symbols	Tree with roots, shell, seed pod
Personification	Earth Steward/Reverend
Runic	Eh (Ehwaz)
Astrological Correlates	Taurus, Scorpio
Major Arcana Key	The Devil
Archangel	Cassiel (Saturn)
Stone Alchemy	Smokey quartz, petrified wood

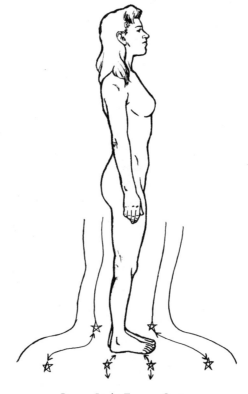

Brown Light Energy Centers

Harmonic

Sound of short o—centered vibration, soft-spoken short o.

**Nature Spirits gathering round,
Devic energies abound,
Walking proudly, feet on ground,
Opening to power profound.**

Or:

From realms of Spirit we are borne,
From boundaries unseen, unknown,
To the Earth on which we're born,
The path of power to be shown.

Amplify by walking slowly, with awareness and mindfulness about your personal connection to the powers of the planet Earth.

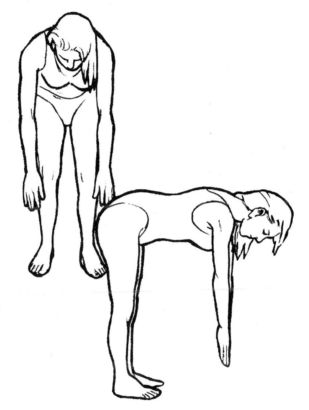

Brown Light Harmonic Posture

Alchemical Properties

Brown Light connects the physical to devic energies of Nature. Brown centers, grounds, and attunes the physical to receive healing in a physical, emotional, etheric, spiritual manner.

Powers	Supportive, direct, tangible, connecting action
Activates	Nature connection, attunement and awareness
Amplifies	Natural devic energies
Balances	Blissy, disconnected spirituality
Releases	Detachments from nature and healing earth energies
Realigns	Positive energy flow between nature and humankind

Harmonious Brown Light Energy Pattern

Shamanic Brown Light Energy Pattern

Sensory Key

(Interchangeable)
The sensory key suggested with Brown Light is a woodsy blend.

> Shared attributes of woodsy blends and Brown Light:
> Connection
> Centering
> Strength
> Devic energies
> The element of Earth

Woodsy blends are available ready-made or can be created quite easily with items such as leaves, herbs, roots, bark, stones, seeds, cones, et cetera. Woodsy scents can be bought or created from blending the Earth Light sensory key oils and others which are personally alchemical for you. Experiment with your blend until the scent evokes the energies of the deep forest for you.

- Buy or create an oil whose scent is deep and woodsy. Rub the oil into an unusual piece of wood, such as a gnarled root, carved figure, wand or staff. Focus on Brown Light infusing the wood with magickal, Earth-connection energies.

  Use the wooden piece ceremonially to evoke the devic energies—the Nature Spirit dimensions closest to the energies of the Earth.

  Use the wooden piece in your everyday environment as a reminder of your connection to the powerful energies of the planet earth.
- Keep a woodsy blend of scented oil on hand for quick centering and grounding of your scattered energies. Rub oil on pulse points.

  Breathe, focus on a clear Brown Light connecting you to the stability and the strength of Earth. Breathe, and imagine yourself in a deep, quiet forest. Take time for an earth journey, deep into the heart of Nature. Breathe and collect your power in connection to Earth.

Symbols

Tree with roots represents the shamanic connection between the elemental energies of the earth and those of spirit. From a rooted connection to the elemental energies of the earth, humankind can securely reach the expansive energies of spiritual evolution.

Shell represents the protective structures Nature provides for our self-development. That which Nature has provided for the development of one's Self cannot truly be duplicated for the development of any other.

Seed pod represents the earthbound structures we rely on for growth, then cast aside as we transform. The earthbound limitations we seek to shed are often the natural protections we coveted when we first began to grow.

Personification

Connection

Brown is the energy of the Earth Steward. It is St. Francis of Assisi teaching the power and pleasure of Simplicity in Spirituality. Brown is the energy which connects us to the deepest spiritual Earth energies.

Musings

Dance to the rhythm of the earth, and you will hear the music of all the spheres.

Power which is not rooted in Nature may be nothing more than disconnected divinity.

Devas are decidedly easier to divine from within their own dimensions.

Our life evokes our character.
—Joseph Campbell

Nature does nothing uselessly.
—Aristotle

Runic Correlate

Eh (Ehwaz)

Shared aspects with Brown Light:

    Practicality   Transportation
    Movement   Vehicle
    Medium for change
    The element of Earth

Eh (Ehwaz)

Eh (Ehwaz) supports the security of the personal alchemist, the connection to nature's energies, and the surest vehicles for transportation in all dimensions. The personal alchemist requires the how and the where-with-all, as well as the essential "why!" Activate personal centering energies and practical methods for your alchemy with Eh (Ehwaz).

The alchemy of Eh (Ehwaz) is activated in proportion to the connection one has to the energies of planet earth. The greater the connection, the greater the vehicle provided for the processes of self-transformation.

Astrological Correlates

Solar Taurus

When the Taurean has determined in his deep and sometimes dark subconscious that his emotional or material security lies there, he goes there and stays there forever.

—Grant Lewi

Lunar Scorpio

A mystic strength enshrouds you even in weakness; you are supported by inner, perhaps unexpressed convictions; you know what you're doing, even when no one else in the world does.

—Grant Lewi

Brown Light relates with Scorpio for issues of centering, focus, expression, and self-empowerment. All signs also correlate with Brown Light according to their elements.

Fire signs   Energy focus
Water signs   Grounded security
Earth signs   Empowerment activator
Air signs   Centering catalyst

Major Arcana Key

The Devil

Shared aspects with Brown Light:

Boundaries   Structures
Connections   Self-criticism
Grounded power   Expectations

> *There is no devil except of man's own creation, and here it is evident that men are chained by their own wrong choices. However, the chains about their necks are loose and can be removed at will.*
>
> —Eden Gray

Musings

It must be terribly convenient to have a devil in one's philosophy; taking all the blame for one's personal failings. Too convenient, I believe.

We can "give ourselves the devil" about something we don't like about what we are—or we can assume all the responsibility for all that we are—and in so doing we acquire the power to change that which we do not like.

Personal boundaries are needed to conserve and ground personal powers and spiritual, shamanic connections.

Archangel

Angelic Dimension Key

Cassiel: Archangel of Saturn

    Alchemy of Earth wisdom, Connection and Karmic pattern

Days	Saturday, Monday
Times	3-4 AM
	11-12 AM
	7-8 PM

♄

And holy Earth, the giver of life, yields to the gods rich blessedness.

—Euripides

Angelic Invocation

Cassiel, ordered light of angelic realm, help me to connect my energies, my heart felt truths and my Spiritual seekings, to the wisdom of this Earth on which I find my self just now.

Stone Alchemy

Placement for Brown stones is between the ankles, preferably while standing on the ground outdoors. Brown stones can also be held in the hands and meditated with quite effectively. This is true in or out of doors. Smoky quartz and petrified wood are the stones chosen here for Brown Light.

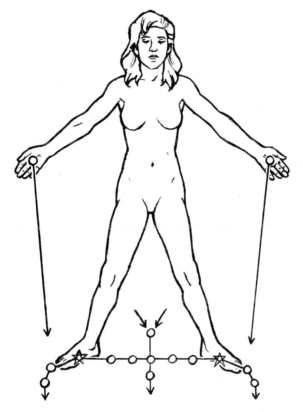

Brown Light Stone Placement

Smoky Quartz: Transmuter Stone
Element: Earth and Air

Smoky quartz is an inexpensive, high vibration stone. Smoky quartz ranges in shades from light to very dark brown. The best shades to use for Brown Light Earth-connection energies are the lighter sorts which are brownish-tan, smoky (almost dirty) quartz.

The dark, smoky quartz is used for heavy releasing of negativity and can be used for Black Light work, as it is similar to Black. This stone can be used for Brown Light for deep emotional or physical release. Focus on releasing these energies into healing Earth energies for transmutation.

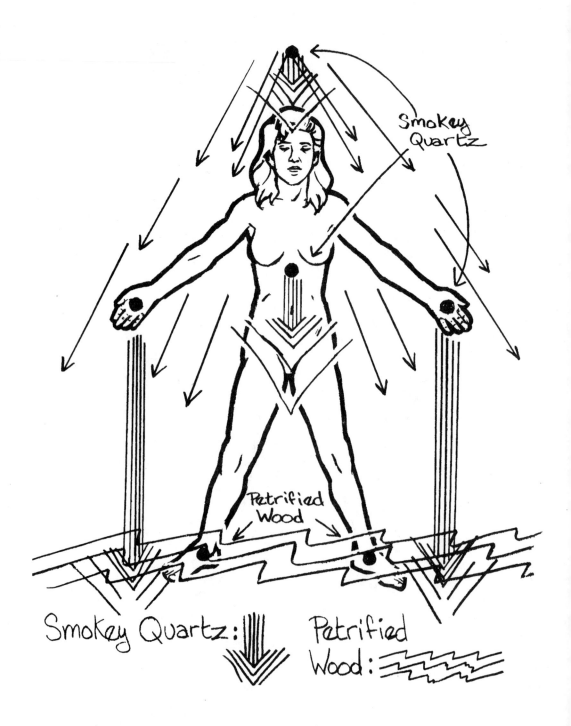

Brown Light Stone Energy Patterns

Alchemist's Note: For connecting with Brown Light Earth energy and Nature awareness, lighter smoky quartz is more effective because they tend to be more sensitive to the Earth rhythm. Take them outside; put them between your feet; stand, and begin to feel not only the rhythm of the earth, but your personal rhythm, as well. By using lighter smoky quartz, it enhances the spiritual connection between Earth, your Self, and Spirit. It is a shamanic sort of alchemy.

Petrified Wood: Bridging Stone
Element: Earth

Petrified wood symbolizes the transformation of all life in Nature. It has a subtle vibration. It is good for drawing support in times of change.

Petrified wood is actually not wood, but the chemical replacement which happened when fossilized matter formed around wood. Petrified wood has become stone and has an ancient, primitive energy. Petrified wood has returned to the earth, so to speak. It has an energy which connects to the earth as well as to the whole process of the Planet Earth changing and moving. Petrified wood bridges the Human, Mineral, and Plant Worlds together.

Alchemist's Note: Energies which are bridges, such as petrified wood and amber, work to help us gain more Earth consciousness and stability on our path.

Alternative Stone

Another stone or object to use with Brown Light work is a fossil. Fossils are ancient preservers of energy, and reminders of the processes of life.

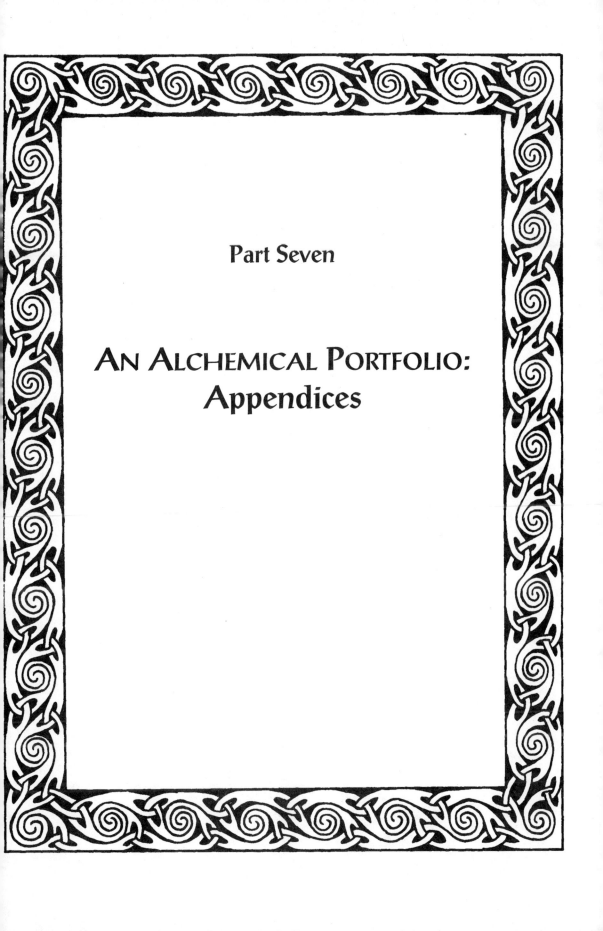

Part Seven

AN ALCHEMICAL PORTFOLIO:
Appendices

Appendix A

Quick Reference: Rays and Lights

Attributes of Rays

Red Ray
      (Primary) Root chakra
- Energies   Lifeforce, physicality, survival, strength
- Placement   Base of spine, pubic bone
- Stones   Ruby, coral, jasper

Scarlet Ray
      (Blended) Etheric to physical
- Energies   Fundamental balance, sex-role expectations, Yin/Yang, receptivity/activity
- Placement   Just above pubic bone, around tailbone
- Stones   Garnet, watermelon tourmaline, cinnabar

Rose Ray
      (Blended) Etheric to physical
- Energies   Emotional growth, temperance, balance connectedness to others, harmony
- Placement   Mid-shoulder blades, mid-sternum on heart, crown of head
- Stones   Alexandrite, rose quartz, rhodonite

Orange Ray
      (Secondary) Sacral chakra
- Energies   Creativity, enthusiasm, self-control, physical and emotional digestion
- Placement   Small of back, three inches below navel
- Stones   Amber, carnelian, fire agate

Peach Ray
      (Blended) Etheric to physical
- Energies   Peace, communication, good will, positive restructuring, humor
- Placement   Above small of back, in navel, on heart chakra
- Stones   Rhodochrosite, unikite

497

Yellow Ray   (Primary) Solar plexus
    Energies   Wisdom, philosophy, contemplation, organization, mental equilibrium
    Placement   On spite at waist level, in front on waist
    Stones   Topaz, citrine, tigereye

Golden-Green Ray   (Blended) Etheric to physical
    Energies   Rejuvenation, metamorphosis, release, renewal, rebirth
    Placement   Bottom of rib cage, midpoint of spine just above waist
    Stones   Peridot, jade, serpentine

Green Ray   (Secondary) Heart chakra
    Energies   Health, abundance, growth, harmony, healing, expansion
    Placement   Heart area, front and back, over all body
    Stones   Emerald, malachite, aventurine

Blue Ray   (Primary) Throat chakra
    Energies   Devotion, expression, inspiration, spirituality, exhilaration, etheric flow
    Placement   On spine between top of shoulder blades, center of collar bones
    Stones   Celestite, sodalite, blue lace agate

Turquoise Ray   (Blended) Etheric to physical
    Energies   Zeal, dedication, service, self-determination
    Placement   Just above heart chakra, solar plexus, over all body
    Stones   Aquamarine, turquoise, chrysocolla

Indigo Ray   (Blended) Brow chakra
    Energies   Synthesis, ceremony, ritual, magick, unity, centering, blending all aspects
    Placement   Third eye area, throat chakra
    Stones   Sapphire, azurite, lapis

Violet Ray   (Secondary) Crown chakra
    Energies   Awareness of choice (karma), connection of physical to spirit, regalness, mastery
    Placement   Crown of head, upper chakras
    Stones   Amethyst, fluorite, royal azule

Attributes of Lights

Sky Lights

Effect from etheric through upper chakras most directly
Includes White, Rainbow, Crystal, Spirit, Silver, Gold

White Light   Reflected light with all spectrum properties, transmitting medium,
                                channel for healing energies
      Placement   Above each shoulder, top of head, outside of ankles,
                                over and around all body
      Stones   Milky quartz

Rainbow Light   Blends and orders all spectrum Rays, focuses for specific
                                Ray programming
      Placement   Four to six inches above head, outside of white stones placements
      Stones   Crystals with rainbow inclusions (rainbow quartz),
                                abalone or mother of pearl

Crystal Light   Evokes clarity, perfection, precision of psychic cosmic energies
      Placement   Between feet, 6 to 12 inches above head
      Stones   Very clear quartz crystals and double-terminated crystals

Spirit Light   Light beyond vision or division, structure or form; representing
                                the All . . . the Oneness . . . the Source
      Placement   Above crystal light stones, all around the body and environment.
      Stones   Clear quartz crystal clusters in groups of four or more points

Silver Light   Receptive light; relates to lunar, feminine, Yin energies
                                of inner peace
      Placement   Right side of head (left brain), any placement to open receptivity
      Stones: Silver, moonstone

Gold Light   Active light, stimulates all other energies, psychic vitamin
      Placement   Left side of head (right brain), base of spine to activate
                                energy flow
      Stones   Gold, rutile (rutilated quartz)

Earth Lights

Effect from etheric through lower chakras
Includes Black, Gray, Brown
Placement at lower chakra points, around legs and feet

Black Light	Absorbs and helps transmute negativity, symbolizes the quest for light, centers and shields
Stones	Apache tears, snowflake obsidian
Gray Light	Balanced Light with positive/negative active/receptive energies, Earth connector with energies of flexibility and stability
Stones	Granite, hematite
Brown Light	Connector Light with deep Earth energies; attunes to Nature, ecological consciousness
Stones	Smoky quartz, petrified wood

Rays of Power

Stimulating Positive Aspects

Attribute	Activates	Amplifies	Balances
Action analysis	Orange	Yellow	Blue
Active intelligence	Yellow	Green	Indigo
Androgynous balance	Scarlet	Rose	Green
Catalyst	Red	Indigo	Yellow
Cleansing	Golden-Green	Red	Peach
Communication	Yellow	Scarlet	Green
Compassion	Blue	Rose	Green
Confidence	Orange	Peach	Blue
Courage	Orange	Green	Indigo
Creativity	Orange	Blue	Yellow
Dedication	Turquoise	Green	Orange
Detachment	Blue	Violet	Yellow
Determination	Turquoise	Orange	Blue
Devotion	Violet	Indigo	Rose
Energy flow	Green	Red	Rose
Enthusiasm	Green	Orange	Yellow
Expansion	Green	Rose	Yellow
Expression	Blue	Yellow	Green
Harmony	Peach	Rose	Green

Attribute	Activates	Amplifies	Balances
Hope	Green	Violet	Yellow
Honor	Red	Scarlet	Indigo
Humility	Rose	Violet	Blue
Humor	Peach	Blue	Yellow
Gratitude	Violet	Indigo	Green
Idealism	Violet	Golden-Green	Scarlet
Illumination	Yellow	Orange	Blue
Implementation	Indigo	Orange	Golden-Green
Independence	Red	Green	Scarlet
Integrity	Turquoise	Scarlet	Green
Inspiration	Indigo	Orange	Turquoise
Intellect	Yellow	Orange	Peach
Justice	Violet	Blue	Peach
Love	Rose	Red	Green
Loyalty	Violet	Blue	Scarlet
Memory work	Golden-Green	Yellow	Orange
Mental discrimination	Yellow	Orange	Turquoise
Mercy	Blue	Rose	Peach
Motivation	Red	Orange	Indigo
Openness	Peach	Turquoise	Blue
Organization	Yellow	Indigo	Blue
Peace	Peach	Rose	Green
Perception	Yellow	Scarlet	Indigo
Prosperity	Green	Orange	Turquoise
Psychic abilities	Indigo	Blue	Rose
Regeneration	Golden-Green	Red	Green
Rejuvenation	Golden-Green	Orange	Blue
Relationships	Scarlet	Rose	Green
Release	Golden-Green	Orange	Peach
Responsibility	Violet	Blue	Rose
Responsiveness	Green	Rose	Peach
Revelations	Violet	Indigo	Peach
Security	Rose	Blue	Orange
Self-respect	Rose	Red	Turquoise
Sensitivity	Blue	Rose	Peach
Serenity	Rose	Indigo	Peach
Service	Turquoise	Red	Indigo
Sharing	Green	Turquoise	Rose
Sincerity	Blue	Yellow	Rose
Soul consciousness	Violet	Indigo	Scarlet
Strength	Red	Orange	Turquoise
Synthesis	Indigo	Peach	Scarlet
Temperance	Rose	Violet	Turquoise
Tenderness	Rose	Peach	Green

Attribute	Activates	Amplifies	Balances
Trust	Blue	Red	Rose
Understanding	Blue	Rose	Green
Unity	Indigo	Peach	Rose
Vitality	Orange	Turquoise	Golden-Green
Vision	Indigo	Violet	Yellow
Willpower	Red	Turquoise	Rose
Wisdom	Blue	Indigo	Yellow
Zeal	Turquoise	Red	Indigo

Rays of Purification

Transforming Negative Aspects

Attribute	Releases	Realigns	Balances
Agitation	Yellow	Violet	Indigo
Anger	Blue	Orange	Peach
Anxiety	Rose	Blue	Yellow
Arrogance	Yellow	Scarlet	Rose
Authoritarianism	Green	Turquoise	Rose
Bitterness	Turquoise	Golden-Green	Peach
Conceit	Orange	Indigo	Golden-Green
Confusion	Indigo	Golden-Green	Scarlet
Contempt	Indigo	Yellow	Violet
Cowardice	Blue	Rose	Turquoise
Criticism	Rose	Yellow	Turquoise
Cruelty	Green	Orange	Rose
Cynicism	Orange	Rose	Turquoise
Delusion	Indigo	Golden-Green	Yellow
Depression	Peach	Blue	Turquoise
Desolation	Orange	Turquoise	Green
Destructiveness	Green	Red	Rose
Deviousness	Orange	Golden-Green	Turquoise
Disorganization	Indigo	Peach	Yellow
Dissatisfaction	Green	Peach	Turquoise
Ego disorders	Yellow	Scarlet	Turquoise
Expectations	Yellow	Turquoise	Indigo
Extremes	Turquoise	Scarlet	Indigo
Fear	Orange	Blue	Golden-Green
Frustration	Indigo	Red	Peach
Greed	Rose	Green	Peach
Hate	Green	Rose	Scarlet
Ignorance	Blue	Orange	Turquoise
Imbalance	Indigo	Scarlet	Rose

Attribute	Releases	Realigns	Balances
Indifference	Orange	Blue	Turquoise
Inferiority	Red	Orange	Golden-Green
Insecurity	Rose	Red	Blue
Intolerance	Yellow	Violet	Blue
Irritability	Blue	Indigo	Rose
Isolation	Peach	Blue	Green
Jealousy	Rose	Green	Scarlet
Judgmentalism	Green	Yellow	Rose
Lack of self-respect	Blue	Rose	Scarlet
Laziness	Orange	Yellow	Turquoise
Martyrdom	Red	Turquoise	Violet
Negativity	Golden-Green	Yellow	Turquoise
Obsession	Yellow	Violet	Green
Perfectionism	Green	Scarlet	Blue
Pessimism	Golden-Green	Green	Violet
Possessiveness	Rose	Blue	Green
Power-seeking	Indigo	Turquoise	Violet
Procrastination	Red	Golden-Green	Turquoise
Psychic vampirism	Green	Golden-Green	Violet
Rebellion	Blue	Red	Scarlet
Regrets	Golden-Green	Indigo	Turquoise
Remorse	Violet	Indigo	Green
Resistance	Red	Green	Blue
Revenge	Golden-Green	Red	Rose
Separateness	Indigo	Blue	Turquoise
Self-rejection	Yellow	Blue	Green
Self-righteousness	Violet	Peach	Golden-Green
Stubbornness	Rose	Yellow	Scarlet
Superiority	Indigo	Orange	Scarlet
Totalitarianism	Green	Indigo	Turquoise
Vanity	Blue	Peach	Rose
Vacillation	Scarlet	Yellow	Indigo
Vengeance	Violet	Red	Peach
Violence	Peach	Red	Rose
Yearning	Rose	Golden-Green	Red

Natural Lights Basic Enhancement Properties

Stimulating Positive Aspects

White	Protects, communicates, assists transmittal
Rainbow	Organizes, blends, balances distribution
Crystal	Amplifies, clarifies, focuses
Spirit	Empowers, connects to Soul levels
Gold	Activates, energizes and inspires
Silver	Receives, reflects and nurtures
Black	Filters, strengthens, aids in manifesting
Gray	Stabilizes, enhances flexibility
Brown	Grounds, opens and attunes to connect

Transforming Negative Aspects

White	Channels release, seals in healing
Rainbow	Disperses, realigns, redirects
Crystal	Purifies, synthesizes
Spirit	Transmutes to highest good
Gold	Activates release, energizes transformation
Silver	Opens receptivity to transformation
Black	Absorbs residue, supports transformation
Gray	Balances flow of positive and release of negative
Brown	Opens the physical to healing, connects to Nature energies

Elemental Alchemy

Spirit	=	Spirit Light
Spirit and Air		White Light
Spirit and Fire		Crystal Light
Spirit and Water		Violet Ray
Spirit and Earth		Black Light

Air and Spirit	=	Peach Ray
Fire and Spirit		Rainbow Light
Water and Spirit		Blue Ray
Earth and Spirit		Golden-Green Ray

Air and Fire	=	Yellow Ray
Air and Water		Rose Ray
Air and Earth		Gray Light

Fire and Air	=	Orange Ray
Water and Air		Silver Light
Earth and Air		Indigo Ray

Fire and Water	=	Scarlet Ray
Fire and Earth		Red Ray
Water and Fire		Turquoise Ray
Earth and Fire		Gold Light
Water and Earth		Green Ray
Earth and Water		Brown Light

For the sake of learning the Rays and Lights in the order in which they relate to each other, let's list the alchemical combinations another way.

Red Ray	=	Fire and Earth
Scarlet Ray		Fire and Water
Rose Ray		Air and Water
Orange Ray		Fire and Air
Peach Ray		Air and Spirit
Yellow Ray		Air and Fire
Golden-Green Ray		Earth and Spirit
Green Ray		Water and Earth
Turquoise Ray		Water and Fire
Blue Ray		Water and Spirit
Indigo Ray		Earth and Air
Violet Ray		Spirit and Water

White Light	=	Spirit and Air
Rainbow Light		Fire and Spirit
Crystal Light		Spirit and Fire
Spirit Light		Spirit and Spirit
Silver Light		Water and Air
Gold Light		Earth and Fire

Black Light	=	Spirit and Earth
Gray Light		Air and Earth
Brown Light		Earth and Water

Foundational Elements and Key Issues

Spirit	Right action, oneness
Air	Perception, communication
Fire	Sensation, regeneration
Water	Intuition, healing
Earth	Knowledge, moderation

Rays	Elements	Key Issues
Red	Fire and Earth	Sensation, regeneration, knowledge, moderation
Scarlet	Fire and Water	Sensation, regeneration, intuition, healing
Rose	Air and Water	Perception, communication, intuition, healing
Orange	Fire and Air	Sensation, regeneration, perception, communication
Peach	Air and Spirit	Perception, communication, right action, oneness
Yellow	Air and Fire	Perception, communication, sensation, regeneration
Golden-Green	Earth and Spirit	Knowledge, moderation, right action, oneness
Green	Water and Earth	Intuition, healing, knowledge, moderation
Turquoise	Water and Fire	Intuition, healing, sensation, regeneration
Blue	Water and Spirit	Intuition, healing, right action, oneness
Indigo	Earth and Air	Knowledge, moderation, perception, communication
Violet	Spirit and Water	Right action, oneness, intuition, healing

Sky Lights	Elements	Key Issues
White	Spirit and Air	Right action, oneness, perception, communication
Rainbow	Fire and Spirit	Sensation, regeneration, right action, oneness
Crystal	Spirit and Fire	Right action, oneness, sensation, regeneration
Spirit	Spirit	Right action, oneness
Silver	Water and Air	Intuition, healing, perception, communication
Gold	Earth and Fire	Knowledge, moderation, sensation, regeneration

Earth Lights	Elements	Key Issues
Black	Spirit and Earth	Right action, oneness, knowledge, moderation
Gray	Air and Earth	Perception, communication, knowledge, moderation
Brown	Earth and Water	Knowledge, moderation, intuition, healing

Appendix B

Keys

Harmonics

The system of harmonics works by attuning the Ray energies through the use of sound and vibration. This is another way of getting into the energy and weaving another thread, strengthening the web.

Primary Rays

Red Ray	Harmonic e as in she
Yellow Ray	Harmonic ah as in father
Blue Ray	Harmonic o as in boat

Secondary Rays

Green Ray	Harmonic a as in say
Orange Ray	Harmonic eh as in bet
Violet Ray	Harmonic u as in sun (also from u as in sun to oo as in moon)

Blended Rays

Scarlet Ray	Harmonic i as in ice
Turquoise Ray	Harmonic aw as in draw
Golden-Green Ray	Harmonic i as in sit
Rose Ray	Harmonic y as in why
Peach Ray	Harmonic a as in sat
Indigo Ray	Harmonic om

Indigo (a synthesis Ray) has the sound of **om**. **Om**, the chant of **ohm**, can be used for any stone to awaken its energy. It is an all-purpose chanting harmonic. In **om**, the **o** is physical and the **mmm** is spiritual. When you make this sound in balance, you balance out these energies. If you need a little more physical energy, stretch out the **o**. If you need a little more soothing or spiritual energy, stretch out the **mmm**.

Alchemist's Note: Another way you can quickly attune your self and your stones or crystals is simply by going through the vowel sounds. We all know these from grammar school: **a, e, i, o, u**. When you get to **u**, stretch it into an **oo** sound.

Lights

The harmonic key for the Sky Lights is the sound of **m** as in **me**. This harmonic is higher pitched and far more variable than the deep **m** of the Indigo harmonic **om**.

The harmonic key for all the Earth Lights is the sound of **o** as in **mom**. This harmonic **o** is moderately deep in pitch but not as much as the harmonic (long) **o** of Blue Ray or the harmonic **om** of Indigo. Variations of this harmonic are best sung or chanted with a sedate, grounded energy.

Sensory Keys

Rays

Red	Cinnamon
Scarlet	Cloves
Rose	Floral
Orange	Ginger
Peach	Fruity
Yellow	Sandalwood
Golden-Green	Herbal or minty
Green	Bayberry
Turquoise	Bay laurel
Blue	Thyme (tranquility)
Indigo	Jasmine (temple incense)
Violet	Lavender, lilac

Sky Lights

(Sensory keys used with Sky Lights are interchangeable)

White	Frankincense
Rainbow	Myrrh
Crystal	Almond
Spirit	Vanilla
Gold	
Silver	

Earth Lights

(Sensory keys used with Earth Lights are interchangeable)

Black	Patchouli
Gray	Sage
Brown	Woodsy

Selected Incense Systems

Red
        Spicy (blends of cinnamon, cloves, etc.) includes:

Red	Rose
Scarlet	Orange

Yellow
        Sandalwood (single note) includes:

Peach	Yellow
Golden-Green	Green

Blue
        Jasmine (single note) includes:

Blue	Turquoise
Indigo	Violet

Sky Lights
        Frankincense/Myrrh (single or blend) includes:

White	Rainbow
Crystal	Spirit
Gold	Silver

Earth Lights
        Woodsy (blend of cedar, evergreen, etc.) includes:

Black	Gray
Brown	

Mind work
        Woodsy (most specifically compatible Ray is Yellow) includes:

Scarlet	Rainbow
Peach	Brown
Yellow	Turquoise
Indigo	

Body work
        Spicy (most specifically compatible Ray is Red) includes:

Orange	Gold
Golden-Green	Silver
Green	Gray
Red	

Spirit work
        Floral (most specifically compatible Ray is Blue) includes:

Violet	White
Blue	Spirit
White	Black
Crystal	

Remember, any one incense which is personally alchemical for you will always work best. These divisions are arbitrary, useful to focus, but not fixed in their effect. Experiment.

Symbolic Keys

(Illustrations of symbols may be found in the chapters on specific color Rays and Lights)

Essential Energies of Vitality and Lifeforce

Red	Feathered arrow, drum, drop of blood
Scarlet	Double-edged sword, justice scales, Yin/Yang symbols
Rose	Wreath, links in a chain, full-blown rose
Orange	Flame, control panel, cauldron

Creative Energies of Heart and Mind

Peach	Peace symbol, handprint, keystone arch
Yellow	Obelisk, pagoda, maze
Golden-Green	Flower bud, spoked wheel, tiny sprout
Green	Heart, evergreen tree, money sign

Spiritual Energies of Service and Devotion

Turquoise	Shield (badge), staff, sword
Blue	Music note, grail, wave
Indigo	Equilateral cross, sailor's knot, Egyptian eye
Violet	Lotus blossom, temple, star (five- or six-point)

Sky Lights: Supportive Energies of Spiritual Evolution

White	Pyramid, clouds, feather
Rainbow	Rainbow, solar system (galaxy), beribboned maypole
Crystal	Quartz crystal point, crystal ball, wand
Spirit	Eight-point star (or personal religious symbol), wings, crown
Gold	Sun, male symbol, rocket (fireworks)
Silver	Moon, female symbol, basket

Earth Lights: Centering Energies of Connection and Stability

Black	Theta symbol, footprint, candle
Gray	Spiral, road sign X, river
Brown	Tree with roots, shell, seed pod

Personification Images

Red	Essential Warrior	*Mars/Ares*
Scarlet	Warrior/Adventurer	*Robin Hood*
Rose	Active Healer	*Mother Theresa*
Orange	Creative Muse	*White Goddess*
Peach	Receptive Resistor	*Mahatma Gandhi*
Yellow	Teacher/Sage	*Gautama Buddha*
Golden-Green	Transcendental Naturalist	*Emerson/Thoreau*
Green	Creator/Nurturer	*Mother Nature*
Turquoise	Revolutionary Humanist	*Thomas Jefferson*
Blue	Spiritual Poet/Bard	*Krishnamurti/Talesin*
Indigo	Prophet/Oracle	*Edgar Cayce*
Violet	Magician/Alchemist	*Merlin*
White	Receptive Healer	*Mary, Mother of Gods*
Rainbow	Artist/Expresser	*Georgia O'Keefe*
Crystal	Guardian Angel	*(Individual)*
Spirit	Christ/Avatar	*Jesus/Buddha/Krishna*
Gold	Provider/King	*Arthur*
Silver	Counselor	*Guinevere*
Black	Shaman/Medicine Teacher	*Hermes*
Gray	Dancer/Athlete	*Greek Olympian*
Brown	Earth Reverend	*St. Francis*

Appendix C

Traditional Systems

Runic Activators

Ray and Attribute	Runes	Runic Attribute	Symbol
Red: Lifeforce	Sigel (Sowelu) Tyr (Ger.) Teiwaz (Brit.)	Essential power, warrior	ᛋ ↑
Scarlet: Balance	Thorn (Thurisaz) Beorc (Ger.) Berkana (Brit.)	Catharsis, chaos balance	ᚦ ᛒ
Rose: Temperance	Os (Ansuz)	Benevolence, communication	ᚠ
Orange: Vitality	UR (Uruz)	Potency, courage, strength	ᚢ
Peach: Peace	Ethel (Othila)	Unity, allegiance, consolidation	ᛜ
Yellow: Intellect	Daeg (Dagaz) Man (Ger.) Mannaz (Brit.)	Study, facts, self-knowledge	ᛞ ᛗ

Ray and Attribute	Runes	Runic Attribute	Symbol
Golden-Green: Renewal	Ger (Jera)	Harvest, cycles, transformation	ᚲ
Green: Expansion	Feoh (Fehu)	Abundance, prosperity, growth	ᚠ
Turquoise: Dedication	Eoh (Eihwaz)	Readiness, service, power	ᛇ
Blue: Expression	Wyn (Wunjo)	Spiritual gain, joy, self-achievement	ᚹ
Indigo: Synthesis	Lagu (Laguz)	Inner wisdom, magic, mystery	ᛚ
Violet: Spirituality	Ken (Kano)	Guidance, spiritual opportunity	ᚲ

Light and Attribute	Runes	Runic Attribute	Symbol
White: Healing	Eolh (Algiz)	Shield, assistance, protection	ᛦ
Rainbow: Blending	Peord (Perth) Daeg (Ger.) Dagaz (Brit.)	Distribution, initiation, chance	ᛈ ᛞ
Crystal: Clarity	Tyr (Teiwaz)	Truth, spiritual judgment	ᛏ
Spirit: Source	Gyfu (Gebo)	Unity of self and Self, gifts	ᚷ

Light and Attribute	Runes	Runic Attribute	Symbol
Silver: Receptivity	IS (ISA) Lagu (Ger.) Laguz (Brit.)	Inner journey, secrets, mystery	I ﾑ
Gold: Activity	Man (Mannaz) Wyn (Ger.) Wunjo (Brit.)	Self-activation, achievement	ᛗ ᚹ
Black: Release	Haegl (Hagalaz)	Transmutation, change, disruption	ᚺ
Gray: Flexibility	Nyd (Nauthiz)	Endurance, persistence, resolve	ᚾ
Brown: Connection	EH (Ehwaz)	Transportation, movement, vehicle	ᛗ

Astrological Correlates

Sign	Ray	Light	Essential Attribute
Aries	Red	Gold	Essential Activator
Taurus	Green	Brown	Grounded Healer
Gemini	Golden-Green	White	Renewal Medium
Cancer	Blue	Silver	Devoted Receptor
Leo	Orange	Gold	Creative Activator
Virgo	Yellow	Gold	Active Organizer
Libra	Rose	White	Harmony Medium
Scorpio	Scarlet	Brown	Centered Balancer
Sagittarius	Peach	Gray	Friendly Peacemaker
Capricorn	Indigo	Black	Synthesis Seeker
Aquarius	Turquoise	Gold	Dedicated Activator
Pisces	Violet	Silver	Spiritual Receptor

We can rearrange elements to create similar alchemy:

Sign	Ray	Light	Essential Attribute
Aries	Turquoise	White	Zealous Transmitter
Taurus	Rose	Gold	Harmony Activator
Gemini	Orange	Gold	Peaceful Activator
Cancer	Green	Black	Healing Seeker
Leo	Peach	Silver	Vitality Receptor
Virgo	Violet	Brown	Grounded Spiritualist
Libra	Scarlet	Gray	Friendly Balancer
Scorpio	Blue	Black	Devotion Seeker
Sagittarius	Golden-Green	Gold	Renewal Activator
Capricorn	Yellow	Brown	Ordered Connector
Aquarius	Red	Black	Essential Seeker
Pisces	Indigo	White	Synthesis Medium

Major Arcana Keys

Ray	Arcana	Attributes
Red	The Emperor	Lifeforce, thrust
Scarlet	The Lovers	Balance, Yin/Yang
Rose	Temperance	Moderation, Self-unity
Orange	Strength	Vitality, Self-control
Peach	The Hierophant	Activating right action
Yellow	The Magician	Perceptive ordering
Golden-Green	Transformation (Death)	Renewal, metamorphosis
Green	The Empress	Growth, abundance
Turquoise	The Hanged Man	Service, self-determination
Blue	The Chariot	Idealism expressed
Indigo	Judgment	Integrating wisdom
Violet	Justice	Spiritual Karma (choice)

Light	Arcana	Attributes
White	The High Priestess	Transmitting medium
Rainbow	Wheel of Fortune	Energy distribution
Crystal	The World	Clarity, empowerment
Spirit	The Star	Transcendence, joy
Silver	The Moon	Receptivity, Yin
Gold	The Sun	Activation, Yang
Black	The Tower	Release, transmutation
Gray	The Hermit	Centered flexibility
Brown	The Devil	Earth connecting
Self/Personal Alchemist	The Fool	Open-minded explorer

Angelic Dimensions

Gabriel   Archangel of the Moon

Day	Monday
Times	5-6 AM
	1-2 PM
	9-10 PM
Aspects	Psychic gifts, intuition, the cycles of women (and the female aspects of men, as well)
Color Energies	Silver, White, Rose, Blue, Crystal, Spirit, sometimes Scarlet for Yin/Yang balance
Candle Colors	White, silver, blue

Samael   Archangel of Mars

Day	Tuesday
Times	6-7 AM
	2-3 PM
	10-11 PM
Aspects	Courage, protection (particularly from violence), organization, mechanical affairs
Color Energies	Red, White, Orange, Black, Gold, Crystal, Spirit, sometimes Yellow for order
Candle Colors	Red, orange, white

Raphael   Archangel of Mercury

Days	Wednesday, Saturday
Times	7-8 AM
	3-5 PM
	11-12 PM
Aspects	Communication, writing, mental abilities, intellect and some healing
Color Energies	Yellow, White, Gray, Black, Crystal, Spirit, sometimes Indigo for synthesis
Candle Colors	Yellow, white, gray

Sachiel   Archangel of Jupiter

Days	Thursday, Sunday
Times	12-1 AM
	8-9 AM
	4-5 PM
Aspects	Money, business, social position, luck, opportunities for financial success
Color Energies	Green, White, Violet, Gold, Crystal, Silver, Spirit, sometimes Turquoise for service and zeal
Candle Colors	Green, white, violet

Anael   Archangel of Venus
    Days   Friday, Monday
    Times   1-2 AM
                                  9-10 AM
                                  5-6 PM
    Aspects   Love, relationships, art, beauty, poetry, music, harmony
    Color Energies   Rose, White, Peach, Blue, Silver, Crystal, Spirit, sometimes Orange for creativity
    Candle Colors   Rose, white, peach

Cassiel   Archangel of Saturn
    Days   Saturday, Monday
    Times   3-4 AM
                                  11-12 AM
                                  7-8 PM
    Aspects   Real estate, homes, land, karmic patterns (personal and universal)
    Color Energies   Indigo, White, Brown, Green, Black, Crystal, Spirit, sometimes Rainbow for sorting energy patterns
    Candle Colors   Indigo, white, brown

Michael   Archangel of the Sun
    Days   Sunday, Thursday
    Times   4-5 AM
                                  12-1 PM
                                  8-9 PM
    Aspects   Careers, achievements, ambitions, motivation and life tasks
    Color Energies   Orange, White, Gold, Violet, Crystal, Spirit, sometimes Brown to ground Sun energies
    Candle Colors   Orange, white, gold

Auriel (Uriel)   Archangel of Uranus
    Days   Monday, Wednesday
    Times   2-3 AM
                                  10-11 AM
                                  6-7 PM
    Aspects   Magick, devotion, alchemy, sudden changes and astrology, universal cosmic consciousness
    Color Energies   Violet, White, Indigo, Blue, Spirit, Crystal, Silver, sometimes Rainbow for sudden changes
    Candle Colors   Violet, white, indigo

Asariel   Archangel of Neptune

Days	Monday, Saturday
Times	(none traditional)
	(I use times ruled by **Auriel** or **Gabriel**, whose energies are compatible with aspects of **Asariel**)
Aspects	Vision, inner journeys, personal cosmic consciousness, water, oceans, secrets
Color Energies	Silver, White, Blue, Black, Indigo, Violet, Crystal, Spirit, sometimes Turquoise for clarity and energy
Candle Colors	Silver, white, blue

Azrael   Archangel of Pluto

Days	Thursday, Saturday
Times	(none traditional)
	(I use times ruled by **Cassiel**)
Aspects	Transformation, death, spirit worlds, earth journeys, stones, crystals, minerals.
Color Energies	Black, White, Brown, Silver, Red, Gray, Spirit, Crystal, sometimes Violet for healing with minerals, stones and crystals
Candle Colors	Black, white, brown

Astrological Correlations for Stones and Elements

Fire signs	Aries, Leo, Sagittarius
Fire element stones	Ruby, fire agate
Water signs	Cancer, Scorpio, Pisces
Water element stones	Coral, moonstone, abalone
Earth signs	Taurus, Virgo, Capricorn
Earth element stones	Serpentine, rhodonite, snowflake obsidian
Air signs	Gemini, Libra, Aquarius
Air element stones	Watermelon tourmaline, topaz, peridot, sapphire

Astrological Alchemy Stones

Aries	Carnelian, jaspers, rutile quartz
Taurus	Emerald, chrysocolla, sodalite
Gemini	Blue lace agate, fluorite, unikite
Cancer	Moonstone, red coral, white agate
Leo	Fire agate, gold, malachite
Virgo	Citrine, rhodonite, serpentine
Libra	Watermelon tourmaline, rose quartz, turquoise
Scorpio	Ruby, garnet, lapis
Sagittarius	Amber, rhodochrosite, peridot
Capricorn	Tigereye, Apache tear, snowflake obsidian
Aquarius	Aquamarine, celestite, azurite
Pisces	Amethyst, sapphire, alexandrite

Astrological Correlations of Sun Sign Stones

Aries	Ruby, red jasper, garnet, watermelon tourmaline, rhodonite, carnelian, fire agate, topaz, peridot
Taurus	Amber, carnelian, fire agate, serpentine, emerald, chrysocolla, celestite
Gemini	Alexandrite, rhodonite, topaz, sapphire
Cancer	Red coral, citrine, emerald, abalone, moonstone
Leo	Ruby, garnet, watermelon tourmaline, rhodonite, carnelian, fire agate, topaz, citrine, peridot
Virgo	Yellow jasper, carnelian, fire agate, citrine, serpentine, celestite, sapphire, snowflake obsidian
Libra	Watermelon tourmaline, alexandrite, rhodonite, citrine, emerald, sapphire
Scorpio	Ruby, red coral, garnet, citrine, peridot, azurite, sugilite (royal azule), abalone, moonstone
Sagittarius	Ruby, watermelon tourmaline, fire agate
Capricorn	Yellow jasper, garnet, carnelian, fire agate, chrysocolla, celestite, sapphire, sugilite (royal azule), snowflake obsidian
Aquarius	Alexandrite, rhodonite, citrine, peridot, celestite, azurite, sapphire, sugilite (royal azule)
Pisces	Red coral, citrine, peridot, azurite, sugilite (royal azule), abalone, moonstone

Best Overall Stones for all Astrological Signs

Cinnabar	Rose quartz	Amber
Tigereye	Jade	Malachite
Aventurine	Aquamarine	Turquoise
Sodalite	Lapis	Amethyst
Fluorite	Rainbow quartz	Quartz crystals
White agate	Silver	Gold
Apache tear	Smoky quartz	Petrified wood

Rays and Lights with Stones

Red Ray

Ruby

Ruby carries the element of Fire. It correlates as an enhancer to the Fire signs of Leo, Sagittarius and Aries. It represents lifeforce, so it also relates to the Sun—and to Mars for its active energy. Ruby relates to Pluto, because it has the power of deep transformation. A ruby is especially good for Scorpio people, because it stimulates them to release the karmic debts they have. Scorpio people sometimes come in with an awful lot of work to do, and ruby can be a helper for this.

Coral

Coral has a Water element, with some Fire. Red coral is related planetarily to Mars because of lifeforce, and to Saturn because of its structured aspect. It also relates to Neptune, because it is connected to oceanic consciousness and psychic consciousness. Red coral has a Water element, which relates it to Cancer, Pisces and Scorpio. Red coral gives the Water signs structure in the sea of emotion with which they often have to deal.

Jasper

Jaspers contain the Earth element, with some Fire. They are good stones for all signs and aspects. Jaspers reflect the workhorse ethic of Saturn because they do so many jobs. They have a little bit of the fire of Mars and the transformative energies of Pluto. Red jasper correlates well with Mars energy and is especially good for Aries. Yellow jasper reflects the precision and order of Capricorn and Virgo. Bloodstone jasper enhances Fire and Earth signs and balances Air and Water signs.

Scarlet Ray

Garnet

Garnet combines the elements of Air and Earth together. The more clear the garnet, the more Air; the more opaque the garnet, the more Earth. The garnet correlates astrologically in the same way as rubies. For the most part, its fire is Mars and Sun. Like ruby, it relates to Pluto for deep transformation—but with a little more spiritual effect. Garnet is well matched to Capricorn and Scorpio. It is nice for Leo and Aries by matching then soothing some of their fire.

Watermelon Tourmaline

Watermelon tourmaline carries the element of Air. It is the stone of choice for Libra and issues of balance. Watermelon tourmaline has an interesting correlation with the Fire signs, as well, because of its electrical warmth. It goes well with Aries, Leo and Sagittarius, who are Fire signs. It correlates with the Sun because it has an energizing effect, and with the Moon for receptivity. Watermelon tourmaline relates to Venus for relationships. It also relates to Jupiter for healing and harmony; and to Neptune, because it helps in balancing our intrapsychic expectations of Self.

Cinnabar

Cinnabar carries the element of Earth with a little bit of Water in it. Cinnabar correlates with all of Earth signs (Virgo, Capricorn and Taurus). It enhances these by subtly activating their energies while still matching their earthy aspects. Cinnabar can be quite good for stabilizing Fire signs (Aries, Leo, Sagittarius). It is also stabilizing for Air signs (Aquarius, Gemini and Libra). This is particularly so for Libra's issues of balance. Cinnabar correlates with Saturn for its own balance and order, and for its work. It also relates to Mercury because of the focused-mind meditative effect.

Rose Ray

Alexandrite

Alexandrite carries the elements of Air with a little Spirit. It is good for all Air signs (Aquarius, Gemini and Libra). Alexandrite is especially effective for Libra, because its transformation of moving and changing clearly reflects balance. It is also good for Scorpio, because it helps with some of the sensuality issues Scorpio has to deal with. Alexandrite also reflects the harmony of Venus and Jupiter.

Rose Quartz

Rose quartz, as with most quartz, has the elements of Air and Earth together. The more clear the rose quartz, the more Air; the more opaque, the more Earth. Rose quartz is special for Libra, Cancer, Pisces and Virgo, as they sometimes need tender energies. Rose quartz is also good for Aquarius, who needs to be reattached to community love.

Rhodonite

Rhodonite can be soothing to Leo, because Leo heart energies sometimes move a little too fast. Rhodonite gentles and stabilizes the Mars energy of Aries. Rhodonite is also very good for the mental tension of Air signs, such as Libra, Aquarius and Gemini. Rhodonite has an Earth element which gives a balance to all signs.

Orange Ray

Amber

Amber contains the Earth element, with some Fire. Darker amber is especially good for Taurus, Capricorn and Virgo, as it stimulates these Earth signs without shattering their energies. Their Earth aspects make them strong, but sometimes they can become fixed. Amber is also very good for Air signs (Aquarius, Gemini and Libra) because of the tendencies Air signs have to get into intellect and become stuck in the mental. Amber enhances the Fire signs (Leo, Sagittarius and Aries). It soothes the restless energies that can cause Fire signs to burn out. Deep red amber is especially good for Scorpio. Scorpio needs the dark, fiery warmth that particular ambers can provide. Amber is warming and stimulating to the Water signs (Pisces, Cancer and Scorpio). Amber is useful to give all signs a mental rest. In activation, cleansing and purification, amber is like time in the Sun.

Carnelian

Carnelian carries the elements of Earth and Fire together. It correlates with Mars for its active energy, and with Saturn because it is very ordered in its work. Carnelian correlates with Pluto, because it transforms our systems and our scripts. Carnelian works well for Fire signs (Leo and Aries), but Sagittarius people may find some carnelians make their "friendly fire" rather hyper, and not so friendly. Carnelian is stimulating to Earth signs (Taurus, Virgo and Capricorn). It warms their creative aspects, lights a fire under them and gets them moving. Carnelian can be a little intense for Air signs. The stone's fire and the air of the Air signs together can cause energy to torch out.

Fire Agate

Fire agates have the elements of Fire and Earth together. Fire agate is good for all Fire signs (Sagittarius, Leo and Aries). Fire agate is excellent for Earth signs, as well, because it matches their basic Earth element, then fires them up. Fire agate has an energy that correlates with Mars' essential, active fire. Fire agate also has a deep pattern-making power, similar to the energy of Uranus. Fire agate also reflects the energies of Saturn with its balance and structure.

Peach Ray

Rhodochrosite

Rhodochrosite has no traditional correlates. It does have energies of the Earth element about it, with a a little Spirit and a touch of Fire, as well. The way it operates suggests a lunar/receptive and solar/active balance with a connection to Earth.

Unikite

Unikite suggests the element of Earth with a touch of Fire. It also suggests a correlation with Mercury, because it helps with the ability to communicate. Unikite opens balanced communication between people and their interests psychically from the etheric. Unikite, like rhodochrosite, can be used for the good of all signs.

Yellow Ray

Topaz

Topaz has an Air element, since it relates to the intellect. Topaz has the philosophical, intellectual energy of Uranus, and also carries the activating energy of the Sun. Topaz correlates well with Aries, counteracting impulsivity by giving clarity and order to thoughts before action is taken. Topaz is good for Gemini because it helps with concentration. Topaz is helpful to Leo when the central nervous systems need balancing out. Leo energy is heart-related, and sometimes their central nervous systems get a bit short-changed.

Citrine

The citrine has the element of Air, and some Spirit. It correlates with the sun for its warmth and activation. Citrine also correlates with Mercury, because it is precise and good for positive communication. Citrine is especially good for Leo, as it enhances that golden energy Leos often have. Citrine helps clear out the shadows and doubts Virgos sometimes have. Citrine is good for all Water and Air signs because it increases focus and concentration.

Tigereye

Tigereye correlates to the Sun and to Earth. It is useful to Air signs (Aquarius, Gemini, and Libra) for grounding. Tigereye enhances Earth signs (Taurus, Virgo, and Capricorn). It warms and expands their earthy vibration. Tigereye provides focus for Water signs (Pisces, Cancer and Scorpio). It stabilizes the Fire signs (Aries, Leo, Sagittarius) because it can match their vibration and bring their energy down "to earth" a bit.

Golden-Green Ray

Peridot

The element for peridot is Air. It correlates well with Mercury, because it is intellectual and has to do with communication. Peridot also correlates well with Jupiter, because it focuses more expansive healing energies. Peridot is good for Leos because it strengthens the whole heart area. Because it helps tranquilize their intense emotions, it is great for Scorpio, Pisces, Aries and Aquarius.

Jade

Jade has the element of Earth and some Spirit. Jade reflects the psychic energies of Neptune and also the organized, steady working energy of Saturn. Jade is an excellent overall environment stone for all signs to use.

Serpentine

Serpentine has an Earth element which is beneficial to everyone. It especially good for Taurus and Virgo, and vibrates well with their energies. Serpentine reflects the expansion of Jupiter and also has the gentle harmony of Venus.

Green Ray

Emerald

Emerald carries the elements of Air and Earth together (the more clarity, the more Air). Some perfect emeralds carry the element of Spirit, for healing. Emerald correlates with the Sun because it is a great energizer, and with Jupiter for its abundance. Emerald is also associated with Neptune because it helps balance the intrapsychic self. Emeralds are especially good for Taurus, as it helps expand energies outward. Emerald is helpful to Cancer because it unblocks constrictions. Emeralds are also attuned to Libra's balance issues.

Malachite

Malachite is an excellent overall stone, best reflecting the Earth element. It is enhancing for Earth signs and stabilizing to the Air, Fire and Water signs. It has a steady, Mother Earth, heartbeat energy. Malachite correlates with Pluto's transformative energies. The expanded Green Ray energy suggests Jupiter (although not quite as sharply as emerald or aventurine). In the way that malachite seems to be prepared for change ahead of "schedule," it correlates with the psychic attributes of Neptune.

Aventurine

Aventurine reflects the energies of Earth, with some of Jupiter for luck. It also reflects Neptune, because it stabilizes etherically with psychic consciousness. It is useful for all signs, especially the Earth signs. Aventurine attunes quite well with Taurus.

Turquoise Ray

Aquamarine

Aquamarine has an Air element with a bit of Spirit in it. It reflects the energies of Venus with relationships and balance. It is also attuned to Neptune and to Uranus for its psychic, cosmic qualities. Aquamarine is effective for all signs to use to reach the spiritual, expressive planes. Aquamarine is great for Aquarius, Pisces and Libra, in particular.

Turquoise

Turquoise is reflective of the Earth energies most purely. It is good for all signs who need to connect with the balance of Earth, Sky and Spirit.

Chrysocolla

Chrysocolla has the Earth element, with some Air. It reflects the connection of Earth and Spirit. Also, chrysocolla reflects the harmonious balance of Venus and the quiet determination of Saturn. Specifically, it works well with Taurus and with Capricorn.

Blue Ray

Celestite

Celestite has no traditional astrological aspects, but it suggests the psychic energies of Neptune. It also suggests the more spiritual, cosmic energies of Uranus. Celestite is helpful for Aquarius, often plagued with headaches; and for the Earth signs constricted in their energies. I would say celestite is generally useful to all signs, used gently. It may need to be balanced, though, in the Air signs with something a little earthy, such as malachite. Balance celestite with the Water signs, as well, so the flow does not become excessive. In those cases, use something like sodalite or blue lace agate. These stones will balance, but not interfere with, celestite's beautiful work.

Sodalite

Sodalite shows the reflective energies of the Moon as well as the supportive energies of the Earth. It is a hard worker, a little bit like Saturn. Sodalite is useful in stabilizing all signs, particularly Cancer. Sodalite attunes to the blue energy to which Cancer vibrates, and the earth of sodalite gives stability to Cancer.

Blue Lace Agate

Blue lace agate has the element of Earth, with some Air. It is useful for all signs. It is particularly good with Air signs, as it enhances their natural energies, yet grounds and centers their emotions.

Indigo Ray

Sapphire

Sapphire reflects the element of Air. It also reflects Saturn in its fixed and ordered working manner. I feel it also shows Uranus with the depth of spiritual, psychic and universal awareness. Sapphire can be used for any sign for synthesis and centering. Sapphire is especially good for Libra and Gemini duality issues. Sapphire also enhances the deep cognitive energies of Virgo and Capricorn.

Azurite

Azurite has the element of Earth, with Spirit and Air. It also vibrates to what we call outer-dimensional spatial energies. Azurite correlates with the psychic, universal, cosmic energies of Neptune and Uranus. Azurite is excellent for Pisces, Aquarius and Scorpio, and is useful for all signs in self-transformation.

Lapis

Lapis contains the Earth element, and is excellent for all signs. It reflects the cosmic energies of Uranus as reflected on earth. Lapis vibrates well to the harmony of Venus and the expansive energies of Jupiter. Although lapis has a lot going on in it, I find that lapis is easier to work with than azurite. Lapis has an effect which is a little more gentle and won't sweep you away.

Violet Ray

Amethyst

Amethyst carries the element of Air. If it is very crystalline, it also carries Spirit. Denser amethyst which is rough or tumbled has more of the Earth element. Amethyst reflects the psychic energies of Neptune and Uranus. It is also attuned to the spiritual awareness of Neptune, and reflects Pluto with its transformative, karmic energies.

Fluorite

Fluorite is related to Air and Spirit. It reflects Neptune and Uranus in their most intense, psychic and spiritual aspects. Fluorite is naturally attuned to Aquarius, Pisces, Libra, Scorpio, and Gemini. Fluorite encourages spiritual development and dream work in all signs.

Sugilite/Royal Azule

Royal azule has the element of Earth with Spirit. There are no traditional correlations for royal azule. However, it suggests the karmic energies of deep personal-universal transformation.

White Light

Milky Quartz

Milky quartz reflects the elements of Earth, Air, and Spirit. It is effective for all.

White Agate

White agates reflect the element of Earth with some Spirit, and are effective for all signs.

Rainbow Light

Rainbow Quartz

Rainbow crystals have the elements of Spirit and Air together. They correlate with Spirit in the universe, and with all signs. Everyone can benefit from them.

Abalone

Abalone contains the elements of Water and Earth. It correlates nicely with lunar energy, as well as with Neptune. Abalone is good for all signs, particularly the Water signs (Cancer, Pisces and Scorpio).

Crystal Light

Crystals

All clear and translucent crystals carry the element of Spirit and are useful for all. Crystals carry the highest energies of Spirit and correlate with the universe through the highest realms of consciousness and awareness.

Silver Light

Silver

Silver correlates with the moon and the element of Earth. It is good for all signs, and best for Air and Water, who need to be constantly receptive to their own flow.

Moonstone

Moonstone, of course, correlates most strongly with the moon. It also relates to psychic Neptune and receptive Venus. Moonstone is excellent for all signs, and particularly so for Cancer—the moon child.

Gold Light

Gold

Gold carries the element of Earth and correlates to the solar energies. Gold is good for all signs, and best for Fire and Earth signs. It warms them and matches their energies.

Rutile Quartz

Rutile quartz has the element of Air, and Earth, as well, because it has iron inclusions. Rutile quartz is excellent for activating all signs.

Black Light

Apache Tear

Apache tears have the element of Earth. They correlate with Saturn for release, and with Pluto for transformation. Apache tears can be used effectively for all signs.

Snowflake Obsidian

Snowflake obsidian carries the element of Earth and obsidian correlates with Saturn for release and Pluto for transformation. I find it has a little lunar energy, as well, because it reflects white and the healing medium. Snowflake obsidian is especially good for Virgo and Capricorn.

Gray Light

Granite

Granite carries the element of Earth. Its energies are most useful for all astrological signs, correlating with Earth signs most directly.

Hematite

The element for hematite is Earth. It correlates with Earth as a planet and with the lunar energies, as well. Hematite also correlates with Mars and Saturn as it has a hidden, ordered fire.

Brown Light

Smoky Quartz

Smoky quartz has the elements of Earth and Air. It correlates with the planet Earth and is good for all signs. This is especially true for Earth signs, because smoky quartz heightens their energy. Smoky quartz is stabilizing to Air and Fire energies. It can be a problem to Water signs if it is not balanced with a bit of something golden, with sun aspects, such as amber or carnelian.

Petrified Wood

Petrified wood has the element of Earth. It correlates to Pluto for its transformational energy, and to the planet Earth. Petrified wood is supportive and protective for all signs.

Appendix D

Stone Alchemy Resource

Abalone
Dense vibration, filter stone
Use to filter, balance and distribute Light and Ray energies harmoniously throughout Body, Mind and Spirit

Alexandrite
Intense vibration, transformative stone
Synthetics have very strong properties; transmutes and transforms energies; harmonizes relationships

Amber
Strong vibration, magnetic stone
Purifies system with diffuse, spreading energy; clears negative psychic energies and activates positive; red amber more physical, yellow amber more mental

Amethyst
High-vibration, source stone
Combats addiction, breaks cycles of dependency; relieves insomnia, soothes stress disorders, pain; connects to transformative spiritual energies

Aquamarine
High-vibration, purity stone
Brings clarity of vision to spiritual work; clears expressive blocks in Mind/Body/Spirit; cleanses etherically, reflects onto the physical.

Apache Tears
Subtle vibration, mystery stone
Works by drawing energies out of physical; use for releasing Mind/Body/Spirit blocks

Aventurine
Earthy vibration, good-luck stone
Touchstone for abundance, confidence; stabilizes overstressed pace of physical environment; brings emotional tranquility

Azurite   Powerful vibration, truth stone
                     Excellent for intuition, clairvoyance, meditation; use for ceremony, ritual, spiritual attunement; dramatically increases receptivity to highest wisdom and truth

Bloodstone   Combines green/heart with red/physical
  (jasper)

Blue lace   Subtle vibration, sensory stone
  agate   Opens sensory channels throughout body; aligns receptive/expressive flow; balances lower chakra energies

Blue tigereye   Excellent for deep meditation
  (Hawk's eye)

Carnelian   Earthy, fiery vibration; action stone
                     Nourishes skin, epithelial tissues; helps blood circulation for balanced flow; encourages positive familial relationships

Celestite   Very high vibration, intellectual stone
                     Very mental, strong imagemaker for visualization; excellent for mental/constrictive disorders; i.e., migraines. Works physical and etheric simultaneously

Chrysocolla   High earthy vibration, resolution stone
                     Balances physical using spiritual energies; inspires calm, courage, resolve, determination; combines earth vibration with crystal energies

Cinnabar   Subtle vibration, meditative stone
                     Balances Yin/Yang; effective primarily as focused meditation tool; toxic to skin at times, wear over clothing

Citrine   High vibration, organization stone
                     Activates positive self-image, self-order., breaks up emotional blocks; removes fears, doubts, negativities

Clear quartz   High vibration, clarity stone
                     Opens to the Oneness of highest Self and Spirit

Double-   Intense vibration, direction stone
  terminated   Rotates and maneuvers energies at the highest rates of vibration; breaks
  crystals   congestions and blocked energy flow

Emerald   High vibration, healer stone
Balances heart rate, soothes nervous tension; excellent for healing vital
organ functions; brings Mind/Body/Spirit well-being

Fire agate   Powerful vibration, courage stone
Balances digestive functions; excellent for sugar imbalances, i.e., diabetes;
enhances self-determination, fortitude

Fluorite   Intense vibration, catalyst stone
Stimulates spiritual growth; energizes all levels with positive, spiritual
energy; excellent dream stone

Garnet   High vibration, primal force stone
Transformative of generative, sexual systems; prevents depression,
insecurity, judgmentalism; excellent for spiritual journey, astral plane work

Gold   Earthy vibration, activator stone
Stimulates energies of all stones; provides an ongoing tonic effect

Granite   Dense earthy vibration, foundation stone
Stabilizes and relieves frustrations; provides supportive foundation for
sense of security

Hematite   Magnetic, earthy vibration; guidance stone
Opens channels to inner teacher, intuition; calls forth healing from within,
from earth, from spirit; stimulates brain activity, builds blood

Jade   Deep, subtle vibration; contemplative stone
Radiates harmonious energies for abundance; not receptive, but active
environmentally; strengthens nervous system

Lapis   Powerful, physical vibration; penetration stone
Instills devotion and inspiration; balances lower chakra ego needs;
clears to allow higher spiritual energy flow

Malachite   Strong, steady vibration; strength stone
Supportive for time of transition; imparts deep physical strength, healing,
stability; restores energy to tired eyes and third-eye strain

Milky quartz   High vibration, transmitter stone
Blends Spirit of crystal with the denser vibration of Earth, reflecting a
foundation shield of energy

Moonstone	Gentle vibration, absorbent stone Opens Self to nurturance from all levels; excellent for all female disorders; highly absorbent, clean often
Peridot	High vibration, antibiotic stone Conducive to clear thinking; stimulates mental; combats physical viruses; balances healing; unblocks psychic knots, impediments
Petrified wood	Ancient Earth vibration, bridging stone Use for grounding tensions and drawing support from Earth energies; bridges Mineral and Plant World consciousness in a practical, grounded manner
Quartz clusters	High vibration, Sacred Four Council stones Sacred stones of direct contact with Source; provides a balance of all elements and energies in the Body, Mind and Spirit
Rainbow crystals	High spiritual vibration, order stone Use for an overall balancing from spiritual and etheric energies focused on spectrum points
Red coral	Moderate vibration, shamanic stone Moves energy from root to heart chakra; prevents lethargy and malnutrition; connects earth/physical to etheric/spiritual
Red jasper	Deep, earthy vibration; protective stone Enhances feelings of groundedness and security; works to give strength to depleted energies
Rhodochrosite	Gentle vibration, peacemaker stone Encourages compassionate involvement in life; awakens active connection to Self, Nature, Spirit; spiritual tonic; opens awareness.
Rhodonite	Dense, earthy vibration; physical stone Soothes and stabilizes nervous tension; reduces palpitations due to stress; releases negative buildup; opens to healing
Rose quartz	Gentle, strong vibration; harmony stone Good overall healing stone, uses gentle magnetism; awakens consciousness of love and harmony; heals heart-related disorders; opens heart chakra
Royal azule	Potent vibration, mastery stone Helps recall past life patterns and wisdoms; opens access to genetic codes (DNA); creates pathways to spirituality on Earth

Ruby
Intense vibration, divine fire stone
Activates through bloodstream for a whole-body effect; use for healing and rebuilding; avoid if exhilarated or angry

Rutile quartz
Intense, electrical vibration; power stone
Transmits active healing energies; helps rebuild cells and tissues

Sapphire
High vibration, laser stone
Develops clairvoyance, spiritual wisdom; opens channels to spirit guides; creates purification on all levels

Serpentine
Earthy vibration, centering stone
Grounds scattered energies; centers emotions; affects environment for rejuvenation; stabilizes physical for healing to occur

Silver
Strong, receptive vibration; lunar stone
Symbolizes the receptive aspects of Mind, Body and Spirit unity; opens awareness on all levels; gives serenity, stability

Smoky quartz
High vibration, transmuter stone
Use to release deep emotional issues; transmutes with Earth, absorbent energies; connects to rhythm of Earth, Nature awareness

Snowflake obsidian
Earthy vibration, grounding stone
Use for centering energies before, after and during release of negativities; follow by focusing on positive energies coming into balance; helps draw out viruses and toxins

Sodalite
Dense, earthy vibration; supportive stone
Soothing agent for focusing energy; use to balance orange, red, or yellow energies; best worn or carried for a day or so

Tigereye
Earthy vibration, practical stone
Excellent for goal-setting, prioritizing; connects to earth/physical for stability; balances sensory impulses

Topaz
High vibration, brain stone
Energizes the intellect, sensory perceptions; stimulates focus, clarity, awareness; combats mental exhaustion, repression

Turquoise
Powerful earth vibration, sacred Earth stone
Balances, connects physical and psychic polarities; steadies vibrations, realigns essential energies; possibly the greatest all-purpose healing stone

Unikite	Earthy vibration, healthful peace stone Soothes and uplifts simultaneously; spreads energy diffusely; supports rose and green healing energies
Watermelon tourmaline	High vibration, balance stone Aligns brain impulses, electrical input/outgo; works through central nervous system to heal; use rose-pink to activate, green to heal and seal
White agate	Earthy vibration, transmitter stone Seals holes in etheric, auric energies; supports all other stones as a healing medium

Elements and Attributes

Rays

Red

Ruby   Divine Fire Stone
Red coral   Shamanic Stone
Jasper   Protective Stone

Scarlet

Garnet   Primal Stone
Watermelon tourmaline   Balance Stone
Cinnabar   Meditative Stone

Rose

Alexandrite   Transformative Stone
Rose quartz   Harmony Stone
Rhodonite   Physical Stone

Orange

Amber   Magnetic Stone
Carnelian   Action Stone
Fire agate   Courage Stone

Peach

Rhodochrosite   Peacemaker Stone
Unikite   Healthful Peace Stone

Yellow

Topaz   Brain Stone
Citrine   Organization Stone
Tigereye   Practical Stone

Golden-Green	Peridot	Antibiotic Stone
	Jade	Contemplative Stone
	Serpentine	Centering Stone
Green	Emerald	Healer Stone
	Malachite	Strength Stone
	Aventurine	Good Luck Stone
Blue	Celestite	Intellectual Stone
	Sodalite	Supportive Stone
	Blue lace agate	Sensory Stone
Turquoise	Aquamarine	Purity Stone
	Turquoise	Sacred Earth Stone
	Chrysocolla	Resolution Stone
Indigo	Sapphire	Laser Stone
	Azurite	Truth Stone
	Lapis	Penetration Stone
Violet	Amethyst	Source Stone
	Fluorite	Catalyst Stone
	Royal azule (sugilite)	Mastery Stone

Lights

White	Milky quartz	Transmitter Stone
	White agate	Receptive Stone
Rainbow	Rainbow crystals	Order Stone
	Abalone	Filter Stone
Crystal	Clear quartz	Clarity Stone
	Double-terminated crystals (clear)	Direction Stone
Spirit	Clear quartz clusters	Sacred Four Council Stones
Silver	Silver	Lunar Stone
	Moonstone	Absorbent Stone
Gold	Gold	Solar Stone
	Rutile quartz	Activator Stone

Black	Apache tear Snowflake obsidian	Mystery Stone Grounding Stone
Gray	Granite Hematite	Foundation Stone Guidance Stone
Brown	Smoky quartz Petrified wood	Transmuter Stone Bridging Stone

Appendix E

Elements for Spells and Ceremonies

Monday

Astrological	Moon (Also Neptune and Uranus to support)
Rays/Lights	Silver, White, Violet, Crystal, Rainbow, Spirit
Attributes	Psychic abilities, intuition, inner self, goddess energy, Yin receptivity
Stones	Moonstones, pearls, white coral, shells, fluorite, white agates, marble, milky quartz, selenite, crystals, pale amethyst, mother of pearl, abalone, rainbow quartz, silver, silver-veined turquoise, tourmalinated quartz, hematite
Candle Colors	White, lavender, silver, gray; balance with gold and yellow
Angelic Guide	Gabriel

Tuesday

Astrological	Mars (Supported by Sun)
Rays/Lights	Red, Scarlet, Crystal, Gray, Black (to balance and earth)
Attributes	Strength, leadership abilities, goal-setting, removal of obstacles, energy for achievements, motivation
Stones	Ruby, garnet, red amber, corals, carnelian, red jasper, bloodstone, cinnabar, fire agates, hematite, obsidians, apache tears, onyx, jet-black coral, marble, granite
Candle Colors	Red, white, gray or black; balance with indigo or green
Angelic Guide	Samael

Wednesday

Astrological   Mercury (Supported by Vulcan)

Rays/Lights   Yellow, Peach, White, Crystal, Brown

Attributes   Intellect, communications, specific business transactions, perception, logic, study skills

Stones   Citrine, tigereye, amber, yellow jasper, rhodochrosite, light carnelian, yellow fluorite, creamy moonstone

Candle Colors   Yellow, peach, white, brown; balance with violet or blue

Angelic Guide   Raphael

Thursday

Astrological   Jupiter (Supported by Earth)

Rays/Lights   Green, Golden-Green, Violet, Rainbow, Crystal

Attributes   Health, wealth, law, expansion, success, luck, fortune, friendship, love

Stones   Emerald, peridot, jade, tourmaline, malachite, aventurine, bloodstone, green fluorite, green quartz, turquoise, chryscola, amazonite, aquamarine, amethyst

Candle Colors   Green, turquoise, white, violet; balance with rose or orange

Angelic Guide   Sachiel

Friday

Astrological   Venus (Supported with Moon for receptivity)

Rays/Lights   Rose, Peach, White, Crystal, Rainbow, Spirit

Attributes   Temperance, romance, love, harmony, friendship, beauty, peace

Stones   Rose quartz, pink tourmaline, rhodochrosite, peach carnelian, unikite, moonstone, mother of pearl, abalone, rainbow quartz, opal

Candle Colors   Rose, pink, white, peach; balance with blue or green

Angelic Guide   Anael

Saturday

Astrological   Saturn (Supported by Pluto for transformation)

Rays/Lights   Indigo, Blue, Black, Brown, Gray, Crystal, Spirit

Attributes   Organization, balance, patience, wisdom, security

Stones   Lapis, sodalite, azurite, sapphire, blue lace agate, blue coral, fluorite, blue tigereye, smoky quartz, petrified wood, obsidian, crystal, hematite

Candle Colors   Indigo, blue, gray or brown; balance with white or yellow stones

Angelic Guide   Cassiel

Sunday

Astrological   Sun (Supported by Earth)
Rays/Lights   Gold, Orange, Peach, Crystal
Attributes   Joy, peace, vitality, expressive activity, action, Yang, stimulation
Stones   Gold, rutilated quartz, citrine, tigereye, amber, carnelian, rhodochrosite, fire agate, opal
Candle Colors Gold, orange, yellow, peach; balance with green or violet
Angelic Guide Michael

Stone Shopping List

This shopping list is just a little starter kit for you. There are many places where you can get stones. Some packaged kits are available and have a very good selection. This can be a good way to get started. If you don't really know what you want, there are people who have put these together. If they are fair in price and easier to obtain, then certainly that is a good way to begin. You can always add to your collections as you expand and experience your stones.

Primary Stones

Ray	Primary Attribute	Stones
Red Ray (First Chakra)	Lifeforce	Snowflake obsidian Red jasper Red coral
Orange Ray (Second Chakra)	Vitality	Carnelian Amber Fire agate
Yellow Ray (Third Chakra)	Intellect	Citrine Topaz Tiger eye
Green Ray (Fourth Chakra)	Expansion	Emerald Malachite Aventurine
Blue Ray (Fifth Chakra)	Expression	Blue lace agate Sodalite Celestite

Ray	Primary Attribute	Stones
Indigo Ray (Sixth Chakra)	Synthesis	Sapphire Azurite Lapis
Violet Ray (Seventh Chakra)	Spirituality	Fluorite Amethyst Sugilite (royal azule)

Blended Ray Stones

Ray	Primary Attribute	Stones
Scarlet Ray	Balance	Watermelon tourmaline Garnet
Rose Ray	Temperance	Rhodonite Rose quartz
Peach Ray	Peace	Rhodochrosite Unikite
Golden-Green Ray	Rejuvenation	Peridot Jade
Turquoise Ray	Dedication	Turquoise Chrysocolla

Sky Lights Stones

These primarily affect the higher-level etheric bodies and upper Chakra/power centers, but can be used for all Body, Mind and Spirit work.

Light	Primary Attribute	Stones
White Light	Healing	Milky quartzes White agates
Rainbow Light	Blending	Crystals with rainbows Abalone
Crystal Light	Clarity	Clear crystal point Double-terminated crystal
Spirit Light	Source	Quartz cluster Twin crystals

Light	Primary Attribute	Stones
Gold Light	Activation	Rutilated quartz Gold
Silver Light	Receptivity	Moonstone Silver

Earth Lights Stones

These primarily affect the lower-level etheric bodies and base Chakra/power centers, but can be used for all Body, Mind and Spirit work.

Light	Primary Attribute	Stones
Black Light	Release	Apache tears Snowflake obsidian
Gray Light	Flexibility	Hematite Granite
Brown Light	Earth Connections	Smoky quartz Petrified wood

Stones and Harmonics

If you are very musically inclined, you might want to try to think of keys and notes that reflect your stones' energies. I like to use drums. For instance, malachite has a certain deep kind of steady beat. It is a little bit like a heart beat; and, of course, it relates to that energy. Red jasper, which also relates to that energy, is much faster. These kinds of things help you attune to the energies. Remember that the stones are reflective of our own needs, our strengths and, again, our weaknesses. They help us and they grow with us.

Another way to program stones (particularly crystals) is to simply do what I have heard called "the breath of intent." Hold the stone or the crystal and breathe, or blow the breath of intent, across the stone.

Use your own energies
and the energies of the Lights
and the Rays around you
to create magickal Self-healing and magickal Self-enhancement.

You are the weaver. You create the fabric of energy that is Life . . . that is Creation.

Now it is time for you to make your Magick
and to grow in Power.

You are the magickal alchemist.
You are the creator of your own Life.
So mote it be . . .
and
So it is.

Appendix F

Bibliography

Achterberg, Jeane. *Imagery in Healing*. Boston: Science Library. 1985.

Anderson, Mary. *Color Healing: Chromotherapy and How it Works*. Northamptonshire, England: The Aquarian Press. 1982.

Arroyo, Stephen. *Astrology, Psychology, and the Four Elements*. Reno, Nevada: CRCS Publications. 1975.

Bayley, Harold. *The Lost Language of Symbolism*. Secaucus, New Jersey: Citadel Press. 1988.

Birren, Faber. *Color Psychology and Color Therapy*. Secaucus, New Jersey: The Citadel Press. 1961.

Blum, Ralph. *The Book of Runes*. New York: St.Martins Press. 1982.

Bonewits, P. E. I. *Real Magic*. Berkeley: Creative Arts Book Company. 1971.

Boorstein, Seymour. (Editor). *Transpersonal Psychotherapy*. Palo Alto: Science and Behavior Books. 1980.

Brennan, Barbara Ann. *Hands of Light*. New York; Bantam Books. 1988.

Bulfinch, Thomas. *Bulfinch's Mythology*. New York: Avenal Books. 1979.

Campbell, Joseph (Editor). *The Portable Jung*. New York: Penguin Books. 1971.

Chocron, Daya Sarai. *Healing With Crystals and Gemstones*. York Beach, Maine: Samuel Weiser, Inc. 1986.

Cirlot, J.E. *A Dictionary of Symbols*. New York: Philosophical Library. 1983.

Cornelio, Marie Williams. *Gemstones and Color.* West Hartford, Connecticut: Triad. 1985.

Crowley, Aleister. *777 And Other Qabalastic Writings.* York Beach, Maine: Samuel Weiser, Inc. 1986.

David, William. *The Harmonics of Sound, Color and Vibration.* Marina Del Rey, California: DeVross Publishers. 1980.

Dychtwald, Ken. *Body-Mind.* New York: Pantheon Books. 1977.

Elliot, R. W. V. *Runes: An Introduction.* Cambridge: Manchester. University Press. 1980.

Fortune, Dion. *The Mystical Qabalah.* York Beach, Main: Samuel Weiser, Inc. 1984.

Fromm, Erich. *The Forgotten Language.* New York: Grove Press, Inc. 1951.

Galde, Phyllis. *Crystal Healing: The Next Step.* St. Paul: Llewellyn Publications. 1988.

Glass, Justine. *Witchcraft: The Sixth Sense.* Hollywood, California: Wilshire Book Company. 1965.

Graves, F. D. *The Windows of Tarot.* Dobbs Ferry, New York: Morgan & Morgan. 1973.

Gray, Eden. *A Complete Guide to the Tarot.* New York. Bantam. 1972.

Grieves, Thomas-John. *An Earth Treatise on Practical Magic.* Houston: Moonrise. 1982.

Grof, Stanislav. (Ed). *Ancient Wisdom and Modern Science.* Albany, New York: State University of New York Press. 1984.

Hall, Calvin S., and Nordby, Vernon J. *A Primer of Jungian Psychology.* New York: New American Library. 1973.

Houston, Jean. *Life Force: A Psycho-Historical Recovery of the Self.* New York: Delta Books. 1980.

_____. *The Possible Human.* Los Angeles: J. P. Tarcher, Inc. 1982.

Howard, Michael. *Candle Burning: Its Occult Significance.* New York: Samuel Weiser. 1980.

Jung, Carl Gustav. *Mandala Symbolism.* Princeton, New Jersey: Princeton University Press. 1973.

_____. *Psychology and Alchemy.* Princeton, New Jersey: Princeton University Press. 1980.

_____. *Memories, Dreams, Reflections.* New York: Random House. 1973.

_____. *Psyche and Symbol*. New York: Anchor Books. 1958.

Khatena, Joe. *Imagery and the Creative Imagination*. Buffalo, New York: Bearly Limited. 1984.

Knight, Gareth. *The Practice of Ritual Magic*. New York: Samuel Weiser. 1976.

Kunz, George Fredrick. *The Curious Lore of Precious Stones*. New York: Dover. 1971.

Leek, Sybil. *Astrological Guide to Successful Everyday Living*. New York: Signet. 1972.

_____. *Moon signs*. New York: Berkeley. 1981

Lewi, Grant. *Astrology for the Millions*. New York: Bantam. 1978. (by arrangement with Llewellyn Publications)

Lewis, Ursula. *Chart Your Own Horoscope*. New York: Pinnacle Books. 1988.

Masters, Robert., and Houston, Jean. *Listening to the Body*. New York: Dell Publishing Company. 1978.

_____. *Mind Games*. New York: Dell Publishing Company. 1972.

Mishlove, Jeffery. *The Roots of Consciousness*. New York: Random House. 1975

Nichols, Sallie. *Jung and Tarot: An Archetypal Journey*. York Beach, Maine: Samuel Weiser, Inc. 1986.

Nitsch, Twylah. *Language of the Stones*. Irving, New York: Seneca Historical Society. 1983.

Ornstein, Robert. *The Psychology of Consciousness*. New York: Penguin Books. 1972.

Ouseley, S. G. J. *Colour Meditations*. London: L. N. Fowler. 1967.

Reed, Ellen Cannon. *The Witches Tarot*. St. Paul: Llewellyn Publications. 1989.

Rendel, Peter. *Introduction to the Chakras*. Northamptonshire, England : Aquarian Press. 1981.

Russel, Peter. *The Global Brain*. Los Angeles: J. P. Tarcher. 1983.

Shorr, Joseph E. *Psychotherapy Through Imagery*. New York: Thiem-Stratton, Inc. 1983.

Starr, Kara. *Merlin's Journal of Time: The Camelot Adventure*. Solana Beach California: Ravenstarr Publications. 1989.

Stewart, R. J. *The Merlin Tarot*. Northamptonshire, England: Aquarian Press. 1988.

Thorsson, Edred. *Futhark: A Handbook of Rune Magic.* York Beach, Maine: Samuel Weiser, Inc. 1989.

Tyson, Donald. *Rune Magic.* St. Paul: Llewellyn Publications. 1988.

Uydert, Mellie. *The Magic of Precious Stones.* Northamptonshire, England: Turnstone Press. 1981.

Vaughan, Frances E. *Awakening Intuition.* Garden City, New York: Anchor Books. 1979.

Watts, Alan. *Psychotherapy East and West.* New York: Ballantine Books. 1961.

_____. *The Essential Alan Watts.* Berkeley: Celestial Arts. 1974.

Wolfe, Amber. *Imagery Reflections: An Exploration of Transpersonal Implications of the Active Use of Imagery.* Houston, Texas: University of Houston Press. 1986.

_____. *In the Shadow of the Shaman.* St. Paul: Llewellyn Publications. 1988.

_____. *Moondancing.* St. Paul: Llewellyn Publications. 1987.

_____. *Shamana.* St. Paul: Llewellyn Publications. 1987.

_____. *Rainflowers.* St. Paul: Llewellyn Publications. 1987.

STAY IN TOUCH

On the following pages you will find listed, with their current prices, some of the books now available on related subjects. Your book dealer stocks most of these and will stock new titles in the Llewellyn series as they become available. We urge your patronage.

To obtain our full catalog, to keep informed about new titles as they are released and to benefit from informative articles and helpful news, you are invited to write for our bi-monthly news magazine/catalog, *Llewellyn's New Worlds of Mind and Spirit*. A sample copy is free, and it will continue coming to you at no cost as long as you are an active mail customer. Or you may subscribe for just $7.00 in the U.S.A. and Canada ($20.00 overseas, first class mail). Many bookstores also have *New Worlds* available to their customers. Ask for it.

Stay in touch! In *New Worlds'* pages you will find news and features about new books, tapes and services, announcements of meetings and seminars, articles helpful to our readers, news of authors, products and services, special money-making opportunities, and much more.

Llewellyn's New Worlds of Mind and Spirit
P.O. Box 64383-890, St. Paul, MN 55164-0383, U.S.A.
* * *

TO ORDER BOOKS AND TAPES

If your book dealer does not have the books described on the following pages readily available, you may order them direct from the publisher by sending full price in U.S. funds, plus $3.00 for postage and handling for orders *under* $10.00; $4.00 for orders *over* $10.00. There are no postage and handling charges for orders over $50.00. Postage and handling rates are subject to change. UPS Delivery: We ship UPS whenever possible. Delivery guaranteed. Provide your street address as UPS does not deliver to P.O. Boxes. UPS to Canada requires a $50.00 minimum order. Allow 4-6 weeks for delivery. Orders outside the U.S.A. and Canada: Airmail—add retail price of book; add $5.00 for each non-book item (tapes, etc.); add $1.00 per item for surface mail.

FOR GROUP STUDY AND PURCHASE

Because there is a great deal of interest in group discussion and study of the subject matter of this book, we feel that we should encourage the adoption and use of this particular book by such groups by offering a special quantity price to group leaders or agents.

Our Special Quantity Price for a minimum order of five copies of *Personal Alchemy* is $53.85 cash-with-order. This price includes postage and handling within the United States. Minnesota residents must add 6.5% sales tax. For additional quantities, please order in multiples of five. For Canadian and foreign orders, add postage and handling charges as above. Credit card (VISA, MasterCard, American Express) orders are accepted. Charge card orders only ($15.00 minimum order) may be phoned in free within the U.S.A. or Canada by dialing 1-800-THE-MOON. For customer service, call 1-612-291-1970. Mail orders to:

LLEWELLYN PUBLICATIONS
P.O. Box 64383-890, St. Paul, MN 55164-0383, U.S.A.

All prices subject to change without notice.

IN THE SHADOW OF THE SHAMAN
Connecting with Self, Nature & Spirit
by Amber Wolfe

Presented in what the author calls a "cookbook shamanism" style, this book shares recipes, ingredients, and methods of preparation for experiencing some very ancient wisdoms: wisdoms of Native American and Wiccan traditions, as well as contributions from other philosophies of Nature as they are used in the shamanic way. Wheels, the circle, totems, shields, directions, divinations, spells, care of sacred tools and meditations are all discussed. Wolfe encourages us to feel confident and free to use her methods to cook up something new, completely on our own. This blending of ancient formulas and personal methods represents what Ms. Wolfe calls Aquarian Shamanism.

In the Shadow of the Shaman is designed to communicate in the most practical, direct ways possible, so that the wisdom and the energy may be shared for the benefits of all. Whatever your system or tradition, you will find this to be a valuable book, a resource, a friend, a gentle guide and support on your journey. Dancing in the shadow of the shaman, you will find new dimensions of Spirit.

0-87542-888-6, 384 pgs., 6 x 9, illus., softcover $12.95

ROBIN WOOD TAROT DECK
created and illustrated by Robin Wood
Instructions by Robin Wood and Michael Short

Tap into the wisdom of your subconscious with one of the most beautiful Tarot decks on the market today! Reminiscent of the Rider-Waite deck, the Robin Wood Tarot is flavored with nature imagery and luminous energies that will enchant you and the querant. Even the novice reader will find these cards easy and enjoyable to interpret.

Radiant and rich, these cards were illustrated with a unique technique that brings out the resplendent color of the prismacolor pencils. The shining strength of this Tarot deck lies in its depiction of the Minor Arcana. Unlike other Minor Arcana decks, this one springs to pulsating life. The cards are printed on quality card stock and boxed complete with instruction booklet, which provides the upright and reversed meanings of each card, as well as three basic card layouts. Beautiful and brilliant, the Robin Wood Tarot is a must-have deck!

0-87542-894-0, boxed set: 78 cards with booklet $19.95

16 STEPS TO HEALTH AND ENERGY
A Program of Color & Visual Meditation, Movement & Chakra Balance
by Pauline Wills & Theo. Gimble

Before an illness reaches your physical body, it has already been in your *auric* body for days, weeks, even months. By the time you *feel* sick, something in your life has been out of balance for a while. But why wait to get sick to get healthy? Follow the step-by-step techniques in *16 Steps to Health and Energy,* and you will open up the energy circuits of your subtle body so you are better able to stay balanced and vital in our highly toxic and stressful world.

Our subtle anatomy includes the "energy" body of seven chakras that radiate the seven colors of the spectrum. Each chakra responds well to a particular combination of yoga postures and color visualizations, all of which are provided in this book.

At the end of the book is a series of 16 "workshops" that help you to travel through progressive stages of consciousness expansion and self-transformation. Each session deals with a particular color and all of its associated meditations, visualizations and yoga postures. Here is a truly holistic route to health at all levels! Includes 16 color plates!
0-87542-871-1, 224 pgs., 6 x 9, illus., softcover $12.95

HOW TO HEAL WITH COLOR
by Ted Andrews

Now, for perhaps the first time, color therapy is placed within the grasp of the average individual. Anyone can learn to facilitate and accelerate the healing process on all levels with the simple color therapies in *How to Heal with Color.*

Color serves as a vibrational remedy that interacts with the human energy system to stabilize physical, emotional, mental and spiritual conditions. When there is balance, we can more effectively rid ourselves of all that hinders our life processes.

This book provides color application guidelines that are beneficial for over 50 physical conditions and a wide variety of emotional and mental conditions. Receive simple and tangible instructions for performing "muscle testing" on yourself and others to find the most beneficial colors. Learn how to apply color therapy through touch, projection, breathing, cloth, water and candles. Learn how to use the little known but powerful color-healing system of the mystical Qabala to balance and open the psychic centers. Plus, discover simple techniques for performing long distance healings on others.
0-87542-005-2, 240 pgs., mass market, illus. $3.95

KUNDALINI AND THE CHAKRAS
A Practical Manual—Evolution in this Lifetime
The mysteries of Kundalini revealed! We all possess the powerful evolutionary force of Kundalini that can open us to genius states, psychic powers and cosmic consciousness. As the energies of the Aquarian Age intensify, more and more people are experiencing the "big release" spontaneously but have been ill-equipped to channel its force in a productive manner. This book shows you how to release Kundalini gradually and safely and is your guide to sating the strange, new appetites which result when life-in-process "blows open" your body's many energy centers.

The section on chakras brings new understanding to these "dials" on our life machine (body). It is the most comprehensive information available for cleansing and developing the chakras and their energies. *Read Kundalini and the Chakras* and prepare to make a quantum leap in your spiritual growth!
0-87542-592-5, 224 pgs. 6 x 9, illus., color plates, softcover $12.95

WHEELS OF LIFE
A User's Guide to the Chakra System
by Anodea Judith
An instruction manual for owning and operating the inner gears that run the machinery of our lives. Written in a practical, down-to-earth style, this fully illustrated book will take the reader on a journey through aspects of consciousness, from the bodily instincts of survival to the processing of deep thoughts.

Discover this ancient metaphysical system under the new light of popular Western metaphors: quantum physics, elemental magick, Kabbalah, physical exercises, poetic meditations, and visionary art. Learn how to open these centers in yourself, and see how the chakras shed light on the present world crises we face today. And learn what you can do about it!

This book will be a vital resource for: Magicians, Witches, Pagans, Mystics, Yoga Practitioners, Martial Arts people, Psychologists, Medical people, and all those who are concerned with holistic growth techniques.

The modern picture of the Chakras was introduced to the West largely in the context of Hatha and Kundalini Yoga and through the Theosophical writings of Leadbeater and Besant. But the Chakra system is equally innate to Western Magick: all psychic development, spiritual growth, and practical attainment is fully dependent upon the opening of the Chakras!
0-87542-320-5, 544 pgs., 6 x 9, illus., softcover $14.95